PRAISE FOR C

"Many times evangelical treatments of new religions (pejoratively labeled *cults*)—and at times world religions—consist of doctrinal comparison, usually followed by apologetic refutation. Paul Louis Metzger's volume moves beyond this template to consider new and world religions on their own terms while also relating them to the Christian faith. Not content with mere description, contrast, and rebuttal, Metzger invites representatives of the religious traditions he engages into conversation that includes critique. This dialogical approach is a refreshing addition to evangelical treatments of religion that should be of value to Christians in the academy, the pulpit, and the pews."

—*John W. Morehead, director, Western Institute for Intercultural Studies; and director, Evangelical Chapter of the Foundation for Religious Diplomacy*

"In this wise and stimulating discussion, Paul Louis Metzger calls for evangelical Christians to pursue 'relational, incarnational apologetics' in our engagement with a religiously and culturally diverse society. Drawing upon his extensive personal relationships with those from very different perspectives, as well as his experience in teaching theology, Metzger presents a fresh approach that listens carefully to Christianity's critics while also pointing others to Jesus."

—*Harold Netland, professor of philosophy of religion and intercultural studies, Trinity Evangelical Divinity School*

"In *Connecting Christ: How to Discuss Jesus in a World of Diverse Paths,* my good friend Paul Louis Metzger writes on a topic he daily lives out—connecting Jesus to our post-Christian culture. How can we join the most important conversations of our time, rather than retreating to the comfort of our own subculture? Metzger has labored hard to build bridges here, in very progressive Portland, Oregon, making this a work deeply rooted in real-life experience. In this timely and compelling read, you will learn how to engage the culture more effectively for greater kingdom impact."

—*Kevin Palau, president, Luis Palau Association*

"I have trusted and respected Dr. Paul Louis Metzger so much that over the past several years we have asked him to periodically teach an apologetics course to our Young Life staff in the Northwest. His book *Connecting Christ: How to Discuss Jesus in a World of Diverse Paths* is consistent with why our staff loves his teaching—he weds a message of biblical orthodoxy together with the compassion of incarnational witness. Dr. Metzger's book reads like a field manual for engaging disinterested and even hostile people with both the truth and grace of Jesus Christ."

—*John Franklin, senior vice president, Young Life Western Division*

"Paul Louis Metzger is among a select group of Christian apologists who correctly understands three counterintuitive missiological realities:

+ the United States is a mission field;
+ presenting Christianity as a *religion* reduces the gospel to just one possible choice in an over-saturated religion marketplace;
+ our most effective mission strategy—perhaps our only effective mission strategy—is to talk about Jesus of Nazareth.

"This is the best book available for instructing us all in how to talk about Jesus to people of other religious traditions. Christian witnesses must read it."

—*Terry Muck, dean, E. Stanley Jones School of World Mission and Evangelism, Asbury Theological Seminary*

"We all desire to share the good news of Jesus Christ with our friends, family, neighbors, and even strangers. Yet to share the profound, life-changing message of Jesus Christ effectively, we must first understand these individuals: their beliefs, their questions, and their presuppositions. In short, we must learn to dialogue, to listen, and to respond in a respectful, winsome, God-honoring way.
"In *Connecting Christ* Paul Louis Metzger allows us to eavesdrop on some profound conversations, giving us a glimpse into the mind-set of others from differing faiths and a better understanding of how to share with those who have yet to respond in faith to Jesus Christ."

—*Luis Palau, world evangelist*

"I find *Connecting Christ* to be as robust and clear a statement of evangelicalism as I have recently seen."

—*Phyllis Tickle, founding editor [ret.], Publishers Weekly, religion*

"Paul Louis Metzger loves Jesus, and this book shows that his love for his neighbors is just as palpable. *Connecting Christ* presents the kind of witness to Jesus that participates in the power of the gospel to change the world. The development of a viable and winsome evangelical apologetic in the twenty-first century receives a huge boost in the book you hold in your hands."

—*Amos Yong, J. Rodman Williams Professor of Theology, Regent University School of Divinity*

"Paul Louis Metzger has given us a remarkable expression out of God's very heart. His proposal for a relationally authentic pursuit of engaging others needs to be heard by everyone. In his writing he is clear while not being simplistic, and he is courageous without being arrogant. A relational-incarnational apologetic model will challenge and release all of us to seriously live out of God's heart, to love unconditionally with humility, repentance, and confession."

—*Dr. Randall Y. Furushima, dean and executive officer, New Hope Christian College*

"What's glaringly missing from *Connecting Christ* is anything *hypothetical*: no hypothetical conversations, no hypothetical questions, no hypothetical worldviews—this is real-world apologetics. What is *not* missing from this book: a Christ-centered approach to apologetics, compassion and empathy for the lost, a commitment to truth, and a thorough knowledge of competing worldviews, not as we read about them but in the nuanced manner that we encounter them. This is the manual for evangelism and apologetics for the next decade."

—*Rick James, publisher, Campus Crusade for Christ; and author,* Jesus Without Religion *and* A Million Ways To Die

"The variety of religions and philosophies across the globe is dizzying. The common way to account for such diversity—from the world's perspective—is to say either all of it is false or there are many paths to fulfillment and the hereafter. Paul Louis Metzger, a leading expert on Christ and culture, gives us another perspective, a better way. *Connecting Christ* is a must-read on how to live Christianity in a world of diverse faiths."

—*Michael O. Emerson, Allyn & Gladys Cline Professor of Sociology and cofounding director, Kinder Institute for Urban Research, Rice University; and author,* Divided by Faith, United by Faith, People of the Dream, *and* Transcending Racial Barriers

"In this wide-ranging trinitarian apologetic, Paul Louis Metzger gently but firmly addresses people of various Christian denominations, other religions, and no religion from an evangelical perspective of solidarity with them, presenting the good news that because God is gracious to us in Jesus Christ, God will not let any of us go and will not let Christians separate themselves from anyone, even their enemies, because those who trust in the crucified Savior cannot let anyone else go either. Among other intriguing issues the relation of theology and science; the problem of universalism; how to understand Christianity in a pluralistic market-driven, consumer culture; and how to relate with others over divisive moral issues are also discussed.

"What makes this a very compelling read and an unusual one today is the fact that Metzger never wavers from pointing readers to the only One who can make us truly one and give us genuine hope for the future of humanity, namely, Jesus Christ himself. Anyone reading this book will see just how everything really does look differently in light of a theology of the Trinity."

—*Paul D. Molnar, professor of systematic theology, Department of Theology and Religious Studies, St. John's University*

"Paul Louis Metzger paints a compelling and refreshing picture of our Christian opportunity to both share the good news and grow in love and relationship with others. Neither is negotiable. It is an honest look at how we have missed the mark in evangelism and steers us back to the heart of Jesus. I also love how Metzger lays out a humble and thoughtful display of different religions. He does not belittle or generalize but invites us into real relationships and real conversations with others. What a helpful resource for people who want to grow in their witness!"

—*Vikki Rubens, area director, Oregon, InterVarsity Christian Fellowship, USA*

CONNECTING
CHRIST

CONNECTING
CHRIST

How to Discuss Jesus in a World of Diverse Paths

PAUL LOUIS METZGER

THOMAS NELSON
Since 1798

NASHVILLE   DALLAS   MEXICO CITY   RIO DE JANEIRO

Published in Nashville, Tennessee, by Thomas Nelson. Thomas Nelson is a registered trademark of Thomas Nelson, Inc.

Published in association with the literary agency of Credo Communications, LLC, Grand Rapids, MI 49525; www.credocommunications.net.

Thomas Nelson, Inc., titles may be purchased in bulk for educational, business, fund-raising, or sales promotional use. For information, please e-mail SpecialMarkets@ThomasNelson.com.

Unless otherwise noted, Scripture quotations are taken from the Holy Bible, New International Version®. NIV®. © 1973, 1978, 1984, 2011 by Biblica, Inc.™ Used by permission of Zondervan. All rights reserved worldwide. Unless otherwise noted, quotes are from the 1984 edition. Quotations marked UPDATED NIV are from the 2011 edition.

Scripture quotations marked KJV are from the King James Version.

Library of Congress Cataloging-in-Publication Data

Metzger, Paul Louis.
  Connecting Christ : how to discuss Jesus in a world of diverse paths / Paul Louis Metzger.
    p. cm.
  Includes bibliographical references (pp. 268–327).
  ISBN 978-0-8499-4724-7 (trade paper)
  1. Witness bearing (Christianity) 2. Apologetics. 3. Christianity and other religions. I. Title.
  BV4520.M46 2012
  248'.5—dc23

2012002938

Printed in the United States of America

12 13 14 15 16 QG 5 4 3 2 1

In memory of Dietrich Bonhoeffer, profound witness to the all-powerful weak Word—Jesus.

And to the memorable witness of the Lord's wise fools, Paul Isihara and Yaeko Miyamoto.

Also to the respondents at the end of this volume, whom I will remember for their gracious investment of time and thoughtful engagement.

ACKNOWLEDGMENTS

I am thankful for my connections to numerous others when thinking through how I might discuss Jesus in a world of diverse paths. I am grateful to so many people for their insights, and, in many cases, for their long-suffering patience. When considering the themes developed in this volume, I learned that thorough study depends on dialogue with others. I am very grateful that many people have determined to stay connected with me to discuss these matters, keeping the conversation going and never giving up. Here are some of them.

I wish to express appreciation to the administration of Multnomah Biblical Seminary and University, including present seminary dean Robert Redman, former seminary dean Donald Brake, president Daniel Lockwood, and provost Wayne Strickland for their vision for seeing our institution expand its forms of cultural engagement in connection to Christ. I also wish to thank former and present seminary and university colleagues Albert Baylis, Ron Frost, R. G., Michael Gurney, Brad Harper, Tony Kriz, and Karl Kutz; and students and teaching assistants Michael Badriaki, Gretchen Cain, Wink Chinn, Joe Enlet, Matt Farlow, Ross and Rachel Halbach, Chris Laird, Andreas Lundén, Derrick Peterson, Ronaldo Sison, and Sam and Desiree Titus with their friend Jackson Prakash for their contributions, including keen analysis of the themes and arguments developed in this volume. My world religions class and Young

Life apologetics class at Multnomah have been invaluable experiences as students and I have wrestled through these issues together.

I wish to express thanks and appreciation to Matt Baugher, Paula Major, and their team at Thomas Nelson for their vision and enthusiasm for this project, David Sanford and Tim Beals of Credo Communication for supporting this project, Madison Trammel for his insights and interaction through various stages of the work, and the invaluable assistance of Beyth Hogue Greenetz, my assistant and colleague at the Institute for the Theology of Culture: New Wine, New Wineskins. Beyth and the interns, advisory council, and faculty committee at the institute have been phenomenal ministry partners. I am honored to journey with the New Wine, New Wineskins community and to live into the theology of cultural engagement articulated in this book with them.

I am also grateful for my interaction with religion scholars Harold Netland, Daniel W. Brown, John Morehead, and Randall Furushima, and to the Association of Theological Schools, especially Stephen Graham and Francis Pacienza, for the opportunity and privilege to participate in the project "Christian Hospitality and Pastoral Practices in a Multifaith Society," and to coauthor the evangelical team essay with Sang-Ehil Han and Terry Muck. I also wish to express gratitude for the influence of my doctoral mentor, the late Colin Gunton, who developed a uniquely trinitarian apologetic and who inspired me to develop my own particular trinitarian apologetic framework.

Some of the respondents in the volume have become personal friends. I hope that will soon be true of the other respondents after our continued interaction. They, together with Buddhist priest Takakazu Fukushima, under whom I studied Buddhism in Japan, have enriched my life through the time and energy they have invested in connecting with me.

I am always tempted to dedicate every book to my wife, Mariko, and children, Julianne and Christopher, given their diverse forms of connection to me every day of my life. Their presence, patience, and passion for life— and my wife's particular global theological-cultural instincts—are so dear to me. Still, I have chosen to dedicate the book to the respondents and a few others. There is the late Dietrich Bonhoeffer, whose influence is keenly felt in my heart and mind as I finish this volume. His costly discipleship (like that of friend and mentor John M. Perkins)—bound up with bearing witness to Jesus, who is the all-powerful weak Word hanging in the gallows—inspires me to pursue a more cross-centered apologetic. Few people have demonstrated the cruciform apologetic of Jesus' love better in my midst than friends Paul Isihara and Yaeko Miyamoto. Their witness of staying connected to and supporting my family and me during very difficult times inspires me to connect with others more during trying circumstances so as to develop enriching and life-giving, life-transforming conversations and relationships.

INTRODUCTION

WIRED FOR RELATIONSHIPS

All people long in one way or another to connect with Christ. They may not know him by name—as of yet—but he knows their names. The triune God in whose image everyone is created has wired people for relationship with Christ. Everyone pulls at the wiring in one way or another, but no amount of pulling bound up with the devastating tragedy of our rebellion can remove people from God's reach and the power of his love. As Christians, we don't connect Christ to anyone, or anyone to Christ. The Spirit does all the relational connecting, but we are called to be witnesses to Christ. As his witnessing people and body, we may be conduits for the Spirit, acting as Jesus' voice, his hands, and his feet as we proclaim his good news in word and deed. Such witnessing may involve all kinds of robust ideas and strategies. But we must always ensure that our ideas and strategies are conduits for Jesus Christ's incarnate love.

There is more than one way to discuss Jesus. How can it be otherwise, when the Christian Scriptures include four diverse and harmonious accounts of Jesus—Matthew, Mark, Luke, and John? The gospel writers were overwhelmed and amazed by the mystery of God incarnate, as were the rest of the New Testament authors. Approaching Jesus the Christ from their respective vantage points, they penned for us authoritative accounts of the Lamb of God, Son of Man, Son of God, Messiah, Lord. How could the biblical writers not present Jesus Christ in this multifaceted way when his mysterious being defies singular definition?

As God incarnate, Jesus Christ is no abstract concept or remote figure of the past. When he removes the veil and discloses himself to us, we are undone by his glory, humility, holiness, mercy, and love. Like Peter who experienced Jesus' miracle of breaking the nets with a great catch of fish, we are brought to our knees, realizing how broken and petty and sinful we are: "Go away from me, Lord; I am a sinful man!" (Luke 5:8). Be assured that when we are undone in his presence in this way, he will renew us and call us to himself: "Don't be afraid; from now on you will catch men" (Luke 5:10).

While the Lord Jesus certainly does not fit with static notions and cultural stereotypes of God, we can easily reduce the way we talk about him to clichés. And so it is important that we guard against speaking of Jesus Christ and the Christian faith in a rote manner when engaged in apologetics—that is, presenting a truthful and meaningful account of the Christian faith, especially in an increasingly diverse culture that does not accept pat answers. After all, we are not dealing with intellectual abstractions when we discuss the truth, for the truth is the living God. This truth is God in the flesh (John 1:14), who tells his followers face-to-face, "I am the way and the truth and the life." No wonder he adds, "No one comes to the Father except through me" (John 14:6). He is not simply a way, but *the* way; not simply a truth, but *the* truth; not simply a life, but *the* life. These statements on their own might appear mechanical to some. That is why a person-to-person, heart-to-heart, life-on-life encounter with other people of diverse paths through prayer to God (who is supremely personal himself) is so essential. People are not simply wired to assent to truths; they must live them in relation to this God who is the living truth. As Christ's people, we must continually seek to engage people relationally—case by case, and not in some fixed, packaged manner. There is more than one way to talk about Jesus, given who he is and that we live in a world of diverse paths.

Just as Jesus called Peter, Paul, and John, he also calls us to hook diverse people's lives, hearts, and minds and draw them in, nets breaking. It didn't come easily for the apostles. Just think of Peter: He was set in his good Jewish ways, and he couldn't imagine how Gentiles could come to receive salvation on equal terms with the Jews by simple faith in Christ Jesus. He even told the God of Israel and of Jesus that he was more kosher than God: he wouldn't eat the "ham sandwich" dropped from heaven in a vision (Acts 10:14)! But when God spoke to Peter, when people sent by Cornelius the centurion appeared at his door, and when Cornelius's household experienced salvation in the same way Peter had, Peter made the necessary adjustments (Acts 10:34–35). Jesus works in mysterious ways. The same thing happened to Saul, who became Paul after his life-altering encounter with Jesus on the Damascus Road (Acts 9:1–9): he became all things to all people so as to save some (1 Corinthians 9:22).

It didn't come easily for them then, and it won't come easily for us now. In a religiously diverse America, many of us no longer live in a Bible Belt zone, and where the Bible Belt still exists, it is shrinking. People won't respond if we try to lure them in with *Bible Answer Man* ways. Many of them are also cynical, having been burned by certain TV-preacher types who offer them Jesus to fleece them, getting a lease on their lives and access to their bank accounts.

Certainly rigorous, thoughtful answers have their place, as do meaning-ful attempts at contextualizing the truth in winsome, striking ways. But no matter how good the argument or how contextual, winsome, and striking the message, nothing replaces sacrificial love for others; this is how trust is built. The community of faith must become the apologetic for the faith: a holistic rationale for faith in Christ involving interpersonal and life-on-life encoun-ters. I refer to such interpersonal and life-on-life encounters involving the investment of one's whole person and community as relational-incarnational apologetics. Are we up to the challenge of approaching apologetics relation-ally and incarnationally in a world of diverse paths? Only if we depend on God and one another as Christ's people.

I look forward to journeying with you through the pages of this book. I hope you are as excited as I am about the holistic rationale for the faith to which I allude. One of the striking features of this book is the development of apologetics that goes beyond the mere logical defense of the truth or the Christian worldview. For those of you who have not read apologetic volumes before, some of the terms like *worldview* and *relational-incarnational* may appear foreign to you. I will unpack and develop these terms as we proceed. For now it will suffice to define briefly three basic approaches: worldview, market-driven, and relational-incarnational.[1]

The articulation and rational defense of a Christian worldview or belief system is often what people have in mind when they speak of Christian apologetics. The worldview approach often centers on the demonstration of the internal coherence of the Christian truth claims and the evaluation that these beliefs correspond better to reality than alternative worldviews. Such a defense is important. But I am going beyond simply making a logical defense of Christian truth claims. As stated previously, I am calling for relational-incarnational apologetics in a world of diverse paths.

People—including Christians—are more than their belief systems. We need to engage not simply people's minds but their whole lives. Nor are we settling for appealing to people's tastes, as in a market-driven approach to evangelism and apologetics. I will take the opportunity to describe this approach in a little more detail, given that it is not often as immediately recognizable as a form of apologetics. A market-driven model is reflected in Christians' appeals to affinity groups and their tastes and appetites, not their minds or the deep values of their hearts. This model is often reflected in Christian outreach events that attempt to attract seekers to faith based on the hottest or funniest or most glamorous religious brand, fad, or celebrity. In its most extreme form the market-driven approach does not entail getting to know people's stories and their deepest longings and fears. Rather it focuses on making sure they remain stimulated and entertained by the advertisements and purchase the Christian package. Not everyone who employs the market-driven approach intentionally seeks to be market-driven. Not everyone turns the church into a Christian carnival. It is often more subtle. A lot of hipster Christianity goes on in the emerging/emergent church movement. Even if the emerging/emergent church movement is not banking on its hipster appeal to draw people, it often attracts people based on its hipster ethos and aura. The same thing goes for those boomer megachurches that create family or self-help programs and justice packages to draw people. The hipster churches actually have justice packages too. However, their programs, like their services and their personal appearance, are less polished looking than the contemporary boomer yuppie alternatives—but like the yuppie alternatives, their appearance is carefully constructed. (By the way, not all emergents are hipsters, and not all boomers are yuppies—and neither camp would claim me!)[2]

Of course churches should promote justice, nurture families, and help people with addictions (as well as attend to their personal appearance and hygiene). Still, while they may not mean to do so, the way churches operate these initiatives may attract seekers to the programs instead of into community. Jesus does not want us to use the church to draw families but to draw nuclear families and individuals without families into God's family. Moreover, Jesus does not help us get in touch with ourselves but helps us die to ourselves so that we can truly live in selfless love with him and others as his people. And lastly, what would Jesus do when a particular justice package no longer appeals to the consumer or has served its purpose in drawing the seeker to church? Would Jesus discard that particular justice package and promote another? When a church does so (and churches sometimes do), does it not turn justice into a commodity? How just would that be? Often market-driven proponents don't know they are market-driven, and aren't often aware of the implications or associations bound up with their practices and plans. In this way, too, the market-driven approach differs from the worldview and relational-incarnational models since both of these approaches are more intentional and strategic in their orientation while the market-driven approach can often be more subconscious in terms of the development of an apologetic strategy. Subconscious or not and regardless of one's intentions, the exclusively market-driven approach, like its exclusively worldview-oriented counterpart, is not relational or incarnational at its core. Whether one is engaging primarily or exclusively people's brains (a worldview-dominated model) or their taste buds (a market-driven model), one is not sharing in their life stories and engaging them holistically.

A relational-incarnational model goes beyond simply addressing what people think and want and focuses attention on why they think such thoughts and what it is they truly need. *Relational* follows from the fact that God is personal and calls us into personal relationship with himself through Jesus Christ. As Christ's witnesses we are called to engage people relationally. Encountering people relationally entails addressing them as more than simply rational beings or as cultural creations with religious appetites. God's Word did not become incarnate primarily to share incredible ideas about God or to promote a heavenly marketing plan or business strategy. He became incarnate to share life with us and to take us home to his Father's house through his costly sacrifice. Of course we need to be sensitive to people's intellectual concerns and cultural contexts and make sure we are conduits for Christ on various paths, for one size of apologetic witness does not fit all types of people. That is why we must engage people relationally, heart to heart and life on life. I don't think anyone is truly won to Christ by beating them in an argument or arousing their curiosity and giving them a free meal. You have to win their heart. Winning the heart requires life-on-life sharing in view of Jesus, who became incarnate and gave his life for us. This is why I speak of *incarnational*. We Christians must follow in the incarnate Christ's footsteps here on earth and lay down our lives for those who do not yet know Jesus so that they might respond to his incarnate love and give their lives to him. This relational-incarnational model requires of Christians personal repentance and vulnerability, sacrifice, shared story, and an expansive view of the gospel that goes beyond sin management and marketing strategies and beyond mere assent to religious propositions.

Part I of this book will unpack and develop this model in various ways. Part II will engage other religious traditions and cultural movements in view of this model. Part III will bring this model to bear on pressing issues or "hot topics" that Christians must address today. Part IV includes the responses from representative figures of the traditions I engage in Part II.

The relational-incarnational model of apologetics expressed in this book builds upon the triune God's life story with us. The Father who shares life with his Son gives his Son to us so that we might become members of his family through the Spirit. This God makes it possible for us to share life with others who do not yet know him. Viewing God in this way makes it possible for us to conceive apologetics relationally. You may have heard it said that many Christians live like atheists. I would go so far as to say that many evangelical Christians think like Unitarians, and confess the Trinity in name only. They are often very fearful and reluctant to talk about the Trinity. If they do talk about the Trinity, they often resort to mathematical formulas and recipes: "The Trinity is like 1x1x1=1" or

"Take an egg white, egg yolk, and egg shell, and mix them in a blender; there you have the Trinity." No wonder many Christians find the doctrine of the Trinity irrelevant, with no bearing on life and relationships. But our faith is not based on some formula or recipe. It is based on the good news that the Father and Son invite us to share life filled with selfless love with them in the Spirit. This is no incoherent mystery. While we cannot define love, we can describe and experience it. Divine love is the ultimate life-giving mystery, as the Father gives his Son's life over to sacrificial death to save the world through the Spirit.

In this light our task as Christian witnesses is not to build on some supposed neutral, logical philosophical system but to retell Jesus' story and show in word and deed how the Christian story makes best sense of life in view of Christ's sacrificial love. We must not negate people's customs, traditions, and beliefs but instead negate only that which stands in the way of securing people in profound relationships. So I will negate explanations of the Trinity that resort to illustrations of egg whites, egg shells, and egg yolks. Egg whites and shells and yolks don't have relationships. Persons do. Impersonal notions of the triune God do not sustain people of various paths. Only an interpersonal God can sustain people in relationships. The interpersonal God Christians refer to as Father, Son, and Spirit sustains the best relational intuitions of diverse paths and traditions and invites people on these paths to encounter this God. And so, we invite these diverse religious practitioners to share life with us, just as the Father and Son share life with us through the invitation of the Spirit. To varying degrees, and to the best of my ability, I have sought to do so with my dialogue partners in this volume. While I cannot tell you this approach will be branded a success, I will tell you that I seek to be sensitive and charitable toward the traditions and hot topics I engage.

I believe you will find this relational-incarnational apologetics unique in many respects, including the striking responses by adherents of the various traditions. I am very eager for you to read these exchanges because they have a significant bearing on how to approach apologetics in our contemporary context. In writing this volume I became aware of how significant this relational-incarnational approach to apologetics is: as I got to know various respondents, trust was often established, leading to more meaningful exchanges. Much of the credit goes to the respondents. I am sure they struggled to engage me (and still do). But their relational intuitions have helped sustain our dialogues. The structure of the volume hints at the dialogical nature of this enterprise. For example, I do not provide rejoinders but allow the responses to stand on their own. It isn't always easy, but we who are evangelical Christians must come to realize that being faithful witnesses to Jesus does not always mean that we must have the last word. Some books with rebuttals include rejoinders by their authors, and while there is merit in such approaches, they are not as realistic as the approach taken here. Dialogical, relational forms of engagement allow for space and openness. They reflect the complexity of level-playing-field interaction with those who do not share our perspectives. We must guard against imposing our categories on people of diverse paths and dismissing those who think and believe differently than we. Those who believe differently continue to exist after intense exchanges, and we must learn how to live alongside them for the long haul. Christians must learn to live, navigate, and engage other traditions in the context of such cultural and intellectual complexity, variety, and ambiguity.

As followers of Jesus we will experience frustration, disappointment, and even trauma from time to time. I still remember the pain and trauma I experienced recently when a leader of one religion said to my world religions class and me, "I don't care what you evangelicals think. Just leave us alone." His remark was very hurtful and dismissive; he did not care to engage us. Perhaps he spoke out of pain and rejection. Perhaps he and/or others in his religious tradition had experienced firsthand evangelicals shoving truth claims down their throats and trying to impose on them certain moral codes or worse. In that sense my class and I may have had it coming, given our solidarity with evangelicalism as a movement. Still, we simply wanted to interact with this leader and learn from him. We evangelicals will need to grow in tenacity to give space to others, to be patient, and to love sacrificially, always hoping and praying that they will someday respond to Jesus' love in faith. As witnesses it is not our place to bracket and bookend others but to approach our dialogues and lives with them as open books, where the truth claims come off the page and into people's hearts. If we are open books, people can then get the inside scoop on our lives. This will require humility, vulnerability, and tenacity on our part even as we address hot topics. So we will need to be sure that for all our inadequacies, we seek to live beyond reproach and find our adequacy in God.

My colleague Dr. Philip Johnson, who teaches church history at the seminary where I serve, told me that he seeks to introduce students to Christian figures from the past who found Christ to be their all-sufficiency in facing and overcoming overwhelming challenges, including their own inadequacies. Dr. Johnson explained that so many of our students sense that they are inadequate to serve Jesus Christ, many of them coming from broken homes and lives filled with pain, failure, and disappointment. Like them, I sense my inadequacy even as I write these words; in fact, even now I hope my sense of inadequacy in myself increases so that I might find my adequacy in Christ and not in technique or intellect, however useful they may be. Even the brilliant Paul, the great apostle and apologist, said that his adequacy came from Christ, not himself. No doubt that was one of the secrets of his own ministry's success: "Such confidence as this is ours through Christ before God. Not that we are competent in ourselves to claim anything for ourselves, but our competence comes from God. He has made us competent as ministers of a new covenant—not of the letter but of the Spirit; for the letter kills, but the Spirit gives life" (2 Corinthians 3:4–6).

While I will offer recommendations and seek to model a relational and incarnational approach to apologetic witness, this is not your typical how-to book that states, "Do these three things when your alternative worldview dialogue partner says these two things." As we move forward through this book, I trust that you will be ever more conscious that the ultimate "how to" in speaking about Christ in an increasingly diverse culture is to speak exclusively from the standpoint of dependence on him and his holy love for you and those you seek to reach. Never forget: our adequacy comes from him.

PART I

A Relational-Incarnational Approach

CHAPTER 1

WHAT IS RELATIONAL-INCARNATIONAL APOLOGETICS?

Have you ever seen the movie *As Good as It Gets*, starring Jack Nicholson and Helen Hunt? Nicholson plays Melvin Udall, a man who pursues "Carol the Waitress," played by Hunt. Until he falls in love, Melvin is rude, insensitive, racially bigoted, homophobic, and severely obsessive-compulsive. As his gay neighbor Simon Bishop explains, Melvin is the worst kind of human. As difficult as it is to deal with Melvin, it is perhaps even more difficult to imagine that this man is a best-selling author of romance novels. In fact, when the female receptionist at his publishing house asks him how he is able to portray women so accurately in his works, Melvin tells her that women are like men, only without reason and accountability.

But what does all this have to do with apologetics? Everything. Everything, that is, if you want to engage people truthfully and relationally—and not treat them dismissively. That's what this chapter and this book are about. But it's easier said than done. So often I am like Melvin. I talk about romance novels—usually God's love letter to us recorded as the Bible—but I'll never understand the depth of his love. I talk about relationships with people, but I rarely develop them myself. I lecture on incarnational, life-on-life apologetic engagement, but I often fail to respond to people life-on-life, keeping them at a distance. And I know I am not alone in this social indifference.

Conservative Christians often approach people as Melvin Udall does. We can wax eloquent on romance and relationships, but we rarely experience them. We approach Mormons, Buddhists, and homosexuals as Melvin does: categorizing and dehumanizing them until we are forced to deal with them face-to-face. Only then do we see that they are humans and not stereotypes. We may be able to articulate a homosexual worldview in order to dismantle it or set forth the homosexual demographic of a given locale, accounting for their tastes, educational backgrounds, vocations, hobbies, everything except who they are in terms of their deepest values and life stories. In other words, we can know about homosexuals or Buddhists or Mormons as groups, but never really know or engage the individuals. Instead we simply lump them all into one category, as Melvin unceremoniously labels Carol as a waitress and Simon as a fag. But it isn't so easy to label others once we find out who they really are.

People are complex, mysterious, inconsistent, contradictory, wart-infested, and wondrous to behold. In keeping with how Simon views the matter, the longer you gaze at someone, the more human the individual becomes.[1] And if you stare at someone long enough, that individual becomes more than just his or her worldview or demographic. Like God, in whose image everyone is created, each human is too complex to be classified. True understanding requires what Atticus Finch says in *To Kill a Mockingbird*: "If you can learn a simple trick, . . . you'll get along a lot better with all kinds of folks. You never really understand a person until you consider things from his point of view . . . until you climb into his skin and walk around in it."[2]

What will lead us to take the risk to climb outside our shells, peel away the pretense of false skin, climb into someone else's skin, and walk around in it? Usually it takes a crisis to justify such a risk. Melvin does not get close to Carol until she's suddenly gone from his life: she quits her waitressing job for the sake of her sick child, Spencer. Melvin finds a top-notch doctor to care for "Spence" (as Melvin will later affectionately refer to him) so that she can return to her job. At first, Melvin selfishly wants Carol to remain his waitress at his favorite restaurant, but his interest in her deepens as his contact with her increases.

Melvin's crisis with his neighbor Simon begins when Simon, who is an artist, is beaten horribly. Simon's manager imposes on Melvin and makes him care for Simon's dog. Melvin is forced to get outside his skin and enter into Simon's world. As time goes on and as Melvin's, Carol's, and Simon's lives become increasingly intertwined, Melvin realizes that objective logic won't help him truly understand relational and subjective beings. As a Melvin-like Christian apologist, I need to come to terms with the fact that the individuals to whom I am presenting the faith are more than their worldviews, demographics, and behaviors—far more.

Reason and Market Research Are Limited

Through a relational-incarnational apologetic approach, it is possible to engage all types of people. Combining *relational* and *apologetic* may seem impossible. "Relational apologetics" sounds like an oxymoron, thanks to the modernistic conception of apologetics that involves a hard-core, in-your-face, go-for-the-jugular approach to interaction. Don't get me wrong. I am not saying that all traditional apologists debate this way. Some very brilliant apologists are sensitive and gracious in debate, but I am mindful of how some other apologists function. They win battles, but they lose wars. They win debates, but they lose hearts because of their presentation. Compassion and love are necessary in apologetic outreach, for as Floyd McClung once said and Joe Aldrich often quoted, "People don't care how much we know until they know how much we care."[3]

Imagine two apologists: The first was a young, up-and-coming evangelical scholar who memorized his famous liberal Christian opponent's arguments in preparation for their debate. Most people expected he would be destroyed by his liberal antagonist, but before the intermission, the young apologist had already so dismantled and humiliated his liberal counterpart, relishing every moment of it, that even evangelicals in the audience were feeling embarrassed for the opponent. The young man had won the battle but lost the war. The second apologist was Francis Schaeffer, founder of the evangelical organization L'Abri in Switzerland. After a debate his younger opponent said that Schaeffer gazed upon him during their interaction with the compassion of a father toward a son. Schaeffer won not only the debate but also the person's heart in the process. Which kind of apologist is more effective? Both men recognized the need for engaging in rigorous argumentation involving a solid grasp of the facts. However, the relational apologist could move beyond arguments and initiate life-on-life engagement with his opponent.

The first apologist was using simply a worldview-oriented approach. An exclusively worldview-oriented argument, as I am defining it here, is rational and conceptual in nature. It provides a robust system of thought that seeks to explain the internal coherence and external correspondence of the faith to those who do not yet know Christ. While such logic is important, it does not go far enough. People are more than collections of ideas and belief systems, and in my experience, they do not decide to believe in God based primarily on finding the Christian system of thought the most airtight option. The exclusively market-driven argument has the same flaw: it is not relational. Although it is important to communicate faith in a manner that connects with one's intended audience, it is not enough to do market research to gather facts about their likes and dislikes, including what they would find appealing about Christianity, so that the apologist can shape (or even reduce) the message to win his or her audience over as religious consumers. Consumer-based religion never sticks to people's souls, and it must always remake itself to appeal to consumers' ever-changing and fluctuating desires. The exclusively worldview-oriented approach to apologetics does not address the whole human constitution—only the rational features, turning God-fearers into religious problem solvers. In contrast, the exclusively market-driven approach to apologetics does not address the whole gospel or the soul's needs; it spins the gospel to appeal to what seekers want to hear so as to win them over as fickle consumers of religious products. These one-sided strategies reduce God to logic or propaganda, but a relational and incarnational approach to apologetics frames discussion around God's great love, which causes him to give himself to us wholly and sacrificially in Jesus.

As important and necessary as a Christian worldview is, it does not go far enough. Certainly God has a great argument for his own supremacy.

In fact, he communicates it to us through his eternal living Word (Jesus), through the written Word (Scripture), and through the words of his creatures (especially the church when it lives in obedience to Jesus through Scripture). Jesus—the living, personal Word who now lives in his people by the Spirit—dwelt in our midst. John 1:14 says it best: "The Word became flesh and made his dwelling among us. We have seen his glory, the glory of the One and Only, who came from the Father, full of grace and truth."

It is important that this Christian worldview corresponds to reality. We should not tolerate inconsistencies in our argumentation, although paradox and mystery and personal, life-altering encounters with God exceed the limits of our minds. To borrow a line from Shakespeare's *Hamlet*, where Hamlet speaks of his encounter with his father's ghost to his philosophically minded friend Horatio, "There are more things in heaven and earth, Horatio, than are dreamt of in your philosophy."[4] The great philosopher, scientist, and apologist Blaise Pascal would agree. He said on the night of his conversion, "Fire—'God of Abraham, God of Isaac, God of Jacob,' not of philosophers and scholars."[5] Even the great literary scholar and apologist C. S. Lewis wrote along these lines (when contrasting pantheism and biblical theism) in his book *Miracles*:

Men are reluctant to pass over from the notion of an abstract and negative deity to the living God. I do not wonder. Here lies the deepest tap-root of Pantheism and of the objection to traditional imagery. It was hated not, at bottom, because it pictured Him as man but because it pictured Him as king, or even as warrior. The Pantheist's God does nothing, demands nothing. He is there if you wish for Him, like a book on a shelf. He will not pursue you. There is no danger that at any time heaven and earth should flee away at His glance. If He were the truth, then we could really say that all the Christian images of kingship were a historical accident of which our religion ought to be cleansed. It is with a shock that we discover them to be indispensable. You have had a shock like that before, in connection with smaller matters—when the line pulls at your hand, when something breathes beside you in the darkness. So here; the shock comes at the precise moment when the thrill of *life* is communicated to us along the clue we have been following. It is always shocking to meet life where we thought we were alone. "Look out!" we cry, "it's *alive*." And therefore this is the very point at which so many draw back—I would have done so myself if I could—and proceed no further with Christianity. An "impersonal God"—well and good. A subjective God of beauty, truth and goodness, inside our own heads—better still. A formless life-force surging through us, a vast power which we can tap—best of all. But God Himself, alive, pulling at the other end of the cord, perhaps approaching at an infinite speed, the hunter, king, husband—that is quite another matter. There comes a moment when the children who have been playing at burglars hush suddenly: was that a *real* footstep in the hall? There comes a moment when people who have been dabbling in religion ("Man's search for God!") suddenly draw back. Supposing we really found Him? We never meant it to come to *that!* Worse still, supposing He had found us?[6]

As Pascal and Lewis make clear, God is personal and relational, calling us to account and into covenant relation. Pantheism (the belief that everything is God) and deism (the belief that God is transcendent and distant) allow people to keep God at bay. Keeping a distance from God is impossible when considering the God revealed in Scripture. From all eternity, God as Father encounters God the Son, who as his Word reveals God to us (John 1:1) and through the Spirit brings his truth home to our lives. (For discussion of the Spirit see John 14 and 16.) Interpersonal relation, address, and response go to the core of God's triune being; it is how God and we, his creation, are related and wired. The triune God of interpersonal communion has created us as relational beings: he did not intend for us to exist as solitary individuals but to enter into relationship with the Father and the Son and one another in perfect harmony through the Spirit. We all long to be loved. We were created to connect with this interpersonal God who loves us. All our witness must be framed in such a manner that it bears witness to God's relational engagement of the world.

Christian apologetics must be framed in view of this triune God who is interpersonal and relational. Colin Gunton, the British systematic theologian, explains apologetics in view of the Trinity, equating "the apologetic or missionary function" with "the elucidation of the content of the faith for those outside the community of belief." He goes on to write,

> It is part of the pathos of Western theology that it has often believed that while trinitarian theology might well be of edificatory value to those who already believe, for the outsider it is an unfortunate barrier to belief, which must therefore be facilitated by some non-trinitarian apologetic, some essentially monotheistic "natural theology." My belief is the reverse: that because the theology of the Trinity has so much to teach about the nature of our world and life within it, it is or could be the centre of Christianity's appeal to the unbeliever, as the good news of a God who enters into free relations of creation and redemption with his world. In the light of the theology of the Trinity, everything looks different.[7]

Indeed, everything does look different. The triune God enters into free relations with his world and preserves the entire creation from the enslaving constraints of mechanistic determinism. This God, who exists from all eternity in the freedom of life-giving communion as Father, Son, and Spirit, freely creates the world and endows humans and nonhumans alike with majesty and dignity so they can be all that he designed them to be in the freedom of their respective creaturely vocations. There is no sense of need for communion with us to make up for a lack in the divine life. We do not emanate from God or complete his eternal being. There is no sense of compulsion. Rather the Father connects with us as the result of his overflowing grace and mercy, expressing the abundance and fecundity of the divine love of the triune, interpersonal encounter through the Word—the incarnate Son—and the quickening, life-giving Spirit.

In John's gospel we find the personal Word, Jesus, engaging people heart to heart and life on life, addressing them and calling for response. Unfortunately many of the first-century Jewish leaders in Jerusalem sought to quantify and compartmentalize and enslave spirituality, turning it into dead orthodoxy, locking God in the holy of holies and in the inner court, where the Gentiles could not go, and marketing and commercializing religion and profiting from religious practices. No wonder they were taken aback and reacted strongly when God's Holy-of-Holies Word took up residence in the flesh (John 1:14; the text conveys that Jesus tabernacled in our midst as God's Shekinah glory in the flesh); Jesus confronted them outside the inner sanctum (John 2:13–25; Mark 11:12–19), challenged their exploitation of the temple system, and proclaimed that he had come to replace the temple as the messianic community's center of worship (John 2:18–22). This challenge and declaration was a twofold threat to the Jewish leaders' grasp on power.[8] The same Jewish leaders treated knowledge of the Scriptures the same way. They failed to see that the Scriptures were not collections of special truths to which simple assent and adherence (apart from living, personal faith in God revealed in Jesus) led automatically to salvation. And so Jesus, the Word enfleshed, rebuked them: "You diligently study the Scriptures because you think that by them you possess eternal life. These are the Scriptures that testify about me, yet you refuse to come to me to have life" (John 5:39–40).

Fortunately not everyone responded as those Jewish leaders did. They wanted to kill Jesus because he healed the man on the Sabbath and because he claimed that God is his Father (John 5:18). The woman at the well responded much better. Because Jesus knew so much about her past, she went from hiding behind Samaritan folk religion to embracing Jesus' words as Spirit-filled truth that leads to eternal life (John 4:16–26). How will we respond—like many of the Jewish leaders and scholars or like this lowly Samaritan woman? Jesus offers us eternal life—not as a collection of facts or rules to follow or as a commodity. He invites us to enter into interpersonal communion with his Father and himself through the Spirit for all eternity. (See Jesus' promise of the Spirit of abundant life in John 7:37–39.) Jesus does not market eternal life. Eternal life is not some product or thing that Jesus gives us. Jesus *is* eternal life. He gives himself to us free of charge. Exclusively worldview-oriented and market-driven approaches keep God at bay and do not call for us to move beyond our gray matter or our greenbacks. Relational-incarnational apologetics demands of us our thoughts and money and every drop of our blood, sweat, and tears as a sacrifice of praise in response to God's sacrificial love poured out for us.

Love Is Limitless

In *As Good as It Gets*, Melvin uses his clout as a best-selling author to persuade his editor at the publishing house to ask her top-notch husband-doctor to care for Carol's sick son, Spencer. Melvin and his editor are not friends; their relationship is simply contractual. It is only because he is a best-selling author (which he uses to his advantage in manipulating his editor to help him out) that his editor chooses to help him, and it is only because he has money to cover the high medical costs that Carol goes back to work to wait on Melvin. Melvin goes to great lengths to buy her services as his waitress. It is essentially contractual, not communal. Melvin is persuasive in getting his editor and his waitress to do as he wishes, but his persuasive powers are not about truth or love but about satisfying his base desire to enjoy breakfast. What would happen if Melvin loses forever his creative flair for writing romance novels? What if he can no longer cover Spencer's medical bills? And what if Melvin loses his taste for the food served at the restaurant? The contractual arrangement between all three parties falls apart.

Eventually Melvin falls in love with Carol, and that love changes everything. He will do anything for Carol, despite how often she insults him. He still uses the art of persuasion, but it is not so that he can get her to wait on him—it is to win her heart. Toward the end of the movie, just as Carol is telling him they are incompatible, Melvin takes the biggest risk of all and tells her how he really feels about her. No pretense. No small print. No bait and switch. He no longer resists the pull of the line of his affection for her. He swallows it hook, line, and sinker.

The rest is history. The love that Melvin increasingly experiences toward Carol extinguishes his rudeness and insensitivity, his compulsiveness, his homophobia, and his autonomy.[9] This is what God does with us, when his loving, personal, incarnational truth invades our lives. We no longer try to sell people on God, using gimmicks and bells and whistles to tickle their ears to make them sign up and buy a ticket for heaven. We engage them heart-to-heart, just as God did when he sent his Son to the world. Far from tolerating and enduring us, far from telling us what we want to hear, he told us what we need to hear: we are dearly loved, we are deeply messed up, and he has gone to the greatest lengths imaginable to win our hearts. He is interested not simply in our minds, obedience, and pocketbooks but in every part of us, just as he has given all of his triune self to us, as Jesus and the Spirit are poured out into the world.

An exclusively worldview-oriented model of apologetic witness leaves the discussion at a collection of good ideas designed to show people that the Christian view best explains reality and that people need to exchange their deficient worldview for the Christian one. An exclusively market-driven approach tells people what they want to hear and not what they need to hear, so that the apologist can seal the deal and go on to the next customer. In contrast, a relational and incarnational model of apologetics goes beyond discussion of God's good ideas and away from a great marketing strategy to sharing in the life of a holy, loving God who gives himself to us sacrificially. Relational-incarnational apologetics does include rational discussion of God's great ideas and pays careful attention to context so the truth is communicated meaningfully to others of different faiths. But it goes beyond syllogisms and targeting a particular demographic, and it goes beyond soft-sell. Actually, it can involve hard words, but those words come forth from sharing in hard and messy life whereby one creates space through self-sacrifice on behalf of the other for one's views to be heard. It also involves having hard words to say to oneself even while challenging others, repenting of one's sins that keep people from coming to terms with Jesus for who he is and not what we make him and his message out to be. In the end, a relational and incarnational model will assist in bearing witness to Christ among people in a post-Christendom,[10] postmodern[11] context; such a context is often quite cynical and dismissive of Christian claims and sales pitches. These cynics need to experience the good news, as we share life with them. Such engagement will require far more than rigorous thoughts and careful attention to context. Ultimately such engagement will cost us our lives. Are we prepared to begin this missional journey?[12]

CHAPTER 2

WHAT ARE WE MAKING AN
APOLOGY FOR ANYWAY?

What do I mean by "apology"? I am not talking about saying "I'm sorry." That will come later (chapter 4). Nor am I talking about the compulsion to try to defend God. The kind of apology I am talking about here is bearing witness to the good news of Jesus Christ. So then what is the good news, and why is it so good?

If we are not careful, we can easily turn the good news into a position paper about the faith. While robust confessions of the faith are vital, the good news is much more than a statement of faith. It is a personal relationship with the living God, about whom we confess certain statements. The propositions about personal relationship with God have their place, as long as they don't replace the relationship with God to which we bear witness.

Have you ever been in a heated argument with someone and wondered, "What are we arguing about anyway?" If we are taking the gospel to heart, we should be asking ourselves that same question when engaging in dialogues and debates on the gospel. While propositions of revelation, particular stances on eschatology, and personal views on ethics are important, we must make sure that the main thing remains the *main thing*. We all struggle to get at the main thing. For me, a good way to separate essentials from nonessentials is to ask myself, "What hill am I willing to die on?" I doubt I would be willing to fight and die for my particular stances on the seventy weeks of Daniel and premillennialism, the finer points of the doctrine of biblical inspiration, or the precise moment when human life begins. But the relational bases that undergird eschatology (the doctrine of the future), bibliology (the doctrine of Scripture), and ethics (the principles of moral values) definitely resonate with me as gospel-centric. In keeping with these points, I esteem those early Christians who were willing to die for their belief based on the Bible that Jesus is the resurrected Lord, that he is returning bodily and will judge the living and the dead, and that no one can ultimately take away their value and significance because they have inherent worth and dignity as those created by a God who loves them and to whom they will return. These are hills on which I would die too.

There are two dangers when discussing matters of propositions about God and personal relationship with God. The first is reducing personal relationship with God to a series of propositions, missing the forest (personal relationship with God) while looking at the trees (statements about God). The second is rejecting propositions about God in favor of personal relationship, failing to see that even talk about personal relationship with God involves certain propositional claims, such as: there is a God; I am not this God; and God is personal, not impersonal, and wants to have a relationship with you and me.

When making an apology about God, we must also guard against the tendency of turning the good news into a marketing plan or business strategy with contractual terms of agreement where the small print is really small. All too often, we turn gospel witness into a pharmaceutical commercial. As Christians, we should not be trying to sell people something. We should hope that God uses us to save them from selling themselves and their souls for cheap and/or expensive goods. For what does it profit a person to gain the whole world and yet lose his or her soul (Matthew 16:26; Mark 8:36)?

As witnesses we shouldn't be trying to make people identify themselves with our Christian brand, but we should, rather, be helping them see beyond labels that commodify Christianity and themselves to lasting heart-to-heart connections with Jesus, who longs for communion with them. With this in mind, we should not portray relationship with Jesus as contractual. Relationship with Jesus is an unconditional loving covenant into which Jesus calls us, where he accepts us with all our warts and wrinkles and stains, and where he makes us his own holy people by transforming us from the inside out.

The Christian symbol of the cross is not a logo like the Nike Swoosh or the BMW Roundel, where people purchase the brand's products to gain a sense of prestige or status. By identifying with the symbol of the cross, Christians historically were claiming to move beyond status, unconditionally laying down their lives for Jesus because Jesus had laid down his life unconditionally for them. Unlike a logo you can tear off, you can never tear yourself off of a cross when both your hands and feet are nailed to it. We are not trying to sell people Christian products. Sure, Jesus talks about the kingdom of heaven being like a priceless treasure in a field or a pearl of great price, for which people will go out and sell all they own to buy them. But instead of adding costly possessions to our inventory, we will have to sell everything to purchase this treasure or pearl (Matthew 13:44–46). There is no small print with Jesus. All the print is big; it is even red-letter. "In the same way, any of you who does not give up everything he has cannot be my disciple" (Luke 14:33). We are not talking about selling products but about giving our lives to Jesus just as Jesus has given his life to us. There is no exchange of mere assets but an exchange of lives—where Jesus dies so that we can live—and a marriage of hearts as Jesus rises from the dead to take us to himself to share in his fullness. We belong to Jesus as his holy people and spotless bride, and he is our merciful, loving Lord and royal husband.

CHRIST AND HIS BRIDE

The gospel is a shared story involving priceless sacrifice for the sake of interpersonal communion, even sacred romance. This claim is significant to me. I am willing to die for it, for it is the reason why I live. Everything follows from it, since for me everything is bound up with it.

Why do I say this? Because this is how God's inspired and authoritative Word, the Bible, portrays it. In Ephesians 5:25–33, Paul says that the ultimate relationship outside the Godhead is between Christ and the church. While the relationship between a husband and a wife is profoundly important (harking back to God's institution of marriage in the garden recorded in Genesis 2), it is only a witness to the marriage of Christ and the church. The fruit of that relationship is the rescue of all believers. As Ray Ortlund Jr. once said in a sermon I heard years ago, God was not from all eternity pondering how he would illustrate the marriage relationship between husbands and wives and so determined to send his Son into the world to live, die, and rise again to create the church for marital communion. God determined in the eternal council of the Trinity to create the institution of marriage between men and women to illustrate the ultimate marriage of Christ and the church.[1] As Paul says, God's ultimate concern is not with husbands and wives, but with Christ and his church, to which the former union bears witness (Ephesians 5:31–33).

Jonathan Edwards seemingly bears witness to Paul when Edwards maintains that God's goal in human history is to provide God's Son with a bride: "There was, [as] it were, an eternal society or family in the Godhead, in the Trinity of persons. It seems to be God's design to admit the church into the divine family as his son's wife. . . . Heaven and earth were created that the Son of God might be complete in a spouse."[2] If this is so—and I truly believe it is—then it is vital that Jesus returns. Otherwise, how will that spiritual union be consummated? While one might not accept a literal reading of the seventy weeks of Daniel, one must accept a literal reading of Jesus' visible return for his bride—the church—at which time faith becomes sight and all is transformed.

Now, if this is so, rationalism and moralism have no place, and yet sound rationality and morality certainly do. Regarding rationalism and rationality, John Calvin says in his commentary on Ephesians that we cannot understand the nature of the spiritual union between Christ and the church that Paul discusses in Ephesians 5:25–33. However, that does not mean we should take lightly its profound relational significance. Instead we must seek to experience it. Calvin speaks of Paul's own "astonishment at the spiritual union between Christ and the church." Calvin later comments, "For my own part, I am overwhelmed by the depth of this mystery, and am not ashamed to join Paul in acknowledging at once my ignorance and my admiration." Calvin wants to avoid two extremes: dissecting "the manner and character of this union" and "undervaluing what Paul declares to be a deep mystery." In place of these two extremes, Calvin argues that "reason itself teaches how we ought to act in such matters; for whatever is supernatural is clearly beyond our own comprehension. Let us therefore *labour* more to feel Christ living in us, than to discover the nature of that *intercourse*."[3]

Ephesians 5 also speaks of Christ's profound sacrifice for his bride, laying down his life for the church. We also know how Paul served the church in sacrificial service to Christ. The same kind of sacrificial love is expected of us as we seek to commune with Christ. How can it be otherwise, for participation in Christ's life involves experiencing not only Jesus' sweet joys and supreme delights but also his deep sorrows and dire sufferings? In fact, any deep and profound relationship entails participation in hardships as well as highlights. This is even more so the case for our marital union with Christ. So, while grin-and-bear-it moralism is out, our moral fiber will be tested and cultivated through trials so that we can experience the joyful fullness of Christ's life in loving communion with him as his Spirit of love fills our hearts with faith, hope, and love.

We suffer with Christ so that we might fully participate in his life of love. Not only do sacrifice and suffering take on greater significance when we suffer with Christ in communion with him, but the Bible and ethics also take on greater significance. The Bible's inspiration and authority are bound up with bearing witness to this relationship between Christ and the church rather than in being conceived as a textbook of information about God and the world. (While there is information to be gained, the information is to be framed relationally, not rationalistically.) Therefore, ethical determinations correspond to interpersonal communion and holy love rather than to the unholy and unloving cheapening and commodification of individuals. Anything not done from the vantage point of God's holy love is empty and lacking in lasting value (1 Corinthians 13). Anything not done in view of Christ's precious and priceless sacrifice is unethical, or at least is less than fully ethical; for as Jesus said, "Greater love has no one than this, that he lay down his life for his friends" (John 15:13). And as Jesus also says, we should love our enemies just as God does, being perfect as he is perfect (Matthew 5:43–48). In Romans 5:6–11, Paul says that Jesus laid down his life for his enemies to make us his friends. The Bible teaches that God even transforms a wretched whore to be his spotless bride. (See the book of Hosea and Revelation 19.)

Nowhere is the sacred romance between Christ and his church more profoundly envisioned than in Andrei Rublev's classic icon of the holy Trinity, which is based on his reading of the story in Genesis 18 where Abraham hosts three angelic visitors.[4] This icon "clearly expresses" the "eternal circle of love which opens to the hospitality of the creature, leading it to the eternal trinitarian Banquet."[5] Here in this celebrated icon (which is not intended to be worshipped but to be used in worship, serving as a window into the divine realm), "the circle of the infinite tenderness of 'the Three' opens to welcome the viewer, whom the icon leads into sacred space, to communion at the Table of God, at the very heart of the hospitality of God to which man, in turn, is invited and where, with fear and love, he enters into the intimacy of God."[6] Nowhere is this hospitality better described or envisioned biblically than in the closing chapters of the book of Revelation. God, who judges Babylon and the merchants who committed adultery with the unholy city, makes of a wretched whore a holy bride for his Son, Jesus; and through the Holy Spirit and the bride—the church—God invites all to come and enter into the joy of union with his Son at his wedding banquet.

God has not closed off the circle. The Son, who as Jonathan Edwards says will be made complete in a spouse, has not yet completed his church. Just as Rublev's icon opens up toward the person who is gazing upon it, so God opens up toward the world through his Spirit and the church, and says to all, "Come!" John the apostle bears witness to the Spirit and the bride in Revelation 22:17, where he writes, "The Spirit and the bride say, 'Come!' And let him who hears say, 'Come!' Whoever is thirsty, let him come; and whoever wishes, let him take the free gift of the water of life." This vision of infinite and breathtaking beauty is worth dying for because it is the ultimate reality and is worth living for—even for all eternity. And so I ask you: What are you making an apology for?

MARRIAGE AND ENFLESHED FAITH

I find myself repenting and apologizing for how I often fail to live into this vision of ultimate reality involving relational intimacy, for which I am called to make an apology. The Father, Son, and Spirit who have wired us to participate in their bond of love for all eternity continue to reach out to connect with us. And yet, we so often pull away. But God keeps on pursuing us, rewiring us to be relationally whole and making that reconnection. To this end, Jesus becomes flesh and dwells with his people (John 1:14; Revelation 21:1–4). To this end, he becomes one flesh with his church (Ephesians 5:31; Revelation 19:6–9). To this end, the Spirit opens the circle and invites us in to complete us as he makes all things new (Revelation 21:5; 22:17). As witnesses to this reality, it is our privilege to join the Spirit and invite people to come and drink and be made whole in the new creation. To this end, we must open our hearts to God, our ears to listen, our mouths to confess, and our lives to others. We must put flesh on our faith so that together we can break down barriers and be made whole. This one flesh reality is spiritual. Whereas the letter kills, the Spirit gives life (2 Corinthians 3:6). The Spirit makes old bones live again (Ezekiel 37:11–14) and all things new (Revelation 21:5; 22:17).

MARRIAGE AND THE SPIRIT

While I can share with you information about this reality, even computing it in such a way that you could add it to your Christian worldview, you must come to experience such intimacy in marital union with Christ through the Spirit. And while I can hopefully communicate these truths to you in a winsome and compelling manner that would make you want to experience profound communion with Christ, I will not engage in selling Jesus' church out to the highest bidder, turning her into a whore like the Babylon of Revelation 18, cheapening her by failing to insist that God calls on his people to be holy in preparation for the marriage supper of his Son. Encounter Jesus. Suffer with him to experience his life more fully. Be holy in your love for God and his church as God is holy in his love for you and his church. Imagine what awaits those who now walk by faith, when faith and hope give way to the fullness of love when Jesus appears, when faith becomes sight at the consummation of Jesus' union with his people at the marriage supper of the Lamb.

I am banking everything on Jesus becoming flesh, becoming one flesh with his people, and making new this world of flesh and blood and matter. This book is an apology for the enfleshed Word of the triune God and all that his incarnate life entails for the world and various relationships. As such it is an apology not only for the incarnate God but for humanity and the creation as a whole. This holistic reality to which I point entails holistic witness. Just as the Word became flesh to love this world, we must be enfleshed through words and deeds of love. These themes we will engage throughout the book in different ways.

In the first chapter we set forth the basic meaning of relational-incarnational apologetics. This chapter focuses on the essential gospel message to which we seek to bear witness. The next chapter talks about making sure we are truly bearing witness to Jesus and not serving as a stumbling block to people and keeping them from coming to know him. The fourth chapter talks about our ongoing need to repent of ineffective witness and renewal as witnesses. The last chapter in this opening section focuses on the church as God's ultimate apologetic witness to the incarnate Christ.

In the end you will need to determine what you are making an apology for and how you approach apologetics. In fact, take time to consider what you believe is the biblical, gospel core and decide how you would share it in apologetic witness. You and I must always seek to keep the main thing as the main thing, not getting off on tangents, being distracted by interesting issues, failing to connect everything to the center—which I hope for you is Jesus and your relationship with him and all things in relation to him. Whatever you are making an apology for, make sure you really believe it, and that it is worth dying for because you are convinced that it is worth living for—eternally.

So what hill will you die on? Remember you only have one life to live. Let me encourage you to consider carefully your options and then take aim at the heart, banking everything on Jesus and his undying love for the people to whom you are bearing witness, depending ultimately on the Spirit and not primarily on your reason, marketing strategies, or business plans. If you follow my advice, you will be making a powerful apology for the gospel because your confidence will not be in yourself; your adequacy will come from him (2 Corinthians 5:11–21).

CHAPTER 3

Who's the Stumbling Block—
You and Me or Jesus?

Contrary to what one may think of healthy relationships, a relational apologetic model does not entail rejection of the idea that Jesus is a stumbling block. In fact, it promotes Jesus as a stumbling block. Paul speaks of Jesus as a stumbling block in 1 Corinthians 1:22–25: "Jews demand miraculous signs and Greeks look for wisdom, but we preach Christ crucified: a stumbling block to Jews and foolishness to Gentiles, but to those whom God has called, both Jews and Greeks, Christ the power of God and the wisdom of God. For the foolishness of God is wiser than man's wisdom, and the weakness of God is stronger than man's strength."

Jesus is the crucified God. As such he is a stumbling block and scandalous to those imprisoned by the world system, the flesh, and the devil. When engaging in relational-incarnational apologetics, how can we remove the cross's reminder of his violent and humiliating death? How can we ignore Jesus' call to deny ourselves and follow him? We must accept the whole Christ and nothing but the whole Christ. Jesus is not a power-of-positive-thinking therapist, a Santa-like figure with a bag of toys, or a bobble-head doll that sits on one's dashboard as a good-luck charm. While comforting and counseling and freely giving himself as he sovereignly and providentially watches over us, Jesus is also Lord and God, our divine holy lover who judges sin. He has the right to call us to account, for his love is pure and the Father has entrusted all judgment to him.

Here we find infinite irony and paradox. Religious and secular types alike are often repulsed by the cross, but the cross is the very symbol of God's holy love. The cross demonstrates that God does not hold our sins against us or wall himself off from us. The cross reveals God's open heart toward us, as the God of justice has determined to be judged in our place, opening the door for us to enter into his presence as his people.

How strange is it that the one to whom all judgment has been entrusted seeks us out in his infinite mercy? Rather than seeking to judge and condemn us, the judge has undergone our judgment in place of us. No wonder God has entrusted all judgment to him. By contrast, the Father has not entrusted judgment to us; God has not made us God. And yet we so often want to take the place of God as God. In our idolatry and self-righteousness, we set stumbling blocks in front of people that keep them from stumbling over Jesus and falling into his arms. Self-righteousness and self-interest birthed in self-love are our biggest hurdles in bearing witness to Jesus. When we as Christians fail to live into the fullness of Jesus' love, loving ourselves more than him and others, we become stumbling blocks to people, tripping them up and keeping them from stumbling over Jesus and his holy love.

FALSE WITNESSES

Self-love stands in the way of loving God and loving others. Self-love leads us to reject God's selfless love poured out in Christ at the cross, causing us to despise the cross and to try to take Christ's place as judge. Self-love leads us to seek to displace God and distance ourselves from others. Pursuing power and glory and wisdom from below, we seek to rise up on the backs of others; we marginalize and banish them rather than call them to repent of their rebellious ways as we repent of our own rebellious ways, responding to God's love and mercy as recipients of and debtors to God's grace.

Self-love or narcissism is something each of us must contend against, and how we respond to the cross is indicative of how righteous or selfish we are. Self-righteousness, that is bringing our supposed capacities of righteousness and confidence in our own abilities to the table as if they are helpful, fails to account for Scripture, which calls for clearing and even overturning the table of self-righteousness in view of the cross. There is a reason the very first beatitude in Jesus' kingdom manifesto known as the Sermon on the Mount is, "Blessed are the poor in spirit, for theirs is the kingdom of heaven" (Matthew 5:3). It entails being undone before God, sensing our desperate need for God, boasting only in God and not in ourselves. The cross drives us to boasting in God, the crucified God, the God undone for us to break us of our self-righteousness as he pours himself out for us, making himself a fool, holding nothing back. Let the one who boasts boast not in his or her own supposed righteousness, wisdom, riches, power, or niche groupings; let that person boast in the Lord (Jeremiah 9:23–24; 1 Corinthians 1, especially verse 31).

A people who realize that they are the worst of sinners have the potential to be the best and greatest apologists. I believe Paul was the greatest apologist among the apostles because he realized he was the least of the apostles (1 Corinthians 15:9). He had stumbled over Jesus in his self-righteousness and had fallen apart, coming undone and being remade. As a result, no one else stumbled over Paul because his identity was in Christ Jesus. He got out of the way so that people could stumble over Jesus' loving righteousness rather than Paul's self-righteousness. Instead of making them become like Saul the Pharisee, Paul became all things to all people so that they could know Christ (1 Corinthians 9:19–23) and receive his mercy, rather than stand against him in self-love and pride. Paul wanted Christians to make sure they saw Jesus alone as the stumbling block, and that they themselves did not cause others to stumble.

When Paul wrote his first letter to the Corinthian Christians, they were not done stumbling over Jesus, for they continued to identify themselves in relation to human leaders such as Paul or Peter or Apollos (1 Corinthians 1:12). They thought too highly of themselves (1 Corinthians 1:26–27), flaunted their spiritual gifts (1 Corinthians 12, 14), and boasted in their false forms of wisdom, power, and riches (1 Corinthians 1:31; Jeremiah 9:23–24). As a result of their narcissistic, self-righteous tendencies, they were failing to bear witness to Christ and were themselves stumbling blocks, keeping the people around them from encountering Jesus. All of us must stumble over Christ Jesus and his cross, or we will never fall into his arms and come to know him personally; instead, we will stand in opposition, seeking to be God in place of him. We must die to ourselves daily in him, or we will never find him or our true selves.

A Theology of the Cross and True Witness

German monk Martin Luther was concerned for Christian evangelism and apologetics in the sixteenth century because he thought Roman Catholic theology and practices kept people from being effective witnesses. In place of celebrating a theology of glory apart from the cross, Luther gloried in the cross. Luther's concern paralleled Paul's. First-century Christian Corinthians had factionalized based on celebrity connections (1 Corinthians 1:12) and class divisions (1 Corinthians 11:17–34). Both Paul and Luther understood that works righteousness is based on self-love, and self-love involves spiritual pride. Love is humble, not prideful; it does not seek its own good, but the good of the other, especially the unlovable. Self-love leads to self-righteousness, whereby one boasts in oneself—in one's intellect, skill, and charisma, and in others whom one finds attractive, upstanding, and good. As a result of self-love and pride, we never move beyond ourselves and niche affinity groupings to care for the weak, the foolish, the ugly, and the poor so that they might be saved. For we cannot even see how weak and foolish and ugly and poor and needy we are!

Narcissism

Regardless of the mistakes of first-century and sixteenth-century Christians, how do we respond to God's love revealed in the crucified and risen Christ now in our own lives? Do we boast in our accomplishments and capacities and affinities? If so, we do not have the love of God in our hearts; and as a result, we cannot be effective witnesses who move beyond the love of worldly attractions to faith in God's love revealed in Christ Jesus and the cross. As Luther states in the Heidelberg Catechism, "The love of God does not find, but creates, that which is pleasing to it. The love of man comes into being through that which is pleasing to it." He goes on to write,

> The love of God which lives in man loves sinners, evil persons, fools, and weaklings in order to make them righteous, good, wise, and strong. Rather than seeking its own good, the love of God flows forth and bestows good. There sinners are attractive because they are loved; they are not loved because they are attractive. For this reason the love of man avoids sinners and evil persons. Thus Christ says: "For I came not to call the righteous, but sinners" [Matthew 9:13]. This is the love of the cross, born of the cross, which turns in the direction where it does not find good which it may enjoy, but where it may confer good upon the bad and needy person.[1]

Luther goes on to say that the intellect is not able to grasp this state, for it can only affirm and embrace that which exists as true and good in appearance, not that which exists only as a result of God's creative love—"the poor and needy person" whom God makes good.[2]

Our narcissism keeps us from seeking God and seeing the poor, for God is found only in the weakness and foolishness and suffering of the cross as he determines to serve the poor and needy and humble the strong and wise. Luther writes,

> Because men misused the knowledge of God through works, God wished again to be recognized in suffering, and to condemn wisdom concerning invisible things by means of wisdom concerning visible things, so that those who did not honor God as manifested in his works should honor him as he is hidden in his suffering. As the apostle says in 1 Corinthians 1[:21], "For since, in the wisdom of God, the world did not know God through wisdom, it pleased God through the folly of what we preach to save those who believe." Now it is not sufficient for anyone, and it does him no good to recognize God in his glory and majesty, unless he recognizes him in the humility and shame of the cross. Thus God destroys the wisdom of the wise, as Isa. [45:15] says, "Truly, thou are a God who hidest thyself."[3]

Luther adds,

> He who does not know Christ does not know God hidden in suffering.
> Therefore he prefers works to suffering, glory to the cross, strength to
> weakness, wisdom to folly, and, in general, good to evil. . . . God can
> be found only in suffering and the cross. Therefore the friends of the
> cross say that the cross is good and works are evil, for through the cross
> works are destroyed and the old Adam, who is especially edified by
> works, is crucified. It is impossible for a person not to be puffed up by
> his good works unless he has first been deflated and destroyed by suf-
> fering and evil until he knows that he is worthless and that his works
> are not his but God's.[4]

A theology of God's glory apart from the cross is narcissistic and nihilistic. Let's consider these claims. The cross signifies concern for the other,
especially the weak and foolish and poor and ugly, instead of concern for
oneself. To deny the cross is to affirm the self over the other—both divine
and human. In elevating the self in self-love, one denies the theology of the
cross, for the cross signifies God's Son's death to self and his call on us to follow in his steps. To deny the cross is to deny one's own wretchedness and to
affirm one's illusory beauty and elevate self in place of God. In his discussion
"Excellence of This Means of Proving God," Blaise Pascal writes, "Those
who have known God without knowing their own wretchedness have not
glorified him but themselves. 'For after that . . . the world by wisdom knew
not God, it pleased God by the foolishness of preaching to save them that
believe' [1 Corinthians 1:21 KJV]."[5] Only by holding firmly to the cross do we
guard against narcissism, and with it nihilism.

Nihilism

To deny the theology of the cross is to deny God and meaning because
the God revealed in Jesus is the one and only God. Therefore, the rejection of the crucified God is the attempted denial of God's existence, and
denial of God's existence leads to meaninglessness, no matter how well one
is able to cover it up with personal accomplishments and acquisitions. If we
deny that the God revealed in the cross is the real God, we take matters

into our own hands and elevate self over the other, reveling in self-love. When we do this, we deny true love, for the omnipotent weakness and omniscient foolishness displayed in Jesus at the cross are the true marks of the divine love, and to deny sacrificial love is to deny purpose and meaning and hope in the universe. Without this holy, pure, sacrificial love, everything is meaningless.

The theology of glory elevates the self and affirms its own power and wisdom and self-righteousness. Wherever the self reigns, meaning is no more and chaos reigns, as in the Corinthian church. Wherever the self reigns in its own glory and beauty, all we have is shame, death, and decay, contrary to popular belief. Friedrich Nietzsche—ironically the son of a Lutheran pastor—denied the crucified God, and to deny this God is to deny the lowly other.[6] To deny the lowly other is to deny God, who will only be known in suffering among the weak and foolish. Nietzsche put forth the *Übermensch* or "over-man," which is the mirror reflection of the *Übergott* or "over-god"; both concepts deny Jesus Christ, the crucified God, and both deny meaning in the universe.

Self-love leads one to promote God as powerful and wise apart from the weakness and foolishness of the cross. Such a god is nonexistent, for God in Christ Jesus is the only God there is. A god of power and wisdom that contends against Christ's sacrificial, foolish love is the source of all meaninglessness because life is meaningless without such love. The pursuit of this non-god leads to apologetic arguments that seek to destroy the other through rational prowess, addressing the mind without appealing to the heart and concern for the other. In contrast, Paul made himself a fool to win over the hearts of the foolish and power-seeking Corinthians (2 Corinthians 11–12). As already noted, Paul became all things to all people to save as many as possible (1 Corinthians 9:19–23). Like his Lord, he gave himself sacrificially to others, holding nothing back, bearing witness to the power and wisdom of God found in the weakness and foolishness of the cross.

I am not espousing a denial of reason but an affirmation of reason at its best.[7] Such reason entails basing one's claims on the revelation of God in Christ Jesus. For as Pascal writes, "We know God only through Jesus Christ.

Without this mediator all communication with God is broken off. Through Jesus we know God. All those who have claimed to know God and prove his existence without Jesus Christ have only had futile proofs to offer."[8] Reason at its best involves developing one's claims holistically. Jesus and Paul did not simply argue with people. They exposed their hearts by appealing to their audiences' affections, pursuing arguments that would unveil people's first love. To do so, they had to expose their own hearts, moving beyond indifference and detached objectivity. As Paul said, he and his fellow witnesses did not simply share the gospel with people; they went beyond sharing information to sharing their lives in sacrificial love (1 Thessalonians 2:1–12), revealing their inner selves to reach people from the heart. Here they followed God's example, for God revealed himself to us by Jesus becoming flesh and giving his life for us in sacrificial love (John 1:14, 18; 3:16).

Jesus is a stumbling block to people—the right kind of stumbling block. He brings them to the end of themselves, to the end of boasting in vain speculation, and to the end of boasting in all that they have accomplished in their own strength, by dying in their place for their sins. Jesus' cross shames the wise and breaks the powerful; left to ourselves we so readily shame the foolish and break the weak and encourage the worldly wise to reason for reason's sake rather than for the sake of the other, especially the foolish and the weak. But when Christ gets hold of us and frees our hearts from the shackles of self-love and self-righteousness, we become like Saul who became Paul and who no longer sought after a righteousness of his own according to his own merits and capacities. Paul spoke out against those who put up false stumbling blocks for people such as circumcision of the flesh as a means for Gentile converts to be accepted by Jewish Christians (Philippians 3:1–14). Such false-teaching Judaizers were leading these Gentile converts away from faith in God's love, causing them to stumble in sin by attempting to attain righteousness on their own. The Gentile believers were being forced to attain righteousness in their own strength and wisdom rather than founding their hope on the mercies of God. Only as they attained their own righteousness according to Jewish means would they be seen as valuable and acceptable to these false teachers and many in the Jewish Christian community.[9]

Niche Communities

Narcissism, which involves self-righteousness, also leads to niche communities that exclude others. In Corinth the problem of celebrity-affinity groupings surfaced around the notorious super-apostles and even the sound leaders like Paul, Peter, and Apollos who radically opposed such idolatry. Although Paul did not address the problem in 1 Corinthians, nepotism and nationalism were very real problems in the first-century religious community. In John 8, the people who believed in Jesus later sought to kill him because he claimed to be the God of Abraham (vv. 58–59). They honored and believed Jesus previously, but they did not worship him as Lord and God. When he spoke of their need to be set free, they claimed to be children of Abraham and never slaves of anyone (John 8:31–41). As a result, they could not accept Jesus as their Savior and Lord. They placed greater value on their familial pedigree and national identity than on allegiance to God revealed in Jesus. Not only did this rejection of Jesus hurt them, but these supposed disciples were also stumbling blocks to the people at large, especially as they sought to destroy Jesus (John 8:42–59).

When we find our identities in anything other than the crucified God, we are denying the gospel and marginalizing those who do not meet our own standards, like the Gentiles who came to faith in Jesus but who were being enslaved to the law of self-righteousness. The false teachers who proclaimed that the Gentile Christians needed to be circumcised to be saved were stumbling blocks, causing these Gentiles to depend on their own strength and merit, and to succumb to the false wisdom of the flesh (Acts 15; Galatians).

How ironic is it that the one who was truly holier than you and me became sin so that we could leave behind our holier-than-thou ways and repent and become the righteousness of God (2 Corinthians 5:21)? How ironic is it that we who are unrighteous would seek to be self-righteous, rather than cling to Jesus, and exhort others to attain righteousness on their own to gain the approval not of God but of their peers and the religious establishment? How often do we lead people to stumble today?

I doubt if anyone today is urging "pagan Gentiles" to be circumcised to be saved, but perhaps we are adding other requirements to faith when the only requirement should be total dependence on God revealed in Christ Jesus for one's life and salvation. Performance-based spirituality is alive and well in North American Christianity. While spiritual maturity is crucial, we often settle for consumer preference and/or religious performance and call that spiritual. And so we judge people if they don't dress the way we do, if they don't use Christianese or other insider language, if they wear tattoos (or don't wear tattoos, based on what the niche group esteems), if they don't vote the way we do, or if they don't promote American interests here and abroad. We easily wrap the Bible in red, white, and blue, or make people wear our brand, or honor celebrities rather than wrap ourselves in Jesus' love, wear his cross, and honor him as God's despised glory (1 Corinthians 1).

JESUS IS THE TRUE STUMBLING BLOCK

Self-righteousness leads us to despise and suppress others, marginalizing them if they are not as noble and as profound as we are, forgetting that God did not choose us because of our significance. In fact, many who are chosen were not significant in the world. And even if we were significant by the world's standards, human wisdom, power, influence, and nobility have been crucified on the cross. Remember Paul's words, and you will be sure that Jesus alone is the stumbling block:

> Brothers, think of what you were when you were called. Not many of you were wise by human standards; not many were influential; not many were of noble birth. But God chose the foolish things of the world to shame the wise; God chose the weak things of the world to shame the strong. He chose the lowly things of this world and the despised things—and the things that are not—to nullify the things that are, so that no one may boast before him. It is because of him that you are in Christ Jesus, who has become for us wisdom from God—that is, our righteousness, holiness and redemption. Therefore, as it is written: "Let him who boasts boast in the Lord." (1 Corinthians 1:26–31)

Self-righteousness leads us to despise and suppress others who don't measure up to our standards. God chose us before we were righteous, before we had good behaviors, before we loved him. Yet like the Corinthian Christians, we so often forget. Remember that God loved us when we hated him. Jesus died for us, though we despised him, ridiculed him, and found him weak and foolish. Only as we know God's sacrificial love will we turn from our foolish rebellion and sinful behaviors. Only as we reach out to people as drink offerings of God's sacrificial, holy love on their behalf will they be led to repentance. Only as we stumble over Jesus and lead others to do the same, laying down our lives for them in the weakness and foolishness of Jesus' all-powerful and all-wise love (rather than being stumbling blocks by condemning them in self-righteousness), will they fall at his feet in repentance and respond in faith and be transformed.[10]

PAUL ON MARS HILL

Paul was a *world* Christian. He not only traveled the known world of his day to places such as Corinth, Athens, and Rome, but also lived in the world, even though he was not of it. As a world Christian Paul did not go around his Christian convictions to engage those outside the church. Nor did he stop short at his convictions. Rather, he went through his convictions to engage those outside the faith.

In contrast to world Christians like Paul, *worldly* Christians are in the world and of it. As such, they lose sight of their distinctive identity in Christ and their distinctive Christian truth claims. Often their rationale is that they do not want to be a stumbling block to people, but in leaving their truth claims at the door, they keep Jesus from becoming the stumbling block so others can't repent of their autonomy and respond to his loving call for relationship with them.

There is one other group—*otherworldly* Christians. These Christians are not really in the world. They stop short at their convictions and fail to connect with the people around them. These Christians will only engage those outside the faith if the latter are willing to change their views and accept Christ.

As a world Christian Paul engaged people where they were, though he did not leave them there. Take for example his interaction with the philosophers on Mars Hill. Paul was critical in mind, though charitable of spirit. We must not get these two mixed up: it is not good to be critical in spirit (where we are judgmental of people and do not hope for the good) and charitable of mind (where we do not critically discern if the perspectives of others resonate with Scripture). As a biblical Jewish monotheist, Paul grieved over the idolatry that surrounded him in Athens (Acts 17:16). But that did not keep him from thoughtful and gracious interaction with the philosophers on Mars Hill. He approached them in a spirit of charity, hoping to find points of contact even while discerning their errors in judgment. Along with his critical reflection and charitable spirit, Paul creatively engaged them. The statue of the unknown God served as a bridge for Paul as he creatively sought to build rapport and connection to Christ (Acts 17:23). There was already a connection from God in Christ, for as creator and redeemer of the world, he is in constant pursuit of us. And so, he had wired the pagan philosophers whom Paul quotes to say: In God, "we live and move and have our being" and, "We are his offspring" (Acts 17:28).

Paul continues to make points of connection when he speaks of God judging the world through Jesus, whom God raised from the dead. While many of those gathered there scoff at Paul's teaching, some want to hear more (Acts 17:32). Even those who do not cannot rightly claim that Paul distances himself from them, for God's judgment of the world includes all people, including Paul (Acts 17:30–31). As such, Paul was not the stumbling block. He recognized that everyone's rightful place was on their faces at the foot of the cross of God's judgment on sin; as such, Paul had already stumbled over Christ and is here inviting others to meet him there.

We should not seek to avoid situations where people might scoff at our Christian truth claims involving Jesus' death and resurrection. Jesus is the stumbling block, and when people scoff at him, they are only hurting themselves. They can only receive the life that Jesus offers by being humbled and stumbling over him and falling on their faces at the foot of the cross of God's judgment on sin: Jesus' foolishness and weakness are the wisdom and power of God, whereas our wisdom and power are foolish and weak in our self-isolation bound up with our pride. Like Paul, we all must constantly recognize our need for Christ's mercy as our judge who has undergone judgment for us. Paul moved through his convictions as a world Christian in charity of spirit, critical in mind, and creative in imagination. Paul made sure that he engaged people and led them to experience Jesus as the stumbling block. Will we do the same?

CHAPTER 4

Why Should We Apologize?

A few years ago, I was asked to do a four-week series at a church in Portland on how the people at that church could become more missional in their community. By the time the first class ended, I thought I was on a mission to reach that church for Christ! On the last night, I spoke of the need in post-Christendom for Christians to be redemptive in their witness and make apologies for the past and present failures of the church. I claimed that such confession has a significant role to play in our Christian witness today. This deeply troubled some people. One man reacted immediately. He stood up and interrupted my talk, exclaiming, "Why should we apologize? We're Christians!"

Why should we apologize? Whereas the man that evening indicated by his remarks that we *shouldn't* apologize because we are Christians, I believe we *should* apologize because we are Christians. So many evil things have been done over the millennia in the name of religion, including the Christian religion. While we should not forget that Christianity has made important contributions to humanity (including gains in the spheres of health and education), and that Christians have acted courageously and compassionately throughout the ages (including playing a lead role in the abolition of slavery in the United Kingdom and the United States), nonetheless the church and Christians have a spotted record. Take for example the church's roles in the Inquisition, the Wars of Religion, and the Holocaust. At various levels and in various ways, individual Christians and church movements have been guilty of committing or allowing hateful and oppressive incidents over the years. We bear the same family name—"Christian" or "Christ-follower"— as these religious perpetrators of evil and/or evil masterminds, and so we should apologize as representatives of the same faith.

Why Should We Apologize?

Rather than taking ownership and repenting of past evils committed in the name of Christianity, Christians often rationalize those actions by saying that those who committed horrible acts were not truly Christian. For example, this rationalization has been made about the Christians who were involved in atrocities against Native Americans or First Nations people to achieve the United States' Manifest Destiny. Countering the claim that those guilty of genocide against indigenous people were not Christians, Native American author Vine Deloria Jr. argues,

> They really were Christians. In their day they enjoyed all the benefits and prestige Christendom could confer. They were cheered as heroes of the faith, enduring hardships that a Christian society might be built on the ruins of pagan villages. They were featured in Sunday school lessons as saints of the Christian church. Cities, rivers, mountains, and seas were named after them.[1]

Is it any wonder then that Deloria perceives the cross—that ancient Christian symbol of liberation—this way: "Where the cross goes, there is never life more abundantly—only death, destruction, and ultimately betrayal"?[2] We must repent of acts that have led to such horrible associations with the cross. How do we repent? Not by dismissing the associations or by rationalizing that such people who were guilty of such heinous acts were not

Christians. To those who remain unconvinced by Deloria's claim, I would add that whether or not such victimizers were truly converted Christians, they confidently claimed to bear Christ's name; at the very least they were confessing Christians. That alone gives Christians today sufficient grounds to repent and make confession of sin in their stead. By claiming to bear Christ's name and to speak in his stead, they negatively impacted Christian witness, the effects of which can be forcefully felt today in many sectors, including among Native Americans.

The dominant church culture must side with indigenous people today by speaking out against their present exploitation by forces such as the negative effects of global capitalism. As Deloria has said, "At this point in the clash between Western industrialism and the planet's aboriginal peoples we find little or no voice coming from the true Christians to prevent continued exploitation."[3] For as long as I don't speak out against their oppression, my culpability increases, especially if I benefit from harm done to our indigenous brothers and sisters. Anglo believers such as me must stand in solidarity with indigenous people today in the face of ongoing oppression, if our own cries for forgiveness and repentance are to be more than words and empty rhetoric.

The dominant Christian culture in North America should not approach our Native brothers and sisters from a position of strength, relating to them from a charity mind-set and not sensing our mutual need for them; but we should come to them from a position of weakness, vulnerability, and shared need. One of the most profound apologetic arguments today is witnessing indigenous and minority Christ-followers who, though victimized, live victorious lives of forgiveness and mercy in and through Christ, even toward their Anglo victimizers.

Such is the life of the African American Christian civil rights and community development leader Dr. John M. Perkins. Dr. Perkins has had an impact on countless lives across the ethnic and economic spectrum through his own life that bears authentic witness to the power of the gospel of reconciliation and kingdom justice. Dr. Perkins was beaten within inches of his life by white supremacists when he was a young man ministering among the black poor in Mississippi. Instead of seeking revenge, Dr. Perkins allowed God to use that victimizing ordeal to transform him into a catalytic force that bears profound witness to how Jesus' victorious love breaks through racial and class divisions to bring about lasting reconciliation and redemption.[4]

Such victorious victims teach us how great our need in the dominant Christian culture[5] is for Christ's reconciling power to invade our lives, for we often have a hard time forgiving others and asking for forgiveness due to fears of vulnerability and loss of control. Sometimes it is so bad we don't even sense our need to repent. To conclude this point, when members of any victimizing dominant church culture repent and are reconciled to victimized brothers and sisters in Christ (including voluntarily and mutually sharing power and resources and talents), the church bears profound witness to Christ. For Jesus himself suggests the world will know we are his disciples when we live as one in God's love, as he and his Father are one (John 17:23).[6]

Moving on from arguing that we should repent because we bear the same name as those guilty of victimization, we should also apologize because confession of sin is viewed in Christian Scripture as a mark of growth in righteousness. Confession and repentance reflect humility and a broken and contrite spirit, which (paradoxically, perhaps) are signs of spiritual development. God will never despise such a spirit, as David acknowledges in his confession of sin in Psalm 51 (see verse 17). John also calls all Christians to confess their sins (1 John 1:9). Jesus honors the hated tax collector Zacchaues by visiting his home and affirms him for repenting of his sins (Luke 19: 1–10).

Lastly, we should apologize given that the Lord of the church became sin and died in our place as our substitute and our representative; as the apostle Paul writes of Jesus and his work, he who knew no sin became sin so that we could become God's righteousness (2 Corinthians 5:21). If Jesus can apologize, so to speak, in that he died our death, taking our penalty to himself as his own as the sinless one, then how in the world can we think we shouldn't apologize for the church's actual and inherited sins? These were the types of things I said in response to the gentleman that evening at the church.

The one thing I appreciated about the man's response that evening was that at least he saw Christians as living in solidarity with one another. He said, "Why should *we* apologize? *We're* Christians!" So many Christ-followers today do not recognize their solidarity with any movement; they see themselves simply as individual believers.

Why Should I Apologize?

Recently in a seminary class I spoke of the need for Christ-followers to repent of what the church has done through the ages in failing to bear true and redemptive witness. A very bright student who is also a genuine Christian said in response, "Why should I apologize? I'm not them." While well-meaning, the student in question failed to understand that as Christ-followers we live in solidarity with one another, and with humanity in general.

So many believers fail to recognize this biblical teaching of corporate solidarity. Perhaps one reason is because of the Enlightenment's influence on our thought. For all of the strengths of the Enlightenment, such as safeguarding the role of the individual in society, it failed to safeguard against the extremes of individualism and with it autonomous forms of freedom. For instance, there was a widespread rejection of the doctrine of original sin and with it corporate solidarity and responsibility for humanity's sin. Robert Jenson, in his book on early American theologian Jonathan Edwards, comments on this doctrine and what is at stake in the Enlightenment rejection of this teaching. The modern doctrine of humanity dismisses the idea that each individual should "accept responsibility for human history's total act as my act." Jenson argues that this modern dismissal of original sin (that is, humanity's solidarity in Adam's sin and corporate responsibility) is "morally corrosive." Jenson claims, "If I cannot take responsibility for humankind's act, how can I take it for that of my nation? If not for my nation's act, how for that of my family?"[7] In discussing Jenson's claim in my book *Consuming Jesus: Beyond Race and Class Divisions in a Consumer Church*, I comment,

> It is ironic that many evangelical Christians claim that they are not responsible for the sins and lives of others, whether it be those monstrous forebears who enslaved blacks or committed genocide against Native-American people or those criminal forces today that enslave

women to lives of prostitution and who rob the poor of their homes through enforced gentrification and "urban renewal." Taken far enough, it will undermine their patriotic concern for the nation and their veneration of the family, as Jenson's argument suggests.[8]

Not simply seminary students fail to comprehend this matter but also Christian leaders. Christ entered into corporate solidarity with all of humanity in its fallenness, and in the face of his own moral purity. So, too, the righteous prophets of old identified with the people in their sinful state. Righteous Moses told God to strike him down if God was going to destroy unrighteous Israel (Exodus 32:31–32). Righteous Ezra and Daniel also identified themselves with the people, repenting of collective sin (Ezra 9; Daniel 9). This is a far cry from the outburst of the late Reverend Jerry Falwell after the events of September 11, 2001. He denounced materialists, secularists, homosexuals, and atheists (among others) as responsible for the attacks on America. Possibly likening himself to an Old Testament prophetic figure, Falwell seemingly failed to recall how the prophets of old always identified with the people in their sin, leading the people into repentance through their ownership of evil and repentance of sin as prophetic leaders. The church in the United States has been guilty of racism, materialism, sexual impurity, and other gross sins; yet Reverend Falwell did not mention them.[9] Judgment always starts in the household of God, and he failed to realize this biblical perspective; moreover, Falwell failed to recognize that he is responsible (as someone claiming to be a prophetic voice speaking God's Word in society) for the atheists, secularists, materialists, and others, just as the prophets of old were responsible for the unrighteous people, not just the righteous ones.

As a result of the late reverend's outburst (for which he later apologized), more damage was done to the church's public witness across the nation, intensifying the culture war divisions in our country and undermining the sense of America's corporate solidarity in sin. While I am grateful to the late Reverend Falwell for his concern for the plight of the human unborn and his efforts to bring evangelicals together with other religious groups over shared moral concerns, he could have done a lot more to bring people together if his prophetic stance would have been truly prophetic—speaking to the surrounding secular culture from a standpoint of solidarity in fallenness and brokenness rather than in hostility and alienation. Christ-followers can make a great amount of headway with others in terms of addressing human sinfulness as long as we are pointing the finger first and foremost at ourselves.

WHY IS IT DIFFICULT TO APOLOGIZE?

The same night when the man in that Portland church interrupted and exclaimed, "Why should we apologize? We're Christians!" I shared about the power of confessing the church's personal and corporate sins, even with those who do not claim to follow Christ, as I recalled the Reed College confessional booth story outlined in Donald Miller's *Blue Like Jazz*. I take that story as an illustration of apologizing in our apologetic for the faith.

Reed College is well-known as a secular and irreligious school.[10] Miller writes about how he and other Christ-followers serving at Reed built and used a confessional booth during Reed's Renn Fayre celebration at the end of the school year to reach out to others. Miller says of Reed's Renn Fayre: "They shut down the campus so students can party."[11] However, the confessional booth was used not for Christian apologists to take confessions from the "partying pagans" at Reed, but for those partying to hear the confessions of Christ-followers who apologized for their participation in the church's sinning against society, and against individuals in a variety of ways. These Christians' authentic and humble encounters with the Reed students opened doors for meaningful and profound exchanges.

When I reflected later on all four sessions at that church, I realized that a key reason why it is so difficult for us to ask for forgiveness is because we Christians often struggle with uncertainty, anxiety, and even arrogance, making it virtually impossible for us to engage others heart to heart. Our fears and pride keep us from being authentic and profound gospel witnesses: we fear exposing ourselves as imperfect, and our pride is bound up with self-righteousness and seeking to impress or please everyone. Of course we should never delight in revealing the church's dirty laundry to those who don't know Christ; we should guard against such revelations that would keep people from faith. But often enough those who do not yet know Christ are already aware of the church's brokenness. So who are we kidding? There are no sufficient grounds *not* to apologize.

WHY IS IT IMPORTANT TO APOLOGIZE?

Fear and pride and arrogance keep us from depending on Christ Jesus for our security, and from participating in his broken-though-full life through which the Spirit is poured out on his people. It is only when we are broken and contrite in spirit that we experience his profound healing presence. What an opportunity to experience intimacy! Now, of course, there are many Christians who are very humble and dependent on the Lord. But even they must remain diligent and not boast in their humility and how much they depend on him. As for the rest of us, we must regain that sense of fully depending on Jesus and of fully participating in his life, thereby experiencing intimacy with him.

Fear and pride and arrogance keep us from participating not only in Jesus' broken-though-full life and from experiencing intimacy with him but also in other people's broken lives and bearing witness to Jesus' ability and desire to heal them with his mercy and love. People do not feel safe around us if they sense that we think we are better than they are. But if and when we are broken and contrite in spirit, they will be exposed to God's mercy poured out on us as we confess and experience his healing touch, and hopefully they will respond to him too. What an opportunity for missional engagement! All ground is level at the foot of the cross, and all are welcome there.

If we are not willing to confess, how will those who do not yet believe in Christ or other believers ever truly confess? We must not broker power or try to cover up our faults because when we hide from sharing our faults, we are only kidding ourselves. Those who don't know Christ do know that we are far from perfect. As members do in recovery programs such as AA, we need to confess to others, "Hello, I'm Paul, and I am a recovering sinner." Profound, transformational heart change involves making that confession.

Donald Miller, Tony "the Beat Poet" Kriz, and the other Christians with them really did it up with the confessional booth at Reed College, as recounted in *Blue Like Jazz*. It was as if they had returned to the Middle

Ages, as they were ringing cowbells and wearing monk's robes. Tony shared with me later how one of the Reed student revelers entering the confessional booth thought the whole thing was staged and a spoof. As he was making fun of it and mockingly confessing his "sins," Tony said to the student, "This is a confession booth, and I would like to begin. As a Christian, I want to ask your forgiveness for all those times when my fellow Christians judged you and condemned you. . . ." After Tony shared with him the bankruptcy and total brokenness of his own life, the Reed student who was sitting only a few inches away responded, "That is the most beautiful thing I have ever heard." The young man then began sharing his own empty life with Tony, and how, like Tony, he was also in great spiritual need.[12]

Tony went to all this trouble because he was burdened by his own brokenness and because God had given him such a heart for the students at Reed. He did not see them as stoned and pagan intellectuals. He saw them as beautiful people created in God's image who were what I would call "ruined Rembrandts." Like the rest of us fellow humans, they were masterpieces horribly marred by the fall and in need of restoration. Even as masterpieces—ruined masterpieces, but masterpieces all the same— they were fearfully and wonderfully made. I believe they could sense Tony's admiration. In the end, people will never be drawn to us if we don't recognize their inherent beauty. People will not confess to us from the heart if we do not confess to them our brokenness.

All of us are Rembrandts ruined by the fall, but total depravity does not wipe out the image. As Karl Barth says, our fallen condition cannot cause us to lose something we never possessed: "What man does not possess he can neither bequeath nor forfeit."[13] While we have capacities (such as reason), these capacities are not to be equated with the essence of the image—which is each person's being constituted in relation to God and others. All of our capacities are constituted in these relationships, as we come from God and exist in relation to God and the rest of the creation.[14]

All people cry out for God. They cannot get out of the matrix of God's framing of life. Whether they are in confessional booths at churches during Lent or in confessional booths on Reed's campus during Renn Fayre, they cry out for God. No matter where they go, in one way or another, they are looking for God. A statement often attributed to G. K. Chesterton puts it well: "Every man who knocks on the door of a brothel is looking for God"—not just those who enter churches and confessional booths. In fact, some may even argue that we shouldn't presume that all those who knock on the doors of churches are necessarily looking for God any more than those who knock on other doors. Some knocking on church doors might be trying to make sure that God is looking in their direction, trying to get him to take note of how righteous they are, and how great the need is for people like them. What they (and often I) fail to account for is that it is not the Pharisee in the temple standing proudly and thanking God for his self-righteousness who goes home forgiven and justified but the tax collector beating his breast and asking God for mercy (Luke 18:9–14).

Total depravity does not imply that we have lost the image or that we can never do anything that is good or true or beautiful or that we have no dignity. Rather total depravity implies that sin impacts every area of our lives, including the affections, will, and reason,[15] and we can do nothing to cooperate with God to save ourselves. We are in a state of total desperation and dependence on God's mercy for forgiveness, cleansing, and new life.

Having said all that, God is not left without witnesses in the creation. No matter how far we run away or how well we hide and pull on the wires, God pursues us and finds us and reaches out and rewires and restores us. In fact, as his creation we are wired to glorify him in one way or another—even though we have fallen. We cannot escape his goodness. Those of us who are Christians must repent of our brokenness bound up with religious pride and with it our failure to see the beauty of those who are not yet believers in Christ. We need to approach them—no matter their belief system and behaviors—with faith and hope and love, always hoping for the best (1 Corinthians 13:4–13), always longing for God to make all things and all people new. In view of God's transforming work of the creation in and through Jesus in the Spirit, we must never look at anyone from a merely human point of view (2 Corinthians 5:16), be they Christians or not, for Christ's work impacts all creation in various ways.

Fear and pride and arrogance surface in our refusal to see not only our own brokenness but also the good and beauty in others. In fact, that willful blindness is part of our brokenness. First Corinthians 13 has something to teach us. We must always hope and look for the good and not fixate on evil or the differences between other traditions and our own (although significant differences should still be noted).[16]

We can learn a lesson or two from Jesus, who sees good in others (even those outside the religious elite), including Gentiles in general (Luke 4:22–30), the Canaanite woman (Matthew 15:21–28), the centurion (Matthew 8:5–13), and the shrewd manager in one of his parables (Luke 16:8–9). Jesus was even struck by something significant in the rich young ruler, who eventually departed downcast in spirit for choosing wealth over Jesus. The text tells us that Jesus loved him and was impressed by the ruler's love for the Law (Mark 10:21). Remember God's love ultimately creates all attraction, but that love is not only present in the rewiring of God's creation after the fall in God's saving work in Christ; it is also present in the initial wiring of the creation. Despite the various forms of wiring, the Lord often uses the examples of these outsiders to challenge insiders to pursue authentic spirituality. Indeed, I am often challenged by "outsiders" to connect more with Christ as I connect with them.

We should not be surprised when we find faith outside religious boundaries or when we find truth outside the confines of the Bible and church. While Paul grieved over the idolatry in Athens, nonetheless, he was still cognizant of the Athenians' sense and limited knowledge of God, as reflected in his conversation with the philosophers on Mars Hill (Acts 17:16–34). They were aware of the real possibility (indeed, actuality) that God eluded their cognitive grasp, so they had erected a monument to the Unknown God to cover their bases. They had the suspicion that there was more in heaven than what they could dream of in their philosophy (to commandeer the phrase from Hamlet to Horatio), and their own poets understood that we all live and move and exist in and through God. Paul recognized that the Athenians knew this truth about all people's relation to God, but so often we Christians are surprised when we find people outside the walls of the church who have insights about God. While those insights don't save them, and can even be brought forth by God as evidence to condemn them,[17] God will not be left without witnesses in their midst. We should not be surprised and should repent of any hint of arrogance. Here is what Lesslie Newbigin has to say about the matter:

> The Christian confession of Jesus as Lord does not involve any attempt
> to deny the reality of the work of God in the lives and thoughts and

prayers of men and women outside the Christian church. On the contrary, it ought to involve an eager expectation of, a looking for, and a rejoicing in the evidence of that work. There is something deeply wrong when Christians imagine that loyalty to Jesus requires them to belittle the manifest presence of the light in the lives of men and women who do not acknowledge him, to seek out points of weakness, to ferret out hidden sins and deceptions as a means of commending the gospel. If we love the light and walk in the light we will also rejoice in the light wherever we find it—even the smallest gleams of it in the surrounding darkness.[18]

We should expect to find points of connection to Christ outside the church. God has wired all people to seek him, and he continues to pursue all people—including Christians!—through Jesus and the Spirit.[19] We should be wary of intellectual works righteousness, and we should be amazed that any of us has any clue as to God's character and ways. Revelation is a gift of God's grace, not a work that we produce.

These points about our oft-repeated failures to value those who do not yet know Christ personally and to see how great our own need for Christ is have been impressed upon me through various encounters with fellow evangelical Christians and leaders of other faith traditions. My world religions class and I had just watched an interview with a leading representative of another religion. Among other things, this person's humanity was so profound, yet I later told the class that I feared that we could not recognize how profound this man is given how incomplete and weak our movement's doctrine of humanity is. One student shared after class that, sad to say, we often view those who do not yet know Christ as mere souls to win over, not people to befriend.

Our apology or defense for relationship with Christ must involve an apology or defense of our fellow humans and relationships with them. As the God-Man, Jesus is fully divine and fully human. We confess this truth, but do we really believe it? Jesus grounds every instance of human creativity and beauty and profundity as our Creator who became human. I am not calling for a secular humanistic approach to humanity that denies the fall and everyone's need for Christ, but for a biblical humanism that grounds our understanding of humanity in view of Christ who became human and who does not eradicate our humanity but rather preserves it from decay and transforms it through his incarnation, crucifixion, resurrection, and ascension.

We must apologize for our condescension toward our fellow humans and must move toward the celebration of their humanity. Even now Jesus preserves and prepares the creation and humanity at large for the possibility of its ultimate transformation. I find breathtaking glimpses of Jesus' masterful work in the lives of those who do not yet profess faith in him as God incarnate. Instead of feeling pity for leaders of other traditions, as a few of my students exclaimed after hearing the lecture of a representative of another religion, I feel privileged. These friends could only sense the pain and hurt and confusion in the lecturer, whereas I could also hear the passion and healing and clarity bound up with this person's honest and vulnerable and brilliant reflections. I long for this person to respond to Christ and receive from his fullness, but I am also made all the more aware of how great my own need for Christ is when I encounter this spiritual leader.

This person's profundity puts me to shame and leads me to take a long, hard look at myself. I come away from these encounters amazed that God would see fit to choose me. How arrogant I am when I can only pity the brilliant and passionate leader of another faith tradition on the one hand or the homeless beggar on the other hand. These people don't need my pity but my sense of longing for relationship and affirmation of their dignity and priceless value as objects of Christ's creative and sacrificial love, and I need the same from them. They are not worthless objects of pity but priceless masterpieces of creation that God longs to restore even as he restores you and me. When I pity my neighbor, I am not loving my neighbor as myself as God's Word commands (Mark 12:30–31).

Whether we are talking about dehumanizing ideas or actions, we all need to apologize. We all are guilty. We cannot be good witnesses without realizing how much we fall short and are in need of God's and other people's mercy. We all are in need of the Savior to save us from our false redemption and filthy rags of works righteousness and illusions of grandeur pertaining to self and repudiation of others. Moreover, there are times when we don't even give the appearance of performing well at the game of religion. At times we even come across as victimizers even though many of us might seek to portray ourselves to others as the victims. With this in mind it is worth saying that the victim in one system of evil is the victimizer in another system. Rowan Williams puts it this way in his discussion of victimization and violence:

> I am, willy-nilly, involved in "structural violence," in economic, political, religious and private systems of relationship which diminish the other (and I must repeat once more that the victim in one system is liable to be the oppressor in another: the polarity runs through each individual). Yet I find, through the resurrection gospel, that I have a choice about colluding with these systems, a possibility of belonging to another "system" in which gift rather than diminution is constitutive. I am thus equipped to understand that structural violence is not an unshakeable monolith: critical action, constructive protest, is possible. My involvement in violence is most destructive when least self-aware, and simply understanding that involvement is a crucial first step. But to understand it in the presence of the Easter Jesus is to understand that violence is not omnipotent, and that my involvement in it does not rule out the possibility of transformation of my relations.[20]

Taking on board Williams's point, I must confess that I am no better than slave traders putting people in chains, US colonels slaughtering innocent Native American women and children, and TV preachers passing violent judgment on pagans. And you, no matter who you are, are really no different from me. Given the right—or rather, wrong—circumstances, we would inflict similar if not more subtle forms of dehumanization on others. Whenever I elevate myself over others, thinking I am fundamentally better than other sinners, I am falling prey to falsehood and oppression. I must realize that I am so like them, and they are so like me, and all of us are in need of Jesus.

We All Must Apologize

I remember talking about our shared spiritual need a few years ago at a civic gathering at a Buddhist temple in Portland. Those in attendance recognized the need to cultivate compassionate coexistence so that we might move beyond the culture-war hostility so prominently displayed in America. During the meeting, several left-of-center individuals began pointing fingers at President Bush and accusing him of all kinds of evil.

Finally, a liberal-minded Buddhist priest and I intervened. It sounded as if the priest was quoting Jesus when he told his liberal parishioners that they needed to get rid of the dirt in their own lives before they could judge others, including President Bush. I then shared how I am no different from the worst perpetrators of wrongdoing, how given the right—or rather, wrong—circumstances, I would likely have done what they did. I recalled the recent disclosure of the grave injustices of abuse and humiliation committed by Private Lynndie England and other members of the US Forces against their prisoners at the Abu Ghraib prison in Iraq. One liberal-minded person said that she would never do what Private England was found guilty of doing; this Portlander spoke of being a person of justice and integrity (supposedly unlike Private England in Iraq). In response I shared with this person in the presence of the entire gathering there in Portland what a Christian theologian from South Africa had told me after news of the Abu Ghraib scandal broke. The theologian in question was struck by how many Americans were in a state of shock about how supposedly upstanding young American soldiers like Private England could commit such horrible acts against those imprisoned. The theologian from South Africa who had fought against apartheid and had witnessed horrible atrocities committed by both sides during and immediately after the apartheid reign said to me, "You Americans are so naive. You wonder how this normal, decent, likable young lady could get caught up in such evil. Put any one of us in a situation like that, and we would likely end up acting just like she did."[21]

In other words, the real Abu Ghraib prison is within my own heart and in yours too—no matter who you are. We are all enslaved and needy, whether we know it or not. We are all ruined masterpieces in need of restoration. We must all repent. Otherwise, we might do something worse. We must apologize and make connections to other ruined masterpieces. Instead of painting by numbers, we must paint by hearts. The mosaic is restored as we connect heart to heart and life on life. Only then do we participate in God's transformative work. But will we take such actions and make these relational connections as the church?

CHAPTER 5

How Is Christ's Church
God's Apologetic?

J osh McDowell famously wrote that the evidence demands a verdict that Jesus is Lord.[1] While affirming his point, I would also argue that the verdict that Jesus is Lord demands evidence in our lives as his community that he is Lord. In a culture that is increasingly dismissive of rational arguments for the faith isolated from life-on-life engagement, it is vital that we set forth those rational claims in embodied ways. In other words, our lives as Christ's community must create the space for our views to be heard.[2] G. K. Chesterton exclaimed, "The Christian ideal has not been tried and found wanting. It has been found difficult; and left untried."[3] As followers of Christ we must make sure that we are demonstrating to the world that we have tried the faith, as difficult as it is, and found it fulfilling. In turn, we must create space and invite the surrounding world to press into the difficulty and try the faith with us and experience its fullness in the incarnate Christ's community.

The Word became flesh as Jesus. As John writes, "The Word became flesh and made his dwelling among us. We have seen his glory, the glory of the One and Only, who came from the Father, full of grace and truth"

(John 1:14). There was no divorce between word and action, between proclamation and presence, in Jesus' life. In fact, the proclamation included and
continues to include presence, for the personal Word who became flesh is
God's embodied presence in the world through the Spirit.

Why is it so important from the standpoint of relational-incarnational
apologetics to personalize truth? It is because people long to be touched,
for they are embodied souls created in the image of the triune God, who
is interpersonal: the Father, Son, and Spirit in communion. As the image
of God, Jesus comes close and touches us (John 1:14; Colossians 1:15–20).
This is especially true today, as more and more people miss being touched in
a culture that is increasingly virtual.[4] We are all wired for relationships. We
are all wired to want to hear the truth rather than the lie, even though we
often live the lie as a result of the fall. We are all wired to want to be touched,
even though we often pull away in our present state of alienation. Without
concern for relationality involving honesty and life-on-life engagement in an
increasingly virtual culture, people will think we're fake or unreal. They'll
look at us as virtual Christians.

Here are a few illustrations of this problem concerning the virtual. In
the poem "The Vacation," Wendell Berry writes of someone who spent
his entire vacation recording his vacation on video in order that it might
live forever on film. However, the man failed to realize that although he
went *on* vacation and recorded it on video, he was never *in* his vacation.[5]
The use of the video camera along these lines is not the only instance of
this technological dimension to the problem. People on cell phones often
ignore the physical presence of others, denying face-to-face embodiment
in favor of near out-of-body experiences with people miles away.[6] The
problematic use of the video camera and cell phone are current phenomena. The movie *Avatar* envisions and celebrates a future where people can
operate human hybrid bodies called "avatars" by mental link. While fascinating, an avatar in this mode signifies the separation of the mind/soul
and body, similar to Platonism. From a biblical perspective, it does not
affirm the vital, inseparable link between spirit and body, which among
other things signifies that you, he, she, and I as human subjects are actually connecting with others when we make physical contact with them
through hugs or handshakes.

BODY AND SOUL

According to a biblical perspective, we are embodied souls. Thus we must not disengage from people by loving them simply with words and sentiments and failing to love them with our deeds in life-on-life encounters. We create space for life-on-life encounters with people when we engage them in embodied actions and not simply with our words and sentiments. As 1 John 3:18 asserts, "Dear children, let us not love with words or tongue but with actions and in truth." John's model is God's divine Word—the second person of the Trinity—who is always active and who became embodied truth (1 John 1:1–4; 4:7–21). Over against both the teaching of the antichrist, which denies that God has come in the flesh (1 John 4:1–3), and those Christians who claim to love God, who is spirit, but do not evidence love for fellow Christians who live alongside them in the flesh (1 John 4:19–21), John makes it quite clear: we are to reflect Jesus, God's incarnate Word of truth and love, with embodied acts of true love toward those around us. Never does Scripture call the church Jesus' spirit; Scripture calls the church Jesus' body, which lives out his incarnate life in the Spirit as God's missional community in the world.

We are not simply taking up space with our bodies as one might claim from a Platonic perspective (according to which the soul migrates eternally from body to body). From a biblical perspective humans are embodied souls. After this life as we know it is over, our souls will be clothed in immortal bodies at the resurrection of the dead (1 Corinthians 15; 1 Thessalonians 4:13–18; Revelation 20). Our embodiment and future resurrection do not exist in isolation from Christ. Jesus is the firstborn over all creation and the firstborn from the dead (Colossians 1:15–18). He is the firstfruits of the resurrection (1 Corinthians 15:20). Orthodox Christology claims that God's eternal Word is embodied in history. The difference between Jesus and an avatar incarnation is that "the Word became flesh" (John 1:14). There is no separation of the second person of the Trinity from his embodiment; he exists from the inception of his incarnation unto eternity as the Word who became flesh (1 Corinthians 15). Another way of thinking of this is to consider that Mary is the mother of God. In keeping with orthodox Christology at large (and not simply Roman Catholic theology), Mary is the God-bearer (*theotokos*). This claim guards against Nestorianism, which divides Jesus' deity and humanity into two separate persons. From a biblical and orthodox Christian perspective, God *became* human; he did not simply take up residence in human flesh.

Scripture affirms our need for touch; the vital connection of one human to another involves embodiment, and God became flesh to connect with us, to love and heal us. Whether we are talking about small children in Romanian orphanages or elderly people in retirement homes, people often dwell in isolation and long for connection. I am told that those small children in those orphanages will eventually hit their heads against the walls because they long to feel touch. In the case of at least one elderly person I know, he will keep others on the phone as long as possible because he hates to hear the deafening silence when the conversation is over. Even on the phone we can "reach out and touch someone," as the old Bell telephone company jingle claimed. For we touch not simply through our hands but also through our eyes and our voices, as well as through other means. I am told that young people who cut themselves do so to know that they exist: in place of Descartes's dictum, "I think; therefore I am," they subconsciously claim, "I feel pain; therefore I am."

The Sense of Touch

We live in a culture where touch is seldom found, and when we do experience contact, it is often by crashing into one another on the expressways of life. This statement calls to mind the claim of Detective Graham Waters in the movie *Crash*, who at the beginning of this movie on contemporary forms of fragmentation and objectification involving racism, ponders a crash in which he was just involved: "It's the sense of touch. In any real city, you walk, you know? You brush past people; people bump into you. In LA, nobody touches you. We're always behind this metal and glass. I think we miss that touch so much, that we crash into each other, just so we can feel something."[7]

In LA they simply crash into one another on matters of race and other issues. In other places we may endure one another. Diversity trainer Tim Wise speaks of Minnesota Nice. Where I work—Portland, Oregon—we experience what one friend calls Portland Cool. We often tolerate one another—including those of different ethnicities—in our niceness and in our coolness, depending on the place. But such tolerance typically cloaks indifference, perhaps even disgust; all too often we simply endure one another through the veil of tolerance and detachment.

I am very thankful that God does not simply tolerate us. Certainly tolerance has its place: I would not want to go back to the days of the religious wars in Europe, the Spanish Inquisition, or the Salem witch trials. But tolerance does not go far enough. There is a saying: "I would rather be loved than tolerated." Indeed I would too. Tolerance does not involve touch. It does not address our vital need as humans to be taken so seriously that we move toward face-to-face, heart-to-heart, life-on-life encounter. I am grateful that the Bible does not say, "For God so tolerated the world that he chose not to send his Son"; rather, it says, "For God so loved the world that he gave his one and only Son" (John 3:16). God gave his Son sacrificially. There was no holding back. God did not crash into us but came alongside us. He "moved into the neighborhood"[8] and took up residence in our midst: God's glory was embodied as Jesus of Nazareth. God gave his soul to us when he gave to us his first love—his Son. There is nothing the Father could give that would cost him more—not even his own person, for his Son was the object of his undivided, eternal affection. We are the objects of his affection in his beloved Son and experience his embrace, just as John did when Jesus touched him (1 John 1:1–4).

In contrast to cities like LA and Portland, the city of God champions love. In place of lobbying and violently protesting to take back America in urban centers of power, Jesus comes close and touches our ideological enemies just as he touches us—we who were once his enemies (Romans 5:6–11). Jesus can say anything to me because he has created space with his life in my life for his views of me to be heard. He can bring the hard truths home to me because he has lived the truth in order to save me. Jesus doesn't simply have views. He embodies his views and lays himself down—not for an ideology—but for individuals who are more than their worldviews, ideologies, and behaviors. I firmly believe we can say anything to people when they know that we truly love them, when they believe we would do anything for them, when we move inside their hearts even if we have not yet convinced their minds or moved them to change their behaviors. For they know that we are concerned about them personally, and not simply about their beliefs and behaviors, tastes and abilities.

When we live as Jesus lived, inhabiting space with people and laying down our lives for them, we can share our lives and words with them. But do we want to? Are we willing to pay the price for relationship—namely, relational sacrifice? Just as Jesus gave his life for his enemies, Paul was willing to go to hell for his countrymen who opposed him so that they could be saved in place of him:

> I speak the truth in Christ—I am not lying, my conscience confirms it in the Holy Spirit—I have great sorrow and unceasing anguish in my heart. For I could wish that I myself were cursed and cut off from Christ for the sake of my brothers, those of my own race, the people of Israel. Theirs is the adoption as sons; theirs the divine glory, the covenants, the receiving of the law, the temple worship and the promises. Theirs are the patriarchs, and from them is traced the human ancestry of Christ, who is God over all, forever praised! Amen. (Romans 9:1–5)

As forceful in personality and persuasion as Paul was, he didn't crash into people; he touched them. He didn't sacrifice them for his cause; he gave himself for them because of God's living, cruciform Word. Paul lived in view of this Word at great cost to himself for the sake of others.

Jesus as the living Word calls on us to bear witness to him. The book of Acts indicates that Jesus continues to act in history even after he ascended to the Father's right hand, continuing his ministry through his church (Acts 1:1) in the power of the Spirit (Acts 1:8). The church participates in the missions of the triune God, as believers participate in the Son and Spirit whom the Father sends out to touch and heal the world. The church then and now is to be the hands and feet of Christ, for we are his body. Of course, literally speaking, Jesus only has one physical body. However, through our union with Jesus by the Spirit, we participate in his incarnate existence as we reach out and touch one another within the church and as the church reaches out and touches the world at large.

The Church as Embodied Witness

This church, which is Christ's lived community, is *the* apologetic of the gospel. The church derives this legitimacy from its participation in the life of the triune God. Actually it is the triune God who is the great apologetic; he is "our social programme."[9] The doctrine of the Trinity is not reserved for intellectual theology; rather it has practical importance for the church's life (and I would add its mission) because the triune God, who is three eternally holy and loving persons in communion, is the basis for healthy relationships and sociality. The church *is* called to witness to this divine community as salt and light in society at large. As the triune God is the church's social programme, the church, as it participates in God's life, is God's "social ethic"[10] lived out in this world. The church does not simply have a social ethic or apologetic. The church *is* a social ethic and apologetic as it bears witness in life and in death to God's love, peace, justice, and mercy demonstrated in Jesus' life story in which it participates.[11]

How does this have a bearing on apologetics? Simply look at the church in the book of Acts. Rather than crashing into people as the Sanhedrin physically attacked Christians, the church lived sacrificially among the people, touching and healing and caring for the sick, possessed, and dispossessed. In the face of growing opposition and persecution, we read of Christ's kingdom community continuing to live a holistic apologetic, touching rather than crashing into others:

> The apostles performed many miraculous signs and wonders among the people. And all the believers used to meet together in Solomon's Colonnade. No one else dared join them, even though they were highly regarded by the people. Nevertheless, more and more men and women believed in the Lord and were added to their number. As a result, people brought the sick into the streets and laid them on beds and mats so that at least Peter's shadow might fall on some of them as he passed by. Crowds gathered also from the towns around Jerusalem, bringing their sick and those tormented by evil spirits, and all of them were healed. (Acts 5:12–16)

Ironically, as a result of this holistic apologetic for the faith and the fruit of salvation that it bore, the Jewish religious hierarchy persecuted them all the more (Acts 5:17–18).

No one dared join the apostolic community as it lived out the kingdom of God missionally in the public square, and yet they were highly regarded by the people. The people brought the sick and the possessed to them so they could be healed and released. As a result of the apostolic community touching their lives, the good news was received. God continued to build the church as the surrounding culture witnessed the transformation of people's lives.

How does God extend his healing touch today? Certainly God heals people of physical ailments and delivers the tormented from bondage to demons, as demonstrations of God's kingdom power. Spiritual healing occurs in various forms—deliverance from "personal" demons, deliverance from physical pain, and deliverance from emotional suffering, among other things. God also uses us to heal others of their suffering, enlivening us to suffer with them for the faith and anointing us as we suffer hardship in the faith. God's healing touch is often most apparent as we are weak and suffering, for it is then that God's grace abounds most profoundly in and through us and to us (2 Corinthians 12:7–10).

If redemptive suffering is a vital aspect of the faith—and it is—then I suggest that the church is at its best when it is not wielding the power of the world (the sword) but the power of God (the cross), which involves being healed through suffering as God works his way into our broken, weak, and wounded lives to transform us. It is here that God's healing power is most clearly demonstrated. We extend God's touch through our wounds, wounds that God is healing, finding our victory in him in the midst of victimizing life circumstances as he transforms us from the inside out. Suffering is providential, and it is significant in the context of apologetic witness for the faith—a faith born out of suffering.

THE CHURCH AS A WOUNDED HEALER

One of the great exponents of this way of thinking and being was the late Henri Nouwen. In *The Wounded Healer* Nouwen wrote, "A minister is not a doctor whose primary task is to take away pain. Rather, he deepens the pain to a level where it can be shared. . . . Ministry is a very confronting service. It does not allow people to live with illusions of immortality and wholeness. It keeps reminding others that they are mortal and broken, but also that with the recognition of this condition, liberation starts. . . . Hospitality becomes community as it creates a unity based on the shared confession of our basic brokenness and on a shared hope."[12]

It is difficult for us to understand this in the developed West. In our comfort-driven culture, we seek to avoid pain and suffering. Pain and suffering are marks of God's judgment, so we often think. Instead of sensing that suffering is providential, we are driven to paranoia—"Why does God hate me so? Just look how much I'm suffering!" However, when the church lives within the sufferings of Christ, when the church does not flee from suffering but embraces Christ in the midst of it and through it and shares in other people's sufferings, the church becomes a profound social ethic and apologetic for the faith. Instead of causing suffering that destroys, instead of suffering other people's existence by way of tolerance that is veiled indifference, the church that suffers redemptively with and for others becomes an agent of God's transforming and healing presence in the world. We must think more creatively when suffering innocently, for suffering in and for the faith is the way in which our faith grows and gains ground, especially in a culture where through power politics the church is arguably losing ground.

Perhaps the greatest personal living example of apologetic witness in and through suffering in my experience has been my friend and mentor John M. Perkins, whose story of victory in the midst of victimization I share in chapter 4. In fact, Perkins speaks of how the church and individual Christians experience greater anointing and creativity in ministry by suffering through God's transformative presence in their lives. Perkins also speaks of the need for Christians to enter into people's suffering, to live among the oppressed and marginalized, to relocate, reconcile, and redistribute their lives, talents, and resources voluntarily for the sake of the downtrodden and depressed so that they might experience God's renewal.[13] Perkins's words are surrounded, undergirded, and energized by his deeds in the midst of suffering, which are themselves energized by Christ's healing love. Perkins is a living witness to God's Word become flesh, who enters into our neighborhoods, homes, and hearts, transforming them from stone to flesh through God's Spirit of love poured out.

LIVING THE WITNESS

Our lives as God's people must create the space for our views to be heard. As we journey through the second and third sections of this book, we will engage in various forms of apologetic strategy and argumentation yet always seeking to be relational-incarnational. We will seek to move beyond crashing into Buddhist, Hindu, and Mormon persons; seek to move beyond objectifying them; and seek to abandon demonizing language that marginalizes and ridicules them. When encountering those who do not yet know the eternal Son who became human, we must bear witness to God's Word that may cut like a surgeon's knife as the Spirit pierces the soul, but we must never employ words of condemnation and hopelessness that cut and destroy those with whom we share the truth; nor should we ever look down on those outside the church, pushing them away. We should long to share life with them and to experience shared faith in the person of Jesus.

To engage most effectively in this relational strategy, our words must be accompanied, undergirded, and energized by lives lived with the people with whom we are sharing. Christ's church as a lived and living community of holistic care that suffers for others and even at the hands of others, while seeking to do them good, is one of the greatest testimonies to the truthfulness and power of the gospel. Our road is not easy. Even though we love, many people with whom we share our words and lives even at great cost to ourselves will not always accept our message. But let us never give them the excuse to hate us because they sense that we hate them. Martin Luther King Jr. said that although his white oppressors hated him and his people, he and his people would love them back.[14] Remember King's predecessor Martin Luther's words: "He who does not know Christ does not know God hidden in suffering. Therefore he prefers works to suffering, glory to the cross, strength to weakness, wisdom to folly, and, in general, good to evil. . . . God can be found only in suffering and the cross."[15] As the apologetic of God's kingdom, the church will enter into redemptive suffering for the sake of those who do not yet know the saving power of the gospel of Jesus. For there is no better way to bear witness to the gospel except through suffering, for as Luther wrote, God's true glory is "found only in suffering and the cross."

John M. Perkins, Martin Luther King Jr., and Martin Luther understood well this reality.[16] So, too, did the early church. When the plague of Cyprian hit the Roman Empire in AD 250 (and lasted for many years), the church emerged as a "volunteer corps" that was the "only organization in Roman cities that cared for the dying and buried the dead." The church experienced persecution during this time. In fact, as the church "dramatically increased its care, the Roman government began persecuting the church more heavily." The church even cared for its persecutors who suffered from the plague. According to historian Gary Ferngren, Dionysius, the bishop of Alexandria, wrote, "Presbyters, deacons, and laymen took charge of the treatment of the sick, ignoring the danger to their own lives. . . . Their activity contrasted with that of the pagans, who deserted the sick or threw the bodies of the dead out into the streets."[17]

I see increasing signs of this kind of living today—not just in iconic John Perkins, but also among common Christians such as those who gave sacrificially of themselves and continue to do so in the Katrina-ravaged South. Even among big and small churches in the Portland metro area, I find compassionate outreach through various holistic means and care for those without health and dental insurance. I see such signs in various other places too.[18] The more we as Christ's church exercise sacrificial love so our views about Christ can be heard, the more we will be heard. It does not matter if people end up hating us, as the Christians were hated during the plague of Cyprian. What matters is that our enemies know we love them back. If we are hated for loving, we are in good company—with Jesus, Dionysius, King, and Perkins. No matter what happens, may we never stop sharing Jesus' sacrificial, redemptive love in word and deed, for Jesus is calling us as his community to live into and out of his life as the ultimate apologetic.

PART II

An Engagement of Diverse Traditions

CHAPTER 6

THE JEWISH QUESTION (JUDAISM)

In a 1933 piece titled "The Church and the Jewish Question," German Lutheran theologian Dietrich Bonhoeffer addressed the subject of Israel and the church's relation to it as he reflected on the church's struggle in the face of Hitler and his attack on the Jewish people.[1] At the time, Nazi Germany was challenging the Jews' right to existence as a distinct people by releasing a series of Aryan Clauses that disqualified those of Jewish origin (no matter their religious affiliation) and those married to Jews from holding public office in the German state. Given the close relation of the church and state in Germany at the time, it also excluded those of Jewish origin from church appointments. These clauses were the most grievous of the disabilities Hitler imposed on the Jews and preceded their mass extermination.[2] For Bonhoeffer, the Aryan Clauses forced Christian theologians to address two fundamental issues: "What is the church's attitude to this action by the state? And what should the church do as a result of it? That is one issue. The other is, what attitude should the church take to its members who are baptised Jews?"[3] Bonhoeffer called on the church to oppose the Nazi attacks on the Jewish people. He eventually died at the hands of the Nazis for his courageous witness and defiance of the Hitler menace.

With Bonhoeffer, I contend that the church has a fundamental responsibility to promote the well-being of the Jewish community. And while the "Jewish Question" as I am using it here takes on different form, I would highlight my agreement with Bonhoeffer that God's covenantal purposes in Jesus signify that "no nation of the world can be finished with this mysterious people [the Jewish people], because God is not yet finished with it."[4]

The Jews' Jewish Question

What we may consider to be the "Jewish Question" is probably not the primary question that Jews have asked themselves. Perhaps the primary question for Jews throughout their history centers on how to follow God's law. As Louis Finkelstein writes,

> It is impossible to understand Judaism without an appreciation of the place it assigns to the study and practice of the talmudic Law. Doing the Will of God is the primary spiritual concern of the Jew. Therefore, to this day, he must devote considerable time not merely to the mastery of the content of the Talmud, but also to training in its method of reasoning. The study of the Bible and the Talmud is thus far more than a pleasing intellectual exercise, and is itself a means of communion with God. According to some teachers, this study is the highest form of such communion imaginable.[5]

In the analysis of any religious tradition, one must differentiate between questions asked by the adherents of a particular tradition and questions an outsider asks of that tradition.[6] This is not intended to relativize one's Christian concerns, but to particularize them.

My Question

The Jewish Question, as I am using it here, has particular pertinence given how Christians have grievously approached the Jewish community throughout church history. In this essay my own particular concern as an evangelical Christian is to maintain that Jesus Christ is the ultimate revelation of God and Jewish Savior of the world and to guard against anti-Semitism. How does one maintain this balance? This is no easy task. Take for example Martin Luther, who in 1523 wrote the tract "That Jesus Christ Was Born a Jew," wherein he hopes and believes that the Reformation view and approach to the gospel will be instrumental in leading many Jews to faith in Jesus (while maintaining that Roman Catholicism has approached the Jews in a very dismissive and thoughtless manner). Twenty years later Luther wrote a condemnatory piece, "On the Jews and Their Lies." No doubt offended by the Jews' unresponsiveness to the gospel message, Luther claims that God has not listened to their cries for over fifteen hundred years of suffering. Given that God promises in the Psalms and the Law to listen to the righteous and deliver them because they are his people, Luther raises the question: Why won't God listen to the Jews and deliver them? Luther answers his own question by claiming, "They must assuredly be the base, whoring people, that is, no people of God, and their boast of lineage, circumcision, and law must be accounted as filth."[7] Luther did not stop at uttering such a monstrous declaration. Later in the volume Luther asks, "What shall we Christians do with this rejected and condemned people, the Jews?" Luther lists several abominable action points:

> First, to set fire to their synagogues or schools and to bury and cover with dirt whatever will not burn, so that no man will ever again see a stone or cinder of them. This is to be done in honor of our Lord and of Christendom, so that God might see that we are Christians, and do not condone or knowingly tolerate such public lying, cursing, and blaspheming of his Son and of his Christians. . . . Second, I advise that their houses also be razed and destroyed. . . . Third, I advise that all their prayer books and Talmudic writings, in which such idolatry, lies, cursing, and blasphemy are taught, be taken from them. . . . Fourth, I advise that their rabbis be forbidden to teach henceforth on pain of loss of life and limb. . . . Fifth, I advise that safe-conduct on the highways be abolished completely for the Jews. . . . Sixth, I advise that usury be prohibited to them, and that all cash and treasure of

silver and gold be taken from them and put aside for safekeeping. . . . Seventh, I recommend putting a flail, an ax, a hoe, a spade, a distaff, or a spindle into the hands of young, strong Jews and Jewesses and letting them earn their bread in the sweat of their brow, as was imposed on the children of Adam.[8]

According to Rabbi Joseph Telushkin, Hitler made horrific use of Luther's most lamentable piece in justifying his actions against the Jewish people, and he considered Luther an ally. Rabbi Telushkin notes that the Nazi propagandist Julius Streicher said in his defense at the Nuremberg trials that he had not said anything against the Jews that Martin Luther had not said first.[9] It is also important to point out that the Nazis had displayed "On the Jews and Their Lies" during their reign of terror at the Nuremberg rallies. Moreover the city of Nuremberg presented a first edition of the treatise to Streicher, who had served as editor of the Nazi newspaper *Der Stürmer*. The paper described Luther's treatise as the most fundamentally anti-Semitic piece ever published.[10] While all the blame for acts of aggression in Nazi Germany cannot be leveled at Luther, and one must account for the particular dynamics of German history as a whole,[11] Luther is certainly worthy of much blame for fanning the flames of anti-Semitism in Germany.

Anti-Semitism is by no means dead and gone.[12] If we are to guard against anti-Semitism today and not recommit the sins of the past, evangelical Christians must maintain that the Jewish people and their faith tradition today have enduring value in and through Jesus Christ. He is their destiny and the ultimate truth of God.

Those who care very little for the Jewish people and care only for their own well-being as Gentiles should think again: if the Jews are dead and gone, the threat of nihilism looms large over all of us. I do not mean to assert here that the Jewish people only have instrumental value, that is, that their existence serves to safeguard Gentile existence. I am addressing the threat of anti-Semitism inside and outside the church and claiming that those who think they can exist without the Jews (and are better off without them) should think again: the Gentiles and Gentile Christians have no ontic basis for their own existence without the Jewish community. I would go even further: the church exists for the Jewish people.[13]

The apostle Paul hoped that his ministry among the Gentiles would arouse his fellow Jews to envy so that they might long for Jesus (Romans 11:14). From the standpoint of the New Testament, any cosmic or symbolic role that the Jewish people have is bound up with Jesus. Jesus of Nazareth—born of woman and under the Law (Galatians 4:4) and from the line of David and of Abraham (Matthew 1:1–17)—is the cosmic redeemer. He is the God-forsaken Son of God on the cross, whom God raised from the dead to bring life to all people, Jewish and Gentile. Furthermore, Jesus' identity is also bound up with Jewish identity; Jesus comes from the Jewish people and belongs to them (Matthew 1). The cry of dereliction on the cross, "My God, my God, why have you forsaken me?" (Matthew 27:46), which most if not all of us also ask at one time or another and which the Jews have exclaimed repeatedly throughout their long and tortuous history,[14] finds its crisis point and resolution in Jesus' own cry and cosmic work of God-forsaken presence as God on the cross and the God who is with us forever as the resurrected Jewish Messiah.[15] Given God's covenant history with the Jews centered in Jesus, how can anyone begrudge their existence?

I grew up in a Christian home, one that loved the Jewish people. And yet, I live in a world that has so often begrudged the Jews' existence and has frequently sought to do away with them, finding them peculiar and perverse. To its shame, this attitude and agenda have often been manifested in the church's own engagement of the Jewish community. I have often wondered: Why such a reaction—why are the Jews dismissed and rejected so, even by the church?

Christianity has been corporately guilty of atrocities committed against the Jews. As Christians, we must not distance ourselves from those who committed crimes against the Jewish community in the name of Jesus; in other words, we must not claim that such criminals weren't really Christians and so their acts should not be counted against Christianity. While I maintain that anti-Semitic theology in the church is a denial of the New Testament witness, it is impossible to separate anti-Semitic figures and their views from Christianity, as in the case of Luther already noted. Such figures were often hailed as great Christians during the Holocaust, the Inquisition, and the Crusades. We Christians today often react and try to distance these figures and their atrocities away from Christianity. But as a movement, we have failed grievously. I do not intend to distance myself or Christianity from these figures in the sense of not feeling or sensing responsibility, although I do maintain that anti-Semitism has no biblical grounds. I am deeply sorry and burdened for what *we* as the church have done to the Jewish people. Referencing a Pauline point of view (Romans 9–11), my only hope is that the Jesus in whom I believe, and in whom I long for the Jewish people to believe, will make them jealous for him. The Jewish people boast a history of the Patriarchs, the Law, and the Prophets. The past and the future and the present all belong to them in Jesus.

While I hold that Jesus is the fulfillment of the Jewish Scriptures, I also believe that the Jewish faith tradition today (and not simply Jewish people) has inherent value. From my perspective ultimate inherent value is never to be found apart from Jesus. Indeed the truths that one discerns in other religions find their basis and telos in Jesus, whom the New Testament discloses as the ultimate truth of God[16] (just as the Jewish biblical tradition maintains that all truths find their ground in relation to the God revealed in the Hebrew Scriptures). Still, I believe that Judaism is a living religious tradition, and that God is at work there.

As I define *God*, I need to make clear that I am speaking of the triune God—the God revealed in Jesus and revealed in the Hebrew Scriptures and the New Testament, just as many of the church fathers reasoned. In light of Jewish and Christian history, it is clear that Judaism has often been more righteous than Western Christianity in their dealings with one another. The Jewish faith community's ongoing hope in the God of the Bible throughout their troubled history and superior virtue in the face of the church's extreme failure should humble us and drive us to repentance. The church has failed miserably to be a witness to Jesus among his Jewish people. The church was to make the Jewish people jealous for Jesus (according to Paul in Romans), but we have done just the opposite. We Gentile Christians have not heeded Paul's words in Romans 11:

If some of the branches have been broken off, and you, though a wild olive shoot, have been grafted in among the others and now share in the nourishing sap from the olive root, do not boast over those branches. If you do, consider this: You do not support the root, but the root supports you. You will say then, "Branches were broken off so that I could be grafted in." Granted. But they were broken off because of unbelief, and you stand by faith. Do not be arrogant, but be afraid. For if God did not spare the natural branches, he will not spare you either. (vv. 17–21)

May we Gentile Christians heed Paul's words, turn from our arrogance, be afraid, and repent.

In addition to claiming that the Jewish people and the Jewish faith tradition have inherent value in and through Jesus, I must also account for the fact that my family has been personally enriched by Jewish friends. These friendships have enriched our lives and our faith. Given our concern for anti-Semitism (which entails the objectification of Jewish identity), meaningful exposure to the Jewish tradition and its people guards against such objectification and the marginalization of the Jewish community.

Ever since I was a small child, my family has been close to a Jewish family. They have invited us to special family events, including their kids' bar and bat mitzvahs and weddings, and we have invited them to our own family weddings. A few years ago they even traveled halfway across the country to attend my niece's funeral, following her tortuously slow death to cancer that left my young son asking, "Where is God, and why doesn't he answer our prayers?" Their friendship causes us to view the Jewish community and Judaism in a very positive light.

There have been other relationships and encounters that have had an impact on my family and our faith. Many years ago during my seminary studies on the North Shore of Chicago, my wife and I lived in the home of an elderly Jewish woman, not far from my family's Jewish friends. Every day I would entertain theological questions in my classes, including questions about God's existence and the problem of evil. One theologian addressing the problem of evil challenged us to read the celebrated Jewish author Elie Wiesel's *Night*. *Night* is the story of his family's horrific ordeal during the Holocaust. The instructor informed us that this volume would severely challenge our notions of God's providence. Indeed, the book did and still does, causing me to be more observant of the world's suffering, especially the suffering of the Jewish people.

Every day after school I would return home to our attic apartment. I would pass through the elderly Jewish woman's large, spacious quarters on the first and second floors. In the dining room and on the staircase, I would view brass rubbings she had made years earlier of Jewish gravestones from Europe. I often wondered about the causes of the captioned souls' deaths; the Hebrew characters etched on the stones and paper did not tell the whole story.

One day this elderly Jewish woman invited us to a dinner she was hosting for a distinguished rabbi. We were honored, and we happily accepted the invitation. During the dinner in the dining room, surrounded by brass witnesses from the past, the rabbi asked us what we as Christians made of the Holocaust. In my response I spoke of Wiesel's *Night* and Bonhoeffer's *Letters and Papers from Prison*. The rabbi was, of course, familiar with both Wiesel, the winner of the Nobel Peace Prize and author of numerous acclaimed literary works,[17] and Bonhoeffer, the great Lutheran theologian who helped Jews escape Germany during the Holocaust and who was hung in the gallows for his involvement in assassination attempts on Hitler's life.

In one way or another Wiesel and Bonhoeffer asked from their own particular vantage points what I take to be one of the ultimate Jewish and Christian questions—the psalmist's cry, which Jesus uttered on the cross: "My God, my God, why have you forsaken me?" (Psalm 22:1; Matthew 27:46). Where is God? Why does he not deliver his people?

In *Night* Wiesel recounts how a beloved and beautiful Jewish boy, whom Wiesel calls "the sad-eyed angel," was hung with two men in Wiesel's concentration camp. The boy's crime was that he would not divulge the names of people who were plotting an insurrection in the camp. The two men had been found to possess weapons. Thousands of camp inmates witnessed the executions. Wiesel tells of how the boy lived on long after the two men because of how light his body was: "And so he remained for more than half an hour, lingering between life and death, writhing before our eyes." During the executions, weeping onlookers asked, "Where is merciful God, where is He?" "For God's sake, where is God?" After the latter question was uttered, Wiesel recalls, "And from within me, I heard a voice answer: Where He is? This is where—hanging here from this gallows . . ." Wiesel closes the account with these words: "That night, the soup tasted of corpses."[18]

For Wiesel the "God" who would deliver his chosen people from death at the hands of their enemies was "dead" (not that God was really dead, as according to a secularist or atheistic perspective).[19] Shortly afterward, the Jewish community in the camp celebrated Rosh Hashanah, but Wiesel could not bless God with them. He writes,

> Blessed be God's name? Why, but why would I bless Him? Every fiber in me rebelled. Because He caused thousands of children to burn in His mass graves? Because He kept six crematoria working day and night, including Sabbath and the Holy Days? Because in His great might, He had created Auschwitz, Birkenau, Buna, and so many other factories of death? How could I say to Him: Blessed be Thou, Almighty, Master of the Universe, who chose us among all nations to be tortured day and night, to watch as our fathers, our mothers, our brothers end up in the furnaces? Praised be Thy Holy Name, for having chosen us to be slaughtered on Thine altar?[20]

Wiesel later remarks in this passage that he felt very strong, as he became the accuser and God became the accused.[21]

God the accused and humanity the accuser. This is exactly what happened—not simply in Wiesel's life or in his concentration camp, but on the public stage of world history. Yes, God became the accused, and we all became the accuser. But far from this signifying God's impotence, Christians must realize that God is very strong in his weakness and powerlessness (1 Corinthians 1). God can absorb our grief and outcries, and he can endure being subjected to profound questioning by such individuals as Wiesel and Bonhoeffer. In fact, from a Christian vantage point, he presupposes them in Jesus—the God-forsaken God on the cross—who questions God and lives the question of God-forsakenness.

THE QUESTION OF SUFFERING

While Wiesel does not recognize Jesus as the Messiah who lived and died the question, "My God, my God, why have you forsaken me?" on our behalf and for our sins on the cross, Wiesel teaches that God permits intense questioning. God is able to bear our grief and our struggles. In fact, Wiesel's profound reflections in various works of wrestling with God in the face of horrible suffering are some of the most significant accounts

I have read on the subject. I grew up hearing that Christians are not to wrestle with God or question God when facing trials and tribulations. It is as if we think that God is not strong enough or big enough to handle our questions in the face of tragedy, or that somehow it weakens and ruins faith. However, the opposite is often the case. As a result of suppressing our questions, we frequently diminish faith. Here we could learn a great deal from Wiesel, who as a modern-day psalmist and prophet wrestles vigorously with God.[22] In keeping with traditional Jewish thought, Wiesel maintains that "to challenge God is permissible, even required. . . . One can say anything as long as it is for man, not against him."[23]

Bonhoeffer also wrestles with God. He struggles over the reality of the God-forsaken God on the cross who is with us in his forsakenness, and Bonhoeffer writes about it in *Letters and Papers from Prison*. In view of his own sense of being abandoned by the *deus ex machina*—the God of the gaps, the God who rides into town and saves the day by delivering us from evil (*this* God was now dead to him), who was supposed to deliver Germany from the Nazis—Bonhoeffer writes,

> God would have us know that we must live as men who manage our lives without him. The God who is with us is the God who forsakes us. . . . The God who lets us live in the world without the working hypothesis of God is the God before whom we stand continually. Before God and with God we live without God. God lets himself be pushed out of the world on to the cross. He is weak and powerless in the world, and that is precisely the way, the only way, in which he is with us and helps us. . . . Christ helps us, not by virtue of his omnipotence, but by virtue of his weakness and suffering.
>
> Here is the decisive difference between Christianity and all religions. Man's religiosity makes him look in his distress to the power of God in the world: God is the *deus ex machina*. The Bible directs man to God's powerlessness and suffering; only the suffering God can help.[24]

According to Bonhoeffer, God is with us as the God-forsaken God on the cross. So often we Christians consider God in his resurrection power and dismiss him as demonstrating power in the weakness of the cross.

Bonhoeffer took special note of this latter sense of power. For Bonhoeffer, God wants us to grow up and be adults and not look for him to deliver us from all suffering and to give us our best lives now. Bonhoeffer also held that God identifies with us in our suffering and weakness through his work on the cross. And yet I do not think Bonhoeffer ever lost sight of the resurrection in the midst of his suffering, the suffering of Germany, and the world at war. I believe it was his belief in the resurrection along with his conviction that God identifies with us in his suffering power that sustained him in the face of approaching death in the gallows. As the Nazis came to take him away to be executed, Bonhoeffer told a fellow prisoner, "This is the end. . . . For me the beginning of life."[25] Bonhoeffer took comfort in the fact that God identifies with us in our suffering, and that God suffers. No doubt he also took comfort in the fact that we will participate in Jesus' resurrection from the dead, through which he will deliver us from suffering in the future and redeem and transform history. God sustains us as we cry out the cry of dereliction leading to faith, and he will redeem our suffering not only in his identification with us in our suffering but also in his eventual removal of suffering in the life to come, which involves the transformation of history through Jesus' resurrection.[26]

It is almost impossible to compare Wiesel and Bonhoeffer given the context of their suffering. It is true that both men suffered imprisonment. Like the Jewish boy in *Night*, the innocent Bonhoeffer also died in the gallows. The Christian Bonhoeffer died in the prime of his life: thirty-nine years old, engaged to be married, and one of Germany's brightest young theologians. Yes, Bonhoeffer suffered greatly at the hands of the Nazis. But as Wiesel notes, many others suffered horribly during the Nazi reign of terror, but not in the same way as the Jews: "Were Jews the only victims of German Nazism? There were others, of course—in war actions and in the concentration camps. Polish, Russian, French, and Dutch people; Gypsies and gay people; people who resisted Nazism. But if not all the victims were Jews, only the Jews were all victims."[27]

So how did each man approach suffering, and what undergirded his respective hope?[28] Wiesel rightly saw God's silence in the face of his chosen people's suffering as a cause for his own silence about God. This silence should be taken not as a rejection of God's existence, but as the struggle of faith in view of God's existence.[29] Wiesel would eventually come to write about his questions bound up with his faith. These living questions of faith have not removed from him an acute sense of hope; perhaps living those questions rather than suppressing them has made it possible for Wiesel to have a deep sense of hope in the future.[30] But from a Christian vantage point, I would ask, what is the ultimate ground that ensures such hope as truly lasting? Is it the youth, a future generation, God, a combination of them? I do not know how Wiesel would answer.

I do know what provides certain hope for the New Testament church with which Bonhoeffer identified. The Christian claim that God died with us and for us and even in our place (Revelation 5) assures us that death is not the last word. The last word—a word that involves us, all of us, Jew and Gentile—was not spoken at Auschwitz, Buchenwald, Flossenbürg, or at Golgotha, for that matter; but at Jesus' empty tomb in the garden. This belief inspires comfort, confidence, and courage for one such as Bonhoeffer to contend against the Nazis and anti-Semites of any era on behalf of the Jews. Our labor is not in vain. From a Christian vantage point the resurrection of Jesus grounds Bonhoeffer's and Wiesel's hopes in a future beyond holocausts. My prayer is that this last word of life would create faith and swallow up our doubt and despair in enduring hope. This last word is good news—first for the Jew, then for the Gentile (Romans 1:16–17).

The Question of Salvation

The one who rose from the dead was Jesus Christ—the God of the Jews and a Jewish man. God will fulfill his purposes for his chosen people—the Jews, whose history precedes and prepares the way for Jesus Christ and whose eternal destiny is bound up with his own. The Jewish people's destiny has a bearing on the rest of us. If God does not fulfill his purposes for Israel, how can we ever have the assurance that he will fulfill his purposes for us Gentiles in the church, which involves the salvation of Israel? In Romans, Paul assures us that God will fulfill his purposes in election for the Jews: Israel will be saved. If God were not to fulfill his purposes for Israel, how would we know that he would fulfill his purposes for us—the nations who have come to trust in Jesus for salvation, a salvation that will not be complete until it includes the salvation of the Jewish people and that will entail great riches for Israel (Romans 9–11)? As Paul declares, "But if their transgression means riches for the world, and their loss means riches for the Gentiles, how much greater riches will their fullness bring!" (Romans 11:12).

Our destiny as Gentiles grafted into God's family is bound up with Israel's own destiny, just as their destiny is bound up with the one whom many of them have rejected—Jesus—but who will never reject them. Theirs is the future, and we Gentiles not only live because of them, but also for them to make them jealous for Jesus (Romans 11:14). The day will come when Israel will look on the one they have pierced—and whom *we all* have pierced—and will grieve over him as one grieves over a firstborn son (Zechariah 12:10).[31] Their mourning will give way to joy at his coming, and the nations will enter into that joy (Revelation 21). On that day, they will realize that Jesus is God's Suffering Servant who has borne their sins and our transgressions and has removed all guilt and shame (Isaiah 53).

My students have often asked rabbis in guest lectures on Judaism to share their views on Isaiah 53 and the Messiah. The rabbis have generally interpreted that text to refer to the nation of Israel, not the Messiah.[32] While my students and many evangelicals take the text to refer only to the Messiah, I believe it refers to both the Messiah and the nation of Israel. Israel bears witness to Jesus' rejection in its own rejection of him[33] and in its rejection by the nations. Israel also participates in his life beyond rejection. God rejected our rejection of Jesus when he was on the cross so that he can accept us to himself in the resurrection of the dead as he creates faith in us—resurrecting us to life, even we who were dead in our trespasses and sins.

The Christians' Jewish Question

Just as Israel's existence is bound up with Jesus as the cosmic Savior, the church must come to see that its existence is fundamentally bound up with the Jewish people. Just as the Jewish question is Jesus' question, so it is our question. The answer that Jesus lived in his resurrection is the Jews' answer and our answer too. From Paul's perspective in Romans

9–11, when the Jews reject Jesus, they reject themselves. When the church rejects the Jews—as the church so often does—the church rejects Jesus and itself. We are inseparably bound together in death and in life with the Jewish community. Only together do we conquer the threat of nihilism, as we find it conquered in Jesus' rejection, death, and resurrection. His resurrection alone offers the answer to the question of meaninglessness that he uttered on the cross as he was threatened with annihilation in his identification with all humanity—Jew and Gentile—as he underwent our rightful judgment for our rebellion against God.

As a result of Jesus' death and resurrection and his affirmation of his people in the midst of their unbelief in him, we are not threatened by the rejection of and indifference toward Jesus by Jewish people, and we must not abandon them in their abandonment of him through unbelief. Instead, we can identify with them in the hope that they, too, will be saved. For we, too, have gone astray, and God has delivered us from our rejection of him through Jesus.

This brings me back to that night after dinner, after having talked about Wiesel and Bonhoeffer with the rabbi. During the course of the conversation, I spoke in passing of Jews who had become Christians. The rabbi immediately interrupted by saying that Jews who believe in Jesus are no longer Jews. I don't remember saying anything in return; at the time, I was shocked, bewildered. But my response at this moment is, how could that be? Because of Jesus, the Jews will be. And because he is for them, we Gentiles will be. We must live with the Jews and identify with them in their abandonment, disregard, or indifference toward Jesus through unbelief; believing for them, hoping and longing for that day when all Israel will be saved.

A great example of such identification and acceptance in the face of Jewish unbelief concerning Jesus is exemplified in Wiesel's interaction and friendship with the novelist and Nobel laureate François Mauriac. Mauriac would become an advocate for Wiesel and his book *Night*. The honest, humane, and humble Wiesel recounts their first encounter:

> The problem was that [François Mauriac] was in love with Jesus. He was the most decent person I ever met in that field—as a writer, as a Catholic writer. Honest, sense of integrity, and he was in love with Jesus. He spoke only of Jesus. Whatever I would ask—Jesus. Finally, I

said, "What about Mendès-France?" He said that Mendès-France [the French prime minister], like Jesus, was suffering. . . .

When he said Jesus again I couldn't take it, and for the only time in my life I was discourteous, which I regret to this day. I said, "Mr. Mauriac," we called him Maître, "ten years or so ago, I have seen children, hundreds of Jewish children, who suffered more than Jesus did on his cross and we do not speak about it." I felt all of a sudden so embarrassed. I closed my notebook and went to the elevator. He ran after me. He pulled me back; he sat down in his chair, and I in mine, and he began weeping. I have rarely seen an old man weep like that, and I felt like such an idiot. I felt like a criminal. This man didn't deserve that. He was really a pure man, a member of the Resistance. I didn't know what to do. We stayed there like that, he weeping and I closed in my own remorse. And then, at the end, without saying anything, he simply said, "You know, maybe you should talk about it."

He took me to the elevator and embraced me. And that year, the tenth year, I began writing my narrative. After it was translated from Yiddish into French, I sent it to him. We were very, very close friends until his death. That made me not publish, but write.[34]

I am sure Mauriac empathized with Wiesel's intense pain and legitimate angst. Mauriac was not threatened by Wiesel's reaction to his talk of Jesus. We Jesus lovers have much to learn from Mauriac in his loving response to Wiesel (in contrast to how the older Martin Luther might have responded). All too often we feel as if our faith is being threatened when Jewish people do not believe in Jesus, but we fail to realize that from a Christian perspective they are rejecting themselves when they refuse to believe in him. We also fail to realize that Jesus will never reject them; he loves them with an undying love. To reject them would entail rejecting himself. Jesus belongs to them, and they belong to him. Jesus is their existence and has suffered and lived their question with them.[35] Jesus was there in the gallows as the boy in Wiesel's *Night* suffered and died and in the gas chambers with the countless other children as they suffered and died, just as he suffered and died on the cross. That death includes all deaths. And so in view of the suffering and crucified Jesus, who now in his resurrection lives the answer to the Jewish question, we must not reject them but pray for their reception of Jesus, who is their own destiny as the resurrection and the life.[36]

The Answer

I recall talking with a Jewish man in Skokie, Illinois, back in the early 1990s. I was working in Skokie at the time to help make ends meet for my seminary studies. (It is worth noting that Skokie was identified for years as a very Jewish town; Skokie was chosen as the logical site for the Illinois Holocaust Museum and Education Center, which was built in Skokie in 2009.) I remember saying to this Jewish man in Skokie that the Jews are God's chosen people. Almost as if he were borrowing a portion of a line from Tevye in *Fiddler on the Roof*, he responded, "I wish he had chosen someone else."[37] God has. He has chosen me, and the church as a whole, to pray for the Jewish people, to believe for them, to suffer with them, and not to make them suffer more except to make them jealous for Jesus as his chosen people. The church's existence has not yet made the Jews jealous for Jesus, but I long that someday it will (Romans 11:11–12).

A year ago a rabbi in Portland told my world religions class that if Jesus revealed himself as the Messiah, he would believe in him. Until that time he wouldn't believe. Jesus will reveal himself again and again. Until my rabbi friend believes in Jesus, I will believe for him and hold on to hope for him. And even if he never comes to believe in Jesus, though it will grieve me, I must never reject him (and his people), but love him, defend him, and even be willing to lay down my life for him in the face of anti-Semitism. He is dearly loved by God as one of his chosen people. God will never reject him or his people. May we Christians never reject them either but love them and esteem them.

There is so much enduring value to the Jewish people's tradition and experience: the Jewish community's profound sense of mystery, observance of Torah, and celebration of life even in the face of so much hardship and death over the centuries. While we evangelical Christians must be sensitive to the questions Jewish people today pose, and must seek to engage them meaningfully, we must continue to approach Jewish people with our distinctively Christian questions too, just as they must raise questions of us from their own particular vantage point. Of course, Jewish people do not define their existence in negative relation to the questions Christians pose regarding Jesus. But my enduring hope and prayer as a Christian is that they will come to view themselves in positive, eternal, life-giving relation to Jesus as their Messiah.

CHAPTER 7

WHACK JOBS (ISLAM)

I have had the privilege of interacting with a few leaders of Rizwan Mosque in Portland, Oregon, over the past several years. I have always found them warm and inviting and hospitable. Former president of Rizwan Mosque, Dr. Mirza Luqman, and current president, Mr. Richard Reno, have always taken time out of their busy schedules to interact with my world religions class. In addition to a stimulating lecture and discussion of Islam, I can always count on our hosts at the mosque to prepare tea, coffee, and cookies for us to enjoy during our time together.

One year Mr. Reno told my world religions class that Muslims and Christians should stop arguing with one another over the question, "Who has the most whack jobs?" Mr. Reno was referring to the tendency by Christians and Muslims alike to try and prove that the other side has been guilty of more bloodshed and animosity in religious warfare. He finds this move misguided and irrelevant. "The focus should be on theology," he said. Mr. Reno also argued that we need to block out the media and the politics and get to the heart of the matter. "This is harder in the post-9/11 world."[1]

Mr. Reno is on target in his assessment of the situation and of what needs to be done. He was responding in the affirmative to my reflections based on an article from Islamic studies scholar Daniel W. Brown. In the article Brown says that we need to move beyond dealing with a clash of cultures to dealing with a clash of theologies. Even there Brown argues that orthodox Christians and Muslims agree more than we often realize.[2]

CLAIMS OF MAINSTREAM ISLAM

Before getting to the central points of agreement and disagreement, it would be beneficial to consider some key tenets of Islam from Mr. Reno's perspective. This is not a definitive statement about Islam, but an introduction to this world religion from one of its practitioners. Islam is multifaceted and complex. It is easy to generalize and say all Muslims think and act in one particular way, but they do not. As with the diverse Christian groups, it is important to engage a variety of Muslims if we are to better understand Islam.[3]

According to Mr. Reno, *Islam* means "submission to God." Muslims claim to believe in the one true God, who is holy and transcendent and infinite in mercy. Muslims also believe in angels, who often serve as intermediaries between God and humanity. A key difference between angels and humans is that the former do not have free will. In addition to angels, Mr. Reno says Muslims believe that God has special messengers. Allah (the Arabic word for God) has been faithful throughout time to provide people with messengers who give them divine direction. Other than Muhammad, all the prophets had jurisdiction over particular regions. Muhammad is the culmination of the prophets, the great prophet. By accepting Muhammad as the culmination of the prophets, Islam affirms all previous prophets. According to Mr. Reno, Islam does not reject any religion, but is the ultimate religion for all peoples everywhere.

Mr. Reno claims that the Quran is the ultimate written revelation of God. All previous Scriptures have their place, but the Quran is supreme. The Bible is a revealed Scripture given to a specific people, not all people. He believes that the Bible either was corrupted or was incomplete, so Islam completed God's message to the world and fulfilled it. The Quran that we have is the same as what was revealed to Muhammad, Mr. Reno argues. Each word in the Quran is the same as that revealed originally.

Jesus plays a very important role as a messenger of God in Islam. He is not a divine being but a man. He lived and died as a human being. As with all prophets he was kept pure by God and did not commit any major sins in his life.[4] Jesus escaped death on the cross because a true prophet could never be defeated by the enemies of God.[5] As the Messiah, he was responsible for delivering God's message to Israel to reform the people. The Quran refers to Jesus' followers as Muslims because they accepted God's message and followed him.

The Day of Judgment requires faith and works for salvation. All that is required for salvation is sincere faith coupled with putting forth the effort not to commit the same sins again. Based on God's holy and merciful judgment, one either goes to heaven or hell.

Allah is in control of all things, and Islam affirms the notion of divine decree. And yet, humanity has been given its own free will to do things in keeping with God's laws, including his laws of nature.[6] Mr. Reno told the class that he believes in calling people to God, but not by force. Unfortunately the belief among large groups of Muslims (not simply extremists) is that apostates should be punished and killed. They maintain that God will punish apostates in the next life. By contrast Mr. Reno argues that hell is reformatory. It is long and hard but not permanent. Mr. Reno does not believe one can have a full assurance of salvation, namely, that one can be assured of going to heaven when this life is over; however, he is confident that he will experience heaven given that he is on the right path and given God's infinite mercy.

Five Pillars of Islam

While not exhaustive, the Five Pillars of Islam are the foundations of all Muslim belief and practice:

1. *Shahada*: Muslims must bear witness that there is no God except Allah, and Muhammad is his messenger or prophet.
2. *Salat*: Muslims must pray at least five times daily.
3. *Ramadan*: Muslims must fast during the daylight hours of the holy month.
4. *Zakat*: Muslims must give alms to the poor.
5. *Hajj*: Muslims must attempt to make a pilgrimage to Mecca.[7]

CLAIMS OF AHMADIYYA ISLAM

Mr. Reno and Rizwan Mosque belong to the Ahmadiyya movement.[8] The main difference between Ahmadiyya Islam and other traditions is that it maintains that the second coming of Jesus (whom Mr. Reno calls the Mahdi—the one guided by God) has already occurred. This sect emerged among followers of a spiritual leader, Ghulam Ahmad, in the Indian subcontinent during the nineteenth century. The Ahmadiyya focus on Islam as a spiritual tradition, not a political reality; so religion and politics are separated. Ahmadiyya rejects the politicizing of the faith, which is common in other branches of Islam.

Mr. Reno asserts that jihad has been abused. Ahmadiyya Islam says that you can only use force to defend yourself. The root meaning of *jihad* is "striving, exertion,"[9] and this struggle has three forms:

1. The struggle within oneself to overcome evil (the great jihad);
2. The struggle to reform society, including speaking on behalf of the rights of women and children, and seeking to free slaves (the greater jihad);
3. The struggle to defend oneself and one's own people from those who are persecuting them for their faith (the lesser jihad).[10]

Mr. Reno maintains that Islam did not fight back at first against its persecutors while at Mecca in the early days of the movement. He also claims that freedom of religion is very important in Islam.[11] Mr. Reno points out that Ahmadiyya Islam's emphasis on the separation of religion and politics stands in stark contrast to those Muslim groups that have politicized the faith against them. He notes how his movement has been severely persecuted in Muslim countries where the Sunni and Shiite traditions of Islam struggle to recognize each other as orthodox while rejecting the Ahmadiyya tradition entirely. No doubt Mr. Reno highlights this separation of religion and politics all the more, given how many Muslims politicize the faith and how Christian groups in America have politicized Islam with Christianity in contradistinction to Islam since 9/11.

Conflicts Between Christianity and Islam

Where do our disagreements lie? Is it in the historic Christian claim that God is by nature complex, that God's Word is eternal and descends to earth, and that God's full revelation necessitates appearance in human form? Daniel Brown answers no in each instance. Christianity and Islam involve belief in all three tenets.[12] Among other things Brown claims that Muhammad reveals God's purposes in human form:

> [Muhammad is] the essential exemplar whose words and actions form the authoritative commentary on the Qur'an. Muhammad has been described by some Muslims as a "living Qur'an." Add to this the role of Muhammad as the cosmic "Perfect Man" in Sufi neoplatonist cosmology—the interface between the one and the material world—and it seems quite evident that Muhammad fills a number of the roles that Christians find fulfilled in Christ.[13]

For Brown the real theological disagreement centers on Jesus and the cross. While it is disputed that the Quran denies the crucifixion, the contrast reflected in this question is undisputed: "Is the eternal Word ultimately revealed in flesh or in sounds and letters, on a cross or in a perfect law, in suffering or in success?"[14] Muslims reserve for the Quran what Christians reserve for the crucified and risen Jesus, to whom Christians respond by faith, declaring him to be Lord. While Brown is quick to point out that Shiite Islam theologians teach the doctrine of redemptive suffering based on the passion and death of the figure Husayn, the following disagreement stands as definitive: "Ultimately, Muslims and evangelical Christians are divided over whether the character of God is most clearly revealed in a perfect life culminating in redemptive death or in a perfect book giving rise to a perfect life."[15]

If this difference is truly central, then it is important that Christians approach Islam from the vantage point of the cross—both as a doctrine and as a way of life. We cannot affirm the cross doctrinally—which sees weakness as the power of God and foolishness as the wisdom of God—and then resort to lifestyles affirming power over weakness and a carnal wisdom that is rationalistic rather than relational. And yet, for Brown, the polemical nature of much contemporary evangelical reflection on Islam actually contradicts the core Christian message, and it moves in a nonredemptive direction. For example, Brown draws attention to leading evangelical apologists' critiques of Islam, including their repudiation of Islam for what they believe to be a religion of violence.[16] Little consideration is given by such critiques to how Christianity is often viewed in the non-Western world. Chapter 4 mentions Vine Deloria Jr.'s claim that Christians participated in the genocide of the First Nations peoples in America and gave rise to the following way of thinking among Natives: "Where the cross goes, there is never life more abundantly—only death, destruction, and ultimately betrayal."[17] In other words, it is all a matter of perspective; if we engage other views relationally, we will try to understand the other from within his tradition and not stereotype him; we will also take note of our own brokenness and failings. After all, we have all been guilty of "whack jobs" throughout our own journeys, guilty of not loving our neighbors as ourselves.

This point came home to me a few years ago when my class visited Rizwan Mosque. One of my students asked the former president of the mosque, a Muslim from Pakistan, if he renounced violence, and why Islam appeared so violent, as illustrated by 9/11. The former president of the mosque responded with a passionate denunciation of Western aggression in the world, and suggested by his arguments that Christianity in the West has been guilty of violence against Islam and the non-Western world through its participation in, affirmation of, and identification with American power in various ways. In the evangelical Christian community, we are often blind to our affirmation and identification with American power, but our nearly universal support of American military campaigns suggests to the Muslim world some level of participation.

It is not just the Quran that speaks of violence. Our Christian Bible, with which Muhammad was at least somewhat familiar, does as well. Take Israel's conquest of the promised land and the destruction of God's enemies at the end of the book of Revelation. Muslims find it problematic that many Christians are quick to call Islam a violent religion, when our own Scriptures and history are filled with accounts of violence, even genocide—past (the Bible and the Crusades), present (the expansion of the *Pax Americana*), and quite possibly future. Here is a sobering and eye-opening assessment of the problematic history between Christianity (especially in the West) and the Muslim world:

> Another set of concerns relate to the relationship of the Islamic world to the non-Islamic world, or, in its sometimes more contentious formulation, the relationship of Islam to the West. If many in the West see Islam and Christian-Muslim relations through the stereotype of jihad and religious extremism, many in the Muslim world see a militant Judeo-Christian West, confronting them in a series of successive Crusades. Thus Western images of a militant Islam are countered by Muslim charges that the real culprit is a militant Judeo-Christian tradition, witnessed in history from the Christian-initiated Crusades and Inquisition to European colonialism and American neocolonialism. Critics of U.S. actions in the Muslim world condemn "anti-Muslim" policies: the creation of Israel, support for authoritarian Arab and Muslim regimes during the cold war and post-cold war, a failure of nerve and will in Bosnia[,] support for Russia's occupation of Chechnya, and of (what they charge is) a bias towards Israel in the Palestinian-Israeli conflict and towards Indian rule over a Muslim majority population in the conflict in Kashmir, and finally, a propensity to equate Islam with radicalism and extremism. These issues have been reflected in what some on both sides perceive as an "Islamic threat," or an impending clash of civilizations or global confrontation between Islamic countries and the West.[18]

Mr. Reno would agree that both sides in the conflict have been guilty of committing innumerable "whack jobs" against one another. We in the Western church need to focus on theology, not politics, and to make sure that we have not politicized our theology in favor of Western and American policies.

Of course these matters concerning the West are not black-and-white. Not all American military campaigns are illustrations of imperialistic aggression: American might during World War II helped liberate the world from the Nazi menace; during the first Gulf War, the United States helped liberate Kuwait from Saddam Hussein (and received the support of numerous Muslim countries); in the Bosnian-Serbian conflict, the American military helped mediate tensions. Still, it is doubtful that America or any nation has ever acted devoid of self-interest. The church in America also has been tainted sometimes by overzealous nationalism, allowing American foreign policy to overshadow the church's missional concern for the world. So how should we move out from beneath this shadow and engage missionally today?

RICK AND AHMED: BEYOND CONFLICT TO CONNECTION[19]

One beautiful illustration of the church's rightful missional approach took place in the post-9/11 world in Baghdad, Iraq. An American friend of mine, Rick, was living in a war zone in Baghdad in the days immediately following the overthrow of Saddam Hussein. Rick was helping assess and meet the needs of the poor, distributing food and caring for children and the elderly, renovating schools, and helping with a transition from emergency relief to community development in the war zone.

As time went on, Rick decided to try to move into a dangerous, crime-ridden, inner-city neighborhood. Muslims both inside and outside the community doubted those inside this community would ever enter the kingdom of God—everyone knew they were "bad" people. For many, their only perceived hope for release from a near-certain bondage to hell would be to become martyrs for Islam. Most of the people there lived in hopelessness and despair. *Just the kind of place Jesus would go to!* Rick thought, recalling Jesus' compassion for the poor, the broken, and the lost.

God broke Rick's heart for the people in this poverty-stricken neighborhood. He began doing prayer walks through the streets and alleys in the neighborhood. Rick asked God to lead him to the person of peace in the neighborhood—the person whom God was preparing to serve as the ambassador for the gospel of peace in that community, in keeping with Rick's reading of Luke 10:6. Rick told me that we Christians can sometimes be arrogant, thinking that we bring God to places needing outreach, not recognizing that God has been at work there all along, preparing people to experience his redemptive good news. God humbled Rick and spoke to his heart about the need for humility among Christians. Rick cried out to God, "Lord, I surrender my life to you, and I surrender this day to you. Please cross my path with the people you want me to meet, and please give me your words, actions, attitude, and signs for these people. I know you are already at work in this community. Please connect me with the people you have been preparing."

Rick was there to love and serve Muslims and to build relationships with them. Spiritual conversations came about as people wanted to know more of his story as he lived among them. His motivation for being there was to obey Jesus' command to love his neighbor as himself. In the midst of seeking to be salt and light there and elsewhere, Rick found that people naturally wanted to ask him about his story and what motivated him to live in this manner; the ultimate motivation was and is Jesus' profound transformation of his life, cleansing him and making all things new (2 Corinthians 5:17).

There was no trash collection in this neighborhood. Children were playing near raw sewage. Rick was hoping to move into the neighborhood to engage in community development work. The circumstances were dire, and the situation intense. The American military did not like to go into that area because of the frequent attacks. Rick was scared to death, but he put a smile on his face and sang praise songs under his breath, looking for the person or people of peace in the neighborhood, seeking out people who would ask him to have tea with them. In normal circumstances sharing tea is common in the Middle East, but not at this time in this place, and Rick prayed for a sign from the Lord: people who would ask him to sit down to have tea with them would be those individuals God wanted him to meet.

One day Rick was talking to a man in an alley in the neighborhood. Another man with a long beard, one who looked as if he was of the Wahhabi Muslim tradition, came out of a doorway and into the alley with a box in his arms. As soon as he saw Rick, he threw his box down on the ground and got right in Rick's face, flipping him off, cursing America and President Bush in his broken English, and calling for the killing of all Americans. Then he went into a long tirade of "Kill Americans . . . kill Brits . . . kill French . . ." This was the only person who recognized my friend to be an American.

Everyone else had thought he was Russian or possibly Turkish. No one could believe an American would be walking in this neighborhood. This Iraqi man's face was filled with such rage, distorted with hate. He wanted to kill everything.

Rick put his hand on the man's shoulder for two reasons: to connect with him, demonstrating that he was paying attention; and to be ready to resist if the man pulled a gun on him. Knowing a bit about Arab culture and its emphasis on politeness and honor, Rick shared his name and asked the man for his name, even while the latter was ranting and raving. Rick held his hand out to the man and spoke in broken Arabic. Surprised, the man paused momentarily and introduced himself as Ahmed, then continued on with his tirade. Throughout the course of the conversation, Rick believed against all appearances that this was the person of peace to whom God had led him. God has a history of using such unlikely persons of peace to reach their respective communities, among them the Garazene demoniac (Luke 8) and the woman at the well (John 4). Rick sensed that Ahmed was a highly regarded and feared leader in his community. Rick was so glad finally to know his name!

Two other Iraqi men then came up to them. They were friends of Ahmed and were suspicious of Rick. My friend prayed in his heart, *Lord, I need your intervention. This could get really bad very quickly.* Though Rick had been in a spirit of prayer the whole time, now he was praying even more fervently. From his state of prayer, Rick spoke: "Ahmed, killing is not God's answer. It won't bring peace and prosperity to Iraq. Can I pray that God will bring peace and prosperity for you and your family?" Without waiting for Ahmed's consent, Rick reached out with his hands lifted up, praying for peace in the name of Isa al Masih (Jesus the Messiah), and then received God's blessing, bringing his hands down over his face, as Muslims do. Ahmed's countenance changed, even while still filled with anger.

As Rick prayed and gestured to heaven, Ahmed slanted his head, almost in curiosity. Perhaps Ahmed was struck by Rick's actions because many Muslims think Christians never pray. Seeing Rick pray astonished Ahmed. Then he asked Rick, "Are you Muslim?"

Rick put his index fingers together (an Iraqi symbol of closeness) and said, "No, but I am very close to Muslims. I love Muslims."

"Are you a Christian?" Ahmed asked, crossing himself.

"Not like that. I am a follower of Isa."

It was obvious that Ahmed had never before witnessed anything like this. Still angry, though increasingly astonished, Ahmed asked Rick about the object he was holding: "What is in the bag?"

Rick asked Ahmed in turn, "Are you Sunni or Shia?" wanting to know before he responded. In his bag was a present for a Shiite friend of Rick's—a T-shirt bearing the likeness of a great Shiite religious leader.

Ahmed responded, "Sunni! Kill all Shia!"

"Hmm, you might not like it. It is a present for a Shiite friend of mine." Ahmed's bewilderment increased as Rick explained his reason for buying the present and showed him the T-shirt. Ahmed couldn't categorize or objectify Rick. Rick didn't fit Ahmed's stereotypical classification of Americans or Christians.

Finally Ahmed asked with a bewildered look on his face, "Would you please come and have tea with me?"

Rick said, "I thought you'd never ask!" and prayed silently, *Thank you, Lord!*

At that point Ahmed's two friends left. Ahmed went over to a small shop in the alley and bought a couple of cakes, and then he sat down with Rick at his small workshop space in the alley. Rick said to him, "Ahmed, tell me about your family. Where is your family from? What do you do? What does your father do?" (These are customary questions that show honor, respect, and care.) Then Ahmed asked him the same types of questions. Rick replied, "My reason for coming here and doing relief work and community development is because the Holy Injil [the gospel] tells us to love and serve others. My story is basically that several years ago my life was going one direction; then Isa became the center of my life, and God changed my direction to his path. This happened to me as I was thinking of stories of Isa from the Holy Injil."

Rick then shared the story of the prodigal son that Jesus told (Luke 15:11–32). When Rick got to the part where the son decided to return home after losing all his fortune, he stopped to ask Ahmed, "What do you think the father will do when the son returns?"

Ahmed's response was not surprising: "Kill him!"

Rick then told Ahmed, "I got to the point in my life where I was no longer following God. I knew God through Isa but was going my own way.

God brought this story to my mind when I was far away from God. Instead of killing his returning prodigal son, the father in the story runs out and embraces him and holds a great party for him, rejoicing that his lost son has returned home to him. I returned to God because the story says that God wants us to return home and God comes out and embraces us. And so, I returned to God and surrendered my life to him."

Ahmed couldn't believe this story of Jesus. It did not compute—so unexpected, so incredibly merciful.

As Rick recounted the story to me, he shared lines taken from Stephen Neill's work, *Christian Faith and Other Faiths*: "Our task is to go on saying to the Muslim with infinite patience, 'Sir, consider Jesus.' We have no other message. . . . It is not the case that the Muslim has seen Jesus of Nazareth and has rejected him. He has never seen him, and the veil of misunderstanding and prejudice is still over his face."[20] Rick emphasized to Ahmed that the stories of Jesus are not just for kids. They are for all people—including Muslims and Christians (many of whom, like me, fail to take seriously the radical mercy of God disclosed in Jesus' story).

The wiring in Ahmed's head was short-circuiting. None of this computed well, and it was messing with his heart. Rick told me that throughout the encounter, Ahmed's AK-47 was just a few feet away. But Rick wasn't worried. He was captivated by God's peace (except for touch-and-go moments, as when Ahmed's friends came up to them) because he firmly believed Ahmed was God's foreordained person of peace.[21]

Later when they wrapped up the conversation after a lengthy visit, Ahmed and Rick kissed one another on both cheeks, as is the Arab tradition for close friends and family. Ahmed insisted that Rick return to visit with him. Whenever Rick did come back, he shared more stories, and with Ahmed's permission, prayed for him. Rick always prayed for Ahmed in the name of Isa al Masih. Rick is certain that God was working in Ahmed's life prior to Rick's appearance, and is also certain that God is continuing to do so long after Rick's departure from battle-ravaged Iraq.

As I recall this story, I believe Rick was so willing to risk safety to enter that war zone and unsafe neighborhood because Jesus risked safety to enter the war zone of a world in rebellion against God to surrender his own life in unconditional love on the cross to bring Rick back to God. Rick was so grateful to the Lord for the victory he was experiencing in his own battle-ravaged life that he was willing to risk his life for Jesus and for Ahmed.

Rick always shares Jesus' stories recorded in the Bible with Muslims. What really stands out to Rick is that these stories bear witness to what Daniel Brown calls the fundamental distinctive mark of the Christian faith: the character of God is most clearly revealed in Jesus' perfect life culminating in his redemptive death.[22]

Beyond the discussion of Jesus' perfect life culminating in his redemptive death on the cross and enemy love, one must also account for the distinctive being of God as triune in Christianity, and how the belief in the triune God safeguards consideration of God's love as truly free. God is secure in the divine communal love within the Trinity, so that the love of creation is an overflow bound up with abundant life within the Godhead, and not based on some need for people to fulfill God through our reciprocating love. This is one reason why God loves his enemies and prodigals in his beloved Son whom he gives over to death on the shameful cross for them, shaming himself, so as to bring them home through the Son to participate in his glory. God does not need for us to love him for him to love us; God is loved within the Godhead as the Father and Son dwell in one another through the Spirit of love.

The father in Jesus' story who shames himself by picking up the end of his robe; running to his prodigal son (the same son who had earlier wanted him dead to gain his inheritance); throwing his arms around him; kissing him; putting a ring on his finger, a robe on his back, sandals on his feet; and preparing a feast in his honor reveals the God who shames himself on the cross in his humble act of love for rebels like Rick and me.

I fear that I often act more like the prodigal son's older brother than the father. How often do I begrudge God's love for those drawing near to the Father from distant lands? How easily I forget that I am so much more the prodigal than these sojourners from foreign lands are. Like Rick, I turned my back on God and his Son, Jesus, having believed in Jesus as a young child and having been raised in the Father's household as his child from a young age before I rebelled in my youth. I was inside the Father's household through faith in Jesus, and then I rebelled. Muslims, on the other hand, have not yet entered the Father's house through faith in Jesus.

Like Christians, Muslims are people of the book. Muslims respect Jesus and hail him as a great prophet. I long for Muslims to come to faith in Jesus and to know the way to the Father's house, which is Jesus (John 14:1–7). Muslims are not (yet) followers of Jesus saved by faith in him, but they are not Christians' enemies either. We Christians often wrongly stereotype Muslims as God's enemies and at times even support the idea that the West should wage war with them, perhaps mistakenly grouping all Muslims with extreme radicals who become terrorists and plot to overthrow the American state.[23] We American Christians should not lump all Muslims into the same box. Ahmed does not represent all Muslims. He is very different from Mr. Reno, who helps lead a nationwide effort called Muslims for Peace, whose goal is to promote peace and renounce terror. Moreover, Ahmed does not fit the stereotype of an extreme radical, for he becomes friends with Rick as time goes on. He is Rick's person of peace.

American Christians should sympathize with orthodox and peace-loving Muslims' call to holiness and their disgust over the increasing immorality in America. We American Christians should be very intentional about making sure we don't fit Muslim views of Christians as immoral and materialistic. Our fixation in America with materialistic wealth and militaristic power overshadows our faith in an all-powerful God who cares for the weak, marginalized, and poor. We in the American church often fail to realize that the kingdom of God advances by bearing our crosses, not America's sword. Giving US generals the pulpit to talk of how our nation's God is bigger than the Muslim nations' God and how this national God won the war in Iraq (which a megachurch in the Greater Portland area did after 9/11) only increases the clash of cultures in place of the rightful clash of theologies. It mistakenly makes the church an extension of the state and the American state an arm of Jesus' kingdom.

First thing first: I need to wage war within myself—not a jihad of works righteousness, apart from the cross, but a righteousness that battles against the world system and my flesh as I respond to God's gracious love poured out into my heart, which creates faith in the crucified and risen Christ with whom I have been united in the Spirit (Romans 5:5; Galatians 2:20; 1 John 2:15–17). To employ Mr. Reno's descriptions of the various uses of the term *jihad*, the great jihad is not with Islam but with me as I struggle to overcome evil in my own life. The greater jihad for Christians is not combating Islam in society, using social reform to marginalize Muslims; rather it entails caring for orphans and widows in their distress and giving alms to the poor. Just as my great jihad and greater jihad are not with Islam, the lesser or third form of jihad is not a battle of self-defense against the forces of Islam but a battle against being defensive (which involves discounting Jesus and his cross—the cross entailing love of my enemy—in favor of the sword).[24]

The Cross and the Grain of the Universe

We Christians in the West need to go against the grain of our culture in the post-9/11 world and go with the grain of the universe.[25] And what does going with the grain of the universe mean and entail? John Howard Yoder provides an initial answer: "People who bear crosses are working with the grain of the universe."[26] The cross is the grain of the universe, which is centered in Jesus, the kernel of wheat who falls to the ground to die and bear much fruit (John 12:24). Rick's story, the story of the prodigal son and related accounts, which Rick shared with Ahmed, unpack and flesh out the answer of what going with the grain of the universe entails.

Building on Rick's reference to Stephen Neill's work, Muslims have not heard the gospel and rejected it; they have not yet encountered the radical love of God in Christ Jesus that welcomes prodigals home and that welcomes strangers from distant lands and makes them citizens and children in God's house. They have heard of America's Christian God who imprisons them as aliens and enemies of his kingdom. Unfortunately the clash of cultures in the post-9/11 world replaces the all-important clash of theologies and makes it all the more difficult for Muslims to encounter Jesus face to face and heart to heart. In this light we should take to heart Paul's words:

> When I came to you, brothers, I did not come with eloquence or superior wisdom as I proclaimed to you the testimony about God. For I resolved to know nothing while I was with you except Jesus Christ and him crucified. I came to you in weakness and fear, and with much trembling. My message and my preaching were not with wise and

persuasive words, but with a demonstration of the Spirit's power, so that your faith might not rest on men's wisdom, but on God's power. (1 Corinthians 2:1–5)

We American Christians can confuse American power with God's power, and desire to confront AK-47s with M-16s, other guns, and grenades. When tensions rise and tempers flare, it is best that we contend in relational weakness, fear, and trembling in view of God's all-powerful love revealed in the weakness of Jesus' cross through the Spirit. It is not our task to succeed against our Muslim neighbors. We are to suffer for them and to love them. Our victory is not the triumphal and successful entry into Mecca, but the triumphal elevation on the cross at Golgotha, as Jesus suffered for his enemies and his friends.[27] Such "contending" for the gospel will entail walking down streets and alleys, "confronting" Muslims with handshakes, blessings, prayers, and stories of Jesus' gracious love as we sit down to tea.[28]

CHAPTER 8

THE JESUS BOX (HINDUISM)

Every autumn in my world religions class, I invite a Hindu leader to speak on his religious tradition. I am always impressed with his spiritual sensitivity, his longing for the experience of God, and how he and Hindus generally approach life in holistic terms. We share a passion for divine mystery, though we approach the divine mystery in very different ways.

The Hindu guest speaker always shares about various Hindu practices and beliefs, including the idea that the one supreme deity is beyond naming; it transcends all names. According to a pamphlet he hands out each year in class,

> Hindus all worship . . . one Supreme Being, though by different names. This is because the peoples of India with different languages and cultures have understood the one God in their own distinct way. . . . Through history there arose four principal Hindu denominations— Saivism, Shaktism, Vaishnavism and Smartism. For Saivites, God is Siva. For Shaktas, Goddess Shakti is supreme. For Vaishnavites, Lord Vishnu is God. For Smartas—who see all Deities as reflections of the One God—the choice of Deity is left to the devotee. This liberal Smarta

perspective is well known, but it is not the prevailing Hindu view. Due to this diversity, Hindus are profoundly tolerant of other religions, respecting the fact that each has its own pathway to the one God.[1]

The Hindu spokesperson claims that God is beyond naming and beyond personhood although God manifests himself through names and persons so that we can make initial connections. After having made these connections, we move beyond naming and personhood toward experiencing union with the ultimate reality, which includes us and is beyond distinctions. Gurus help us get there. Practices help us get there. They are means to the end.[2]

From this vantage point, it should not be surprising that every year the Hindu lecturer exhorts my orthodox Christian students, "Get out of your box." As great as Jesus is to this Hindu leader, Jesus is one of many names and pathways to God (although it is worth noting that Jesus does not merit being called one of the incarnations of the supreme deity in Hinduism, unlike Krishna); God is so much bigger than Jesus. God is limitless—beyond all names and traditions. So the Hindu leader challenges my students to get out of their Jesus box. It's almost as if he's putting a Hindu spin on J. B. Phillips's classic phrase, "Your God is too small."

It is understandable that my students get flustered and frustrated when the Hindu leader makes such claims. One obvious reason is that orthodox Christianity is considered an exclusive monotheistic faith. Hinduism claims to favor inclusive oneness: its innumerable deities are manifestations of one supreme deity, which is beyond naming. All of the gods of Hinduism represent different facets or functions of this one supreme, nameless deity:

> As a universal formulation Hinduism accepts all formulations of Truth. According to the universal view there is only One Reality, but it cannot be limited to a particular name or form. Though Truth is One it is also Universal, not an exclusive formulation. It is an inclusive, not an exclusive Oneness—a spiritual reality of Being—Consciousness—Bliss, which could be called God but which transcends all names. The different Gods and Goddesses of Hinduism represent various functions of this One Supreme Divinity, and are not separate Gods.[3]

Ramakrishna makes this same basic point, but extends it to consideration of all religions:

> God is one only, and not two. Different people call on Him by different names: some as Allah, some as God, others as Krishna, Shiva, and Brahman. It is like the water in a lake. Some drink it at one place and call it *jal*, others at another place and call it *pani*, and still others at a third place and call it *water*. The Hindus call it *jal*; the Christians, water; and the Muslims, *pani*. But it is one and the same thing. Opinions are but paths. Each religion is only a path leading to God, as rivers come from different directions and ultimately become one in the ocean.[4]

This ancient doctrine contends against the ancient Jewish and Christian teaching that God is exclusively one and that God is properly named, not ultimately nameless or beyond naming.

Talk of exclusiveness does not go over well in any day. Throughout ancient history Jews and Christians faced persecution for their belief that the God revealed to Moses is one and they must worship and serve him only: "Hear, O Israel: The LORD our God, the LORD is one. Love the LORD your God with all your heart and with all your soul and with all your strength" (Deuteronomy 6:4–5). The Ten Commandments begin:

> I am the LORD your God, who brought you out of Egypt, out of the land of slavery.

> You shall have no other gods before me.

> You shall not make for yourself an idol in the form of anything in heaven above or on the earth beneath or in the waters below. You shall not bow down to them or worship them; for I, the LORD your God, am a jealous God, punishing the children for the sin of the fathers to the third and fourth generation of those who hate me, but showing love to a thousand generations of those who love me and keep my commandments.

You shall not misuse the name of the LORD your God, for the LORD will not hold anyone guiltless who misuses his name. (Exodus 20:2–7)

The Bible teaches that God is exclusively one and that God is properly named. Exodus makes clear that the God revealed to Moses takes seriously his name, *Yahweh*, which English Bibles often render, "the LORD." It is worth noting that the first explanation of the divine name is in Exodus 3:13–15. God articulates his name in the first person as "I AM WHO I AM." To Israel, he gives the name *Yahweh* ("He is") to remind them that he is who he is: God cannot be compared; God is self-defined. Exodus 6:2–3 indicates that God had never explained himself as *Yahweh* until revealing himself to Moses. His people had known him prior to this as *El Shaddai*.

Exodus 34:1–8 unpacks further what *Yahweh* means. Whereas the name El Shaddai reveals God as all-powerful in a general sense, the name *Yahweh* speaks to how God brings the totality of his essence and character into covenantal relationship, focusing primarily on mercy and deliverance. While God cannot be less than he is in the totality of his being—so that as God he must judge—the context of Exodus 3 and 34 makes clear that God reveals his personal name to display his chief desire: to be merciful, redemptive, and in covenantal relationship. In Scripture God pours out his mercy on Israel and the church as *Yahweh*, creating and redeeming them and offering the promise of redemption to the nations through them.

In the New Testament, Peter reflects the importance of God's personal name: "Salvation is found in no one else, for there is no other name under heaven given to men by which we must be saved" (Acts 4:12). Romans 10:5–13 teaches that Jesus is the Lord. The Great Commission says all authority in heaven and on earth has been given to Jesus and that his followers are to baptize believers in the name of the Father, Son, and Spirit (Matthew 28:18–20): Jesus participates in the divine name; as the compassionate Savior, Jesus is this named Lord.

Many people consider such statements as these oppressive, intolerant, arrogant, and limiting. Oppressive? Intolerant? Those who level these charges often point out that Christianity has a long history of persecuting people: the Inquisition, the Wars of Religion, the Salem witch trials, just to name a few. They claim that based on history, exclusive belief systems lead to excluding those who believe differently—even persecuting and killing them. Arrogant? Those who say Christians holding to exclusive monotheism are arrogant often raise the question, "Who are these Christians who make such claims about the divine? They don't have a corner on the religious market—especially in post-Christendom." Limiting? Those who think this way often maintain that exclusive monotheism straitjackets creative self-expression, among other things.

I certainly empathize with the people who make these charges; I share their fears. Anyone who has been in the sights of those who claim to defend God from a position of power and in a posture of spiritual pride can feel their pain; I have felt such pain. In addition we biblical, orthodox Christians have often failed to live compassionately based on how we have interpreted and applied biblical claims; in other words, we have not always wed orthopraxis (right practice) to orthodoxy (right belief). I don't want to distance myself in the slightest from the biblical claims that have been noted (to do so would be arrogant—putting myself above God's Word), but I do want to distance myself from misappropriation of those claims and from lack of love toward those who believe differently than orthodox Christians do.

The critic of orthodox Christianity might respond, "How can you hold firmly to these biblical claims? Regardless of what you might think of misappropriation, they are still exclusionary." It may surprise and dumbfound you, but I don't view these exclusive biblical claims to be exclusionary; I find them supremely inclusive. I share Hindus' and other people's concern for tolerance. In fact, I believe the orthodox Christian claims about the properly named God revealed in Jesus powerfully promote tolerance and love.

At their origins Israel and the church were excluded, persecuted peoples. While they were later guilty of excluding others, this was never God's intention for them. Israel was always to make room for the alien, the orphan, and the widow and to serve as a blessing to the nations. The same is true of God's intentions for the church. In Exodus 3, Acts 4, and elsewhere in their history, we find that various rulers oppressed Jews and Christians, and this involved discounting their God's name. In opposition to such oppression and discounting, God counted these oppressed peoples as worthy of bearing his name. God included the excluded, and he confronted the exclusive insider elites.

In Exodus 3, God reveals himself to Moses, Israel, and Pharaoh through his personal name, *Yahweh* (the LORD). Pharaoh scoffs at this name, perhaps thinking it references a tribal deity for this mass of slaves. Whatever Pharaoh's reason for scoffing, many ancient imperial rulers would consider names for the deities of the people they conquered to be designations for regional divinities or tribal tags for the one ultimate, nameless deity. Regardless of the designations, the imperial rulers often changed these names and used these religions for their own imperial ambitions, keeping and enforcing their "peace." As Edward Gibbon writes, during the age of the Caesars, the various forms of worship were "considered by the people equally true, by the philosophers equally false, and by the magistrates equally useful."[5] Prior to the Romans, the Babylonians and other conquerors also used religion for their empires' ambitions. One example of this would be changing Daniel's name, giving him the name of one of the Babylonian gods.

As bad as it was, changing the name of a Jew paled in comparison to trying to change God's name. When Antiochus Epiphanes tried to set up worship of Zeus in the temple of Jerusalem in 167 BC, thinking that *Yahweh* was nothing more than a regional name for Zeus, he received a rude welcome. His actions led to the Maccabean Revolt and the ensuing cleansing of the temple. Later, Christians were called "atheists" because they did not ascribe to the pantheon of deities and Caesar worship. Such a charge was not simply doctrinal but also political; for how could the Caesars enforce the *Pax Romana* without the subjugated peoples offering homage and ultimate allegiance to Caesar? Both Jews and Christians often paid the ultimate price—the loss of their lives—but to them it was worth the cost.

The Jews and Christians realized their identities were bound up with their names; the same was true of their God. What's in a name? In the biblical world, parents took great care in giving names to their children. The name chosen often signified a chief quality of the child, the parents' experience, or an indicator of what the child would become. A child without a name is someone without an identity, someone who can be used and abused. Slaves' names were changed in America, symbolizing among other things that they were property. They had no lasting personal identity; they were commodities to be bought and sold and manipulated in accordance with their masters' wishes.

The God of the Bible gives enslaved and marginalized people a name—his name. No longer can they be bought and sold to the highest bidder or ignored and abandoned. The named God cares for a nameless people. This is exemplified in Acts 3–4, where Peter and John show mercy to a nameless cripple, healing him in the name of Jesus. As a result of their compassion, scores of people come to faith in Jesus, and Peter and John are persecuted by the religious hierarchy. While on trial for their offense of healing the lame man and causing a public disturbance with a mass altar call, they are commanded not to preach or heal in Jesus' name. Peter and John—these unschooled, ordinary, outsider men—cry out, "Salvation is found in no one else, for there is no other name under heaven given to men by which we must be saved" (Acts 4:12). This supposed exclusionary text is taken out of context. Here Peter and John are the excluded and marginalized, and they are being persecuted for caring for a nameless cripple in the name of Jesus. In contrast, the authorities show no concern for this nameless, crippled man prior to his healing, or joy for his healing. They do not take seriously their own tradition, expressed in Exodus 3.

Much is at stake in this discussion. A nameless god and a nameless people can be commodified (i.e., treated as objects to use and abuse), but a named God and people cannot.[6] Persecute the named God's people if you wish, but they will never lose their identity. While this position is exclusivist (for this named deity alone is Lord), belief in this named God involves caring for the marginalized and excluded.

My Hindu friend mentioned earlier is a very caring person, and I take his concerns about exclusivism quite seriously. Ironically, for all his talk of wanting my class and me to get out of our Jesus box, he is really urging us (whether he realizes it or not) to get into the Hindu box, for Hinduism teaches that God is ultimately nameless. Any other view is excluded at the outset. And so, for all his concern about exclusivist claims, he, too, is exclusivist. He or someone else from his tradition may claim that the goal of each worshipper is to move beyond the Hindu box, but the idea that God is beyond naming remains central to Hinduism.

Even though the Hindu god is nameless, I find this deity limited. I can mix and match an ultimately nameless deity with this or that tribe's views, choosing this or that label, but I can't get a handle on a transcendent, personal deity who is named and who remains distinct in his immanent engagement of my life. As a personally named transcendent deity, the God of my Christian faith transcends me even while enfolding me in his embrace. I can't put Jesus in a box; he is too mysterious and defies my attempts to define and dissect and dress him in ways that appeal to me or to this or that tradition. While I appreciate Hindus' appeal to divine mystery, there is nothing more mysterious to me than this personal named God who reveals himself to me.

I cannot get a handle on a God who gives himself to me and who will not be known apart from his revelation. Jesus is a divine personal Subject. He cannot be objectified. I must not be so arrogant as to think I can encapsulate or package him. Instead I must always allow him to reveal himself to me through Christian Scripture. Today many Christians have taken the belief in God revealing his name to us as warrant to objectify him—the very opposite of God's intention. By revealing his name to us, God intended to keep us from seeking to objectify and control him. Such efforts on our part lead to distorted vision and the creation of idols. Against this backdrop we must always remember that God's revelation of his name signifies that God always remains a divine Subject.

Daily I must return to the Bible to be reformed by the Word that reveals the Lord Jesus rather than attempt to reform God and thereby make a name for myself. My inability and Christianity's inability to control and objectify God should keep us from trying to compel other people to get inside our Jesus box—where Jesus is made in our image. Rather than trying to increase our market value or force everyone into our Jesus box, we should realize that Christianity is not about getting the corner on the market. In place of us, the triune named God revealed in Jesus Christ to whom we Christians bear witness controls the market and confronts us in our attempts to commodify and control others.

As the church we are not to compel but to appeal—to bear witness, nothing more and certainly nothing less. We must bear witness to Jesus' cruciform and resurrected reality of holy love and power in weakness, and not seek after a Christendom-like corporate takeover. For all the talk of conquest of the promised land through Joshua in the Old Testament, Israel was never to engage in imperial conquest. Israel's rulers never entertained

Alexander the Great or Caesar's ambitions for building world empires. God did not want Israel to conquer the whole earth. God wanted Israel—and God wants the church—to be a blessing to the nations. At the end of the day (or age), God's blessing of the nations comes through the name and person of Jesus Christ, who gave up his life so as to bring life to all people. And so, God calls me to be a blessing to my Hindu friend and neighbor.

My point in all this is not to negate my Hindu friend and neighbor but to affirm his personal identity as having infinite and eternal worth. In view of the eternally named, personal God revealed as Jesus who cannot be commodified or put in a box (that is, placed under human control), I cannot put a price tag on my friend or on our friendship. My faith will not allow for my friend's commodification where I use him for my own selfish ambitions.

My Hindu friend has a name—Bharat. His name matters to me, and he has blessed me with his care and friendship. He has also helped me see Hinduism as more than a nicely wrapped system of beliefs and practices. Hinduism is its people. He is a wonderful representative of his religious tradition in that he is always very caring and relational. While I will still exhort him to believe in the name of *Yahweh*, I can't put him or his religion in a box, and this on account of my Judeo-Christian understanding of the importance of names and persons.

As already noted, I consider my dear friend Bharat in his distinctly named personhood to be of eternal worth and value. While I know that Hindus hold all life as sacred because they believe all is one with the divine,[7] I firmly believe it is only possible to maintain that Bharat is eternally valuable and is never open to commodification because an eternally named God and named people can never be commodified, used, and abused for self-serving ends, demeaned, or dissolved. As named and as eternally particular, Bharat does not lose his individuality, contrary to the Hindu view that the ultimate distinction between his conscious self (ātman) and the formless whole (Brahman) should be removed.

I believe Bharat wants this distinction to be removed. Perhaps he maintains, as multitudes of other Hindus do, that to remove the ultimate distinction between the formless whole and ourselves is to remove suffering. For countless Hindus throughout the ages weighed down by suffering, the afflictions they have experienced are terminated with absorption into the infinite; for these Hindus this belief was and is a great comfort. As the authors of *Religions of the World* put it,

> The universal Spirit is what we are and what we always shall be. Since there is only one Reality, annoyances and afflictions are psychological creations only. Suffering can be real only if dualities are real. . . . To those burdened by the restrictions of the caste system, individual gains and even individual existences had little worth. Many were willing to enter the peace of the universal Oneness forever, disappearing as persons like a dissolving lump of salt. Such a salvation has been the hope of millions of Hindus to the present day.[8]

What these precious people take to be a cause for hope and relief from suffering, I take to be a cause for despair and infinite suffering. I want to spend eternity with my friend Bharat before the face of God, who is forever personal and who removes our suffering at the resurrection from the dead. Rather than being dissolved as persons, we are to be raised, never again to suffer grief and decay. I long for Bharat to enter into the fullness of life through Jesus, not into a pre-boxed religion that is sealed shut and locked away forever, but into Jesus' Father's house (John 14). I long for my friend to share with me in seeing face-to-face rather than being formless— "disappearing as persons like a dissolving lump of salt." I long for him to know eternal face-to-face communion, even as we are now fully known (1 Corinthians 13:12).

CHAPTER 9

THE DEWDROP WORLD (BUDDHISM)

There is a slight drizzle floating in the air this late October morning as I sit reflecting on the subject of Buddhism and Christianity. It is fitting that the moisture in the air falls to meet the dew on the grass while I ponder this topic. Such weather is typical here in the Pacific Northwest, and it often drizzles, rains, and pours here from late autumn to early spring. And while the drizzle and dew make for a fitting backdrop on a typical late autumn morning, the friendship I am thinking of is quite surprising.

My enduring friendship with a Zen Buddhist priest, the Venerable Kyogen Carlson, is something I dearly cherish. It is such a surprising friendship that the Zen Buddhist magazine *Tricycle* did a feature story on us and our work. They posted our picture on the front cover with "The Odd Couple . . ." as the caption. The subheading for the article, "Beloved Community," reads, "What can a Zen priest learn from a fundamentalist theologian? A Buddhist community takes interfaith dialogue beyond common ground with their evangelical Christian neighbors." The only thing missing from the subheading is the statement that this fundamentalist theologian had and has much to learn from this Zen priest.[1] I have learned a great deal about how to live more compassionately based on my shared journey with Kyogen.[2]

Kyogen and I have worked together to build understanding and cultivate compassionate coexistence in Portland among disparate groups. It all started when we met several times during the autumn of 2003 with religious leaders from various traditions and members of the Portland Police Department. The backdrop to the meetings was the fatal shooting of an African American woman by a white Portland police officer. There was intense passion and distrust of the police department at that time, particularly among African Americans but also among some religious communities. Later Kyogen and I, along with members of our own religious communities, met together several times to build respect and understanding among Zen Buddhists and evangelical Christians, as there was distrust and apprehension of each other. The distrust was fueled by the culture war over politics, ethics, and religion.

After the reelection of President Bush and the rejection of the gay marriage ballot measure in Oregon in 2004, Kyogen contacted me and asked me to work with him to build understanding between our respective groups. His temple community is made up of people who are politically liberal. His congregation also includes many gay people. Evangelicals were viewed by many in the community at large as having a key role in the recent political results, given that a large percentage of evangelicals supported President Bush and conservative political policies and moral stances. Nationally known evangelical figures spoke out passionately about taking back America (from the liberals). These events and this climate led one of Kyogen's parishioners to threaten to take matters into his own hands if something did not change. Faced with this warning sign, Kyogen asked me to partner with him "palm to palm," as he is known to say. These meetings, along with occasional get-togethers and annual lectures to my world religions class on Buddhism, have helped build a relationship between Kyogen and me. They have left an indelible impact on me, for which I will remain forever grateful.

Recently my class and I made our annual trek to the Zen Center. Kyogen instructed us that according to Buddhism all things that arise in life are transient.[3] The body itself is transient. We are not our bodies. There is no permanent refuge in *dharmas* or "things," which include careers, children, families, us, and even the sensations of enlightenment. If we try to find permanent refuge in these things, we will be unsatisfied.

For Buddhists, according to Kyogen, enlightenment involves ceasing to grasp after things that have no permanence. This is the negative side of enlightenment. The positive side of enlightenment is to engage in a nongrasping way. The Noble Eightfold Path of Buddhism helps the follower move beyond grasping.[4]

The problem of grasping extends to reflection on God from a Buddhist perspective. Ultimately Buddhists are *apophatic* in orientation; that is, they affirm the way of negation, for ultimate reality is beyond naming. Whatever God is, according to Kyogen, it is beyond naming, beyond what I can get my mind around. With this in mind Kyogen also told my class that he is reluctant to call Buddhism nontheistic. He wants to emphasize that God is beyond naming, categorizing, and objectifying. And so Kyogen reasoned that he does not deny God as such; however, he would add that whatever God is, it is not separate from us.

Just as Kyogen finds talk of Buddhism as nontheistic problematic, he also finds the idea that "all life is suffering" to be a faulty translation of essential Buddhist teaching.[5] Rather than talk of suffering, Kyogen maintains that dharmas are marked by "unsatisfactoriness." Life is a mystery. Ignorance leads us to predispositions to want things or not want things, which leads to contact in name and form (sensation, perception, formations, consciousness—all of which being equal). This orientation leads to grasping.

Rebirth is the process of allowing these things to be objectified. Rebirth has a place because that which is objectified or that with which there is attachment needs to be undone and untied. Without the process of rebirth, we could never move toward undoing and untying the knots of attachment. Kyogen spoke in this context of the Buddhist doctrine of the "no-self." He claimed that "There is no self" means that there is no self-nature. We must undergo the rebirth process known as the wheel of samsara so as to undo the knots bound up with attachment in view of the truth that our true nature is unconditioned. Our original mind does not place conditions on things; we must move toward this state, move beyond attachment, grasping, and conditionality.[6]

Buddhism, like any great religious tradition, is simple yet complex. This is evidenced in Kyogen's claim that Buddhism harmonizes the one and the many. Buddhism is dialectical, affirming the particulars as well as the whole. To objectify the particulars and see them as permanent is mistaken, and yet to discard them in view of the whole is also mistaken. Kyogen also asserted that caring for this self and for other selves that arise now is something of great importance. We must live in the moment and care for the moment even though it is impermanent. While this world will end and there is nothing we can do to change it, everything is deserving of complete attention. While no particular thing is important in itself, every particular thing is important because it contains the whole. In fact, Kyogen added, each of us is configured the way we are because the world is the way it is; as such, each of us is the environment.

I appreciate the internal consistency and complexity of Buddhist philosophy. One could spend an eternity of dewdrop moments reflecting upon its delicate yet rigorous sophistication. I also find that there are many practical lessons in Buddhism that bear upon sanity and serenity and the sanctity of all life. All too often I grasp onto things, living life with clenched teeth and clenched fists. This is not good. My Christian faith as well as Buddhism tell us not to grasp and clutch onto things in this life, making that which is mortal immortal. We do not live compassionately when we live with clenched fists. We need to live with open hands and palm to palm.

Having spoken briefly of Buddhism's brilliance and profundity and a key point of connection between it and Christianity, it is equally important to assert that these two historical religious traditions approach the subject of grasping from very different frames of reference and with different ends in mind. With this latter point in mind, I would add that for all its brilliance, I do not find that Buddhism helps us respond to our mortality and face grave suffering and evil in a compelling and satisfactory manner.

For one, I believe we are wired to seek after attachment, though not for greedy gain and not for making an immortality out of mortality (which is bound up with this fallen world order). We are wired to seek attachment as it reflects sacrificial love and immortality based on the crucifixion and bodily resurrection of Jesus Christ. The Christian faith claims that through the fall into sin and evil we entered into a state of mortality and impermanence, but that through Christ Jesus' death and bodily resurrection we will be raised immortal (2 Corinthians 4–5). This is a bedrock conviction of orthodox Christian faith over the centuries. This conviction has a bearing on all of life, including how we respond to good and evil, personhood, and life and death. We will take each item in turn.

I asked my friend if there is an ultimate difference between good and evil. Kyogen responded that good and evil are not self-existing. Evil concerns the degree to which we are self-attached. The more we move toward self-grasping, the more it leads toward evil. Goodness does not have permanence either. For Kyogen even if there is no ultimate difference between good and evil, we must act responsibly because karma requires that we take responsibility to change our destiny so that we don't act this way again. He used gravity to illustrate his point. Gravity does not care what you do, but you learn to avoid the negative consequences of falling off a cliff.

With this in mind I also asked Kyogen about compassion. In view of our having worked together with great intentionality to address the importance of compassionate coexistence in the community at large, I asked him, "In view of the discussion on good and evil, can we say that compassion itself lacks permanence? Does it have ultimacy?" Kyogen responded by claiming that he is not asking people to be compassionate but to live in keeping with their orientation of life in the world. We should find out what our particular *bodhisattva* quality is, and live in keeping with it. Compassion is the gateway to all other qualities, such as wisdom. So to engage one's own bodhisattva—that is, a personified quality in the form of a divine-like figure—one should engage compassion as the gateway. We all need to work together, bringing our various bodhisattvas together for the good of all.

I appreciate my friend's point, but I would add that bodhisattvas have no permanence either. They are significant means by which people engage ultimate reality, but they themselves are not substantive or real. Reality is beyond objectification and boundedness for Buddhism. So once again there is no permanent quality; good and evil—and with them compassion—are not permanent and self-existing but transient.[7]

The same could be said of personhood. It has no permanence. It is like the dewdrop that evaporates in the heat of the morning sun. And yet even Buddhists struggle with longing for permanence and for personhood. Why is that?

The Japanese haiku poet Issa struggled with thinking of the world as a series of dewdrops that evaporate and are no more. He longed to be with his young wife and three children who died. And although a Zen master to whom he went for counsel instructed him that this life is but a dewdrop world, he struggled to move beyond attachment. Why is that?

Kyogen shared with my class the story of a Californian Buddhist, who rigorously affirms the impermanence of all life and the other cardinal teachings of Buddhism, and yet he chooses to speak of God in personal terms. Why is that?

On another occasion Kyogen told my class that while Buddhists are philosophically astute (and they are), he finds that the evangelicals from Multnomah Biblical Seminary with whom they have fellowshipped are so much more relational in orientation. If so, why is that?

It is not because we individual evangelical Christians are better than our Buddhist neighbors. In fact, I do not find that we evangelicals often live relationally and personably. Unfortunately personal relationship with Jesus does not easily translate into personal relationship with my Buddhist or evangelical neighbors.

Moreover I find that Buddhists of the character of Kyogen have much to teach us about compassion. While I do not share Kyogen's view that the distinction between good and evil is impermanent, I value greatly his nonjudgmental attitude toward others. How I long to believe in the objectivity of goodness and its ultimate differentiation from evil without falling prey to the evil of equating ideal goodness with my own distorted judgments and fallen person.

To the extent we humans participate in the ultimate personal reality, existing in the interpersonal communion of the Father and Son in the all-powerful love of the Spirit through faith, we Christ-followers model effective and essential "relationality." Relationality as defined here involves sensitivity and commitment to building community with all that it entails for self-sacrifice and compassionate coexistence and mutual care for one another. The triune God, who is three divine persons in loving and holy communion as the one God, is the ideal personal ground for the possibility of authentic personhood and relationality. I am grateful to the Lord for his grace and mercy that Kyogen found this dynamic present in my students and me. I hope and pray he finds it in us now as well.

The reason I believe Kyogen found this quality of interpersonal relationality in my community a few years ago is because God is present and indwells our lives through the risen Christ in the Spirit. This is not a teaching that is to be kept from others, as if it is for members only. God longs to be present in everyone in a personal and enduring way. The triune God has wired us all for relationship as those created in his image. Although shorted by the fall, all people cry out to be connected. And now we who are Christ-followers are indwelt with his Spirit. Even though we still pull at the wires in our fears of intimacy, the Spirit is in the process of strengthening and transforming us in our vital connection to God in Christ.

I believe the reason the Californian Buddhist whom Kyogen mentioned speaks of God as personal—and the Japanese poet Issa longed to be attached to his family even after they were gone—is that we humans are wired for relational permanence. As the Bible teaches, God raises the dead from the threat of decay. With this in mind, it is worth stating that Jesus did not mourn at the grave of Lazarus because the mourners could not give up their attachment to the deceased, but because such detachment was never intended (John 11). Through his life, death, and resurrection, Jesus makes possible the world's reconnection to God; no longer must our fallen condition resulting from our rebellion block the path to our experiencing salvation and the fullness of relationship with him for eternity.[8]

Through faith in Jesus whom God raised from the dead to destroy detachment, dissolution, and decay, we are born again to eternal relationship with God and with one another. This is good news. For historical Buddhism, however, rebirth is not positive although people in the West like to turn the Buddhist teaching on rebirth into a positive teaching. Such adherents are smorgasbord religious practitioners, not true to orthodox Buddhism as taught by masters such as Kyogen.

With both Christianity and Buddhism in the West, religious consumers mix and match as spiritual connoisseurs. For example, with Christianity, prosperity gospel preachers proclaim that you can have Jesus without taking up the cross.[9] With Westernized Buddhism you can affirm rebirth as essentially a power-of-positive-thinking construct although rebirth was viewed negatively among the Indian religions historically. Life was hard, and life was full of suffering or, as Kyogen puts it, unsatisfactoriness. To be born as a human was seen as one of the best outcomes you could have. But even for humans, life was suffering or unsatisfactory. The whole point of existence was to break out of the cycle of rebirth. For orthodox Buddhism, what keeps you coming back is desire and craving, and you must eliminate it. You must eliminate any desire, even desire for nirvana; Buddhism requires total death to desire and to any form of attachment. But how can life—even Western life—be truly good if we are to move beyond ultimate attachment to others?[10]

Even more severe than Issa suffering the loss of his loved ones was the suffering he incurred from believing that he was to detach himself from longing for permanent attachment to them in any manner. Why is this teaching even more severe than his experience of loss? Because we were created for permanence in relationships. We were meant to be restored to relationship with our loved ones, not in a permanent state of decay but in a permanent state of wholeness.

Issa wrote a poem about life being a dewdrop world. While he could articulate this perspective philosophically, he could not grasp it existentially. He longed for permanence. The poem closes with him longing for more. Os Guinness's own reflection upon Issa's poem and life merits consideration: "Here is a truth [that] should make Eastbound Western man stand still in his tracks, but it is expressed in such distilled beauty that the fragrance of its pathos and poignancy becomes such a jewel of poetry that its lesson is easily lost. Issa the orthodox Zen believer must say 'that life is only dew,' but Issa the father, the husband, the human being, with his agonized grief and tortured love can only cry into the unfulfilled darkness where Zen sheds no light, 'And yet . . .' He feels the inescapable tension between the logic of what he believes and the logic of who he is."[11]

While I appreciate Kyogen's concern to live in the moment fully and to care for every particular even though the moment is fleeting and the particular is impermanent, this teaching does not satisfy me. It should never satisfy me or Issa. Certainly we are not to hold on to this mortal life, making an eternity out of fallen time and space. But God will swallow up mortality with immortality, bringing transformation through the resurrection of all things from the dead through Christ. Issa's "and yet" makes total sense to me and finds its hopeful satisfaction and fulfillment in the "not yet" when Christ swallows up death in victory: "Where, O death, is your victory? Where, O death, is your sting?" (1 Corinthians 15:55).

I long to share in the resurrection to the eternal future in Christ with Kyogen—who has taught me so much about compassion and concern for every particular of every moment—rather than to say good-bye for eternity when the dew finally covers our earthen graves.[12]

CHAPTER 10

WILL THE REAL JESUS PLEASE STAND UP—AND SIT DOWN? (UNITARIAN UNIVERSALISM)

few years ago I invited a leading Unitarian Universalist minister, Rev. Dr. Marilyn Sewell, to speak at a conference on overcoming the culture wars, hosted by the Institute for the Theology of Culture: New Wine, New Wineskins at Multnomah Biblical Seminary. The title of my distinguished colleague's talk was "Will the Real Jesus Please Stand Up?" By Reverend Sewell's own description, "unitarian" signifies that God is one (and I would add, not triune), and "universalist" signifies that all are saved.[1] It was fitting that she would speak at the conference. By her own admission, her Unitarian Universalist movement emerged from the left side of Protestantism;[2] for my part, I maintain that my evangelical movement represents the right side of Protestantism. Our two camps have often been on opposing sides of the culture wars in North America and in the Greater Portland area.

During the course of the talk, Reverend Sewell explained how Jesus was all about love, not rules, and about taking care of the oppressed and poor. As you might imagine, her message was a striking contrast to other talks I have heard over the years at my seminary. Whereas her talk focused by and large on Jesus' social engagement of the marginalized and how our faith must be externalized, normally speakers at the seminary address Jesus' engagement of each of us personally and how our beliefs are to be internalized. Extreme case in point: recently at the seminary I heard a conservative Christian guest speaker claim that it is a distraction for Christians to get involved in caring for the poor or the creation. He argued that the world is falling apart, and it is poor stewardship for us to address the world's problems. Things will only get worse. If that is the case, why polish the brass on a sinking ship? Instead, we must focus all our energies on reaching as many souls as possible; we should leave care for the poor and the environment to Jesus, who will take care of them when he returns to make all things new. Against the backdrop of this conservative Christian leader's talk, Reverend Sewell's activist message serves as an ongoing and significant challenge. That branch of conservative evangelicalism that affirms a quietist or otherworldly approach to the Christian life needs to reconsider Jesus' claims in Scripture. The Bible teaches that Jesus' followers must be concerned for caring for the body and the whole creation as well as people's souls.

Despite our theological backgrounds, all of us should be asking Reverend Sewell's question: "Will the real Jesus please stand up?" It is so easy for all of us to concoct images of Jesus, turning him into our own likeness, as is humorously illustrated in the Hollywood movie *Talladega Nights*. In the movie, race-car driver Ricky Bobby offers prayer at the family dinner table and petitions the eight-pound, six-ounce baby Jesus to help him win his next race and make loads of money. A conversation ensues with others imagining Jesus differently: from baby Jesus to grown-up Jesus to Jesus singing lead vocals for Lynyrd Skynyrd to Ninja Jesus.[3] Such projections of Jesus shape people's prayers and responses to Jesus. Like Ricky Bobby, so often we allow our cultural backgrounds or upbringings, politics or social agendas to influence and shape our views of Jesus and his work.[4]

I believe this problem surfaces in our view of Jesus as it pertains to spiritual and physical poverty. Conservative evangelical Christians are right in claiming that Jesus is the savior of our poverty-stricken souls, but we must also realize that he is the savior of the physically poor as well. Liberals are right in claiming that Jesus is the savior of the physically poor, but they must also recognize that he is the savior of our poverty-stricken souls too. New

Testament scholars Gordon Fee and Douglas Stuart put the contrast suc-
cinctly and also wisely call for a synthesis of the two trajectories:

> In Matthew the poor are "the poor in spirit"; in Luke they are simply
> "you poor" in contrast to "you that are rich" (6:24). On such points
> most people tend to have only half a canon. Traditional evangelicals
> tend to read only "the poor in spirit"; social activists tend to read only
> "you poor." We insist that *both* are canonical. In a truly profound sense
> the real poor are those who recognize themselves as impoverished
> before God. But the God of the Bible, who became incarnate in Jesus
> of Nazareth, is a God who pleads the cause of the oppressed and the
> disenfranchised. One can scarcely read Luke's gospel without recogniz-
> ing his interest in this aspect of the divine revelation (see 14:12–14; cf.
> 12:33–34 with the Matthean parallel, 6:19–21).[5]

Another example of Luke's emphasis on Jesus caring holistically for the
poor is found in Luke 4, where Jesus stands up in the synagogue to read from
the scroll of Isaiah the prophet. After reading from Isaiah 61, he closes the
scroll, sits down, and says that this text has been fulfilled that day in their
hearing (Luke 4:14–21). Jesus indicates that the Spirit of the Lord is upon
him and that it is the year of the Lord's favor. "The year of the Lord's favor"
refers to the Jubilee in the Old Testament, the fiftieth year when debts were
erased, when property was to be returned to those who had lost their possessions, and when impoverished Jewish people who had sold themselves to
their fellow Jews were to be released (Leviticus 25). Jesus extends this text's
import to include concern for the nations, indicating that he will perform
miracles among the poor and leprous Gentiles, as in the days of the prophets Elijah and Elisha, rather than in his hometown due to their hardness of
heart in not accepting him and his message (Luke 4:22–30). Jesus has come
as God's Messiah to bring jubilee justice to the poor and oppressed, and
to all who long for his appearance. The messianic age has dawned in Jesus'
person and ministry. Far from serving as an escape clause from the world
and its problems, eschatology (theology about the final events of the world)
rightly includes Jesus' care for the poor and marginalized; his eschatological
kingdom that awaits fulfillment is present now.

The Jesus revealed in the Bible calls us to be poor in spirit and to defend the poor. Jesus' view of salvation is not limited to concern for this world, but it is not otherworldly either. Jesus' teaching and work as Savior was and is holistic, caring for every dimension of people's lives as their Messiah, their Savior and Lord. True holistic care involves moving people beyond moralism (legalism) on the one hand and antinomianism (rejection of the law) on the other hand. Reverend Sewell rightly challenged my evangelical movement to guard against a moralistic orientation, which would elevate adherence to laws above caring for and loving people. Reverend Sewell argued in her presentation:

> Jesus said over and over and over again—love is the answer, love is the way. Time after time the scribes and Pharisees tried to trap him into violating the law, because they were afraid of his power—his power coming from God, whereas they had only the authority of their outdated rules and their position as religious leaders.[6]

Reverend Sewell drew our attention to Mark 3 where the rulers watch Jesus, waiting to see if he would heal a man with a withered hand on the Sabbath. In reading her address again I am reminded of Jesus' challenge to the rulers in the preceding passage: the Sabbath was made for man, not man for the Sabbath, for Jesus is the Sabbath's Lord (Mark 2:27–28). In recounting the story of the rich young ruler, Reverend Sewell reasoned that Jesus "was telling this fellow that following the rules was not enough—you have to give *yourself* away—do not come here pre-occupied with your own salvation—don't you get it? It is not about you, Jesus is saying, it is about others." She then confirmed her point about Jesus' concern to move us beyond self-concern by referencing Matthew 25; there Jesus questions us after our lives are over: Did we care for the hungry, the stranger, the sick, and the imprisoned?[7]

I take to heart Reverend Sewell's exhortation to guard against moralism, reflecting as it does a vital aspect of Jesus' teaching. However, I do not share her antinomian assessment that our personal convictions have more authority than Scripture's commands, including the Mosaic Law. She takes, "You have heard it said, 'An eye for an eye, and a tooth for a tooth,' but I say to you, turn the other cheek" to mean,

LOVE TRUMPS EVERY LAW, EVERY RULE—YOU MEASURE
EVERYTHING BY THE PRINCIPLE OF LOVE—do not look in
the scripture, do not go by your traditions, throw your rationalizations
out the window—go straight to the heart—what does your heart say,
what does love demand? That is the Jesus I see in Matthew, Mark,
Luke, and John.[8]

In contrast to this perspective the Mosaic Law was not the problem,
according to Jesus and other New Testament writers. The problem was not
the Law but our calloused hearts and wrongful use of the Law (Matthew
19:8; Galatians 3:1–25). Given our hard-heartedness, we so often wrong-
fully read and apply the Law, including minimizing God's ways of merciful
justice and their import for the people.

The Law, rightly interpreted, always involves loving God with one's
whole heart and one's neighbor as oneself. When tested by a teacher of the
Law, Jesus and the scholar agreed that Deuteronomy 6:5 and Leviticus 19:18
summed up what was required for attaining eternal life: loving the Lord our
God with all our beings and our neighbors as ourselves. What Jesus and
the scholar differed on was the meaning of *neighbor*. The religious teacher
defined *neighbor* as the people like him, especially those he liked. In contrast
Jesus defined *neighbor* as anyone who is in need of mercy, including one's
enemy, including one's oppressor. The person who is the good neighbor is
the one who has mercy on the person in need, including the enemy. In this
account the good neighbor is a lowly Samaritan who cares for the beaten and
half-dead Jew lying in his path. The religious expert must become like this
Samaritan who cares for his enemy, if he is to be righteous; he must not be
like the priest or Levite (his kind of people) who pass the man by, not wanting to become ceremonially unclean. The priest and the Levite held to the
letter of the Law, but missed its spirit (Luke 10:25–37).

Let's return to the text in the Sermon on the Mount to which Reverend
Sewell alludes ("eye for eye, and tooth for tooth" [Matthew 5:38–42]). It
was likely the custom of the Pharisees in Jesus' day to extend *just retribution*
in the courts of law to the realm of *personal relationships*. John R. W. Stott
maintains that "the principle of an exact retribution" (*lex talionis*) pertained
only to the realm of the courts, not to one's personal relationships with

those who had wronged him.[9] According to Stott, Jesus "teaches not the irresponsibility which encourages evil but the forbearance which renounces revenge. Authentic Christian non-resistance is non-retaliation."[10] In keeping with the Law's inner logic of love and mercy bound up with the two great commandments, it is correct to maintain as Stott does that "what Jesus here demands of all his followers is a personal attitude to evildoers which is prompted by mercy not justice, which renounces retaliation so completely as to risk further costly suffering, which is governed never by the desire to cause them harm but always by the determination to serve their highest good."[11]

While I do not concur with Reverend Sewell's antinomian assessment of going beyond Scripture to the authority of the heart in her account of Matthew 5:38–42, I share her antipathy for moralism. How do I balance these two extremes? Scripture's authoritative teachings and commands champion wholehearted, loving obedience to God and heartfelt concern for one's neighbor, including one's enemy. Scripture's propositions, principles, and moral maxims are intended to be applied and engaged interpersonally. Nowhere is this more clearly seen than in the New Testament's depiction of Jesus as the Lord of the Law. Scripture, rightly interpreted, always bears witness to him, and so it is best read relationally and Christocentrically.

In the Sermon on the Mount, Jesus says that he has not come to abolish the Law or the Prophets, but to fulfill them (Matthew 5:17). Jesus is the end of the Law—its goal. Whereas the religious leaders appealed to authority— written and oral—Jesus spoke with authority, unlike the teachers of the Law as the people themselves noted (Matthew 7:28–29). Matthew portrays him as the new—and greater—Moses. Whereas Moses went up on the mountain to get the Law (Exodus 19–34), Jesus went up on the mount to give the Law—the Sermon on the Mount.

While the real Jesus *stands up* in Luke 4 to read from Isaiah 61 and declare that this text on the messianic age of jubilee justice is fulfilled in their hearing, here the real Jesus *sits down* and pronounces judgment against false teaching and false teachers with authority: "You have heard that it was said. . . . But I tell you . . ." (Matthew 5:21–48); "Watch out for false prophets . . ." (Matthew 7:15–20). While sitting, he also declares at the close of the Sermon on the Mount:

"Not everyone who says to me, 'Lord, Lord,' will enter the kingdom of heaven, but only he who does the will of my Father who is in heaven. Many will say to me on that day, 'Lord, Lord, did we not prophesy in your name, and in your name drive out demons and perform many miracles?' Then I will tell them plainly, 'I never knew you. Away from me, you evildoers!'

"Therefore everyone who hears these words of mine and puts them into practice is like a wise man who built his house on the rock. The rain came down, the streams rose, and the winds blew and beat against that house; yet it did not fall, because it had its foundation on the rock. But everyone who hears these words of mine and does not put them into practice is like a foolish man who built his house on sand. The rain came down, the streams rose, and the winds blew and beat against that house, and it fell with a great crash." (Matthew 7:21–27)

Here we find Jesus equating his word's authority with doing the will of his Father. This claim is staggering. The only way Jesus can forgive sin and pronounce someone saved is if he is endowed with the very saving power and authority of God himself.

This brings to mind two other texts from Matthew's gospel to which Reverend Sewell draws attention: Jesus' encounter with the rich young ruler seeking assurance of salvation coupled with Jesus' call on his life to sell all his possessions, give all his wealth to the poor, and come follow him to find life (Matthew 19:16–30); and Jesus' declaration that he will judge the nations, separating the sheep from the goats (Matthew 25:31–46). While Reverend Sewell is correct that the rich young ruler in Matthew 19 and the goats in Matthew 25 are wrongly preoccupied with themselves (I would also point out that the sheep in Matthew 25 are not even aware of the good they have done for Jesus), there is more to each account. The rich young ruler has fulfilled the letter of the Law, and yet does not enter into eternal life in this account because he is unwilling to do what Jesus tells him to do: "'If you want to be perfect, go, sell your possessions and give to the poor, and you will have treasure in heaven. Then come, follow me.' When the young man heard this, he went away sad, because he had great wealth" (Matthew 19:21–22). This text is astounding in its import. Nowhere in the Old Testament does it say that the rich are to sell all their possessions and give the proceeds to the poor to find eternal life. But Jesus is telling this man that in order to love the Lord God with all his heart, he must give away his wealth to his neighbor and follow Jesus. Only then will this rich young ruler find eternal life. How can Jesus make such a bold claim? Because he is the goal of the Law. In John 5:39–47, Jesus declares,

> "You diligently study the Scriptures because you think that by them you possess eternal life. These are the Scriptures that testify about me, yet you refuse to come to me to have life.
>
> "I do not accept praise from men, but I know you. I know that you do not have the love of God in your hearts. I have come in my Father's name, and you do not accept me; but if someone else comes in his own name, you will accept him. How can you believe if you accept praise from one another, yet make no effort to obtain the praise that comes from the only God?
>
> "But do not think I will accuse you before the Father. Your accuser is Moses, on whom your hopes are set. If you believed Moses, you would believe me, for he wrote about me. But since you do not believe what he wrote, how are you going to believe what I say?"

Jesus indicates in this passage that Moses will accuse the false teachers of Israel. The Scriptures also make clear that Jesus has every right to judge Israel and the nations, for he has come in his Father's name and shares in that name (Matthew 28:18–20; John 5:39–47; 8:58). Thus Jesus is able to dictate the terms of salvation to the rich young ruler and separate the sheep and the goats, especially since Jesus is found between every line of the Scriptures and is sovereign over history and the universe. The New Testament's Christocentric ethical and moral orientation extends to stewardship of wealth and care for the downtrodden and oppressed, as reflected in Matthew 19:16–30 and 25:31–46. In the former case the rich young ruler is to invest his resources in care for the poor, divesting himself of anything that would stand in the way of following Jesus; in the latter case, whatever the righteous do for the least of Jesus' brothers, they do for him.

Jesus, as the crux of the Scripture, is the safeguard against moralism and antinomianism,[12] for he is the loving Lord and the embodiment and fulfillment of the Law's aims and aspirations. Jesus is not an illustration of universal truth; he is universal truth. While the Sermon on the Mount may contain incredible wisdom that resonates with a variety of religious and secular traditions, Jesus makes himself this disclosed wisdom's ultimate point of reference. The Jesus who tells the rich young ruler that he must sell everything, give it to the poor, and come follow Jesus to find eternal life (in contrast to Reverend Sewell, I take Jesus' instruction to this man quite literally)[13] is the same Jesus who preached the Sermon on the Mount and on whose word one must build one's life to find eternal life (Matthew 7:21–27). Moses never made such claims, nor could he as a mere mortal. Jesus would have us know that he is greater than the great representative of the Jewish legal code, Moses. In Jesus' Jewish context, no more radical claim could be made to Jesus' lordship in relation to legal codes and laws. Jesus and his heavenly Father are the ultimate lawgivers, and together are the true source of righteousness.

No doubt Jesus' disciples despaired of themselves when they heard Jesus' words in the Sermon on the Mount, just as they despaired when they heard Jesus say that it was almost impossible for a rich man to enter the kingdom of heaven. Jesus expected them to have a righteousness that surpassed that of the Pharisees (Matthew 5:20); how could they ever perform that well? And if the rich—who were in their minds close to God because God had blessed them with wealth—were in grave danger of failing to enter heaven, how would they ever have a chance of making it (Matthew 19:23–27)?

Jesus wants his followers to move beyond self-concern bound up with self-advancement and performance-based spirituality and throw themselves on him, clinging to him, depending on him, guarding against distorting God's Word as the Pharisees did or coveting wealth as the rich young ruler did. Jesus' followers will never attain heaven by self-concern or by their own performance. They cannot ever conjure enough passionate mourning, hunger for righteousness, meekness, mercy, purity, peace, and righteousness leading to persecution to attain salvation (Matthew 5:4–10).

Jesus' disciples came to realize that their performance would never be good enough and their riches and possessions would never gain heaven for them; only poverty of soul—spiritual bankruptcy[14]—proves satisfactory, and it depends completely on God's quickening of our spirits and breaking of our hearts. "Blessed are the poor in spirit, for theirs is the kingdom of heaven" is the first of the Beatitudes, the first words recorded of Jesus' Sermon on the Mount. The revelatory teaching of Jesus that the poor in spirit are blessed introduced everything that followed; everything stated in this sermon presupposed this claim, and the disciples' experience of obedience was dependent on it.

Jesus' followers must depend wholly on Jesus and his Word, not on themselves or their own performance, to find life. Only as we cast ourselves on Jesus will we give ourselves away to others. Only then can we truly be free to give freely—caring for the stranger, the sick, and our enemy as Reverend Sewell so powerfully and passionately exhorts us to do. Only as Jesus and his kingdom values enter our hearts and lives will we be free to do these things, not the other way around.

Mention has been made of Matthew 5:38–42 and John Stott's claim that Christ-followers are to care for their oppressors' well-being and never seek retaliation. One of the most striking instances of that Scripture being lived out in history occurred during the plague of Cyprian, described on page 60.[15] These early Christians took very seriously Jesus' command not to seek revenge but to care for one's enemies. I cannot imagine them doing so unless they believed the Bible they inherited was authentic and trustworthy, that Jesus was the almighty judge of the living and the dead, that Jesus knew God as his Father in a unique and special sense, that he was worthy of their surrendering their lives and talents and wealth to him in total obedience because of his costly sacrificial love for them, and that through him they could truly care for those who could not care for them, even loving their enemies at great cost to themselves. As New Testament scholar Robert Gundry maintains, "If the gospels are not reliable, we draw a blank at the beginning of Christianity. But the dramatic upsurge of Christianity demands an explanation equal to the phenomenon."[16] And as Stott argues about Jesus' integrity and authority in keeping with C. S. Lewis's claim, Jesus either suffered from megalomania, or he really was who he claimed to be. Stott is right in concluding that the Jesus who delivered the lofty ethics of the Sermon on the Mount and who is the subject of the four canonical gospels could not be a megalomaniac, but must be Lord and God.[17] Lewis puts it well:

> The historical difficulty of giving for the life, sayings and influence of
> Jesus any explanation that is not harder than the Christian explanation,

is very great. The discrepancy between the depth and sanity and (let me add) *shrewdness* of His moral teaching and the rampant megalomania which must lie behind His theological teaching unless He is indeed God, has never been satisfactorily got over.[18]

Where does this leave us? It leaves us taking up Reverend Sewell's challenge rather than falling prey to complacency and callousness to allow Jesus to take care of the marginalized, the oppressed, and even the oppressor since he is the Son of God. No, since he is the literal Son of God, we must take most seriously the fact that Jesus *stands up* for the orphan and widow in their distress and *sits down* in judgment over the nations, beckoning all of us to care for the sick and imprisoned, the stranger and the hungry too.

Jesus' claims quicken us to take up my distinguished Unitarian Universalist colleague's challenge, but on much surer ground. In no way do I seek to fan the flames of the culture wars between the right and the left. If anything, I wish to support Dr. Sewell in her efforts to care for the imprisoned, the sick, the stranger, and the hungry. It has been my privilege to serve with Reverend Sewell on three separate occasions—one at the culture wars conference at Multnomah; another at a forum on faith, economics, and the environment at Lewis and Clark University; and another at a rally on global climate change at the 2007 Unitarian Universalist national conference in Portland. On each occasion Reverend Sewell's evident courage and compassion and pathos inspired me to take to heart with renewed passion and urgency the Lord Jesus' charge to care for the oppressed and oppressor. Her words and example also broke my heart, for my own evangelical movement is often calloused to the structures that oppress people, settling for distant charity rather than overturning those oppressive structures in solidarity with the oppressed and caring for those who would in turn oppress them for such intervention.

However, I firmly maintain that it is only in believing that the real Jesus who *stands up* for the marginalized literally *sits down* to judge the nations as Lord and God that I have the sufficient grounds and the lasting basis to love the unlovable and the oppressor. As the way, the truth, and the life, Jesus' loving and authoritative life and teachings are ultimately the rightful and victorious way of the world.

CHAPTER 11

THE BURNING BOSOM (MORMONISM)

Recently I was part of a discussion on Mormonism during which another evangelical Christian leader exclaimed that Mormonism is demonic and that the only thing we evangelical Christians share with Mormons is total depravity. When he was asked if he thought that there were bridges of commonality based on such things as the image of God and strong family and moral values, he discounted them, seeing such supposed bridges as outside the bounds of religion. For this Christian leader doctrine was the essence of religion.

Regardless of what one wants to make of this leader's problematic statements about Mormonism, it is a misstep to reduce religion to doctrine. Mormonism itself cannot be reduced to a set of beliefs. It is also wrong to claim that strong family and moral values can be ignored when engaging Mormonism or religion generally. One must account for family and morals as well as ritual, sacred narrative and experience in addition to doctrine in assessing any religion fully. If evangelical Christians want to engage Mormons meaningfully, we must account for all these spheres.

Why do we evangelicals often focus primarily on doctrinal tenets to the exclusion of other matters when assessing religion? As with any religion, doctrinal beliefs don't exhaust who Mormons are. Human identity, religion, and spirituality cannot be reduced to a doctrinal formula. How can it be otherwise—especially for orthodox evangelical spirituality—when truth is not simply a biblical proposition but also and ultimately the life-giving person of Jesus Christ, the eternal Word of God made human flesh? We are not seeking to relativize absolute truth, but to approach truth interpersonally in keeping with the personal Word made flesh, who alone is the way, the truth, and the life.

Our faith and our identity are more than thoughts. Faith and identity involve experiences, relationships, and an entire web of cultural particularities. While Mormonism has traditionally been called a cult in evangelical circles, it is more meaningful and missional to consider Mormonism a religious culture or subculture with different beliefs and distinctive religious practices.[1] When we view Mormonism from this perspective, we are better able to build relationships and share our respective views in meaningful ways.[2] And when we think of Mormons as people like us seeking life-changing spiritual experience, relational security, and vibrant and lasting community, we are better able to see ourselves in them, and to journey with them in pursuit of the truest understanding and richest experience of Jesus.

When we are better able to see ourselves in Mormons, we will be less prone to stereotype and demean them. We will come to see that if we demean Mormon teachings and their customs, we are demeaning them as persons as well as their familial and tribal ties. I must confess that I have tended to look at Mormons with suspicion and consternation, treating them as "the other" whom I can objectify and classify and don't need or want to know. This distorted perspective now causes me grief.[3] Jesus never objectified, labeled, or wrote anyone off. He always got beyond stereotypes and moved through doctrinal formulas to engage people graciously and truthfully, to bring the good news home, and to bring people home to be with him in his Father's house in eternity.

We all need to see past the stereotypes if we are to connect with people as Jesus did. What do you think of when you hear the word *Mormons?* Young men going door-to-door? Polygamy? Salt Lake City? Temples? Governor Mitt Romney? Football great Steve Young? Strange beliefs about human origin and destiny and Jesus? Do you think of Mormons as normal people with hopes, fears, and concerns? Do you ever think that to those outside the evangelical movement, our own beliefs are strange and weird? Our beliefs make good sense to us based on the web of our own experiences, communal network, and cultural context in addition to our reading of Scripture.

Although ecstatic experiences are less familiar in our tradition, evangelical Christians have much in common with Mormons. We all long for profound spiritual experience, relational security, and meaningful community centered in Jesus. If we are to engage Mormons meaningfully as well as truthfully, we need to move beyond simply addressing them from the standpoint of propositions to experiencing and performing the faith powerfully in their midst and participating fully as an evangelical community and family in the life-giving reality of the triune God.

Mormonism as a way of life and common experience involves internal testimony, such as the shared "burning in the bosom." *The Doctrine and Covenants of the Church of Jesus Christ of Latter-Day Saints* reads, "But, behold, I say unto you, that you must study it out in your mind; then you must ask me if it be right, and if it is right I will cause that your bosom shall burn within you; therefore, you shall feel that it is right."[4] This experience provides an internal testimony and assurance as to the veracity of the truth claims Mormons are evaluating.[5] With this in mind, Mormons claim that their experience is not anti-reason; instead experience coheres with rationality.

Mormon missionaries, such as those portrayed in the fascinating movie *God's Army*,[6] convey the significance of this experience for Mormons. While evangelicals and Mormons will differ on the relation of this experience to the identity of Jesus and authority of the Bible in relation to other texts, such as the Book of Mormon, we all maintain that God's love transcends knowledge (Ephesians 3:18–19) and that spiritual wisdom cannot be equated with human wisdom (1 Corinthians 2:6–16). The Spirit reveals spiritual truths to us, so I share Mormons' concern for spiritual wisdom. I agree with them that such truth is not lacking for rationality but goes beyond sheer factuality, requiring the Spirit's testimony.

Our different beliefs about Jesus speak to profound spiritual encounters concerning eternal life and death; they are important, and so, too, are the ways we engage those with whom we dialogue and debate. Jesus never separated beliefs from practices, and he cared deeply and compassionately for those in error, breaking down boundary walls and centering their attention on him. My bosom now burns that I would become a more redemptive Christian witness to my Mormon neighbors. With this in mind, I seek dialogue on three key questions.

THREE KEY QUESTIONS OF MORMONISM

Three key questions Mormonism seeks to answer are: "Where have we come from?" "Why are we here?" and "Where are we going?" Their overarching perspective on the beginning and the end of human destiny can be summed up in Lorenzo Snow's classic statement of Mormon doctrine: "As man now is, God once was. As God now is, man may be."[7] Although at times controversial as a summary statement both in Mormon circles and in Mormon-evangelical interaction, it would appear to be an accurate summary of the Mormon doctrine of exaltation or eternal progression.[8] This couplet is useful in unpacking Mormon answers to these three important questions.

Where Have We Come From?

Mormons believe we all preexisted as spirit children of God and his wife prior to coming to this earth. Jesus and Lucifer were also preexistent children of God. Lucifer and Jesus favored two competing plans to "save" humanity: Lucifer called for saving everyone regardless of their will; in accordance with God's will, Jesus favored the plan that saved those who chose God. Jesus' plan was selected, not Lucifer's. Lucifer and his host rebelled. A part of the judgment given to those who rebelled and were cast out was a denial of embodiment, a punishment given to Lucifer, who became Satan, and those spirits, who became demons.[9]

According to the Mormon Plan of Salvation, we come here to receive a body, to receive the gospel as understood by Mormons, to learn how to return to the Father, to exercise our human agency, and to do all the things we need to do to achieve exaltation as worthiness. This entails being like the heavenly Father.

Why Are We Here?

Here we must account for the Mormon notion of exaltation. The goal of Mormonism is not salvation, but exaltation.[10] We are to obey the gospel as delineated by Mormonism so that we can achieve likeness to God. Just as God was once human who then achieved deity, we, too, can live obedient lives and achieve perfection with God. Obedience requires attending the Mormon church in one's ward, obeying Mormon teaching, and being involved in the practices at the temple. One of the temple practices is baptism of the dead. Mormons of good standing are baptized for the dead so that these people who have passed away can hear the gospel as understood by Mormons after death and accept it postmortem. Mormons also have weddings, called "sealings," that unite couples for time and eternity. Being sealed, the husband and wife will have their own planet and spirit children after this life. Their children who are sealed later in this life will be sealed to them for all eternity.

Where Are We Going?

Mormons have a three-level view of heaven: telestial, terrestrial, and celestial. Beyond heaven is the outer darkness. The telestial level of heaven includes those "who continued in their sins and did not repent in this life."[11] The terrestrial level includes people of good faith, those who "do not accept the fullness of the [Mormon] gospel of Jesus Christ but live honorable lives."[12] The celestial level is for those who have become like the heavenly Father and who have been exalted,[13] having achieved the status of divinity.

Mormonism includes a variety of definitions of hell, one of which is understood as the "second spiritual death." It "refers to the realm of the devil and his angels, including those known as sons of perdition (2 Peter 2:4; Revelation 20:14; Doctrine & Covenants 29:38; 88:113). It is a place for those who cannot be cleansed by the Atonement because they committed the unforgivable and unpardonable sin (1 Nephi 15:35; Doctrine & Covenants 76:30–49). Only this hell continues to operate after the Resurrection and Judgment."[14]

Mormons have a difficult time conceiving of life in a disembodied or immaterial manner. This is evident in their belief that they existed as children of God and his wife, and that they themselves will be gods who inhabit and populate future planets. I appreciate Mormons' emphasis on corporeality in that Christianity rightfully conceived does view perfection for humanity in embodied form. We will not become immaterial and disembodied in the afterlife, but we will be raised immortal in an embodied state (1 Corinthians 15:12–58; 2 Corinthians 5:1–10).

Three Responses of Historic Christianity

Where Have We Come From?

While orthodox Christianity does not espouse that God was at first human who later became God, it definitely does embrace the belief that the second person of the eternal Trinity became human. Jesus will forever be human as the God-Man, and we must always think of him as the eternal Word enfleshed rather than as the eternal Word apart from the flesh. As the eternal Word who became enfleshed, Jesus has always existed with the Father and has no present existence apart from his humanity. Mary truly is the mother of God incarnate, so there is no division between his divinity and humanity. The two natures remain distinct though inseparable in his person, so the Word became flesh in time while continuing to remain the eternal Word of God.[15]

The orthodox claim that the eternal God became human flesh serves as the supreme affirmation of concrete human embodiment, which Mormons also value. Rather than rejecting the doctrine of the Trinity, it would make sense for Mormons to affirm this historic teaching of the church; for we do not worship a human who becomes God, but the almighty God who becomes human. In the words of St. John of Damascus, we do not worship human flesh, but he who became human flesh: "I do not worship matter, I worship the God of matter, who became matter for my sake, and deigned to inhabit matter, who worked out my salvation through matter."[16] The claim that the second person of the eternal Trinity became human is the ultimate affirmation of our concrete particularity and embodied state. Matter is not evil by nature (in contrast to Gnostic spirituality old and new) but is good and blessed of the eternal God who became human flesh.

Why Are We Here?

Jesus as the second person of the Trinity became flesh (John 1:14), and he will never be separate from his body for all eternity. Not only that, but Jesus became one flesh with his church by faith. It is not husbands and wives who ultimately represent the goal of human history, as in Mormon thought, but Jesus and his church. Remember the goal of human history is to provide God's Son with a spouse as Jonathan Edwards remarked: "There was, [as] it were, an eternal society or family in the Godhead, in the Trinity of persons. It seems to be God's design to admit the church into the divine family as his son's wife. . . . Heaven and earth were created that the Son of God might be complete in a spouse."[17]

God was not from all eternity seeking to determine how to illustrate husband-wife relations but to illustrate the marital union between Jesus and his church. Husbands and wives bear witness to this greater reality, as Paul makes clear:

> Husbands, love your wives, even as Christ also loved the church, and gave himself for it; that he might sanctify and cleanse it with the washing of water by the word, that he might present it to himself a glorious church, not having spot, or wrinkle, or any such thing; but that it should be holy and without blemish. So ought men to love their wives as their own bodies. He that loveth his wife loveth himself. For no man ever yet hated his own flesh; but nourisheth and cherisheth it, even as the Lord the church: For we are members of his body, of his flesh, and of his bones. For this cause shall a man leave his father and mother, and shall be joined unto his wife, and they two shall be one flesh. This is a great mystery: but I speak concerning Christ and the church. Nevertheless let every one of you in particular so love his wife even as himself; and the wife see that she reverence her husband. (Ephesians 5:25–33 kjv)

While I certainly admire Mormons for their profound and sacred regard for the human family, the Bible teaches that men and women will not be given in marriage in the eternal state (Matthew 22:30). As great as marriage is to my spouse and me, our marriage is to bear witness to the ultimate marriage—Jesus and his church. As great as the Mormon community is, given its profound affirmation of family relations, even more profoundly communal is God's people existing as Jesus' bride.[18] Of course, we are speaking of a spiritual union of hearts through the Spirit of love, who joins our hearts with Jesus' heart, rather than physical union; but this spiritual union involves the God who became human flesh and his earthly people transformed by his Spirit at the resurrection of the dead, which he inaugurated.

As with the nuclear family, Mormonism places great emphasis on its extended faith community, prizing its tradition and distinguished leaders throughout the history of the movement. Just as Mormons draw from leaders in their tradition, I may draw from leaders in my own tradition, including Calvin, Luther, and Wesley. Each of these Christian leaders speaks to an experiential faith that exceeds reason, that won't be straitjacketed by rationalism, and that does not fall prey to moralism or what might be termed "sin management."

The great Protestant Reformer John Calvin speaks of the profundity of the sacred romance between Jesus and his community in his commentary on Ephesians 5. As noted in chapter 2, Calvin reflects upon Paul's own "astonishment at the spiritual union between Christ and the church." He later notes, "For my own part, I am overwhelmed by the depth of this mystery, and am not ashamed to join Paul in acknowledging at once my ignorance and my admiration." Calvin avoids following the drive of the flesh to attempt at dissecting "the manner and character of this union" or "undervaluing what Paul declares to be a deep mystery!" Over against these extremes, "reason itself teaches how we ought to act in such matters; for whatever is supernatural is clearly beyond our own comprehension. Let us therefore *labour* more to feel Christ living in us, than to discover the nature of that *intercourse*."[19] Although Calvin elsewhere reflects upon the meaning of our union with Jesus, it is important to stress here Calvin's keenly felt awareness of mystical intercourse between Jesus and his church.

Those of us in the Protestant tradition have often failed to account for Calvin's experiential orientation, approaching union with Christ primarily in rational and forensic or legal terms. For all our differences from Mormons, we should take to heart their profound emphasis on experiencing their faith. We can also learn a thing or two from Mormons concerning their affirmation of the sanctity of marriage. Marriage does indeed have lasting and eternal significance—bearing witness to the spiritual union of Jesus and his church—and so we must guard against secular and mundane views of marriage.

Marriage between men and women must be configured in terms of their witness to Jesus' marital union with his church. This is the ultimate union, the ultimate experience, and the ultimate form of communion. My wife and I will someday die (unless the Lord returns before then). Even now we are included as members of Jesus' bride in his marriage to his church. In contrast to our union, the church's union with Jesus lasts for eternity. Unlike even the best of marriages, this union will be without sorrow and free from pain and disappointment. Though my wife and I experience marital bliss with each other, our union with Jesus exceeds our expectations for marriage here below. The love of God and the experience of God in Jesus through the Spirit transcend knowledge and all other forms of experience. Mystical union with Jesus according to the Bible is far greater than union with a spouse and will supersede it and the family. God's community, his family, will be mystically united to him through Jesus in the Spirit.

The most intimate marriages are those formed in relational security, wherein both partners have faith in the other's love for them. Mormons are certainly right to emphasize the importance of performing the faith. Mormons are not ultimately captive to rational configurations of the faith, but the embodiment of it as they perform it in relation to others. But what is to guard against a performance-based spirituality whereby one finds one's worth and significance not in God's love for us but in our living up to God's expectations and demands of us? There is no relational security in living one's life with the aim to be found worthy and adequate. Calvin's contemporary—the father of the Protestant Reformation—Martin Luther espoused that relational security was based on viewing union with Jesus not as an unsure goal but as a sure ground based in faith in God's loving promises.[20] Far from making us lack concern for living righteous lives, this confidence that we are united to Jesus through the love of God poured out through the Spirit in faith makes us work all the harder—not to attain God's favor, but because we have already experienced it. Thus there is no opposition between faith and works and no such thing as cheap grace, for works follow from saving faith as God's love is poured out in our hearts and lives, creating faith and faithfulness as we serve God and others. As Luther says, "Therefore, if we recognize the great and precious things which are given us, as Paul says [Romans 5:5], our hearts will be filled by the Holy Spirit with the love which makes us free, joyful, almighty workers and conquerors over all tribulations, servants of our neighbors, and yet lords of all."[21]

Our relational security is not based on the man Jesus becoming God or on our becoming like him but is based on God's Son becoming human and the eternal Spirit being poured out into our lives in holy love. We are concerned for exaltation but not that form of exaltation that depends on our performance for relational security. How will I ever perform adequately enough? I can never love as God loves or work to attain to the highest heaven. Not only does this framework cause me to be anxious about my eternal state, but also it keeps me from truly loving my brother and sister and everyone else. Only as I am secure in God's exalted love through Jesus in the Spirit am I free to care for others, cultivating profound community.

For Luther union with Jesus does not come about as a result of our acts of love as medieval Catholic monasticism often claimed.[22] Nor does it arise from an act of faith in God as Protestant scholasticism with its bilateral view of salvation often argues.[23] Rather, union with Jesus occurs by faith in God's act of love for us, in and through Jesus' cross and resurrection, and as the Spirit of love is poured out into our hearts, thereby creating faith. This leads us to love God and others, not to gain salvation or be exalted. Having already been exalted through union with Jesus, we are free to lay down our lives for others.

All too often we struggle with sin management, trying to win God's approval rather than living life with the sense that in and through Jesus we have experienced God's approval. We are now God's children, and the Spirit testifies with our hearts that God is our Abba—Daddy-Father (Romans 8:16; 1 John 3:1). Faith is our assurance. Such trust in Jesus' Father is engendered through the Spirit. Faith is not something we bring to the table, nor do we bring our works to the table so as to get God to love us. We don't live this life to manage sin, but to experience God's mercy and grace and joy in holy matrimony with Jesus through faith in God's loving promises as the Spirit of God is poured out into our hearts.

Luther had sought to acquire union with God through acts of love before coming to terms with the promises of God revealed in the Bible that we are saved by grace through faith. It is not our love for God that justifies us, but God's love that creates faith in God's promises as the Spirit of God is poured out into our hearts. Luther writes of our marital union, whereby we become one flesh with Jesus through faith:

> Who then can fully appreciate what this royal marriage means? Who can understand the riches of the glory of this grace? Here this rich and divine bridegroom Christ marries this poor, wicked harlot, redeems her from all her evil, and adorns her with all his goodness. Her sins cannot now destroy her, since they are laid upon Christ and swallowed up by him. And she has that righteousness in Christ, her husband, of which she may boast as of her own and which she can confidently display alongside her sins in the face of death and hell and say, "If I have sinned, yet my Christ, in whom I believe, has not sinned, and all his is mine and all mine is his," as the bride in the Song of Solomon (2:16) says, "My beloved is mine and I am his."[24]

As with Mormons, Luther himself was wary of abstract reason and sterile and static formulations divorced from human experience.[25] In the very essay in which he talks about union with Jesus by faith, he sets forth this paradigm of joyful exchange; here he uses the striking image of Jacob's ladder: "Christ descends from Heaven, and the Christian ascends to be united with God."[26] And so, the believer does not live "in himself, but in Christ and in his neighbor. Otherwise he is not a Christian. He lives in Christ through faith, in his neighbor through love. By faith he is caught up beyond himself into God. By love he descends beneath himself into his neighbor. Yet he always remains in God and in his love."[27]

Here we find that salvation is exaltation, whereby we are united by faith with Jesus who is God; such exalted union with Jesus by faith leads to self-sacrifice for our neighbors in love. While Mormons are to be commended for their profound care for their communities, there is a burden for them to perform the faith to attain to the exalted state. Instead of Jesus descending in love to lift them up in faith, they must ascend by human effort. Joseph Smith uses a ladder to speak to this matter:

When you climb up a ladder, you must begin at the bottom, and ascend step by step, until you arrive at the top; and so it is with the principles of the Gospel—you must begin with the first, and go on until you learn all the principles of exaltation. But it will be a great while after you have passed through the veil before you will have learned them. It is not all to be comprehended in this world; it will be a great work to learn our salvation and exaltation even beyond the grave.[28]

Former LDS president Spencer W. Kimball claims, "Each command we obey sends us another rung up the ladder to perfected manhood and toward godhood; and every law disobeyed is a sliding toward the bottom where man merges into the brute world."[29] He also writes, "However powerful the saving grace of Christ, it brings exaltation to no man who does not comply with the works of the gospel."[30] Mormons believe they experience exaltation by exercising free agency to avoid evil and attain perfection by choosing the right, climbing the ladder toward perfection.

I find this approach to exaltation burdensome. I would never have assurance in this life that I am relationally secure before the Father, given my propensity to disobey and slide down the ladder into the brute world to which Kimball refers. I for one would not be able to care for my neighbor if I were seeking after relational security with God; in fact, I would use my neighbor as a means to the end of acquiring merit before God to attain security. I am extremely grateful to God that I am already assured of exaltation based not on my merit but on that of the eternal Word enfleshed, who took away my sin at the cross and rose from the dead to bring me new life. As Peter says, "For Christ died for sins once for all, the righteous for the unrighteous, to bring you to God. He was put to death in the body but made alive by the Spirit" (1 Peter 3:18). Given that Jesus has already brought me to God and that I am already united with Jesus by faith and receive rather than attain salvation as exaltation through that union, I am now in a position to give myself freely to others, unburdened by anxieties bound up with my performance.

John Wesley and his brother Charles came to experience this same reality. They talked and wrote at great length of salvation and exaltation.

John Wesley, the founder of Methodism, created a movement known for systematic methods, rigorous morals, and social action. His revolutionary movement would not have arisen if he had not undergone spiritual transformation. Earlier in life Wesley did not experience the love and peace and joy that would later energize his missional movement. After training for ministry and completing his seminary education as a young man, Wesley left England to reach for Christ the First Nations peoples in the Americas. Eventually he left the Americas, shipwrecked spiritually and emotionally. It wasn't until May 24, 1738, when he heard Luther's work on Romans being read aloud in London, that he experienced the affectionate assurance so vitally necessary for living an abundant life of radical discipleship. Wesley wrote an account of his conversion experience at Aldersgate in his journal:

> In the evening I went very unwillingly to a society in Aldersgate Street, where one was reading Luther's preface to the *Epistle to the Romans*. About a quarter before nine, while he was describing the change that God works in the heart through faith in Christ, I felt my heart strangely warmed. I felt I did trust in Christ, Christ alone for salvation; and an assurance was given me that He had taken away *my* sins, even *mine*, and saved *me* from the law of sin and death.[31]

The assurance of salvation revolutionized Wesley's life and work. The good news of Jesus' love and assurance sped across the globe through Wesley and his Methodist movement as they called on people to repent of their sins and trust in Jesus alone for their salvation—which for them was exalted union—and cared for orphans and widows and slaves in their distress. Wesley and his movement faced many obstacles, including persecution and marginalization, but they persevered in view of God's sustaining and securing love. Wesley took to heart the assurance that flows from knowing that the eternal Word of God became flesh and that we become one flesh with him through faith. Such union, such exaltation, makes it possible for us to flesh out our faith in service to one another as God's love is poured out into our lives.

I have drawn attention here to noted Christian leaders from my tradition. It is not that they were perfect witnesses or experienced fully what they came to understand as true. Luther continued to struggle with anxieties, paradoxes, and tensions. I have written elsewhere of Luther scholar Heiko Oberman's study *Luther: Man Between God and the Devil*:

> The work portrays Luther as a complex thinker with an equally complex personality and personal history. As already suggested, Luther is a man torn by tension, caught in a whole series of infinite contradictions: pulled by two powers—God and the Devil, dangling from heaven over the depths of hell; a bridge between medieval and modern times; struggling in two spheres—piety and politics, divided between doctrines of law and gospel; and pained by warring passions of dread and delight. The study shows that Luther was not a hero of mythic proportions, but a very human and honest, frail and fearful man. He was so often insecure. Yet he was never shaken of the conviction that God had chosen him to battle it out with the Devil on center stage of the divine tragedy. Luther was born along by the conviction that the earthly powers of the prince of darkness grim (empire and ecclesia) pale in comparison to the prowess of God and His gracious presence in Luther's life.[32]

Luther himself struggled to hold true to his own best instincts, but he often fell short. Catholic and Orthodox Christians for the most part have failed to account for the doctrine of justification by faith in the One who secures our faith, and they have championed synergistic or cooperative models of salvation. Protestants also have often failed to focus on Jesus, trusting in their faith rather than in Jesus' faithfulness. My aim with Mormons (as with Catholics and Orthodox, the conflicted Luther, and myself) is to point all of us to Jesus as the center so that we might fix our gaze on him and experience the fullness of life with him, who is the fullness of deity in human embodiment or flesh (Colossians 2:9–10).[33] To my Mormon friends in particular I would say that the only way we can experience such fullness is if Jesus in eternal communion with his Father is, from all eternity past to eternity future, the one and only true God in the fullness of the Spirit, making it possible for us to participate in the fullness of the one and only true God. We can only be relationally secure in God if the Father and Son are from all eternity perfect and secure and in no way pursuing divine self-realization.

And what is the particular challenge to me? I have come to realize that it is not enough for me to draw attention to leaders in my tradition who have experienced what I refer to in this chapter as the burning in the bosom. Like them, I must seek to fix my gaze on Jesus. The faith must become personal in my own life. It must move from being my founders' faith to being my faith. Each of us must experience the burning in the bosom as expressed in the Bible. Like Paul in Philippians 3, who reflects upon his previous life as a Pharisee and the goal of his present life, which is to be centered in Jesus and experience the consummation of union between Jesus and the church, I have come to realize that I so often place my confidence in what I can do, in what I can attain and achieve. I am becoming more and more conscious of how daily I must cast aside everything that causes me to seek to base my worth and value on my acts of righteousness and pursue only the exalted Christ as my salvation and hope. I have come to realize with Paul that whatever was to my profit is loss compared to the surpassing greatness of knowing and experiencing Christ Jesus my Lord. I consider all those things rubbish and press on toward the goal, which is experiencing the fullness of exalted life in him (Philippians 3:1–14).

All too often I come crashing down from the ladder, seeking to ascend by self-righteous works rather than ascending by faith in Christ's love as he descends from heaven and works for me and in me. While some may find talk of assurance of salvation/exaltation mistaken and even arrogant, I believe it is even more audacious to claim that one could attain one's salvation or exalted state through one's works. I cannot believe the pride that I so often experience as I try to attain to the exalted state by my human efforts. Now, if assurance were based on me rather than on Jesus, then I could understand the charge of arrogance. But our assurance is based not on what we do but on Jesus' finished work on the cross that freed me for the exalted life of participating in him and his righteousness. He who came down the ladder is the only one who can bring us up the ladder.

Where Are We Going?

Evangelicals speak of the gospel in terms of personal faith in the death, burial, and resurrection of Jesus Christ, who is God from all eternity. Mormons agree, but they often seem to imply more (even while maintaining that Jesus is God, but not from all eternity). This is what concerns evangelicals. Mormons and former Mormons have shared with evangelicals that they lack assurance of salvation. Often it appears that they do not trust in Jesus Christ alone, but in other things as well—including involvement in the ward and baptisms for the dead.[34] Many Mormons may indeed claim to experience such assurance, but why do so many fail to experience it? I do not mean to corner them, or to discount the experience of those who claim such profound assurance. I simply ask this question, along with one other: Can one truly experience assurance of salvation if one does not realize that Jesus is God from all eternity, eternally secure as God?[35] From my vantage point in view of the Bible, there is no growth or development in Jesus whereby he becomes God. True fullness and assurance in him result from the overflow of divine love, which he himself experiences in the presence of his eternal Father in the intimacy they share eternally in the eternal Spirit of love.

Just as with Wesley on his short-term mission to the Americas that revealed to him his spiritual bankruptcy, I have come to realize that I do not and will not ever measure up, that I can never pull myself up by the boot-straps or climb up the ladder, that I cannot perform the faith as it is to be lived, that I so readily fail, and that managing my sin will not get me to my destination of salvation as exaltation. Thinking right thoughts won't get me there either. Evangelicals must guard against the temptation to place their confidence in the mastery of right doctrine or management of sin, which is legalistic behavior modification. From a biblical perspective—and here I speak to both evangelicals and Mormons—only God's love centered in Jesus' life as the eternal God, who became flesh, and his finished work on the cross and exalted state, where he sits at God's right hand, assures me, creating faith and relational security in the Spirit.

I have come to realize that I am not smart enough, good enough, or rigorous enough to attain God's favor. But I still keep forgetting. God has brought me to the end of myself on more than one occasion, and I am sure that he will do it again, leading me to repeat Wesley's words (upon his return boat trip home to England from his missionary work in America): "I went to America to convert the Indians, but, O! who shall convert me . . . ?"[36] And yet for all my consternation and wavering at sea, I do know the One in whom I have believed. "Yet I am not ashamed, because I know whom I have believed, and am convinced that he is able to guard what I have entrusted to him for that day" (2 Timothy 1:12). Like Paul the apostle and John Wesley, I have come to experience my own burning in the bosom—a heart strangely warmed. The Word of God has come down the ladder in the flesh and has lifted me up to his right hand, not by my works but by his faithfulness. Jesus became what we are so that through faith in him we can become what he is. God has made us one flesh with Jesus through faith as the Spirit of love is poured out into our hearts.

What kind of burning in the bosom do Mormons experience? Would they not long to experience the profound assurance of a heavenly Father who, as God from all eternity, loves them, secures them in his embrace, and exalts them in and through his one and only Son, who experiences the fullness of the divine life from all eternity with the Father in the Spirit? Such an experience makes it possible for them to pour their lives out freely in service to others rather than having to perform to please God to attain to the exalted state. Only as they experience the eternal Word who became flesh, who becomes one flesh with us through faith by the Spirit of love, will they be free to flesh out their faith in sacrificial service to others. I pray that these dear and profound people who care so deeply for God and others will come to experience the Father's embrace and, with Wesley, feel their hearts strangely warmed. May they come to "trust in Christ, Christ alone for salvation," Christ who from all eternity is God, and may they be able to testify with Wesley that "an assurance was given me that He had taken away *my* sins, even *mine*, and saved *me* from the law of sin and death."

CHAPTER 12

ALL IN (NIETZSCHEAN ATHEISM)

S o often I have lived as a closet Nietzschean. So often atheists who accept Friedrich Nietzsche's claim that God is dead have lived as closet Christians, whether they know it or not. There are numerous times when I live as if God is dead, and I have killed him. There are numerous times when these particular atheists live as if God is alive in their altruistic and noble care for others. While it is certainly not the case that all atheists are Nietzscheans, Nietzsche's influence has been broad and profound, manifesting itself ideologically and practically in diverse ways among both theists and atheists, ranging from the ethical egoism of Ayn Rand to the political policies of Nazi Germany. Nietzsche's penetrating words and analysis of our motives, particularly in relation to our motivations and self-interest, highlight a challenge that extends beyond armchair philosophy to our interactions, and most importantly our motivations behind such interactions. For this reason, Nietzsche will always be relevant to everyone, be they atheist or Christian.

In this chapter I will address nominal Christianity, nominal Nietzschean atheism, Pauline radicalism, and Nietzschean radicalism. While there may be other sets, I am centering my arguments on these four groupings, and so my arguments are limited to them.[1] I will challenge both nominal Christians and nominal Nietzschean atheists to get out of their respective closets and go "all in": nominal Christians to live in light of the crucified and risen God, and nominal and inconsistent Nietzscheans who claim that God is dead to live in light of this claim.

I encourage people to take seriously the relation of their worldviews to their lifestyles, thinking through where their convictions would logically or naturally lead them in terms of action. One thing I appreciate about the atheist Friedrich Nietzsche is that he sought to be consistent in this way. He carefully thought through the connection between his belief that God is dead and how people should live in view of this belief.

Now to be sure, I struggle with the notions of atheism and secularism, and not simply in terms of their adherents' denial of theism. For one, even if somebody denies theism, such denial does not mean that one is denying deity. For as Paul Tillich wrote, whatever concerns us ultimately is our god.[2] Based on this definition of deity, even sex, money, power, and fame function as gods. And while secularists may deny sacredness in principle, many secularists affirm the sacredness of human life and nature. From this vantage point, humanity and the world can also function as deities.

While I struggle with the notions and definitions of atheism and secularism, I also struggle with atheists who affirm Nietzsche's claim that God is dead and don't live in light of that claim. I should add that I also struggle with myself—when I as a Christian don't live in an intellectually honest way. The only way that a Christian can rightfully live out his Christianity is the way Paul did (Acts 20; 1 Corinthians 15; Philippians 1).

In Philippians 1:21, Paul is writing from a Roman jail cell and says, "For to me, to live is Christ and to die is gain." In Acts 20:24, 33–35, Paul is bidding good-bye for the last time in his life to the Ephesian church and says,

> I consider my life worth nothing to me, if only I may finish the race and complete the task the Lord Jesus has given me—the task of testifying to the gospel of God's grace. . . . I have not coveted anyone's silver or gold or clothing. You yourselves know that these hands of mine have supplied my own needs and the needs of my companions. In everything I did, I showed you that by this kind of hard work we must help

the weak, remembering the words the Lord Jesus himself said: "It is more blessed to give than to receive."

In 1 Corinthians 15:29–32, Paul continues:

> Now if there is no resurrection, what will those do who are baptized for the dead? If the dead are not raised at all, why are people baptized for them? And as for us, why do we endanger ourselves every hour? I die every day—I mean that, brothers—just as surely as I glory over you in Christ Jesus our Lord. If I fought wild beasts in Ephesus for merely human reasons, what have I gained? If the dead are not raised,
> "Let us eat and drink,
> "for tomorrow we die."

Everything Paul suffered, he did so based on the resurrection of Jesus Christ from the dead, the resurrection hope he had, and the gracious love he experienced as Jesus forgave him for having persecuted the church and made him his ambassador in chains for the gospel. As a result, the least of the apostles worked harder than all of the apostles, and set us an example to follow, living in light of the grace of God and the risen Lord: "For I am the least of the apostles and do not even deserve to be called an apostle, because I persecuted the church of God. But by the grace of God I am what I am, and his grace to me was not without effect. No, I worked harder than all of them—yet not I, but the grace of God that was with me" (1 Corinthians 15:9–10).

Some live as Christians for pragmatic reasons and not because of the resurrection; they would likely abandon the faith if they were to experience the suffering Paul mentions. Paul did not live out his Christian life to leverage Jesus for his own comforts and privileges. Often in discomfort and humiliation, Paul lived out his Christianity based solely on the resurrection of Jesus Christ from the dead. Paul could lay down his life because Jesus had destroyed the power of sin and death by rising from the dead, thereby securing Paul's future and ours. There was no hedging his bets.

All too often, unlike the apostle Paul, I hedge my bets and take calculated risks. I am not alone. Many other Christians do the same. We do not believe in Christianity because we believe it to be true, but because we need it to be true. We often use Christianity for its moral aims and ends, and for how it benefits us in other ways. But what happens when we find that the faith does not benefit but hurts us, and we no longer "need" it? When we hold on to the faith for pragmatic reasons, we are halfway toward abandoning it.

As a Christian, given my belief in the bodily resurrection of Jesus Christ from the dead, I should live as if Jesus' bodily resurrection matters. The bodily resurrection certainly mattered to the apostle Paul, and as a result he cut his ties to calculated risk and went for broke. If Jesus had not been raised and if the world will not be raised through him, Paul would conclude that his own life of costly sacrifice was a total waste (1 Corinthians 15:30–32). With confidence that Jesus rose from the dead and that he would one day be raised too, Paul lived a life of reckless abandon for Jesus and others.

I should live honestly by cutting my ties to self-preservation and self-advancement and throw myself on the mercies of God to care for me while I care for others. After all, I believe that no matter what happens to me, he will raise me and secure me for eternity. My belief is grounded in a transcendent hope that intersects and transforms history.

This is one of the chief lines of demarcation between my beliefs and those of many atheists. My beliefs extend beyond this world order. While an atheist may hope in posterity or in the ideal of humanity, those ideals would perish in a nuclear holocaust that would wipe out humanity. I can hope in humanity even if it were to perish (and me with it) based on the conviction that Jesus will raise the dead. So I believe my hope in humanity is on much surer ground, and the basis for going all in for the sake of others is more credible. And yet I know atheists whose regard for human well-being surpasses my own. Without consideration of the logical basis for their practices, their authentic concern for their fellow humans humbles me. You may ask how they can humble me when they are not being consistent. They humble me by revealing to me my own inconsistency as they live out what I am called to do as a Christian—caring sacrificially for others by helping them up when they fall.

I am not sure I could say the same for their counterpart, Friedrich Nietzsche. For I am not at all convinced that Nietzsche's call for the individual to rise up to new heights as the superhuman (*Übermensch*) was really an affirmation of his fellow man. And still, at the very least, Nietzsche sought to live out his atheistic convictions. This atheist was no closet Christian.

Through his "Madman," Nietzsche proclaimed that God—ultimately the crucified God—is dead and that we have killed him.[3] Nietzsche was troubled that after proclaiming to the masses that God is dead, and although people knew that the church was an imposter, they still lived as if nothing changed with this knowledge; business went on as usual.[4] For Nietzsche and his prophet Zarathustra, given that God is dead and we have killed him, we must see that we are the creators of our own destinies, including morals. There is no objective truth or goodness. There are only truths and moralities we create as expressions of our will to power, as matters of personal preference and taste.[5] Now, if this is so, if destiny and morality are our own creations based on our own tastes and preferences and will to power, what is to safeguard meaning and purpose and life itself? For as Dostoevsky said, "If there's no everlasting God, there's no such thing as virtue, and there's no need of it."[6]

Nietzsche's atheism was not coupled with naive, utopian optimism. He understood that nihilism and the denial of life were right around the corner, for if there is no God to ensure morals and life, we must ensure them by our own courageous activity and creativity. Nietzsche set forth the doctrine of eternal recurrence as an idea worthy of consideration in the attempt to affirm life in the face of nihilism. Eternal recurrence is an oppressive as well as liberating doctrine, for this teaching places ultimate responsibility on our shoulders. One version of eternal recurrence is that we will live this life over and over again for all eternity—an ancient and philosophically robust version of Bill Murray's movie *Groundhog Day*.[7] If we were to live in view of this idea, we would be sobered by its import: what we do at any given moment has eternally recurring implications. While fatalistic, it also suggests that all of what we do always matters and is full of meaning. Nietzsche presented the idea of eternal recurrence as a possible safeguard against nihilism and as an alternative to such Christian ideas as the existence of God, the immortality of the soul, and the judgment to come.

Nietzsche's philosophical program is not for the faint of heart. In comparing and contrasting Nietzsche and William James, one of the fathers of American pragmatism, Edward Craig writes,

James's writing exudes a certain easy confidence that Nietzsche altogether lacked and could never have approved. His optimism, where it is found, is hard-won and precarious. He feels very keenly something of which James shows little awareness and most certainly does not emphasise, that the realisation that a belief is held for pragmatic purposes is halfway to its abandonment. Where pragmatism enters, "Nihilism stands at the door," [taken from *Will to Power*, paragraph 1] and to accept nihilism and to overcome it calls for a degree of inner strength far beyond the normal. Hence the force of its competitors, as Nietzsche well knew.[8]

Like Nietzsche's philosophy, the apostle Paul's doctrine of the crucified and risen God was not for the faint of heart. Neither Nietzsche nor Paul was pragmatic. Pragmatism is not a good alternative to their radically consistent philosophies of life. It is not as personally demanding or as consistent as their views. I may well become nihilistic in my worldview if someday I were to conclude that Jesus did not rise from the dead, that the dead will not be raised, and that God does not exist. I might well follow the apostle Paul into nihilism apart from optimism if he and I were to conclude that these things are not true. For Paul at least, if Jesus has not been raised from the dead, we are the most pitiful of all people; if Jesus is not raised bodily from the dead, those of us claiming to follow Christ should eat, drink, and be merry for tomorrow we will die (1 Corinthians 15:12–34).

We Christians should not try to have our cake and eat it too. However, I find that we often do just this: we believe to the extent that we hedge our bets. We sit on the fence, believing in Christ not because we believe him to be the truth but because it helps us live moral and profitable lives according to Christian standards, including assisting us in raising our kids in a supposedly wholesome way. On my best nonpragmatic days I don't believe in Jesus because I need him to be true. On my best days I believe in him because I believe him to be the truth. However, I am of the conviction that many in the church believe in Jesus because he profits them emotionally, spiritually, and even materially. In other words, we often believe in him for pragmatic and naively optimistic reasons—something Paul would never do, just as Nietzsche would never hold to a belief for pragmatic reasons.

Now, although Nietzsche could not be accused of espousing naive optimism, how does he not disregard certain forms of human life in view of his nontheistic affirmation of the will to power? While Nietzsche could affirm life through consideration of the idea of eternal recurrence, one must still ask, "Whose or which life?" To affirm life in all its particulars throughout history certainly does not lead us to differentiate good and bad. Are we endorsing all forms of the will to power of life? On this view do not good and evil blur into each other? Could not Nietzsche's atheistic model lead to the affirmation of certain forms of life at the expense of others, to the advance of the strong at the expense of the weak? For if our identity and meaningfulness are bound up with our own acts of creativity—and those alone—must we not impose our will on our surroundings and other people? If the world and everything in it is simply the playing field for our own creative exploits, does not the end of exercising the will to power justify the means?

At least Nietzsche was creative. In place of his creativity, many of us have moved toward consumerism and moral mediocrity. It is not always the most creative who are most valuable and who win today; sometimes it is those who consume the most and who get by at the least cost to themselves. We have replaced rigor and moral excellence and creativity with compulsive consumption and moral mediocrity. In one sense many of us in the church have no trouble believing in Jesus for a life of prosperity in the here and now, eating and drinking as much as we can and trying to put off as long as possible the day when we will die and stand before God. Nietzsche knew what he rejected, whereas we Christians often reject with our lives what we believe but do not understand.

Nietzsche rejected the apostle Paul's doctrine of the crucified God (1 Corinthians 1), considering Paul's religion the most harmful teaching ever taught. He believed it kept humanity from rising to new heights because it esteemed the weak, the despised, and the herd. Here is what Nietzsche says in his book *The Antichrist*:

> The Christian movement, as a European movement, has been from the start a collective movement of the dross and refuse elements of every kind (these want to get power through Christianity). It does *not* express the decline of a race, it is an aggregate of forms of decadence of locking together and seeking each other out from everywhere. It is

not, as is supposed, the corruption of antiquity itself, of *noble* antiquity, that made Christianity possible. The scholarly idiocy which upholds such ideas even today cannot be contradicted harshly enough. At the very time when the sick, corrupt chandala strata in the whole *imperium* adopted Christianity, the *opposite type*, nobility, was present in its most beautiful and most mature form. The great number became master; the democratism of the Christian instinct *triumphed*. Christianity was not "national," not a function of a race—it turned to every kind of man who was disinherited by life, it had its allies everywhere. At the bottom of Christianity is the rancor of the sick, instinct directed *against* the healthy, *against* health itself. Everything that has turned out well, everything that is proud and prankish, beauty above all, hurts its ears and eyes. Once more I recall the inestimable words of Paul: "The *weak* things of the world, the *foolish* things of the world, the *base* and *despised* things of the world hath God chosen." This was the formula: *in hoc signo* decadence triumphed.

God on the cross—are the horrible secret thoughts behind this symbol not understood yet? All that suffers, all that is nailed to the cross, is *divine*. All of us are nailed to the cross, consequently *we* are divine. We alone are divine. Christianity was a victory, a nobler outlook perished of it—Christianity has been the greatest misfortune of mankind so far.[9]

Karl Barth contends that Nietzsche understood Christianity better than most if not all its defenders and the rest of its critics in the nineteenth century. Nietzsche understood what Christianity is about at its core—Christ as the Neighbor, who cares for the downtrodden, the weak, the despised.[10] In place of the crucified God, whom, according to Nietzsche, Paul "created" and proclaimed, Nietzsche put forth Dionysius and his prophet Zarathustra—which are really one and the same.[11] In fact, they are realized in Nietzsche himself. They stand opposed to Paul's crucified God.

It should be made clear that in Nietzsche's later works, Dionysius is not the god of pagan revelry and debauchery of ancient Greek culture but the iconic figure who embraces life in all its terror and tragedy. Dionysius and Zarathustra are those who embrace the tragedy bound up with soaring to the mountain heights of azure isolation, despising the herd mentality, the democratic spirit, and care for the weak, which, as Nietzsche sees it, is bound up with a world-negating escapist outlook.

Walter Kaufmann argues that in *Ecce Homo*, Dionysius epitomizes for Nietzsche the heroic figure who embraces a tragic existence:

> Looking for a pre-Christian, Greek symbol that he might oppose to "the Crucified," Nietzsche found Dionysius. His "Dionysius" is neither the god of the ancient Dionysian festivals nor the god Nietzsche had played off against Apollo in *The Birth of Tragedy*, although he does, of course, bear some of the features of both. In the later works of Nietzsche, "Dionysius" is no longer the spirit of unrestrained passion, but the symbol of the affirmation of life with all its suffering and terror. "The problem," Nietzsche explained in a note that was later included in the posthumous *Will to Power* (section 1052), "is that of the meaning of suffering: whether a Christian meaning or a tragic meaning. . . . The tragic man affirms even the harshest suffering." And *Ecce Homo* is, not least of all, Nietzsche's final affirmation of his own cruel life.[12]

In the end Nietzsche and Paul present opposing views of suffering, meaning, and life. While Nietzsche affirms tragedy and suffering, he rejects the view that we ascend by suffering and dying. For him we suffer and die as we ascend. Greatness involves the willingness to go it alone and experience loneliness and the tormenting pain of the pursuit of excellence, forsaking the comforts of the herd. For many of us in consumer Christianity, we ascend by affirming our base passions and by avoiding suffering and tragedy. Against this backdrop those atheists who affirm Nietzsche in principle yet fail to follow through on his logic and, instead, sacrifice themselves by raising up the weak and foolish come much closer than the nominal church and I do to reflecting Paul's Jesus. Having said that, they are inconsistent; they are not cutting off all ties to a Christian worldview.

These Nietzschean-affirming atheists need to go all in and cut off all ties to Christian philanthropic forms and follow Nietzsche's Dionysius. So, too, the nominal church and I need to count the cost and move beyond hedging our bets and die to Dionysius and follow Paul's Jesus. I don't want to settle for a version of Pascal's wager, betting that it is best to side with Paul rather than with Nietzsche, given that we gain or lose much if Paul is correct (eternal rewards or punishments) and gain or lose nothing if Nietzsche is. I need to wager that the best life is lived based not on quantitative rewards or punishments but on the reward of loving my neighbor and living authentically before God because God has laid down his life so that I can truly live.

We Christians can die to our unbridled passions and our compartmentalization of the faith (bound up with comfort and privilege) because Jesus died to affirm life—our lives. We Christians can be truly for God and for our neighbors—secularist, atheist, and theist alike—becoming truly world-affirming rather than world-negating, laying down our lives for others, especially the downtrodden, because of Jesus' loving sacrifice for true life. Jesus' life of sacrificial love makes it possible for me to go all in and live out authentic faith, laying down my life for the weak and despised.

I am grateful to God for Jesus. I am also thankful to God for Nietzsche. Sometimes the worst enemies of the Christian faith are our best friends. His own brutal honesty, consistency, courage, and logic help me come to terms with my faith and move me to struggle to go all in and be broken for my neighbor in need, as his "adversary" the apostle Paul did.

CHRISTIAN CONSISTENCY

While I am thankful for Nietzsche's consistent and courageous logic, I am even more thankful for a modern-day Paul—Paul Isihara. I want to share the story of his care for my family and me when we were in great need, for we are concerned not simply for logic but for life itself. Paul did not hedge his bets with my family and me, but he lived in view of the apostle Paul's crucified God, sacrificially caring for us—the lowly and despised. Though a math professor by trade, and the son of a famous physicist, he didn't use calculations at all. Or, to be more accurate, he used Christ's kingdom calculations. My family and I were Nietzschean dross and refuse at the time. Having been overseas, we suddenly had to return to the States without work or a place to live. Paul let us use his suburban home and his car, and he even paid for our utilities until we were back on our feet. At the time Paul lived in an apartment in the inner city of Chicago, working in a community development project among the poor and commuting to the suburbs to teach at his college. As he gave to us, he also gave to others. He made this his life's ambition—he still does.

Paul never expected for us or the others he would take into his home from time to time to pay him back. No doubt such care hurt him professionally, for it is very difficult to advance one's career when helping others not fall through the cracks. Coupled with others, we did more than tax and inconvenience his life, career, and bank account; we turned his ascent into a descent. But that was what he was about; following his Lord, Paul carried his cross. I am not sure I would ever do the same, for I value comforts, convenience, and privileged status; but with the inspiration of Paul's life, I might. Paul shows me up, but even more important, he shows me how to live a more noble way.

Certainly I could mention other Christians who lived by heavenly calculations that involved great risk to themselves by caring for the distressed—Christians such as St. Francis of Assisi, who abandoned his father's wealth for his heavenly Father's kingdom to father those orphaned by society, or William Wilberforce, who sacrificed his body and his career to free slaves and transform morals in the British empire, or Mother Teresa, who laid down her life daily to touch the untouchables in India's ghettos. But I would rather talk of Paul Isihara—my own St. Francis right here in the States—because at the time of our return to this country, my family and I were the ones in need. We were the ones in danger of falling through society's cracks and in need of a helping hand, not able to pick ourselves up by our own bootstraps. If it had been up to Nietzsche, God might not have been the only one who died; we might have too. Nietzsche's doctrine is for the strong and superhuman, and there are times when I have been all too weak and all too human. Now the philosophically alive question before me is: Will I do for others what Paul Isihara did for me, going all in?

NIETZSCHEAN ATHEIST CONSISTENCY

While I don't believe Hitler's appropriation of Nietzsche's superhuman concept would have pleased Nietzsche in the slightest, I do believe there is nothing in Nietzsche's thought to guard against Hitler's emergence in one form or another.[13] There is certainly nothing in Nietzsche's thought that would give rise to a Mother Teresa or Paul Isihara. They can give sacrificially to their downtrodden neighbors because Christ has risked everything to secure for them life eternal. But if God is dead, and we were the ones who killed him because we no longer need him, how can we not take matters into our own hands to guard against meaninglessness? We must continue imposing our will on our surroundings, continue creating, and continue taking because nothing is given to us.

There is no place for Nietzsche-affirming atheists to live like closet Christians. If Nietzsche's brutal calculus is right, the well-meaning atheist philanthropist cannot exhort us based on a universal, ethical argument or pragmatics that we should care for our downtrodden neighbors by helping them up. Rather the Nietzschean formula dictates that we should leave them to fend for themselves if we truly care that humanity ascends to new heights. On Nietzschean grounds we can never rest but must continue to ascend by continuing to create meaning by imposing our wills; otherwise, we will cease to be, for it is only our own creative action that safeguards meaningful existence. There is no rest on this model and no naive utopian optimism, just precarious life and dangerous logic.[14]

So will I go all in and do for others what the crucified God and his servant/my friend Paul have done for me? Or will I live by nominal Christianity or by Nietzschean consistency? Hopefully I will choose the former and reject the latter two options. Hopefully the atheist who has affirmed Nietzsche's "God is dead" doctrine and his rejection of the crucified God will go all in with his beliefs or, better yet, come to embrace Paul's crucified God. To me, to scorn nominal Christianity and die to myself in view of the crucified and risen God is a risk well worth taking. Will fellow Christians and Nietzschean atheists go all in and do the same?

CHAPTER 13

AVATAR (NEO-PAGANISM)

Box office hits like *Dances with Wolves* and *Avatar* may speak in part to many of our contemporaries' disillusionments with deistic, secularist, and materialistic worldviews. There must be more to life than what our distant deity figures, technological progress, and Manifest Destiny ambitions can provide. There must be more to primitive and pagan peoples and their cultures than we supposedly advanced peoples once imagined. In the movie *Avatar* primitive paganism and civilized materialism clash, and the former is deemed more profound, progressive, and civilized than the latter.[1] In their own way the adherents of neo-paganism are making similar points as they emphasize the sacredness of Nature and the oneness of all life.

Before proceeding to engage neo-paganism, it will be worth developing a few points related to the movie *Avatar*. In Hinduism, "avatar," or *avatāra*, refers to a deity's descent from heaven. It is often translated as "incarnation," but is best translated as "appearance" or "manifestation."[2] It may be the case that director James Cameron has both uses in mind in the movie *Avatar*. Cameron's "avatar" is a three-dimensional representation of a computer user in another world. The movie is a fascinating (though troubling), fictional (yet realistic) tale of life when worlds collide. Actual collides with virtual. Modern collides with primitive. People collide with people.

In the story a paraplegic former marine participates in a mission on the planet named Pandora. The native humanoids on the planet, known as the Na'vi, do not appreciate the alien expedition. The marine is given the task of gathering intelligence for the military about the Na'vi by using a Na'vi avatar identity in exchange for the promise of spinal surgery. The mission turns ugly when it is discovered that the fundamental reason for the expedition is to drive off the Na'vi and mine their sacred habitat for a precious mineral that is coveted back on Earth. Love, science,[3] and religion combine to combat Earth's corporate and military regimes. Accompanied by a humanitarian scientist and a few others, the marine, who falls in love with a female Na'vi, fights against the corporate and military powers to save the land and its native people, at great risk to himself.

The invading people view the habitat of the Na'vi as an "it," as an artifact, as an object rather than a life. For the Na'vi, indigenous peoples generally, and neo-pagans, it is one thing to use Nature; it is quite another to abuse Nature. Wiccan Gus diZerega illustrates this point by comparing how indigenous peoples in the Pacific Northwest harvested salmon for thousands of years and how Westerners have done so over the last hundred years. Within a hundred years of the first Western harvests, the species is extinct or near extinction in many places. He argues that it has nothing to do with technology but with greed. He claims that the Native Americans "most definitely possessed the technology. What they did not possess was the greed unmodified by any ethical restraint. . . . What the modern world did to salmon it is now doing to the oceans."[4] Indigenous peoples and neo-pagans view the abundance of the natural world as a gift to be appreciated and to be given as long as Nature is treated well, rather than as an object to exploit.[5]

For diZerega *Nature* when capitalized signifies that it is treated as subject. When not capitalized, *nature* signifies its objectification by humans.[6] Nature for Wiccans is sacred,[7] as it was for the Na'vi and other indigenous cultures. According to diZerega, Wiccans do not worship Nature: "We respect, honour, serve and love the Sacred as it manifests *in and through*

Nature. Nature is sacred, but the Sacred transcends what we usually think of as 'nature.'"[8]

DiZerega speaks of being a panentheist, not a pantheist. The Sacred is immanent in the physical world, yet transcendent;[9] thus, while there is identification of the Sacred and the world, the Sacred transcends the physical world and is not exhausted by it (hence, *panentheism*—all is in God and God is in all, but God is not the world; not *pantheism*—everything is God and God is everything). DiZerega is a monist, not a monotheist.[10] Deities have individuality, he writes; the One does not.[11] To say that God has a personality is "limiting." "For many of us, squeezing the Source of All into the image of a human being is the opposite of humility."[12]

Like the Na'vi, neo-pagan peoples embody a holistic way of life centered in practice and experience, and they do not privilege a worldview or belief system above practice and experience. In the context of speaking about ritual, diZerega states, "Practice counts far more than dogma."[13] Later he writes, "My 'faith' is based on encounters with the Sacred, not promises in a text. It is more akin to faith in a trusted friend than faith in faith. It is rational because it is based on my own experience."[14] As far as the Na'vi are concerned, they are one with their habitat, and they view the trees that are rooted where the mineral is found as spiritual entities through which they find life and meaning and through which they communicate with their ancestors. They pray to this life source, and they find answers to their prayers through Nature.

COMMON GROUND FOR CHRISTIANITY AND NEO-PAGANISM

Many Christians react strongly to what diZerega refers to as neo-paganism. However, three elements of neo-paganism resonate with a biblical worldview and Christian spirituality.

Taking Care of Nature

Neo-pagans are right to speak against objectifying Nature as nature. It is one thing to use the natural world; it is quite another to abuse it. As biblically grounded Christians, we should affirm that God has given the creation to us as a gift to use, and we are to be grateful to the Lord for the precious gift of the natural world. We are not rulers over the creation but stewards of it, and so we must be careful not to use creation in an objectifying, utilitarian way, where it exists only for us to do with as we please. Creation is God's handiwork, and along with us it is also his masterpiece. God is Lord over creation, and we are his stewards (Genesis 2). We must be attentive to stewarding God's handiwork as God's precious gift to use and shepherd and cultivate to the praise of his glory and for all of creation's well-being.

Christianity in the modern period has often failed to view the creation as a dynamic reality made up of living organisms that exists in vital relation to humanity, which is the pinnacle of God's creative works. Christians have been tempted, rather, to view the creation in a utilitarian and even mechanistic manner: it exists to be used in whatever way we please, as parts detached from us and exploitable for our industrial ends.[15] While this utilitarian view of creation is changing in many quarters, we must be diligent and take serious note of the fact that God has not made us lords over the creation, only lords in the creation: our stewardship of the creation under his lordship signifies that we cannot do with the creation what we please.[16] We must guard against objectifying nature. DiZerega goes so far as to claim that we must come to see Nature or creation as "thou," not as "it."[17]

Sensing God's Glory in Creation

Surely neo-pagans are correct to claim that there is a close connection between creation and the divine. How often have you been in the great outdoors and sensed the presence of your Creator in a unique and intense manner? A person who does not encounter the vast grandeur of the great outdoors is missing a special dimension of God's glory manifested on earth. One does not need to be a pantheist or panentheist to experience the Sacred in creation (what diZerega would refer to as Nature). While I do not identify creation with God or as part of God, I do identify God as present in a special way as I encounter untamed forests, deserts, and mountain ranges. Here I call to mind that classic hymn I grew up singing in my evangelical church, "This Is My Father's World."

This is my Father's world,
and to my listening ears
all nature sings, and round me rings
the music of the spheres.

This is my Father's world:
I rest me in the thought
of rocks and trees, of skies and seas;
his hand the wonders wrought.

This is my Father's world,
the birds their carols raise,
the morning light, the lily white,
declare their maker's praise.

This is my Father's world:
he shines in all that's fair;
in the rustling grass I hear him pass;
he speaks to me everywhere.

This is my Father's world.
O let me ne'er forget
that though the wrong seems oft so strong,
God is the ruler yet.

This is my Father's world:
why should my heart be sad?
The Lord is King; let the heavens ring!
God reigns; let the earth be glad![18]

That song speaks and sings to me. It leads me to worship the Creator in creation (not to worship creation), and to long to go off and be still in God's presence as God speaks to me in the wind whispering through the leaves, as the music birds sing, and as the brook ripples, teeming with life. One does not need to be Catholic to resonate with St. Francis of Assisi when he proclaims in "The Canticle of the Sun":

> Most high, all powerful, all good Lord! All praise is yours, all glory,
> all honor, and all blessing. To you, alone, Most High, do they
> belong. No mortal lips are worthy to pronounce your name.
>
> Be praised, my Lord, through all your creatures, especially through
> my lord Brother Sun, who brings the day; and you give light
> through him. And he is beautiful and radiant in all his splendor!
> Of you, Most High, he bears the likeness.
>
> Be praised, my Lord, through Sister Moon and the stars; in the
> heavens you have made them, precious and beautiful.
>
> Be praised, my Lord, through Brothers Wind and Air, and clouds
> and storms, and all the weather, through which you give your
> creatures sustenance.
>
> Be praised, My Lord, through Sister Water; she is very useful, and
> humble, and precious, and pure.
>
> Be praised, my Lord, through Brother Fire, through whom you
> brighten the night. He is beautiful and cheerful, and powerful
> and strong.
>
> Be praised, my Lord, through our sister Mother Earth, who feeds
> us and rules us, and produces various fruits with colored flowers
> and herbs.[19]

Many in my tradition would feel uncomfortable speaking of Mother Earth. While I do not believe that the earth or other heavenly spheres have personalities, I would argue that they are not static objects but dynamic forces to which we as persons are inextricably bound and that declare God's glory by being what they were created to be (Psalm 19).

Pantheism and panentheism are certainly unorthodox from a historic Christian perspective; however, their total opposite is not historic Christianity but deism. Historic Christianity does not espouse a deistic model of reality according to which God created the world and then departed, putting in place a mechanistic and moral structure that is self-sustaining. While humanity is certainly the pinnacle of creation from a historic Judeo-Christian perspective, we are bound up intimately with the rest of creation as part of it: from dust we come, and to dust we will return (Genesis 2:7; 3:19).

While I would rigorously contend that the fundamental distinction between God and the world and between persons and the world must always be maintained, nonetheless the distinction is never one of separation. God has freely chosen to enter into relation with us in such a manner that he freely exists only in sovereign and loving relation to the world and us. We are only who we are in relation to God, one another, and the world. We are never autonomous, separate, or independent, no matter how often we crave such autonomy in our sinful condition.

The apostle Paul was no pantheist or panentheist, but neither was he a deist or one who claimed that God is radically opposed to us in his identity. Paul certainly concurred with the Athenian philosophers and poets on Mars Hill that in God we live and move and have our being, and that we are his offspring:

> "The God who made the world and everything in it is the Lord of heaven and earth and does not live in temples built by hands. And he is not served by human hands, as if he needed anything, because he himself gives all men life and breath and everything else. From one man he made every nation of men, that they should inhabit the whole earth; and he determined the times set for them and the exact places where they should live. God did this so that men would seek him and perhaps reach out for him and find him, though he is not far from each one of us. 'For in him we live and move and have our being.' As some of your own poets have said, 'We are his offspring.'" (Acts 17:24–28)

As we are part of the creation, God situates our identity in concrete spaces and times. God gives land to people to inhabit and cultivate, beginning with a garden and ending with a garden in a city. We are uniquely and intimately related to the land, just as God is distinct and intimately related to the world. In the same way that we are distinct from the land though not separate from it, so it is with God, in whose image we exist. According to a Judeo-Christian perspective, God did not create the world out of his being, but by his Word. God brought all things into being out of nothing by way of self-declaration (Genesis 1; John 1:1–3), and now mediates the creation to himself through what Irenaeus of Lyons figuratively calls "God's two hands": the Son and the

Spirit. The grandson in the faith of the apostle John, Irenaeus writes against the Gnostics and their views of angelic mediation and emanation from the divine:

> Angels did not make or form us, for angels could not have made an image of God, nor any other but the true God, nor any power far distant from the Father of all things. God needed none of these to make whatever he had foreordained to make, as if he did not have hands of his own. For always with him are his Word and Wisdom, the Son and the Spirit, through whom and in whom he made everything freely and independently, to whom he also speaks when he says, "Let us make man after our image and likeness" (1:26), taking the substance of the creatures from himself as well as the pattern of the things he adorned.[20]

As the Word of creation and also redemption, Jesus the incarnate Word recapitulates or transforms all of creation, offering it up to God in the Spirit as the high priest of creation.[21] God is not confused with the world, but God enters the world that he created (but that has given way to decay as a result of human sinfulness) and transforms it from the inside out through his Son and Spirit.[22] While not espousing pantheism or panentheism, trinitarian theism over against deism and other forms of monotheism maintains that God is uniquely and intimately related to the world that he created out of nothing by his Word and Spirit. Thus on this account there is a close connection between creation and the divine, according to a trinitarian perspective.

Seeing the Importance of Experience

I resonate in part with diZerega's concern to emphasize practice and experience. As I have stated numerous times, worldview has its place but also its limitations. People are more than their worldviews. They are persons who need to be encountered experientially, whereby we view them as "Thou" rather than as "It." In fact, it is fair to say that a fully Christian worldview would include consideration of experience extending beyond worldview. While I would not separate spiritual experience from textual analysis of Scripture (as diZerega seems to suggest he would do), I would argue that our analysis of the authoritative text must serve as a means to the end of knowing God experientially and not be an end in itself; authority for the orthodox Christian certainly includes Scripture but is not exhausted by it. For the orthodox Christian, Jesus—as the living Word whom we worship—is the supreme authority to whom Scripture, as the ultimate authoritative written Word, points and to whom Jesus' followers bear witness with obedient lives.

We will never understand a people or be used by God in the transformation of a people until we take the time to step inside their shoes, their cultures, and their hearts; get to know them; and are changed by Jesus through our encounters with them. One Native American said to a Christian missionary that his people would believe in the missionary's Jesus when the missionary came to live with them and die with them. Not only is the Native American changed through such an encounter, but also the missionary who comes to live and die with him (which is what Jesus himself would do). God uses those of other faith traditions to impact us even as we impact them. They reveal to us who we are in our distinctive faith tradition through our sheer difference. They remind us of what we are and should be, but have often forgotten or forsaken, and put us to shame at times by knowingly or unknowingly bearing witness to the God revealed in the Bible and his ways when we have failed to do so.

My musing on neo-pagan spirituality has led me to reassess my own worldview and life at points in view of Christian Scripture and to realize how truly personal God is and how intimately he is involved in the sphere of creation. I am grateful for this opportunity and can no longer objectify neo-pagans as bizarre but rather see them as significant conversation partners given their holistic vantage point that differs from my worldview in significant ways but which also challenges me to be more biblical and in line with Scripture's relational spirituality, pushing me to become more Christ-honoring and holistic in keeping with orthodox theology and spirituality.

BOUNDARIES BETWEEN CHRISTIANITY AND NEO-PAGANISM

Now, in view of my sustained concern to promote a biblical and holistic framework, I turn to areas of disagreement between neo-paganism and orthodox theology and spirituality.

Relating to God

Let us consider the moral problem. *Avatar* and the neo-pagan diZerega set forth a panentheistic view of the God-world relation: we are spiritually connected to everything, and everything is part of the divine. A pantheistic, panentheistic, or monistic view of reality proves problematic for consideration of sin and evil; for if we are one with the divine, how can we be sinners (that is, unless the divine incorporates sinfulness into its reality and God is in need of salvation)? It also proves problematic for consideration of the need for a Savior; for if we are ultimately one with God, why do we need a Savior to remove the separation? On this view, Jesus simply becomes a significant illustration of an already existing state of affairs involving union with the divine.[23]

From a panentheistic or monistic perspective, separation is not ultimately moral or ontological; it is fundamentally mental. According to this model, our sinful state of moral separation from God is one of illusion: we fail to see things as they truly are, and we must cease living the lie and get in touch with our true selves, which is not beyond us but rather within us (which some refer to as the spark of divinity). I should also add that it is ultimately impossible to differentiate good from evil in a panentheistic or monistic framework: good and evil proceed from one ultimate reality, which is beyond good and evil. In contrast to this monistic perspective, given the injustices committed against Native peoples and against Nature or creation, it is important that we recognize the ultimately moral problem and come to realize that we stand before a holy, loving, personal God to whom we must give account for objectifying his creation.

DiZerega argues that "there is no general fall. Instead there is growth and development. . . . Malice is always rooted in error," and "We tend to be self-centered beings." Now, if there is no general fall, how can one guard against evil finding its origin in God? And while I believe we are self-centered as a result of the fall (and not simply that we tend to be self-centered), our acts of sin are based not on error of judgment but on self-love that leads us toward malice. Ultimately the problem is moral and not mental, arising from our hearts as we turn away from God out of self-love. DiZerega claims that "anger, resentment and the like are emotions. We generate them, based on our beliefs."[24] In contrast, I claim that they are affections that distort our beliefs. Again the problem is ultimately moral—resulting from self-love, leading to malice rather than giving rise to malice based on erroneous mental states. The problem is not ultimately one of a faulty worldview but one of distorted relationality bound up with negative affections rooted in self-love.

If God is not ultimately supremely personal, other, and distinct from us, what objective basis do we have for challenging such apparent injustices?[25]

Relating to Each Other

Having just alluded to the personal nature of God, it is important that we now turn to consider the personal problem. In a monistic framework we don't really see one another; in the end, one only sees and has a conversation with oneself, for there is no paramount distinction between ultimate reality and oneself. To put it another way, from a monistic standpoint that entails the ultimate denial of difference, one can never truly say, "I see you," which is a line in the movie *Avatar*, indicating mutual indwelling and participational knowledge involving two distinct individuals who come to the same perspective.

From a deistic perspective there is no true seeing of the other, for God is removed from everyone and everything, distant and aloof. But from the vantage point of trinitarian theism, which involves the claim that God's very being involves I and Thou as Father and Son exist eternally in holy, loving communion in the Spirit, we find that there is otherness in unity, guarding against the objectification of the other but preserving otherness in relation (so that there is no dissolution of the respective persons' distinctive identities in favor of sameness). From the vantage point of trinitarian theism, we who are created in the triune God's image are ultimately personal beings in relation to all of life, a view that is at the very least suggested in Genesis 1–2 and is explicitly developed as Scripture progresses from the Old to the New Testament. Here is what Kallistos Ware says of trinitarian relationality and its bearing on humans as those created in God's image and what it entails for us truly seeing one another:

Man is made, not only in the image of God, but more specifically in the image of *God the Trinity*. . . . Since the image of God in man is

165

a Trinitiarian image, it follows that man, like God, realizes his true nature through mutual life. The image signifies relationship not only with God but with other men. Just as the three divine persons live in and for each other, so man—being made in the trinitarian image—becomes a real person by seeing the world through others' eyes, by making others' joys and sorrows his own. Each human being is unique, yet each in uniqueness is created for communion with others.[26]

This relational and interpersonal orientation is derived from consideration of the relational and interpersonal being of God. According to Scripture and trinitarian theology, we find that the Father indwells the Son, and the Son indwells the Father through the Spirit while remaining distinct. This interpenetrating way of being in the divine life (called *perichoresis*) is unique to the divine life, and so we do not indwell God, and God does not indwell us in the same manner as the Father and Son in the Spirit indwell one another. We are in Christ Jesus, who is the fullness of God incarnate, as Paul says in Colossians 2:9–10: "For in Christ all the fullness of the Deity lives in bodily form, and you have been given fullness in Christ, who is the head over every power and authority."

Note as well the language of interpenetration in John 17:20–26, where Jesus prays for all his followers and not simply his original apostolic community:

"My prayer is not for them alone. I pray also for those who will believe in me through their message, that all of them may be one, Father, just as you are in me and I am in you. May they also be in us so that the world may believe that you have sent me. I have given them the glory that you gave me, that they may be one as we are one: I in them and you in me. May they be brought to complete unity to let the world know that you sent me and have loved them even as you have loved me.

"Father, I want those you have given me to be with me where I am, and to see my glory, the glory you have given me because you loved me before the creation of the world.

"Righteous Father, though the world does not know you, I know you, and they know that you have sent me. I have made you known to them, and will continue to make you known in order that the love you have for me may be in them and that I myself may be in them."

The Father and Jesus indwell us (through the Spirit) in love through faith in Jesus' word. It is heart-to-heart and life-on-life engagement, where we dwell in God and God dwells in us. He really sees us, and we see him. He knows us from the inside. Thus the I and Thou are safeguarded, for this encounter is based upon the relational, interpersonal being of God.

God is supremely personal, not other than personal. As supremely personal and interpersonal, the triune God is the I and the Thou, making it possible for God not to engage humanity, which is created in his image, as It, and for us not to engage others as things. For the universe to be a Thou, as neo-pagan and First Nations people believe, there must be an I in creation, and an I-and-Thou interpersonal reality beyond creation who grounds all of reality relationally. God is not impersonal, a point with which diZerega would agree, but God does have a personality and does not contain all personalities as the One beyond personality, contrary to diZerega.[27]

The Thou requires an I for us not to objectify otherness. The ultimate reason why we are not to objectify is because the Trinity is I in relation to Thou, as I and Thou mutually exist and co-inhere in the divine life and call for mutual indwelling in our relationships as those created in God's image. Also as supremely personal, God is not content to let us simply coexist. God's Word is incarnate as Jesus Christ. While the incarnation does not exhaust God's presence, it does specify that God truly comes close and sees us, making it possible for us to see God (John 1:18). To me, the greatest act of humility is that God becomes human and makes it possible to know him in such intimate terms.

Relating to Jesus

I appreciate diZerega's concern to guard against limiting God and his concern for humility. You will recall that I quoted him as saying that to claim that God has a personality is "limiting." He claims, "For many of us, squeezing the Source of All into the image of a human being is the opposite of humility." In response to diZerega, I maintain that Jesus as God in the flesh is not impersonal or beyond personal but supremely personal. As he is supremely personal, his personality cannot be limited to what we normally think of in terms of personality, including affections. He is constant and pure in all his ways, not like us with our fleeting and erratic emotional states. Moreover, while Jesus' divinity extends beyond his embodied state (and so he is not exhausted by it even while being inseparable from his body as integrally one with it), the second person of the Trinity is embodied and mediates us to God. Jesus is no avatar—if we mean by that an appearance or manifestation, one partial embodiment among many. No, Jesus is God enfleshed, coming down to us from above in humility and self-sacrifice from the Father who gives sacrificially of himself in giving his Son up to us. So when we see Jesus, we see his Father (John 14:9), for he and the Father are one (John 10:30) from and to all eternity. Now for us to be truly humble, we must recognize Jesus as the One he claims to be and live in light of his self-sacrificial reality as the one and only Son of God, who makes it possible for us to truly see, know, and obey God.

The points we are making here go beyond worldview analysis, for we are taking our cue not from a logos principle or ideal but from God's personal logos or Word who becomes incarnate to give himself to us in sacrificial love.[28] It is not only neo-pagans who go beyond worldview in their affirmation of faith. The Bible leads me to emphasize the need for personal experience of Jesus. Jesus transcends the rational categories of Christian worldview even though that worldview rightly identifies him as the personal subject that he is. While one can have knowledge of Jesus, the experience of Jesus exceeds rational categories describing him. Jesus and his love transcend our understanding (in keeping with Paul's claim that the love of God transcends knowledge in Ephesians 3:18–19). In Jesus, God comes off the shelf: Jesus is the Word enfleshed, the myth that becomes fact, as he comes from the Father in humble and sacrificial love to give himself for the transformation of our lives and the entire creation in the Spirit. (Romans 8:18–30 speaks of the entire creation groaning, believers groaning, and the Spirit groaning in anticipation of the redemption of all things.) The Word incarnate penetrates our lives and hearts as his indwelling Spirit moves us beyond mere reason to an experiential faith that both involves and transcends rational expression. The same God who said, "'Let light shine out of darkness,' made his light shine in our hearts to give us the light of the knowledge of the glory of God in the face of Christ," who is the image of God (2 Corinthians 4:4–6). Here we find that trinitarian faith is rational and experiential, interpersonal and cosmic.

Relating to Creation

The preceding points on interpersonal relations and personal experience in view of the triune God demonstrate why diZerega and I call for moving beyond objectification to relational and personalized forms of communication and interaction: we are wired for relationality. Neo-pagans and others illustrate this point clearly through their longings for wholeness and oneness. Ridiculing them for their care for the world is a grievous thing, and such mockery magnifies shallowness and cold detachment from God's creation and desperate need for relational wholeness on the part of Christians in view of the triune God who invites us to participate in his interpersonal communion. I believe it is because God has ultimately wired us personally and interpersonally to want to experience life relationally that some people— neo-pagan and non-pagan alike, consciously or subconsciously—personalize the nonhuman creation or prized possessions.

Martin Buber, to whom diZerega refers for his seminal reflection on I-Thou versus I-It, speaks of different ways of observing a tree: one is to approach it scientifically as a botanist; the other is to approach it relationally, perceiving their interconnection.[29] In his own account of Buber's philosophy, the famous Christian medical doctor and author Paul Tournier shares the story of a psychoanalyst approaching a tree as a confidant when growing up, of poets personifying the moon as a woman, of a child treating a favorite teddy bear as a person, and of Sigmund Freud recounting the tale of a child hiding and retrieving a cotton reel, realizing that the child was acclimating himself to his mother's absences by making the cotton reel his mother. Tournier also shares that in André Haynal's study of despair, Haynal claims that Buber developed his I-Thou philosophy out of longing for his mother, from whom he was separated at the age of two when his parents divorced.[30]

With this set of experiences in mind, and in the effort to restate and extend points already made, these stories and Scripture prove that we are wired to approach the whole of life relationally, for we are created in the image of an interpersonal and relational God and are called to experience all of life relationally. Ultimately the I-Thou relationship requires an interpersonal grounding to life. Any concept of reality that is not ultimately personal and interpersonal will be unable to safeguard otherness but will objectify it or at least eradicate its distinctive particularity.

Remember *Avatar*'s paraplegic marine, his beautiful princess, and beloved Na'vi. The paraplegic marine uses an avatar to analyze the Na'vi, but this marine then moves from objectifying the Na'vi to becoming one with them relationally after he senses his need for them. He is transformed as he is circumscribed in their bodily form and experiences life from their vantage point. It is only as the paraplegic marine steps inside the Na'vi culture, using his avatar legs and falling in love with their princess, that he is able to understand the Na'vi. Only then can he truly see them. It is then that he finds communion with them, realizing how they enrich him relationally. The transformation is so radical that the marine is willing to risk losing his life fighting alongside the Na'vi as they resist the foreign invaders.

Without seemingly intending to do so, James Cameron's *Avatar* bears witness to Jesus' incarnation and redemptive suffering. The incarnation of Jesus Christ is no appearance or manifestation but the one and only incarnation. His incarnation is no three-dimensional representation; it is no avatar. It should be clear in view of what has been claimed to this point that I am not arguing that the paraplegic marine in *Avatar* is the spitting image of Jesus; he isn't. But in a manner similar to this story, God has wired the world's people groups to talk of saviors who come to earth and die only to rise and bring new life. The ancients declared this hope in their oracles and myths. As C. S. Lewis has said, the gospel story is the myth that became fact: "If ever a myth had become fact, had been incarnated, it would be just like this."[31]

We are wired to tell these stories, just as we are inclined at times to dress this God up in creaturely forms so that we can truly see him. But we do not need to do so because the one and only God, and not some emanation of a distant and beyond-personal deity, becomes creaturely. The Lord's Supper itself bears witness to the reality of a personal and cosmic redemption as God has replaced the shedding of the blood of animals with the shed blood of Christ, who transforms the human creation and the entire cosmos. We celebrate this reality at the Lord's Table, participating in the life of the triune God as we consume the food and drink taken from grain and grape in anticipation of the consummation of all things.[32]

How can I see and experience this reality if God is beyond personal being and not revealed ultimately through Jesus Christ? If all is one and Jesus is not the incarnation of God, I am ultimately looking in a mirror rather than experiencing a foretaste of the beatific vision. If all is one and God is beyond personhood and there is no unique incarnation but only emanations of the One, we haven't really experienced the revelation of God or a revealed affirmation of the creation by God in the flesh. The greatest affirmation of Nature or creation is that God Almighty became humble human flesh and blood taken from the dust of the earth as the microcosm of the creaturely realm,[33] rather than simply taking on an avatar from which he removes himself time and time again, not being indissolubly linked to the creaturely sphere. Only in the incarnate Jesus, who forever remains the divine Word enfleshed, do we truly see and know experientially the one and only true God and become one with him and with one another through faith. This very Jesus reveals God and the goodness of creation to us as the image of the invisible God and firstborn over all creation (Colossians 1:15). In light of him we can truly say: "I see you."[34]

PART III

An Engagement of Hot Topics

CHAPTER 14

ALL ROADS LEAD TO WALL STREET

This essay addresses key tenets of religious pluralism in the context of a market-driven, consumer culture. The religious pluralist maintains that "all roads lead to Rome" and that "God is beyond knowing."[1] This means that various religions point toward the divine reality that is beyond description and apprehension. As J. A. DiNoia puts the pluralist position, the "transcendent Center . . . remains always beyond and greater than apprehensions of it or even the sum total of such apprehensions."[2]

Despite the apparent humility of the pluralist position, the pluralist, as defined here, claims to know much more than any of the adherents of historic orthodox traditions combined; for such a pluralist asserts that God cannot be identified with any one tradition and judges the various traditions' approximate correspondence to the divine reality. Here is how John Hick frames the pluralist appraisal of the great religions of the world:

> The great world religions appear to me to constitute, in their different
> ways, more or less equally effective—and, alas, at the same time more or

less equally ineffective—contexts of human transformation from self-centredness to a new orientation centred in the divine Reality. Each is, historically, a unique mixture of good and evil; but none stands out on balance as morally and spiritually superior to the others.[3]

If the basis for judgment lies with the pluralist (or the devotee, for that matter), rather than the alleged revelation claim, what is to serve as a prophetic rebuke against projecting onto God one's own preferences for what God should be like? Some projections may appear to many of us to be more honorable than others in terms of what they value, such as what Hick refers to as the move from self-centeredness to divine Reality centeredness.[4] But in a market-driven, consumer culture that prizes the individual's desires as authoritative and conceives value in economic and consumer terms, what is to safeguard against such abuses? Not everyone frames self-centeredness as the problem; some see it as the solution to the world's problems, as the popularity of Ayn Rand's rational selfist philosophy suggests.[5] While the religious consumer or selfist of various sorts can certainly refuse to adhere to the claims of those religious traditions that place others' interests above one's personal passions, such refusal is deemed immoral and subject to rebuke based on transcendent grounds (and therefore is not subject to human preference for legitimacy).[6]

Wherever the starting point, the situation is increasingly complex for all sides—pluralist and nonpluralist alike—given how the political and cultural climate in our society no longer favors religion as providing the moral cohesiveness for society at large. Even religion has undergone democratization and commodification in the free-market age. Economics and the market, not religion, are hailed as providing the reigning salvific narrative. Here is how Gordon Bigelow frames the discussion:

Economics, as channeled by its popular avatars in media and politics, is the cosmology and the theodicy of our contemporary culture. More than religion itself, more than literature, more than cable television, it is economics that offers the dominant creation narrative of our society, depicting the relation of each of us to the universe we inhabit, the relation of human beings to God. And the story it tells is a marvelous one. In it an enormous multitude of strangers, all individuals, all striving alone, are nevertheless all bound together in a beautiful and natural pattern of existence: the market. This understanding of markets—not as artifacts of human civilization but as phenomena of nature—now serves as the unquestioned foundation of nearly all political and social debate.[7]

As a result of this change in perspective and reframing of sacred story, each of the religions or even a particular synthesis of religions is often viewed as a consumer product that one picks and chooses from a vast assortment of options. The reconstruction of religion in a market age has led Lesslie Newbigin to argue,

> Different religious traditions lose their capacity to be the binding element of societies and become instead mere options for religious consumers to select for their own private reasons, reasons which are not to be argued about. Thus "democratized," religions enter the marketplace as objects of subjective choices in much the same way as brands of toothpaste and laundry soap.[8]

This is the context in which the religious pluralist and nonpluralist alike must function. In this light one must ask: What will provide the adequate moral grounds for furthering the flourishing of human life and the cosmos in a consumer culture, where all of life is threatened with commodification, and value is framed by way of marketability and supply and demand? If religious pluralism wins out as the dominant model for approaching religious truth and ethical claims, will it be able to guard against all roads leading to Wall Street, where religion (and human life) only has value to the extent it benefits the GNP?

FROM CONFUSION TO CERTAINTY

Many people function as if nothing is sacred in a market-driven culture. Those of us who hold firmly to one religious tradition for faith and practice (whether we are nonpluralists or pluralists) find that others often mix and match various religions to satisfy their own whims, appetites, and preferences. The following story symbolizes the struggle we all face today—religious pluralist and nonpluralist alike.

I had just graduated from college in Minnesota and had moved to the Chicago area, where I was planning to attend seminary. During my last year of college, I had developed a real interest in ministering to Muslims. So after my move I got connected with a group of people working among Muslims as States-side missionaries. One of the men in the ministry, Joe, was of Italian descent. Joe was street-smart but not formally educated, and he had been an evangelical Christian for only a few years. He knew Chicago like the back of his hand, and so he offered to take me around one day to see Muslim-related sites. Although Joe knew Chicago well, I am not sure how well he knew orthodox Islam. The experience we had at the mosque we visited was not very orthodox.

There we stood knocking at the door of the mosque: my new Italian American friend and me—a Swedish-German-Hungarian-French-Irish American. Someone else also came knocking at the door of opportunity at the same time as us—an Irishman who sounded as if he had just crossed the Atlantic. The man who opened the door of the mosque was a bit suspicious. Another man appeared at the door a second later. Both men wanted to know what brought us there. My friend and I told them that we simply wanted to see the mosque and to get their take on Islam. The Irishman said he was looking for a large space to rent so as to open a discotheque. I don't think he came to the right place.

I can't recall what happened to the Irishman, but I don't think he stayed long. He had traveled across the Atlantic to Chicago in search of the almighty dollar, and he quickly saw that this mosque was a dead end, given the cold reception to his business plan. He probably went next to a church down the block. Now, as suspicious of us as the two men who opened the door were, I think they were even more suspicious of the discotheque entrepreneur with the thick Irish accent.

As a result of our genuine interest in learning more about Islam, they gave us a tour of the place and sat down to talk with us about religion. The entire experience turned out to be one of the most memorable exposures I have had to the American religious and cultural scene, though I don't think

I learned all that much about Islam that day. Not only were we knocking at the door of the mosque with the Irish businessman who seemingly had no real appreciation for the sacred or sacred space, but also one of the two hosts was clearly not a traditional Muslim. I am not sure what he was. He seemed more like a schizophrenic combination of the old-school evangelist Billy Sunday and a Baha'i devotee. While the man who first answered the door was a true adherent of Islam, "Billy Baha'i" was changing his perspective every few minutes. Not only was he confusing us, but also I think he was really frustrating the faithful Muslim. He kept interrupting his fellow host's lecture on Islam, going back and forth between giving a hellfire-and-brimstone message about Moses, Jesus, and Muhammad (each in turn being the only way to God) and talking about all roads leading equally well to God.

As a missionary-among-Muslims-wannabe, I left the mosque that day as if I had been baptized with fire. My head was spinning so fast that I didn't know any way leading to Rome or even to my own home. I didn't learn so much about orthodox Islam, but I did learn something—at least symbolically—about the Swedish smorgasbord or Hungarian goulash or Irish stew of religion we taste in America today.

Though I didn't think we evangelical Christians had much in common with either of our hosts at first, I found that we shared something in common with the true Muslim. Neither he nor Joe nor I wanted to mix and match religions. Neither he nor we saw all roads as leading to Rome or to Wall Street—or to a discotheque, for that matter. The Irishman and Billy Baha'i didn't seem to care too much about transcendent truth claims of particular historic traditions or sticking with a particular tradition,[9] but our orthodox Muslim counterpart and we sure did. As I look back, I find him rather refreshing, as exhausting as the interaction with him and his friend was. I also find his rather lofty claims about Islam's finality rather humble and measured. He stuck to the script and didn't go beyond the road laid out for him by those who preceded him.

What would an outsider looking in have thought? If the Irishman were his guide, he may have thought dollar signs were religious symbols. If Billy Baha'i walked him through the mosque, the observer may have thought that one size of religion fits all or that one can mix and match various religious rituals and belief systems according to one's appetites and consumer preferences. I don't want to make too much of this mosque story, but it bears witness to the diversity of approaches to religion in the context of North America today. Gone are the days when evangelical Christians had a corner on the market. Even the orthodox Muslim has to find his way in this consumer wasteland.

Before moving on, please understand that I appreciate the Baha'i tradition's concern for religious tolerance. My naming of the one man in the mosque as Billy Baha'i is no reflection on the Baha'i tradition's affirmation of tolerance.[10] In a society deeply marred by culture wars, we cannot affirm strongly enough the need for tolerance. Having said that, what I don't appreciate about many pluralists (beyond the consistently agnostic sort) is that they often talk as if they know ultimate truth better than all the historic religions combined. As humble as it sounds to say that God has many names, and that all roads lead to Rome, I don't find these particular claims very humble.

FROM TOLERANCE TO LOVE

While many pluralists claim we are ignorant of the transcendent and are like blind men stumbling about in the dark, many in their ranks also claim to know God's chief attributes, such as love and goodness. How do they know that God is beyond total knowing? Who told them God is loving and good? To use the rhetoric some religious pluralists aim at evangelicals, who made them God or God's spokespeople? At least the Muslim in the mosque that day was claiming to have received the ultimate revelation through the Quran and was not feigning ignorance. Whether right or wrong at the end of the day, he explicitly claimed that we can know something and that religious speech is not to be rendered mythological; doctrinal statements are claims about transcendent reality and open to comparative judgment with other such claims, and thus not reducible to emotive, existential states of figurative expression.[11]

I am not saying that all religious pluralists are disingenuous. Many pluralists hold to pluralist claims such as "all roads lead to Rome" and "God is beyond knowing" because they truly do want to be humble people, are put off by arrogant adherents of particular traditional religions, and want to wage war against the intolerance of those who bully people into holding to the party line. Although a strong critic of pluralism, W. A. Visser 't Hooft accurately conveys the basic sentiments of pluralism:

> We need today more than ever a world faith which will provide an effective basis for human solidarity in a shrinking world. For unless we seek to harmonize the religions how shall we ever find that common "ethos," that universally accepted system of spiritual values and moral principles which we need in order to overcome our confusion, to end the war of ideologies and give international law and morality a solid foundation.[12]

I appreciate the sentiments of religious pluralists who want to safeguard against oppression and promote social cohesion. But I am not sure they can guard against the pragmatic position that religion and people only have value to the extent that they benefit the GNP or me. In other words, I am not sure the well-meaning pluralist has enough artillery in his arsenal to wage war against negative forms of globalization given its own homogenizing tendencies, for religious pluralism itself undermines the distinctive, literal claims of various traditions regarding beliefs and with them morals in favor of "metaphorical" or "mythological truth."

Those particular claims about the transcendent have something very important going for them: they are all about particularity. While it is important to go in search of common ground and build bridges between the various traditions where appropriate, it is best to go through the various traditions' truth claims rather than go around them or above them. In my partnership with the Zen Buddhist priest Kyogen Carlson, we never water down our religions' distinctive qualities and ultimate truth claims. In our efforts to build beloved community, for example, we draw from our particular traditions' views on compassion—as different and as distinct as those grounds for compassion often are. The scandal of Jesus' particularity does not deny the particularity of my Buddhist neighbors, for Jesus lays down his life for all people.

Surely Hick is right in claiming that many adherents of Christianity, who have contended that Jesus is literally the Son of God and that he alone provides salvation for sins, have been guilty of oppression as in the forms of imperialism and anti-Semitism. But that does not mean that one must go the route of Hick and claim that the way to read Scripture and approach its theological categories is metaphorical or mythological.[13] Metaphorical or mythological readings are contrary to how these texts were intended to be read and applied and how multitudes of religious practitioners from various religions approach these texts today. As such, is not Hick guilty of hermeneutical imperialism or at least of privileging his method of interpretation over others? To claim that the particular truth claims of various religious traditions are not to be taken as literally true but as mythologically true signifies that Hick believes the particular claims are literally false.[14] So from the standpoint of the same logic applied by many religious pluralists to exclusivists, Hick's rejection of the literal truth claims of these traditions is a form of imperialism.[15] In the end the key here is not to remove consideration of Jesus' uniqueness but rather to affirm Jesus' uniqueness as disclosed in the New Testament. Instead of oppressing his enemies, Jesus laid down his life for them. Instead of calling on his followers to hate their enemies, he exhorts them to love and care for them.[16] In the case of Jesus and those who follow his example, there is no hint of imperialism.

The tolerance Hick argues for but appears to lack certainly has its place, but love and compassion are even more profound. As stated earlier in this volume, I for one would rather be loved than tolerated. With this point in mind I am so thankful that John 3:16 does not read, "For God so tolerated the world that he chose not to send his Son." I am so grateful that it reads, "For God so loved the world that he gave his one and only Son." Tolerance allows for the opportunity to remain at the far end of an outstretched hand; love requires embracing the other. Tolerance does not entail having to get to know the other; love means being hospitable, which would include welcoming the person into one's home. Tolerance and love alike do not entail having to agree with someone; tolerance and love entail heart attitudes and behaviors that involve making space, and in the case of the latter, cherishing the other even when there is radical disagreement concerning such vital matters as faith claims.[17]

As strange as it may sound to some of us, many people in America today cannot give a good reason why a Muslim community wouldn't want to rent out its mosque to a businessman wanting to use it for a discotheque on off-prayer hours of the day. As an evangelical I can think of many reasons why the keepers of the mosque would never want to hand over the keys to their kingdom—even during the off-hours of the day. Fortunately they can think of such reasons too, and it has nothing to do with making a fortune. Rather it has everything to do with safeguarding the sacred from becoming profaned and protecting the sanctity of life in the public domain. Traditional Muslims can teach American Christians a thing or two about the need to view our church's faith as a public reality, not a private sphere marginalized by the secular state and market. For all too often American Christians view the church as a voluntary association of religious individuals while pledging their true allegiance to the state or market and maybe to their nuclear families as well.[18]

Is there a connection between pluralism and secularism? In my estimation the mythological reading of sacred literature by pluralists and the privatization of religion by the secular state go hand in hand. Pluralism and secularism remove the faith from public scrutiny, where religious claims can no longer be judged as right or wrong based on universal grounds. Of course, many religious pluralists want to keep the sacred from being profaned. But I don't think they have adequate safeguards or moral grounds.[19] While one cannot necessarily keep Antiochus Epiphanes from entering the temple and desecrating it, at least one can protest verbally and with civil disobedience. By no means were the first-century BC Maccabean martyrs under the Seleucid Empire's rule arrogant or oppressive. By no means were the twenty-first-century AD Muslims who protested the French government's call for removing headdresses religious bigots. If they were, then so, too, are those secularists and pluralists filled with bigotry who would minimize religious symbols of the various historic traditions as being banal, mundane, and parochial.

Such minimizing occurs in the States, where we claim that the removal of religious objects or practices from public settings is simply a matter of the separation of religion from the secular sphere. What we fail to realize is that secularism, or the secular state, is by no means void of religious claims. Often secularism, like pluralism, appears to promote neutrality—not favoring one religion over another—but actually these ideologies promote their secular or pluralist claims as being superior to explicitly religious traditions that affirm a personally transcendent God. In addition to the seemingly disingenuous claim to neutrality, adherence to these perspectives often causes more disastrous effects than their religious alternatives. The twentieth century gave rise to more death and destruction than any previous century and often at the hands of total secularists.[20] In the case of the secular state, it claims that it has authority in the public sphere and religious traditions can have autonomy and authority in the private sphere as long as they don't infringe on the rights and privileges of the state (so even their claims to transcendence in the private sphere of the soul are overshadowed by Big Brother).[21] While I appreciate America's historic stance to guard against any particular religious tradition monopolizing America, we have allowed secularism, with its transcendent claims concerning the neutral void, to dominate the span of particular religious heritages. I am for prayer in school, but I also recognize that if Christians are allowed to pray, Muslims should be allowed, too, and Buddhists should be allowed to meditate—even in public settings. The same goes for the display of religious symbols, including Muslim headdresses; they should be allowed in public, just like symbols of the state and Wall Street: Why should the religious symbolism of the almighty American flag or the hallowed Golden Arches be given space and not nativity sets? Such freedom of expression is what helped make this country truly great.[22]

Secularists and religious pluralists alike hold to transcendent claims that compete with those who adhere to orthodox religious traditions. If you press the logic, many pluralists really don't think that all roads lead to Rome and that ultimate reality is beyond knowing. They think they have a handle on it, or at least many of them do. I would rather say (as one who believes in revealed religion) that ultimate reality has a handle on me. Let's be honest. The pluralist is just as exclusivist as the traditional adherent of religion who claims to believe in the one true faith, competing with the historic orthodox for bragging rights to having the majority share of the religious market today.[23] In the end, pluralism may become the new orthodoxy. Maybe it will also give way to the free market of the not-so-free consumer pragmatism and secularism on Wall Street, where only that which benefits the market has value, like an Irish discotheque.[24]

From Selfishness to Faithfulness

The church has no way of controlling how the consumer reports will evaluate the Christian community's significance and import. Regardless of the evaluation, the best way for the church to contend against the homogenizing tendencies bound up with certain globalizing forces increasingly present in our society is for us to embody the language of our particular faith claims in honor of Jesus. In this way, we also honor others, for Jesus the named God makes it possible for all of us to be named and have particularity in a culture of homogeneity.

With the previous point in mind, we should focus on faithfulness rather than financial or numerical success. We should not be surprised if persecution results from our claim that God has but one name, that Jesus bears that name, and that the church participates in this reality when it bears authentic witness to Jesus. Such honesty is not an option among many in the American marketplace of religion (Acts 4–5).[25] Remember that the early church Christians were called atheists in the empire, for they would not worship the pantheon of the Roman gods. The apostolic community suffered for bearing witness to this name among their own people, and yet there was no resulting paranoia or passivity, only a sense of providence and renewed power because they had been found worthy to suffer disgrace for the name (Acts 5:41–42), just as Jesus had suffered.

This same sense of providence will lead us to rejoice in the midst of suffering. Over against paranoia, it will also free us to lay down our lives for those who reject us, just as they rejected Jesus. Captivated by his Father's providential care for him, Jesus laid down his life for others—including his enemies—in personal sacrifice. Even when we as Christians experience marginalization and banishment from the public square, we must not react and seek to take back our place on center stage. We must create space with lives of sacrificial love so our views may be heard from the margins, praying that our public witness to Jesus will be seen and heard and embraced in faith by all. In view of Jesus' literal incarnation, we must engage holistically and self-sacrificially for the sake of the common good, for Christian and non-Christian, religious pluralist and secularist alike. In fact, from an incarnational and relational vantage point, there really is no other way.

CHAPTER 15

DEAD METAPHORS AND LIVING HELL

In our day many people fail to take hell seriously. Perhaps they think of hell and devils and demons as dead metaphors, as primitive and medieval constructs that are no longer necessary images to ensure morality in our sophisticated, contemporary era. What is one to make of the sophisticated theologian Jonathan Edwards, who sermonized at great, fiery length in his "Sinners in the Hands of an Angry God"? To quote Edwards,

> The God that holds you over the pit of hell, much as one holds a spider, or some loathsome insect over the fire, abhors you, and is dreadfully provoked: his wrath towards you burns like fire; he looks upon you as worthy of nothing else, but to be cast into the fire; he is of purer eyes than to bear to have you in his sight; you are ten thousand times more abominable in his eyes than the most hateful venomous serpent is in ours. You have offended him infinitely more than ever a stubborn rebel did his prince; and yet it is nothing but his hand that holds you from falling into the fire every moment.[1]

Perhaps when Edwards delivered that sermon in New England back in the 1700s, he failed to account for his own concept of God as a holy, loving deity who invites us into the joy of his communion.[2] However, his sermon is surely a refiner's fire for contemporary pop-psych messages that can be likened to "Consumers on the Lap of a Feel-Good God."[3]

Not all moderns ridicule hellfire preaching and the doctrine of hell as crude, primitive, and despicable. In fact, sometimes we need to go outside the Christian faith to see the faith for what it is. Sometimes we have to listen to our critics rail against the faith to know the essence of it. Sometimes we need to inquire of masters of metaphor to know if our metaphors are dead or alive. This inquiry has led me to conclude that hell, while horrible, is true and right and affirming of human value and dignity. My exhortation to each of us is to be human and choose—and to do so wisely.

THE NECESSITY OF HELL

C. S. Lewis is not writing metaphorically when he claims that hell, while a horrible doctrine, is nonetheless a moral teaching.[4] It is righteous and morally good that God does not allow people to live in the lie or illusion of their rebellion against their Creator for eternity. God brings closure to sin and rebellion by bringing deeds done in the darkness into the light of day. God is morally upright, and I would add, even merciful to condemn people to hell. How is God being merciful by sending people to hell for their rebellion against him? God does not give us what we deserve in our alienation and hostility toward the Almighty. God takes us so very seriously that he judges us for our rebellion rather than abandon us in indifference. It is a severe mercy that God brings us into the light of day to bring closure to our living of the lie, bringing resolution rather than allowing us to live in the intolerable state of forever enduring divine indifference toward us.[5]

I would never say that God gloats in punishing people, for Scripture itself says that God does not delight in the destruction of the wicked: "Say to them, 'As surely as I live, declares the Sovereign LORD, I take no pleasure in the death of the wicked, but rather that they turn from their ways and live. Turn! Turn from your evil ways! Why will you die, O house of Israel?'"

(Ezekiel 33:11). God delights in doing right toward us. Certainly he judges us because of our rebellion and dismissive and abusive treatment of his Son. However, such judgment is bound up with his good plans for humanity, which are centered in his Son. God is not a glory-grabbing deity who pours out wrath on humans because we have slighted him in some manner. God is a jealous lover, who will never take lightly our rebellion because he loves us so and takes us very seriously. God's anger burns brightly over people taking lightly his Son's sacrificial love poured out for them and closing their hearts to the Spirit's embrace. The author of the epistle to the Hebrews warns his church against abandoning the faith because of increasing persecution. The following warning, which is alluded to in Edwards's sermon, speaks of God's jealous love for his Son in the Spirit:

> If we deliberately keep on sinning after we have received the knowledge of the truth, no sacrifice for sins is left, but only a fearful expectation of judgment and of raging fire that will consume the enemies of God. Anyone who rejected the law of Moses died without mercy on the testimony of two or three witnesses. How much more severely do you think a man deserves to be punished who has trampled the Son of God under foot, who has treated as an unholy thing the blood of the covenant that sanctified him, and who has insulted the Spirit of grace? For we know him who said, "It is mine to avenge; I will repay," and again, "The Lord will judge his people." It is a dreadful thing to fall into the hands of the living God. (Hebrews 10:26–31)

Indeed it is a dreadful thing to fall into the hands of the living God. But it is also a divine mercy. Unlike a fickle deity who judges us erratically, or a distant deity who abandons us in our autonomy and rebellion, this God judges us and does so fairly. We do not deserve to be judged fairly or to be judged at all. Why bother? Doesn't God have better things to do with his time? The Almighty is never unaware or uncaring, even in his wrath. He is never far off—even in judgment, even in our darkest and deepest hell.

As those created in the divine image, as those created for communion with God through his Son in the Spirit, God dignifies us by judging us in our rejection of him. God honors us by taking us so seriously that he judges and condemns to hell those who rebel against him. The noted atheist Bertrand Russell goes so far as to call hell a flattering, human-affirming doctrine:

> If Christianity is true, mankind are not such pitiful worms as they seem to be; they are of interest to the Creator of the universe, who takes the trouble to be pleased with them when they behave well and displeased when they behave badly. This is a great compliment. We should not think of studying an ants' nest to find out which of the ants performed their formicular duty, and we should certainly not think of picking out those individual ants who were remiss and putting them into a bonfire. If God does this for us, it is a compliment to our importance; and it is even a pleasanter compliment if he awards to the good among us everlasting happiness in heaven.[6]

I have the sense that Russell would have become a Christian if he had believed the doctrine of hell to be true. But perhaps for him it was too good—morally and relationally—to be true.

Russell strikes me as having been a brave man, a courageous man, for having denied the faith because he couldn't believe. It is far better to deny the faith because one finds it unbelievable—perhaps even too good to believe—than to hold to it superstitiously as a fallback plan, viewing faith as fire insurance in the event that the atheist has gambled wrongly and there is a God, a judgment, and a populated heaven and hell. For Russell, all is random. Everything is by accident in a universe of scientific data devoid of divine providence. Even humanity's purposeful endeavors are meaningless. Russell courageously (though mistakenly, in my estimation) maintains in the face of these and related atheistic convictions that "only within the scaffolding of these truths, only on the firm foundation of unyielding despair, can the soul's habitation henceforth be safely built."[7]

In keeping with the claim that God flatters people by judging and condemning them to hell, we dignify ourselves when confirming that God is right and merciful to condemn us; in other words, we dignify ourselves when we take responsibility for our actions before God. These are the deeds of mortals who will be raised immortal, and so our actions are of eternal value and significance—one way or another. John Steinbeck would agree that human value and dignity are related to human responsibility. While Russell speaks of God flattering us by condemning us to hell, Steinbeck speaks of God's judgment and hell as doctrines that affirm our dignity. In *Travels with Charley in Search of America*, Steinbeck reflects on having visited a "John Knox church" in Vermont one Sunday morning during his cross-country travels and hearing a fire-and-brimstone sermon:

> It is our practice now, at least in the large cities, to find from our psychiatric priesthood that our sins aren't really sins at all but accidents that are set in motion by forces beyond our control. . . . For some years now God has been a pal to us, practicing togetherness, and that causes the same emptiness a father does playing softball with his son. But this Vermont God cared enough about me to go to a lot of trouble kicking the hell out of me. He put my sins in a new perspective. Whereas they had been small and mean and nasty and best forgotten, this minister gave them some size and bloom and dignity. I hadn't been thinking very well of myself for some years, but if my sins had this dimension there was some pride left. I wasn't a naughty child but a first rate sinner, and I was going to catch it.[8]

If the universe is sheer accident and our actions are the results of that accident, we lose all dignity. The psychiatric priesthood to which Steinbeck refers certainly desires to affirm human value and dignity, but such priests end up unintentionally undermining our value by rejecting the doctrines of personal guilt and eternal judgment. Ironically to some (but perceptively to me), Steinbeck points out that our self-worth as humans is integrally connected to a sense of personal responsibility, and that our actions as free, moral agents truly matter—eternally matter. Steinbeck's perception and firm affirmation of our personal responsibility as moral agents is one reason why I find him to be a true humanist—not the atheistic kind who denies God and unwittingly denies us when viewing our actions as mere accidents of nature, but the kind who affirms our eternal worth by sensing our moral responsibility and culpability before a transcendent, personal deity who cares deeply about our lives, actions, and hearts.

As already suggested in our brief consideration of Edwards, it is possible to go too far in the other direction. One may go so far with talk of moral culpability and judgment and hell as to come across as claiming that God despises humans as worthless and pitiful creatures who have no value. Of course we have value as those created in the image of God. Even though our sins may be abominable, even though we may radically sin against God and against his image, we can never destroy God's regard for us as the pinnacle of his creation and the object of his redeeming love in his Son.

Guilt is not simply a psychological state of the soul and mind; it is also reality. We don't simply lie on psychiatrists' couches; we also stand before a transcendent personal deity who is the source and substance of all justice, who comes close to us, and whom we have personally offended by our rejection of his Son and what his Son has done for us in providing a way out for us from the hellish horrors of God-forsakenness. We are responsible, moral agents, even when we act immorally, and God will honor our choices and human dignity. If God honors our choices to rebel against him and reject him, why do we fail to treat God and ourselves with dignity when we denounce God's judgment, denying our responsibility, trying to have our cake and eat it too? It is critical for our standing before God and for our own value that we see God's judgments concerning us as moral and just. We are not playing fair when we say we have the right to reject a relationship with God, but God does not have the right to allow us to live out the consequences of getting what we want.

We all want justice to be done when it benefits us. But do we long for justice to be done when it involves righting our wrongs and the wrongs of those we love? We want to define who and what is worthy of judgment and who and what is not. We are often arbitrary. Sometimes we judge to get even. God is impartial, and his ultimate aim in judging is not to destroy but to make right. How just are we when we make ourselves out to be the arbiters of justice, claiming that God does not have the right to judge us or pardon us? How dignified are we when we try to take the place of God? By not acknowledging our moral culpability and accepting his mercy by believing in Christ Jesus—who as our divine judge underwent judgment in our place—and by trying to judge in place of God, we claim to be better than

Jesus and his Father. Arrogance is never dignified. We take the place of God and so lose our human dignity in the process.

This leads us to the next point. It is not enough to experience the dignity to which Steinbeck refers by gaining a sense of one's moral culpability as a first-rate sinner. Nor is it enough to sense that one is going to catch hell for one's sins. What is enough is to throw oneself on the mercies of God revealed in Christ Jesus, who entered this world to seek and to save the lost and who calls us to respond to his invitation to accept the free gift of eternal life through personal faith and live in communion with him from this point forward to eternity: "For God so loved the world that he gave his one and only Son, that whoever believes in him shall not perish but have eternal life" (John 3:16). God did not send his Son to condemn us but to save us from our sins (John 3:17). If we only think we are to acknowledge our misery and responsibility as sinners to safeguard human dignity, neglecting to acknowledge God's mercy and grace poured out for us in Christ, we are not being humanistic enough. For what greater affirmation of our human dignity could God demonstrate than to send his Son to give his life for us so that we could experience eternal life with him, in communion with the Father through the Spirit for all eternity? All we need to do is repent and respond in faith.

The great Steinbeck did not go far enough, but Jesus went as far as he possibly could—as far away from God as we can possibly go—to hell. And so we can never truly depart from God's omnipresence even though relationally we can create infinite distance between God and ourselves for eternity. Not only did Jesus become incarnate; not only was he crucified, killed, and buried; but also he descended into hell before rising from the dead and ascending to heaven as the Apostles' Creed proclaims:

> I believe in God the Father almighty,
> maker of heaven and earth:
> and in Jesus Christ his only Son our Lord,
> who was conceived by the Holy Ghost,
> born of the Virgin Mary,
> suffered under Pontius Pilate,
> was crucified, dead, and buried.

He descended into hell;
the third day he rose again from the dead;
he ascended into heaven,
and sitteth on the right hand of God the Father almighty;
from thence he shall come to judge the quick and the dead.[9]

Jesus went as far as he possibly could without undermining our personal worth and value by taking away our freedom to choose or reject him.[10] Lewis calls it a miracle that God permits his creatures to reject his will.[11] Far from being a denial of God's omnipotence, God demonstrates his omnipotence by allowing us to resist his affection and reject his provision for forgiveness and salvation through repentant faith in Christ Jesus. God will never condone sin; he will never simply ignore it. Otherwise he would not be holy or true or loving, for he would no longer see sin as the evil that it is or view his creatures' actions, no matter how reprehensible, as having import. (And not to view someone's actions as having import is to despise that person.) While God has done everything possible to forgive us our sins, we must respond.[12] Lewis puts it well: "Forgiveness needs to be accepted as well as offered if it is to be complete: and a man who admits no guilt can accept no forgiveness."[13] One cannot experience forgiveness unless one responds to God's invitation, repents of rejecting God, and enters into relationship with God by trusting in him for eternal life. "God did not send his Son into the world to condemn the world, but to save the world through him" (John 3:17). But many reject him because we do not want to come into the light of his truth (John 3:18–21); we would rather live and die as a result of the inhumane lie that God is not right, and that we are not responsible or guilty of personal sin. How foolish, self-deceived, and inhumane can we possibly be?

Will we live forever in this state of illusion? Many will. Hell is locked from the inside, not from without.[14] Even though the gates of the kingdom are forever wide open (Revelation 21:25), those in hell will eternally shut themselves off from God and others. Hell is other people, according to one of Jean Paul Sartre's characters in the play No Exit.[15] Hell is an eternal loathing of others, as one exists in a state of solitary confinement and self-absorption, set apart from God revealed in Jesus—the God-Man who ever exists for others—and from everyone else. Hell is within the human soul, as we cut ourselves off from God and others. This life is not simply a testing ground for the next life; it is part of that life.[16] What is done here continues forever, not as good or bad karma but as the continuous trajectory of an embodied soul bent toward or away from the God revealed in Jesus. Eternal life with Jesus as well as death apart from him begins now.

The Necessity of Jesus

So who is in, and who is out? I remember a Buddhist philosopher posing a similar question to me several years ago during a debate at a secular university. We had just finished our respective presentations on Buddhism and Christianity, and we were beginning to ask questions of each other. His first question to me was a "conversation stopper," to use his words. He asked, "Do you think I am going to hell?" This is never an easy question to try and answer, especially when it is intended to serve as a conversation stopper at the beginning of a time of interaction in a public debate, and especially when the person with whom I am interacting is not some carnal pagan who despises religion, but a very spiritual and thoughtful person. I responded by drawing from points collected from Lesslie Newbigin's writings: God makes the decisions—I don't. Jesus alone is Lord, and there will be many surprises.[17]

My intention in responding in this manner was not to blow the Buddhist philosopher off or sidestep the question, but to place us on level ground and move his question beyond a debate item between him and me to a question he should pose directly to Jesus. God called me to be a witness, not a gatekeeper who determines who is in and who is out. My work is to point people to Jesus, not myself, and to invite people to journey with me to meet Jesus. I am not this man's judge. Jesus is *our* judge. Only Jesus can— and will—answer the question of our eternal state. Each of us must come face-to-face with him. There will be many surprises. Simply consider the haunting account of the sheep and the goats recorded in Matthew 25:31–46. Those who presumed they were in were out, and those who realized they lacked self-sufficiency to save themselves (and who depended on Jesus) were in. Newbigin goes so far as to state, "The question of eternal salvation and judgment is not a basis for speculation about the fate of other people; it is an infinitely serious practical question addressed to me."[18]

Presumption is never a good thing and is different from assurance. Assurance is based on what the Lord has done for you and me in spite of ourselves, whereas presumption is based on what you and I think we have done for the Lord on our own merits. I have a confident assurance that I am saved based on what Jesus has done in love for me in living and dying and rising again to break the bonds of sin and death so that I may enter into the fullness of life with him forever. Jesus is my confidence, not me, and I cling to the hope he provides. I have no other basis for hope, for there are so many people so much better than I, so much brighter than I, so much more spiritual than I. All I have is Jesus, and I cling to him like the repentant tax collector, not the haughty, self-righteous Pharisee (Luke 18:9–14). What about you?

Anyone who wants Jesus can have him. He never pushes us away as some fickle, cliquish deity would. We are the fickle ones, pushing him away. He offers us forgiveness, but will we respond, accept his forgiveness, and enter into communion with him? The real question is not, "Do you think I am going to hell?" The real question is the one Jesus posed: "Who do you say I am?" (Mark 8:29). A question that follows from it is also worthy of consideration: "How will you respond to him?" God is judge, and he has entrusted all judgment to the Son (John 5:22)—not a son who stands far off and aloof as the representative of a distant father figure, but the loving Son of the Father who comes close to us, longing to bring us prodigals home to be with him forever (Luke 15:11–32).

What is this forever life with Jesus about? And for that matter, what about its opposite—eternal damnation? I can find no better living metaphorical description of this eternal state of affairs than what C. S. Lewis gives us in *The Screwtape Letters*. God desires to have communion with us, so he frees us to become who we truly are in relation with him and one another. This expands and completes our identities. The demonic forces do just the opposite, shrinking our identities and devouring us, leaving us nothing more than shells and shadows of what we once were and could have been. The demon Screwtape writes to his nephew-apprentice Wormwood, instructing him in the ways of demonology:

To us a human is primarily food; our aim is the absorption of its will into ours, the increase of our own area of selfhood at its expense. But the obedience which the Enemy demands of men is quite a different thing. His love for men, and His service being perfect freedom, is not (as one would gladly believe) mere propaganda, but an appalling truth. He really does want to fill the universe with a lot of loathsome little replicas of Himself—creatures whose life, on its miniature scale, will be qualitatively like His own, not because He has absorbed them but because their wills freely conform to His. We want cattle who can finally become food; He wants servants who can finally become sons. We want to suck in; He wants to give out. We are empty and would be filled; He is full and flows over. Our war aim is a world in which our Father Below has drawn all other beings into himself: the Enemy wants a world full of beings united to Him but still distinct.[19]

It is one thing to be fixated with dead metaphors.[20] It is quite another to focus on lively metaphors like those created by Lewis in *The Screwtape Letters*. We must choose between absorption of our wills into the demonic and the affirmation of our humanity whereby we choose to pursue communion with God instead of consumption. If we choose the former road, we become less than slaves; we become shadows and shells of human existence. If we choose the latter road, we become sons and daughters of the Most High God, who will crown us with glory and splendor in our union with his ascended Son, who sits at God's right hand and who will judge the living and the dead—even the angels and demons.

Lewis does not force someone to take a stand on the actual existence of *personal* demons—that is not his concern. Lewis's concern is for us to consider what his demonic characters represent in relation to eternal matters involving the human, "not to speculate about diabolical life but to throw light from a new angle on the life of men."[21] Hell is no laughing matter. Consideration of our eternal state is a live question each of us must engage if we are to be truly human—considering the ultimate questions of our human existence and not simply questions about what we will eat or drink or wear. Lewis, the literary master and Christian humanist, reflects upon what many people will experience on the other side of the grave: the loss of their dignity, individuality, and personhood as they are swallowed up by the forces of darkness through the consumption of self-love and self-expression rather than self-abandonment.

Choosing self-abandonment over self- or selfish love creates loving, interpersonal communion with Jesus, who gave his life for us, even to the point of God-forsakenness in hell so that we would not have to suffer the horrors of that demonic state of nihilism and nothingness. This demonic state attacks us like a cancer that gnaws away at our humanity and our eternal souls. Jesus lived the question of God-forsakenness on the cross and in hell so that we would never have to experience its horror. As those who are called to be truly human, we should be humane and consider eternal and not simply mortal worth, for we have eternal significance before God. Hopefully, we all will choose self-abandonment over against selfish fulfillment, so we can experience the Father's embrace and receive from his fullness for all eternity. It is a live question: Which road will you take—the road to heaven or the road to hell?

Metaphors come and go but not heaven or hell or you—no matter which state you choose to experience. God will honor your decision, no matter which way you choose, given his miraculous affirmation of your human value and dignity. Heaven or hell—which will it be? Whatever you do, choose wisely.

CHAPTER 16

THE MISSING LINK

Many have sought to chronicle what they take to be historic tensions between modern science and faith. It would take us too far afield to challenge some readings of the history of science's exchange with religion. But it is important to note that many of the presumed tensions may indeed be misreadings of the history of that interchange.[1] One common solution to reconciling God and science has been the "God of the gaps": wherever science does not have an answer, faith proposes that God is the missing link. This goes back to ancient times: when the heavens rained, the gods were crying; when lightning struck and thunder rumbled, the gods were fighting. Slowly science has proposed answers for these and numerous other previously unresolved issues. In fact, Cambridge physicist Stephen Hawking has argued for some time that we don't need God to explain the origin of the universe: in Hawking's estimation, the universe is self-caused.[2] Could it be that there are no more gaps for God to fill, and God is redundant, perhaps even nonexistent?

What is God's relation to the world? During medieval times, it was generally maintained that God intervened in creation and culture throughout history. In the early modern period, it was often claimed that miracles were confined to the biblical period in history, after which it was frequently argued that they are confined to the beginning and end of history. Later even this view was challenged, giving way to the stance held by many that miraculous interventions were confined to the recesses of the human heart. This view was also eventually challenged, as the Freudians deemed religion a neurosis.[3] Is religion a neurosis, or is a religionless universe one without meaning and value? More specifically, is a universe void of interpersonal spirituality and subjectivity without ultimate meaning and value? I answer in the affirmative.

What is needed is a worldview that affirms both the merits of scientific analysis and the merits of interpersonal experience with God, which transcends worldview and scientific procedure. A trinitarian doctrine of creation makes space for the free exercise of science while also providing what science cannot provide—space for interpersonal relations; in short, this trinitarian framework is the missing link. In speaking of the missing link, I should make clear that I am not ultimately about safeguarding gaps or filling gaps, but about creating space or freedom for science and interpersonal communal spirituality to flourish respectively.

Many people are disillusioned with talk of which fish is bigger and bites harder—the Darwin fish or the Jesus fish. I for one am disillusioned by such bumper-sticker rhetoric, but I am not disillusioned by talk of Jesus' significance and import for scientific inquiry. Natural science that is truly natural affirms the subjective and the spiritual, because the spiritual can exceed the bounds of objectivism and mechanical necessity. As the Word through whom God creates all things out of nothing, Jesus makes space for free scientific inquiry of natural objects; the world does not emanate from God, but can be freely investigated as God's distinct creation. Jesus also safeguards space for us to approach all of life in relation to the Father in the Spirit. Such a spiritual approach prohibits the objectification of people or creation as things, and it emphasizes their dignity.

SCIENCE'S FREEDOM UNDER GOD

As we proceed, it is worth drawing attention to a text of Scripture that serves as inspiration for this quest—John 1:1–5, 10–14:

In the beginning was the Word, and the Word was with God, and the Word was God. He was with God in the beginning.

Through him all things were made; without him nothing was made that has been made. In him was life, and that life was the light of men. The light shines in the darkness, but the darkness has not understood it. . . .

He was in the world, and though the world was made through him, the world did not recognize him. He came to that which was his own, but his own did not receive him. Yet to all who received him, to those who believed in his name, he gave the right to become children of God—children born not of natural descent, nor of human decision or a husband's will, but born of God.

The Word became flesh and made his dwelling among us. We have seen his glory, the glory of the One and Only, who came from the Father, full of grace and truth.

According to historic orthodox Christian theology, God creates all things out of nothing by his personal Word, who is incarnated as Jesus. God does not create out of his being, but through a divine declaration. Though God creates the world through his personal Word who becomes flesh, humanity does not recognize or accept him. Yet God intervenes, and those who do receive his Word become his children based on the freedom of his interpersonal grace and truth (John 1:12–14). God's declaration of creation and redemption are free and in no way necessitated by the order of things.

How does this view of creation relate to science? For starters the creation of all things out of nothing safeguards free scientific inquiry. Harold Nebelsick has claimed that the Christian doctrine of creation (especially the Reformation emphasis) was critical in the development of modern science. Given that God created the universe out of nothing by his Word, science has the freedom to investigate nature or creation on its own terms. There are grounds for free, scientific analysis given that there are two distinct spheres: the uncreated (that is, God) and the created (everything but God). Christian theology enumerated along the lines of the voluntary creation of all things out of nothing by God's logos or Word safeguards the rational coherence of the universe and provides the space for natural science's freedom of inquiry.[4] This view has not always been upheld. A view of the world as sacrament and the monistic viewpoint (monism entails the belief that God and the world are ultimately one, that the world evolves from God or is one with God, and that by way of necessity, the study of nature requires a deductive accounting for the divine in the particular objects under investigation within the creation) are its chief competitors.

Inherent in sacramentalist perspectives is a failure to come to terms with the teaching that God created all things out of nothing by his Word. As the creation of the God who is Other, the universe is truly distinctive and is as secular as it is sacred. Where this conviction is not affirmed and integrated into one's overarching framework, the effect is the straitjacketing of free scientific exploration. In a similar vein, William T. Jones reflects critically on a dominant and problematic medieval outlook:

> What makes Augustine and Thomas and all the other medieval thinkers so fundamentally alike, despite all differences, is the sacramental outlook they shared. What makes us differ so markedly from them is that we have largely lost this outlook and that we share the basically secular point of view of the Greeks. When we say that medieval men looked on this world as a sacrament, we mean, first, that they conceived this world to be but the visible sign of an invisible reality, thoroughly impregnated, as it were, with the energy, the purpose, and the love of its Creator, who dwells in it as He dwells in the bread and wine on the altar. And we mean, second, that medieval men conceived this world to be a sacrifice which they freely and gratefully dedicated to the all-good, all-true Giver. Thus, while to us and to the Greeks the world by and large means what it is, to the Middle Ages it meant something beyond itself and immeasurably better. While for us and for the Greeks our life here is its own end, for the Middle Ages life's true end was beyond this world.
>
> That this sacramental point of view was a block to progress— progress in knowledge of how to control the environment and utilize it for this-worldly purposes—can hardly be denied.[5]

While Jones draws attention to some problematic features of the medieval period, he is wrong to attribute this perspective to all medieval theologians and philosophers.[6] One may also question Jones's appraisal of the Greek philosophers. Plato and Aristotle approached reality differently than did their Greek predecessors in view of their logical and psychological models and their doctrines of universals. For Plato this world shadows the ideal realm that exists beyond time and space; this world is real to the extent that it images or participates in that ideal realm. Aristotle's own logic and metaphysics shaped his approach and understanding of physical reality in that the universals impregnated the concrete particulars.[7] Such impregnation was deemed problematic to Francis Bacon.

In contrast to Jones's affirmation of the Greek philosophers, Bacon points to the Greeks as guilty of slowing the progress of science, placing particular blame on the system of "the Philosopher"—Aristotle. Bacon takes aim at Aristotelian logic and scientific analysis that proceed by deductive or syllogistic reasoning and axioms instead of by simple evaluation of the physical. According to Bacon, science can only reach its potential when it is freed from abstract speculation: "The understanding must not therefore be supplied with wings, but rather hung with weights, to keep it from leaping and flying. Now this has never been done; when it is done, we may entertain better hopes of the sciences."[8]

The creation of all things out of nothing by the personal Word of God safeguards science's search for unity according to the canons of reason (affirming the link between minds and the universe as rational) as well as science's free reign to pursue its course unhindered by an ideology that demands one recognize vestiges of God in creation or presumes that one must pursue science religiously. In his famous article on how Christian theology was instrumental in the rise of modern science, Michael Foster claims that modern science was able to arise and flourish when the quest for timeless frames of reference gave way to an empirical approach that focused on space and time forms. This involves the claim that God's voluntary activity, which goes beyond the determination of reason, brings forth the creation in a dependent and contingent manner.[9] What Foster points to as the voluntary will of God resonates in my estimation with the trinitarian doctrine of the creation of all things out of nothing by God's Word. Just as God has relational space within his own being for otherness, God grants space for the creation to be the creation through the voluntary activity of God's declaration by his personal Word.

Science's Enslavement to Observation
and Repetition

The scientific method claims to use *objective* observation and repetition in search of the same results;[10] however, it cannot objectify the realm of dynamic, spontaneous, relational experience. No matter how hard it may try, science cannot provide answers for what spirituality, personal identity, and relationality entail—participational experience. It cannot construe everything by way of scientific procedure and experimentation whereby only that which is observable and repeatable has meaning. Life is too mysterious, and the realm of interpersonal relationships involves grace and participation and not necessity and objectification. Jonathan Edwards once wrote that we cannot define love, only describe it.[11] I would add that we can only truly describe it if we experience it relationally. To experience love, we must move from two-dimensional black-and-white to three-dimensional color. Life becomes 3-D color as we experience the participational grace of God flowing freely from communion with him. That communion is indicative of profound relationships, not blind impersonal necessity, just as God's voluntary creation of all things out of nothing by his personal Word safeguards free scientific inquiry.

Just as it is true that for science to be objective, it must not look for God in creation (for God is beyond the creation and grants freedom for free scientific inquiry according to the rational coherence of all things and voluntary creation by God's personal logos or Word), so it is true that one cannot disprove God by way of science either. That is not to say that there is no integration, for modern science might never have developed freely without the Christian doctrine of creation. There is space for free scientific inquiry, when it does not exceed the spatial and temporal spheres of natural science, just as there is space for an analysis of spirituality and interpersonal communion, when it does not undercut free scientific inquiry in the natural sphere of evaluating objects. The trinitarian doctrine of creation preserves both dynamics in inseparable relation.

We now turn to consider the need for safeguarding such space for a relational and interpersonal ontology that cannot be jeopardized by a mechanistic philosophy of science. The ultimate reason for doing so here is not pragmatic but scientific: scientism—or perhaps better, physicalism—does not account for the fullness of life; what is required is a holistic account of every dimension of life. Scientism or physicalism is not scientific enough, going beyond its rightful bounds of addressing objects, and imposing on other spheres a mechanistic framework that does not make sense of the holistic framework of reality involving subjectivity and interpersonal relations of participation. This truly scientific approach outlined here in this essay not only grants space for the natural scientific method, but also allows the human and interpersonal to flourish, thereby demonstrating its validity as truly creaturely and natural.

Science has its place, a very significant place. How would we care for people if we did not treat the human body according to the objective canons of modern science? However, a doctor still needs a good bedside manner. Physiological analysis alone is not sufficient to care for the person. The two spheres are complementary, and do not stand in opposition to each other. As the medical doctor Paul Tournier remarks,

> the most scientific of doctors, men like Eric Martin, for example, remind us continually that when it comes to treatment, patients can no longer be treated as things, or with the lack of respect which we feel appropriate in handling things. And that the patient has as much need of his doctor's personal contact as of his scientific knowledge.[12]

The doctor must struggle to remain objective and not let personal affection get in the way of treatment (and so it is very difficult to treat one's own loved ones) but at the same time show personal care toward the patient.

This is the ongoing dilemma. The medical profession recognizes the value of caring for the "person" and not just the patient as an animate object. We must guard against reducing the person to a thing and also separating the person from the thing or body, as with Descartes's "ghost in the machine." (Descartes did not view the soul and body as integrally connected.)[13] What happens when we reduce the person to a thing or see the person and body as divorced from each other (and grace from nature and faith from knowledge)? Tournier along with Hans Urs von Balthasar speak to these matters. Here is what Tournier has to say:

From nursery school to university we are taught to adopt the scientific attitude; but science by definition knows only the world of things. Nature, history, society even, are seen as an endless round of phenomena which are rigorously linked in a chain of cause and effect. It is just an enormous mechanism in which we are inexorably caught, a sort of merry-go-round which gets us nowhere. For in the eyes of science nothing has meaning, since everything happens automatically at the whim of chance and necessity, as Jacque Monod has said.[14]

Without the personal and subjective, without the I-Thou of personal encounter in a universe of I-It relations in which we treat subjects and things as mere objects of analysis, we are left with blind chance and necessity, a world without personal meaning and interpersonal participation. In his reflections, Tournier draws from Martin Buber's classic discussion of I-Thou and I-It, which is found in Buber's famous work *I and Thou*.[15]

To say as some might that personhood is an emergent property of matter will not suffice. Once viewed in this way, we can be objectified. While I would not divorce the realm of the noumenal (involving God, moral freedom, and the things in themselves outside of space and time forms) from the phenomenal (the things as they appear to us in sense experience through the categories of the mind in space and time forms) as Immanuel Kant did, Kant was right to safeguard room for faith and moral freedom in a universe of fact and necessity.[16] Such reasoning is not pragmatic but rather holistic. There is more to us than what the scientific method can capture. Ultimately life is a gift, not a necessity, though like divine will and human freedom, the two can be viewed in inseparable and compatible relation. And while we can never know this gift (which is dependent on God's freedom in a direct and dynamic manner), as we know the object of matter as necessity (bound up with the laws of the natural order), our hearts and minds are naturally led to ponder that there is more to life than I-It relations.[17] We naturally long to approach life by way of I-Thou relations, though we also so easily gravitate (given our propensity to sin) toward reducing people to things.

What creates this longing for something beyond the material sphere and the realm of objects? This is not an esoteric question. Multitudes of people throughout the history of the world have had a religious sense that transcends the material sphere.[18] We must account for their experiences in an overarching treatment of what makes us human. Again this is not pragmatic reasoning but truly holistic. There is a spiritual, emotional, subjective component to humanity that cannot be reduced to the raw material of nature and observation. Occam's razor should not be put to theology's neck, demanding the simplest answer to be correct. In fact, it may be harder at times to make sense of things without recourse to theology. While God may not be "necessary" to explain things scientifically in the sphere of I-It relations, explaining life without God is not simpler than explaining life with God, for the triune God alone makes sense of the I-Thou relational framework as God is I-Thou. The rationale for this perspective involves the claim that the Word who comes from God becomes one flesh with us, participating in our lives through the Spirit, turning two-dimensional black-and-white into 3-D color, making it possible for us to enter into the fullness of participation in life, not being limited to the sphere of I-It relations.

We must never separate the two—science and religion, nature and grace—because if we do, nature gets the upper hand. As Hans Urs von Balthasar remarks, such a divorce leaves a devastating impact. Balthasar argues that there can be no "dialectical opposition between 'knowledge' and 'faith'" because while "God's sovereign freedom" does not come "under the judgment of human reason," as if the cross were necessitated by the worldly order and reason, "the light of the Cross makes worldly being intelligible" as it illumines the imprint of God's love on every aspect of creation.[19] Without this integration, without the integral relation of nature and grace along the lines of knowledge and faith,

> worldly being will necessarily fall under the sign of the constant dominion of "knowledge" and thus science, technology, and cybernetics will overpower and suffocate the forces of love within the world. The result will be a world without women, without children, without reverence for the form of love in poverty and humility, a world in which everything is viewed solely in terms of power or profit-margin, in which everything that is disinterested and gratuitous and useless is despised, persecuted, and wiped out, and even art is forced to wear the mask and features of technique.[20]

One can still affirm a scientific explanation of reality, just not one exclusively framed along solely naturalistic lines. I agree with the New Atheists who challenge Stephen Jay Gould's framework of the non-overlapping magisteria (NOMA), which claims that science and religion exist in separate spheres of total sovereignty (science deals with how, whereas religion deals with why).[21] The New Atheists want to address everything, and they also argue that religion wants to oversee everything as well.[22] It is certainly appropriate for the New Atheists to seek to cover everything from the standpoint of their methodology, that is, the sole observation of data. However, it is a mistake for science to think that it can reduce everything to the mere observation of data. It cannot investigate personal relations in this way, and for knowledge to be complete, it must account for participation in the divine love as revealed through the knowledge of faith through the cross, as Balthasar argues.

Trinitarian theology as articulated here does not insist on science having to frame its investigation in such a manner as to go in search of vestiges of the Trinity in creation. It affirms science's free inquiry. It also affirms and champions an embodied empiricism of mutuality and multifaceted and intimate relations with the world. Such a perspective is bound up with the divine love revealed in the Word made flesh, crucified, and risen. This Word of God opens us up to a new way of being in the world as we participate in his life as the firstborn over all creation through the Spirit.

Sheer observation is in two-dimensional black-and-white while experience and participation (bound up with trinitarian thought forms) are in 3-D color. Experience is essential, even to God. Objectively speaking, God knows all things, but until his Word became human, he did not have experiential or participational knowledge of humanity. While God created the universe and could observe and classify and define it exhaustively in his omniscience, he could not experience it as human until he became human. God himself experiences life as human in 3-D color. If the scientist would see life in color, he or she could move beyond rudimentary forms of knowledge, bound up with sheer observation, to participational knowledge, including the wisdom of relational faith.

A scientist can observe another person, but observation is not enough. In order to understand and experience truly all that life entails, a scientist must enter into relationship with the other person. Science can analyze relationships, but its methodology is that of an outside observer. There are important dimensions of interpersonal relationships that can only be understood from the inside, as a participant, not as an observer. The same holds true of spiritual realities.

It is worth noting here that a deistic view will not allow such participation, for in this view God is detached from the world as mere omniscient observer. A monistic view does not allow science its space to operate its laws and canons objectively because the world is God. Nor does it allow for interpersonal relations since everything is one; ultimately in a monistic universe, I am the other, and I look only at myself. Only the trinitarian model of creation and relationality grants space for science's free inquiry while placing limits on science's inquiry to the sphere of data observation. Science is free to observe everything, so there is no limit there. But science does not involve subjective participation and mutual indwelling. Not only do I want to observe, but also I want to participate. In fact, one might even go so far as to ask if there can be full knowledge without participation in any sphere.

The World Isn't Flat

In a discussion of the pull toward generalization over against particularization in science in the modern period, which actually harks back to the Parmenidean and Platonic Greek emphasis on the one over the many, Colin Gunton discusses P. S. Laplace and Michael Polanyi, where Polanyi speaks of Laplace's "decisive sleight of hand" substitution of "a knowledge of all experience for a knowledge of all atomic data." Gunton remarks that Polanyi sought to make clear that "the basis of knowledge is a form of particularity: not the particularity of a disembodied empiricism but that of an embodied mind in particular and determinate relations with the world."[23] If correct, even science in its analysis of things from an I-It vantage point proceeds not from detached objectivity but from encounter at one level or another. Thus science, despite its objective I-It framework, may still end up resting on a participational I-Thou foundation.

From a biblical vantage point one should not be surprised by this situation, for God has wired the universe relationally.[24] Over against disembodied empiricism and all that this philosophy entails for knowledge, the organizing principle of the world—from a truly Christian perspective—the personal logos or Word of John 1, who exists in interpersonal encounter with the Father from all eternity in the Spirit and through whom God creates the world freely, became flesh, not limiting his engagement of the world to creation and observation but moving beyond them to participation in life in the world, in and through the Spirit. The Father mediates all things to himself in space and time through the Son and Spirit, who enter space and time fully while remaining transcendent in their supra-temporal and supra-spacial relations in the Godhead, not being collapsed into the world, thereby safeguarding distinction in relation. God is closer to us than we are to ourselves, while remaining transcendent in relation to us, making it possible for us to observe and engage in I-It as well as I-Thou relations.

The disembodied empiricism of knowledge of data may be phenomenally successful at observation and analysis when it comes to I-It relations but is not able to experience I-Thou relationality. While science is able to study and observe the I-Thou in the sphere of the social sciences, it should only be silent when addressing the subjective experience of I-Thou. As such it is flat compared to the participational, experiential, intimate framework of personhood. While not undermining science's access to discovery of all spheres by way of observation and analysis, the trinitarian model of discovery transcends science, changing life from two-dimensional black-and-white to 3-D color. Trinitarian thought provides the missing link, not simply in terms of allowing science freedom to analyze data but also in terms of granting freedom to experience life in its fullness by participating in it. Such a perspective opens us up to the third dimension and beyond.

Perhaps you have read E. A. Abbott's *Flatland*. It is the tale of Square, an inhabitant of Flatland, who receives an alarming visit by Sphere, an inhabitant of the third dimension. After much effort Sphere finally convinces Square that there is a third dimension by pulling Square out of Flatland into Spaceland. No one in Flatland believes Square when he returns and tells them there is a third dimension. So it is with the physicalists. Of course they believe in a literal third dimension, but they refuse to believe or at least take seriously that there is a vitally significant dimension of life beyond the materialistic mundane. While it is said that the old dark-aged Christians superstitiously rejected the notion that the world is round, insisting that the world is flat, they were certainly right to claim that there is a world beyond the physical. They saw in color even though some have claimed that they did not see in 3-D.

Today's flatlanders are science-minded physicalists who see in two-dimensional black-and-white, rather than with the three-dimensional colored wisdom of interpersonal subjectivity and participation. They will not leave Flatland to participate in the multidimensional nature of reality as a result of a lack of wisdom ("the fear of the LORD is the beginning of wisdom" [Proverbs 9:10]), vision, and imagination. And so, they reject God's Word, for they are enslaved to their reductionistic framework. Fortunately for the rest of us (and still for them, too, if they will simply look and listen), Sphere has come to us as a participant in the infinite dimensions of love and truth and goodness and beauty of the triune God. Sphere opens this reality up to us from beyond as the Father communicates to us his love and goodness, grace and truth, joy and beauty through his Word and Spirit so that we might respond freely and participate in God's spacious life and experience the wondrous harmony of all.

The Flatlanders, as I term the New Atheists, appear to be winning the day in some circles. But I would encourage those who know the dimension of interpersonal subjectivity and who experience participation in the life of the triune God to persevere, to take to heart, and to live in light of the inspiring words of Flatland Prometheus (as Square refers to himself after having returned to Flatland, convinced of the reality of the third dimension). Although "absolutely destitute of converts" and in perpetual prison, he lives "in the hope that these memoirs [*Flatland*], in some manner, I know not how, may find their way to the minds of humanity in Some Dimension, and may stir up a race of rebels who shall refuse to be confined to limited Dimensionality."[25] Let us be that race of rebels and refuse to be confined.[26]

CHAPTER 17

HOMOSEXUALITY, HOLY MATRIMONY, AND HOSPITALITY

My heart hurts for the homosexual community. A dear friend of mine told me that his family member who is gay would have never wished to be gay. All the pain it has caused him—in terms of the internal turmoil, concerning his identity and the stigma associated with it in many of his circles—is so severe. I recall Oscar Wilde's words that no doubt refer in part to his own painful experience of being despised because of his homosexuality: "I never came across anyone in whom the moral sense was dominant who was not heartless, cruel, vindictive, log-stupid and entirely lacking in the smallest sense of humanity. Moral people, as they are termed, are simple beasts. I would sooner have fifty unnatural vices than one unnatural virtue."[1] Wilde and my friend's family member are not alone in the abuse and pain they experienced. History is marked by innumerable instances of abuse and pain experienced by those who struggle with and through homosexuality, including people close to me.

In spite of my own pain in recounting such instances that happened to my homosexual friends and acquaintances, I cannot go against what I believe Scripture reveals about God's heart on the subject of homosexuality. My problem is not homophobia; if anything, it is something I have chosen to call "herme-phobia"—the fear of interpreting or, more accurately, the fear of misinterpreting God's Word. Interpretation is itself a moral enterprise: I must apply the golden rule and seek to understand the biblical text as I would want to be understood, just as I should treat a homosexual the way I would want to be treated.

All people are created in God's image—male and female—and that includes everyone (Genesis 1:27). While the Genesis account speaks specifically of the first man and woman in their marital union, I do not believe the text is exclusively focused on male-female marital union. What does one make of those who never marry? Are they not created in God's image?[2] All people are created in God's image—male and female, heterosexual, homosexual, transgender, and the like.

All people are sinners, and Christ died for everyone (John 3:16; Romans 3:23), not just heterosexual people. All people are ruined Rembrandts—broken yet beautiful. Even God's saints are still sinners—fully righteous and fully sinful as Martin Luther maintained. With this in mind it is worth noting that the biblical prophets and other spiritual leaders were aware of their own need for God, identifying not only with their holy God but also with an unholy people. They had a heart for their people and saw themselves as part of them, even confessing corporate solidarity in the sins of the nation (Ezra 9; Nehemiah 9; Daniel 9). What a contrast to Jerry Falwell after 9/11, who, as noted earlier in this volume, went on record claiming that gays, lesbians, materialists, secularists, and the like had a vital role in causing the attack.[3] If they did, so did evangelicals who, in various quarters, have avoided addressing injustices and favored gaining affluence, comfort, and success, a point the late James Montgomery Boice brought home with prophetic force.[4]

All people stand under God's judgment in one way or another. God's prophets and other leaders of old identified with the people, even while identifying their sinful behavior and the like. Such prophetic identification involved compassion and conviction. To the extent we do not challenge sin and reach out to those whom God would judge, we judge ourselves to be guilty of greater sin and of lesser love for God and them. Action is what

Scripture condemns and what God will judge, not the temptation. It is one thing to be tempted. It is another thing to sin, especially in a purposeful and habitual manner.

Jesus' witnesses must speak on behalf of God and others, even appealing to people to be made right with God. Biblical conviction without compassion is empty, and compassion without biblical conviction is blind. The two extremes are easy ways out; finding middle ground is the truly difficult path. We must wed knowledge to zeal and sincerity, truth to grace, conviction to compassion (Romans 10:1–4). May God give us Paul's prophet heart for people (Romans 9:1–5)!

It is a constant struggle to guard against problematic forms of interpreting the Bible. There is no such thing as "presupposition-less" observations or exegesis, contrary to what some think. And yet, it must be maintained that irreconcilable interpretations are not equally valid. One must ask which presuppositions and interpretations are right in view of constant thoughtful engagement of the biblical text along with a diversity of readers.

It is important to pause and express empathy (not condescension) for the homosexual exegete who believes Scripture affirms certain forms of homosexual behavior. We all want to be affirmed, and no doubt the homosexual hermeneutic is driven at times by homosexual people's desire to seek affirmation from God for who they feel they are in their sexuality. While that desire easily moves toward self-justification—something with which I also struggle—there is that shared basic human desire to seek affirmation and acceptance, which is often present behind various hermeneutical moves. Having said that, homosexuals must come to terms with this propensity to frame their approach to Scripture based on this desire to be affirmed in their sexual orientation. Those repulsed by homosexuality must also come to terms with how their reactions fail to mesh with God's heart revealed in the Bible concerning all people, including homosexuals.

All people must make sure we are asking the right questions, which involves separating primary questions of significance from secondary ones. Concerning homosexuality, the real question is not if one can be both a Christian and a homosexual or if one can experience God in a homosexual church, but rather "Is homosexual behavior right? Is it biblical?"[5]

Homosexuality in Scripture

Creation

In Genesis 1–2, the Bible sets forth marital union as being between one man and one woman, which is God's design for the natural, created order. Genesis 1:27–28 reads,

> So God created man in his own image,
> in the image of God he created him;
> male and female he created them.

> God blessed them and said to them, "Be fruitful and increase in number; fill the earth and subdue it. Rule over the fish of the sea and the birds of the air and over every living creature that moves on the ground."

We also are told in Genesis 2:18–24,

> The LORD God said, "It is not good for the man to be alone. I will make a helper suitable for him."

> Now the LORD God had formed out of the ground all the beasts of the field and all the birds of the air. He brought them to the man to see what he would name them; and whatever the man called each living creature, that was its name. So the man gave names to all the livestock, the birds of the air and all the beasts of the field.

> But for Adam no suitable helper was found. So the LORD God caused the man to fall into a deep sleep; and while he was sleeping, he took one of the man's ribs and closed up the place with flesh. Then the LORD God made a woman from the rib he had taken out of the man, and he brought her to the man.

> The man said,

> "This is now bone of my bones
> and flesh of my flesh;
> she shall be called 'woman,'
> for she was taken out of man."

For this reason a man will leave his father and mother and be united to his wife, and they will become one flesh.

God created man and woman in the image of God as human. God created woman as a companion for the man. Woman was taken from man, and they were to become one flesh. Together they were to rule over all living things as they filled the earth with the progeny of their marital union.

Looking back to Genesis 1–2, Jesus confirmed in Matthew 19 that the standard for marriage is heterosexuality, with one partner, and "until death do us part." He also speaks against divorce and fornication, which would include, among other things, homosexual behavior. Here is the question on divorce that the Pharisees ask Jesus, followed by Jesus' response concerning marriage and divorce:

> Some Pharisees came to him to test him. They asked, "Is it lawful for a man to divorce his wife for any and every reason?"
>
> "Haven't you read," he replied, "that at the beginning the Creator 'made them male and female,' and said, 'For this reason a man will leave his father and mother and be united to his wife, and the two will become one flesh'? So they are no longer two, but one. Therefore what God has joined together, let man not separate."
>
> "Why then," they asked, "did Moses command that a man give his wife a certificate of divorce and send her away?"
>
> Jesus replied, "Moses permitted you to divorce your wives because your hearts were hard. But it was not this way from the beginning. I tell you that anyone who divorces his wife, except for marital unfaithfulness, and marries another woman commits adultery." (vv. 3–9)

Apart from how we handle marital conflict and divorce, the biblical norm for marriage set forth in Genesis 1–2 and Matthew 19 is one woman and one man until death separates them.[6] The biblical norm tells us how to live. Here it is worth drawing attention to the claim Jeffrey Satinover makes about homosexuality: science can tell us about *what is*; but the Bible tells us about *what should be*.[7] Even if someone believes his or her nature is structured a certain way or predisposed toward a certain end, that nature does not justify a sinful lifestyle. I may be predisposed toward a number of things, but I should not, dare not, act them out. Besides, given God's intended design in creation as revealed in Scripture, such "natural" or nurtured orientations or propensities should be viewed in light of the fall of humanity in Genesis 3. Some people may say that homosexual behavior is actually an "unnatural" sin. I disagree. On the one hand all sin is natural from the standpoint of our fallen condition. On the other hand all sin—not just homosexual behavior—is unnatural from God's standpoint. All sin reflects human failure to live in view of God's norms and ideals.

Sodom and Gomorrah

Consideration is often given to the story of Sodom and Gomorrah recorded in Genesis 19. Some pro-homosexual lifestyle interpreters argue that *yadah*, which means "to know" in this text, may be translated in a way that suggests to know *socially*, rather than *sexually*. It is further argued that the word is wrongly translated along sexual lines in this text.[8] In response, what does one make of Lot's suggestion to give his virgin daughters in place of his guests to the gang? It was certainly not so that Lot's daughters could serve beer and pretzels to the boys before the big game! Other interpreters claim that the text before us condemns aggression (rape), not homosexual behavior. Now the text certainly condemns aggression in the form of gang rape.[9] But that does not mean the text commends homosexual behavior along other lines.

Some interpreters claim that Scripture never explicitly mentions homosexuality in its condemnation of Sodom's wickedness.[10] In particular it is argued that when Jesus speaks of Sodom's sin in Matthew 10:14–15 and Luke 10:10–12, "he does so in the context of instructing his disciples on how to respond to inhospitality." It is important to note that the ancient Hebrew culture placed great importance on the sacred call to hospitality.[11] Having said that, inhospitality expresses itself in the crowd's homosexual desire to gang-rape the visitors. Robert Gagnon puts it well: "Ultimately . . . since the story is used as a type scene to characterize the depth of human depravity in Sodom and Gomorrah and thus to legitimate God's decision to wipe these two cities off the face of the map, it is likely that the sin of Sodom is not merely inhospitality or even attempted rape of a guest but rather attempted homosexual rape of male guests."[12]

Law of Moses

The Law is one of relation, not legalism. It is intended to promote sound relations between God and others within the created order, and so in this way, it transcends the Old Testament era (take, for example, the great and universal commands of relational harmony set forth by Jesus in Mark 12:30–31). Some commentators who believe that the Bible affirms (or at least does not condemn all forms of) homosexual behavior will argue that the Old Testament Law is out of commission today. This assertion certainly seems plausible from one angle. For example, what does one make of the Holiness Code in Leviticus? Paul Jewett and Marguerite Shuster set forth the difficulties surrounding this matter:

> Everyone agrees that homosexual acts (at least male homosexual acts) are unequivocally condemned and assigned the death penalty [in these texts]. The problem comes with the placement of these verses in the "Holiness Code," which intersperses matters of the highest ethical concern with those related to ritual purity, including proscriptions of wearing clothing made of mixed fibers or sowing one's land with two kinds of seed (19:19). That all these regulations had importance to Israel in keeping it separate from the customs and idolatrous practices of surrounding nations may be granted; but which remain valid today? Jesus abrogated the food laws. We take it as somehow "obvious" that blended fabrics and mixed crops are unobjectionable. Few see anything morally wrong with coitus during menstruation, forbidden along with homosexuality in Leviticus 18 and 20 and treated, it seems, as a moral and not just a ceremonial matter in Ezekiel 22. Where to draw the line between the moral and the ceremonial is by no means clear. Thus many evangelicals have felt some nervousness about relying in an unqualified way on these texts, even when what should be given weight and what should not *seems* self-evident. They have to acknowledge how strongly culture conditions these assumptions of self-evidence, manifested, for instance, in the tolerant views many have come to have of masturbation and oral sex—unthinkable, not so long ago, that these should be seen as permissible and even advocated by some affiliated with the conservative wing of the church.[13]

In spite of the complexity it is important to argue that those who would relativize such texts as the Holiness Code must still contend with the fact that Jesus gives strong affirmation to the whole Law in the Sermon on the Mount (Matthew 5:17–20). Moreover Paul takes the two Greek words in Leviticus, αρσενος (from αρσην—meaning "male") and κοιτην (from κοιτη—meaning "bed") to make one word, αρσενοκοιτης (meaning "sodomite, homosexual"). This is found in two places in the New Testament: 1 Corinthians 6:9 and 1 Timothy 1:10.[14] In the end, even if one believes there is radical discontinuity between the Mosaic Law and the New Testament witness at key points, the Old Testament Law is binding in those instances where the New Testament adopts and promotes the law in question. For example, the two great commandments are certainly universally binding (Mark 12:30–31), as are the Ten Commandments, according to the New Testament witness. These are not the only texts that are universally binding.

Jesus' Teachings

At this point the question arises in the minds of many: What did Jesus teach about this subject? Since he is the head of the church, it is critical that we consider what Jesus has to say. It is often argued that the Gospels do not record Jesus saying anything about homosexuality. While it is true that Scripture does not set forth explicit statements by Jesus about homosexuality, Jesus does hold up heterosexual union between two people for life as God's intent.[15] Divergence from this norm is adultery. By the way, the only exception in this text for remarriage is "marital unfaithfulness" (Matthew 5:32; 19:9). Jesus also speaks against sexual immorality in Revelation 22:15. In keeping with his charge for one woman to remain married to one man for all their life, all other forms of sexual behavior, including the lust of the eye (Matthew 5:28), are sin. Far from having a more lenient view of sexual behavior and attitudes, Jesus' remarks on sexual sin demonstrate that his view is more severe than the Old Testament's.[16]

Just because Scripture does not record Jesus as specifically saying anything about homosexuality, it does not exclude the possibility that Jesus spoke about the subject. Jesus said so much more than what is recorded in Scripture. Even though Scripture does not record Jesus as specifically saying anything about extreme acts such as bestiality, it would be a mistake to conclude from such silence that the Lord was in favor of these behaviors.

Given that we are dealing with arguments from silence, it is worth noting that there are no same-sex role models in Scripture. The claim that Jesus and his disciples or David and Jonathan had sexual relations with one another is to stretch inference beyond credulity. There is no piece of proof in favor of this stance. In the case of David and Jonathan, the context reveals that it was their mutual zeal for the Lord that bound them together with a love that was greater than that between a man and a woman (2 Samuel 1:26; cf. 1 Samuel 18:1). It was a spiritual-relational-brotherly union, not a sexual one. The idea that they had sexual relations with each other (sometime after 1 Samuel 18:1) would signify fornication. David would later marry Michal, Jonathan's sister, while her brother was alive (one could not use this as an example to promote monogamous homosexual relations).

Paul's Teachings

Moving on to Paul, some pro-homosexual lifestyle interpreters would argue that the exchange of natural for unnatural relations in Romans 1 refers not to those for whom homosexuality is natural but to those for whom heterosexual relations are natural but choose homosexual relationships.[17] From this perspective it is wrong for heterosexuals to engage in homosexual behavior. In response it is helpful to look to 1 Corinthians 6:9 and following, where Paul (who also authored Romans) distinguishes homosexual sin from adultery and sexual immorality. As Paul declares, "Or do you not know that wrongdoers will not inherit the kingdom of God? Do not be deceived: Neither the sexually immoral nor idolaters nor adulterers nor men who have sex with men . . . will inherit the kingdom of God" (1 Corinthians 6:9–10 UPDATED NIV). Paul is not making allowances for such forms of behavior; adulterers, sexually immoral people, *and* men who have sex with men— whatever the circumstances—are in grave danger.[18]

But what if we are speaking of monogamy? Would sexual immorality include monogamous homosexual relations? The argument is sometimes made that Paul and others were against illicit homosexual relationships, not monogamous (legal) ones.[19] However, one cannot find a shred of textual support in favor of this position in the Bible. In view of Paul's dependence on Genesis 1 and 2 for his exposition in Romans 1 and Ephesians 5, where he addresses homosexuality and marriage respectively, one cannot relativize

Paul's claims by arguing that he simply spoke by way of his cultural pre-suppositions.[20] Paul's condemnation of activities and behaviors commended or accepted by the Greco-Roman society at the time of writing suggests that Paul's response is to be taken as universally binding on the church, and not as a culturally relative reaction. If Paul is condemning something that is widely accepted in culture, he cannot be condemning it for cultural reasons. His condemnation of generally accepted activity must transcend that given culture. Given Paul's very clear and strong affirmation of marital union between one man and one woman, one cannot argue that the case for heterosexuality over against homosexual marital union is an argument from silence. Paul is very clear on the matter: marriage is to be between one man and one woman.

Moreover, Paul does not single out homosexual sin. Though Paul argues in 1 Corinthians 6:9–10 that those who engage in homosexual behavior (and other such sins) will not inherit the kingdom of God, he says the same thing about what we often consider to be "normal" or "good flesh" sins in Galatians 5:19–21. Good flesh and bad flesh are still flesh, neither of which will inherit the kingdom of God; God hates gluttony and greed too (though not the glutton or the thief). In this context consider Paul's claims in Romans 2:1 and following. We must read statements about homosexual sin, such as those found in Romans 1, against the backdrop of his overarching argument in texts such as Romans 3:23: "for all have sinned and fall short of the glory of God." Paul has a way of leveling everyone at the foot of the cross. Therefore, we should guard against one-upmanship in terms of grading various sins.[21]

HOMOSEXUALITY AND GOD

It is now time to step back from looking at the trees to get a panoramic view of the biblical forest: Why does the topic of sexuality and homosexuality matter so much to God? To answer that, we must move beyond what the text says to why the text says it. To answer the why question, it is important to note that God's love is creative, expansive. Procreation illustrates this reality and is bound up inseparably with it, although it does not image this reality exhaustively. Sin is the denial of such divine creativity and goodness. All sin is idolatry and involves a turning inward toward self away from God. While homosexuals often display sacrificial love, homosexual behavior does not signify the sacrificial love of "the other"—the sexually different—in marital union, which is bound up with marriage's imaging of the divine life that entails communion involving otherness (which is what we see in Eve being taken from Adam and given to Adam as his helpmate—one who is one with him as sexually different from him).

Moving on, we often think of God as male. If so, what does one do with Genesis 1 as it concerns the image of God? The created being, which is both male and female, bears witness to the relational and participatory makeup of the Godhead (the Father and Son share life with one another in the Spirit) in a way that no other human relation does. Differentiation and interpenetration, in which the Father and Son indwell one another in the Spirit, are part of wholeness in the Trinity. Differentiation and interpenetration of a kind are also true of the male-female relation in marriage. Our entire race's existence hinges on this male-female relationship, not male-male or female-female. Each of us is who we are as the result of the union between one man and one woman. Thus human identity throughout time, while including I-Thou relations such as friendships within a given gender, is founded upon and originates from the primal I-Thou relation of a man and woman.[22]

The male-female relation images something not found in Genesis. The Genesis 1–2 account foreshadows the union of Christ and the church in Ephesians 5 and Revelation 19. "The two will become one flesh"—Christ and the church—so woman is introduced to signify union within the image of God. The male-female relation not only bears witness to the divine reality of Father and Son in the Spirit but also images that which is to come—Christ and the church in the Spirit before God! Thus the male-female relationship images something not found in the Godhead prior to the drama of history. We find here an interpenetration of a new kind, not that of the Father and Son in the Spirit but that of Christ and the church in the Spirit, as imaged by husbands and wives to the glory of God. Indeed the man will leave his father and mother and be united to his wife, and the two will become one flesh, bearing witness to Christ and the church (Ephesians 5:31–32). Just as woman comes from man's side and returns to man as his sexual other, the church comes forth from Christ (in his saving work) and returns to him as his relational other.

Results of Sexual Sin

As important as it is that we discuss Scripture and theology, we must also account for relational scars. Certainly the Bible is concerned for such matters. People experience individual and familial scars through inappropriate sexual behavior. We are not spirits imprisoned in bodies. We are embodied souls. Sins against the body haunt us as individuals and those with whom we are intimate, unlike most if not all other sins. I am speaking here from personal experience. I experienced relational scars as a result of sexual promiscuity when I was younger. Such encounters scar us not only physically and emotionally but also spiritually. Paul speaks against inappropriate sexual behavior, heterosexual or otherwise, claiming that such behavior violates our spiritual union with Christ. May it never be! Only the marriage between a man and woman signals and foreshadows the mystical union with Christ (1 Corinthians 6:15–20).

It is important that we approach these issues relationally rather than behaviorally with people. I do not believe people's hearts change based on changing their behaviors. Relational problems require relational solutions. The whole "Get your act together, and then we will include you" orientation is behavioral, not relational, and is counterproductive to healing. We must engage sexual sin from the standpoint of relationality and spiritual union with Christ.

It is very difficult to engage our homosexual friends and acquaintances relationally. People in the church often are too uncomfortable to discuss the matter, and they often do not want to address this difficult topic in a gracious and loving way. Some want to make it a ministry for a select few. To those who would say, "It's not my ministry," or "This ministry is abnormal," I would say, "You fail to understand that we are called to love our neighbors— all neighbors—and every ministry is about ministering to those who fail to live into the fullness of what God intends for us."

It should be clear that relationships go beyond warm fuzzies. Relationships are often quite costly, especially when it concerns Jesus. Jesus does not promise us comfortable lives. But he does promise to comfort us. Jesus would have us care compassionately and sacrificially (moving beyond our comfort zones) for those who struggle with homosexuality inside and outside churches. He would also have us care compassionately and sacrificially for those with HIV/AIDS—heterosexual and homosexual alike. Jesus promises to comfort us as we comfort others. How are we doing today?

Historically the evangelical movement has failed miserably in its response to the HIV/AIDS epidemic. Donald Miller has claimed that the evangelical movement's historical lack of interest in HIV/AIDS as a social issue told the world, "If you don't do it our way, die. Just die. I don't want anything to do with you."[23] He was reacting to a figure Bono referenced in an interview with *Rolling Stone* magazine. Asked to comment on the evangelical movement, Bono said he was appalled by a 2001 study indicating that only 7 percent of evangelicals believed they needed to do something about the AIDS epidemic. Based on this information, Bono reached out and met with as many evangelical leaders as possible and exhorted them in view of Jesus' example in Scripture to get involved in contending against this modern-day leprosy. To his surprise and delight, these evangelical leaders did take redemptive action. Bono informed the interviewer that based on this dramatic change he now saw the evangelical movement as a redemptive agent in America with a healthy desire to transform the world.[24] Apart from the causes that lead to the disease—which are many—we must engage compassionately in view of the sacrificial, holy love of Christ. Gratefully, as Bono indicates, we are moving in this direction in various spheres.

We need to move beyond pointing the finger toward group participation whereby we stand in the gap on behalf of others (Ezekiel 22:30). No one should point a finger, especially if that person fails to lift a helping hand. When one points a finger, there are three more pointing back. We are all in this together. Thus we need to move past Jerry Falwell to Jesus, move beyond pointing the finger to standing in the gap with God on behalf of the people. Let us love the Lord God with all our hearts and our neighbor—whoever he or she may be—as ourselves, as Jesus instructs us in Luke 10.

Relating to Homosexuals

I will close with a story about one of my best friends and his neighbors, who are lesbians. Brad Harper is one of my colleagues at Multnomah University. When his neighbors and their two children moved in, he and his wife, Robin, tried to discern how they could love their new neighbors: "When they moved in, we engaged them in conversation, helped where we could, and treated them like we would anyone else."[25] Brad and Robin decided not to raise the subject of homosexuality, and they determined only to discuss it if their neighbors did. One day, one of the lesbian neighbors stopped Brad as he was on his way out the door and asked him what he taught at the university. When Brad indicated that he taught theology, she responded, "Oh, I love talking about theology because I'm still trying to find out exactly what my place is in this world."[26] Their ensuing conversation was deep and meaningful. She shared with Brad about painful experiences with the church and with individual Christians about her sexual orientation. He could tell that she wanted to know what he and Robin thought about her and her partner. (What Brad does not specify in his written account is that their lesbian neighbors had been troubled when they found out soon after moving in that Brad taught at Multnomah, a conservative Christian institution.) Here is how Brad responded to her:

> "My worldview on homosexuality, the one I get from the Bible, is very different from yours. But the Jesus of the Bible, the one who loves me and gave his life for me, says that I can honor God by loving my neighbor . . . we are so glad you are our neighbors. We want to be part of your lives and want you to be part of ours." [She] threw her arms in the air and yelled, "Yes!" Since that day we have been in each other's homes. We share food, tools, and yardwork. We have had several conversations about faith and sexuality. I believe they feel safe with us, as we do with them. As a believer in Jesus Christ, I pray that [my lesbian neighbors and friends] who do not profess faith in Christ, will one day be confronted with both his magnificent love and his absolute lordship. I pray that they will receive his gift of forgiveness and surrender every aspect of their lives to him, including their sexuality.[27]

Brad approaches his lesbian neighbors and friends as those created in the image of God. While he does not believe their sexual union reflects the glory of God, as humans they are "infinitely more capable of reflecting the glory of God" than anything else in creation. Brad does not view them as "disgusting, not-quite-human" or as "disgusting perverts," as he has heard others refer to homosexuals.[28]

In his written account of their relationship, Brad closes his reflections on the subject by asking and answering a question: "What does it mean for us to love our lesbian neighbors? We should simply love them as we would love anyone: Find needs and meet them, share our goods and homes, rejoice in the good things in their lives, share our stories of life and faith, and affirm God's love for them."[29] Brad goes on to say that we should never hide from the issue of homosexuality or make it a primary focus for the relationship. While Brad cannot affirm their homosexual union, he does affirm self-sacrificial love between humans wherever he finds it, and encourages us to do the same.

I share Brad's approach and views on the subject, and I admire him greatly. As you can tell, this is not an esoteric issue for Brad. What you don't know about Brad is that one of his own family members is gay. The pain his family member has experienced as a result of internal and external conflict and the pain that Brad experiences with him are severe and deep. In view of the Bible and in view of his personal experiences, Brad encourages us to speak out against speech that degrades homosexuals. He also encourages us that "while we must reject the idea that homosexual partnerships are marriages in the biblical sense, we must also be sensitive to social and legal benefits often kept from homosexuals. These are issues where compassion should lead us to address the problem—not by redefining marriage but by changing other laws."[30] As I see it, it is not a matter of affirming homosexual marriage, but of affirming fellow humans and fellow citizens' equal rights for such benefits as health care for the children raised by gay couples.[31]

Above and beyond laws we must deal case-by-case with individuals. As important as a biblical worldview is, we are dealing with particular persons who have unique stories and life experiences. There are various complexities bound up with homosexuality and various forms of it. The Bible cannot be taken to affirm homosexual behavior and marriage; however, the Bible does affirm loving our homosexual neighbor as ourselves.

Remember the story involving the Samaritan of incredible compassion recorded in Luke 10? Unlike the high-and-mighty Sodomites, whom the Bible denounces as inhospitable, here we find a lowly Samaritan who relates to others in a most hospitable manner. Jesus does not tell the Jewish religious leader in Luke 10 to think like the Samaritan or to follow the religious and cultural customs of the Samaritan but to sacrifice himself for his enemy as the Samaritan does when caring for the presumably Jewish man left for dead on the side of the road. Prior to the Samaritan man's arrival and help, two Jewish religious leaders pass by the left-for-dead man and choose not to help him. The rationale behind their failure to help is likely that they do not want to break the Law. From a letter-of-the-law standpoint, by touching and helping the man, they would become ceremoniously unclean and fear being displeasing to God. But by refusing to help him, they actually break the Law. The heart of the Law is to love one's neighbor as one's self. In this account, only the Samaritan truly obeys the Law. Only he is hospitable.

How would I want to be treated if I were left on the side of the road to die? How would I feel if I were a homosexual, maligned and treated with scorn? Wouldn't I want to be cared for and loved regardless of my sexual orientation? Indeed I would. How do I know? Because that is how I always want to be treated, no matter what differences exist between others and me. So I should do the same and treat others as I would have them treat me (Matthew 7:7–12). While I cannot affirm homosexual behavior and homosexual marriage based on Scripture, I must affirm caring for my homosexual neighbor based on Scripture's esteemed regard for hospitality. In fact, I must do more than affirm—I must care for my homosexual neighbor.

My hope for homosexuals is that they will come to experience God's healing mercy and love and enter into sexual wholeness. My hope for the church is that we will grow in hospitality and care for those in our midst who struggle with homosexual behavior. The church has come a long way in assisting alcoholics with their addictions, but we have a long way to go in terms of coming alongside and caring for those who struggle with sexual sin. I look forward to the day when pastors and other leaders can say publicly, "Here is Bobby (or Susan), who struggles with homosexuality and who wants to honor Jesus. We want to help him as he seeks to honor Jesus in his sexuality." One ministry that assists people wanting to leave behind a homosexual lifestyle in obedience to Christ has informed me that it is so difficult to find mature, sexually whole Christian believers who will come alongside and mentor these people. Instead of passing by them on the side of the road, we need to care for them, loving our neighbors as ourselves.[32]

CHAPTER 18

Beyond Ned Flanders and the Fascists

Do you know Ned Flanders of *The Simpsons*? He represents the stereotypical evangelical to many Americans: nice though naive. This view of those of us who are evangelical Christians is changing. Many of our critics view evangelicals as being more like Adolf Hitler or the fascists. In fact, one of my colleagues mentioned how even Rick Warren was labeled a fascist by a fellow scholar at a recent symposium. Why the change? A key reason for it is that many view evangelical Christianity as "the opponent of the common good," to quote Michael Spencer in his op-ed piece in the *Christian Science Monitor*.[1] Perhaps the greatest antagonist against religion in any form today was Christopher Hitchens, who in his book *God Is Not Great: How Religion Poisons Everything* speaks of religion's courtship with fascism over the centuries.[2]

Fascism and other related evils have indeed grievously marked the church throughout its history, as illustrated by the church's oppression of other faiths during the Inquisition, its association with the Hitler regime during the Holocaust, and its execution of "witches" in Salem, Massachusetts, in the 1600s, to mention but a few. Of course not all of the church was involved in committing evils during these times, and, in fact, many Christians gave themselves sacrificially in confronting the powers over these atrocities, as in the case of Dietrich Bonhoeffer. Nonetheless, fascist ways have horrifically impacted the church's witness over the centuries; such evils committed in the name of Jesus actually deny Jesus, failing to account for the triune God's identity, claims, and ways.

Freedom from Oppression

The triune God's identity revealed in the life, death, and resurrection of Jesus creates space for otherness because God has relational space within his own being for otherness. Over against fascist and totalitarian tendencies present in various monistic ideologies, which champion the one over the many, the triune God, whose being signifies unity in diversity, creates relational space so that we can be one yet many as God's people and give space to those outside the church to live freely in relation. It is important that God's people live into this reality and make relational space for otherness in sacrificial love, just as the triune God has made relational space for us in and through his holy, interpersonal love revealed in Christ through the Spirit.

In his treatment of divine omnipresence in the *Church Dogmatics*, Karl Barth writes of the danger of "the absolute non-spatiality of God." Barth goes on to state that "non-spatiality means existence without distance, which means identity." In contrast, "God possesses space, His own space, and that just because of His spatiality, He is able to be the triune, the Lord of everything else, and therefore the One in and over all things." Barth presupposes that there is no division between God in himself and God in his revelation in Jesus. This conviction is central to his claim about God being spatial in his divine being:

> If in and with His creation God is the same as He is in Himself, revealing Himself to us in His revelation as not less or other than Himself, then it is characteristic of Him to be here and there and everywhere, and therefore to be always somewhere and not nowhere, to be spatial in His divine essence.[3]

Going beyond Barth, it is as the triune God that God has space (and not simply because of his spatiality that he is able to be triune). Such spatiality must be viewed in relational rather than geometrical terms. God has relational space within his being as Father, Son, and Spirit in loving and holy communion from all eternity. God's space is the loving and holy communion of the three in relation. Given the event of revelation, wherein God becomes spatial in Jesus, we see that God has space within his self and therefore is able to make space for otherness outside himself. The Word becomes incarnate and takes up residence in our midst (John 1:14), winning us over not by oppression but by crucifixion and resurrection of life to a new state of being in and for the world. As Jesus declares of his own ensuing passion: "I tell you the truth, unless a kernel of wheat falls to the ground and dies, it remains only a single seed. But if it dies, it produces many seeds" (John 12:24). Lastly, the Spirit whom Jesus sends from the Father pours God's love into our hearts (Romans 5:5), not compelling us with brute force but winsomely appealing to us to respond in loving freedom to his call.

The church today must be attentive to God's engagement of the world. The apostle Paul certainly was. Whereas he sought to destroy Jesus and the church, enslaving and killing Christians before meeting Jesus on the Damascus Road, he later accepts Jesus and lays down his life for Christians as he is imprisoned on their behalf. Moved and compelled not by hostility but by the love of the crucified and risen Jesus who laid down his life for Paul (John 12:24; Galatians 2:20; Philippians 2:5–11), and animated by the Spirit through whom God's love is poured into his heart (Romans 5:5), Paul's life is poured out like a drink offering in love (Philippians 2:17; 2 Timothy 4:6). When the church is not attentive to this trinitarian trajectory and reality in word and deed, the door opens for oppression to occur in various forms. We must stick to our story and never change the script. We must not simply bear witness with true words but also in loving actions. How can it be otherwise when God's gracious and true Word became incarnate? The Word became deed.

For whatever reason, sticking to the script is easier said than done. Michael Buckley argues that Christian apologists in the medieval and modern eras failed to account for trinitarian frames of reference in their debates with their opponents; this failure was critical to the development of the modern doctrine of atheism. Beginning with Christian apologists' defense against Baruch Spinoza (whose naturalistic teachings on God, humanity, and the world won him censure from his Jewish community and harsh criticism from the church), Buckley writes,

> One of the many ironies of this history of origins [of modern atheism] is that while the guns of the beleaguered were often trained on Spinoza, the fortress was being taken from within.
>
> The remarkable thing is not that d'Holbach and Diderot found theologians and philosophers with whom to battle, but that the theologians themselves had become philosophers in order to enter the match. The extraordinary note about this emergence of the denial of the Christian god which Nietzsche celebrated is that Christianity as such, more specifically the person and teaching of Jesus or the experience and history of the Christian Church, did not enter the discussion. The absence of any consideration of Christology is so pervasive throughout serious discussion that it becomes taken for granted, yet it is so stunningly curious that it raises a fundamental issue of the modes of thought: How did the issue of Christianity vs. atheism become purely philosophical? To paraphrase Tertullian: How was it that the only arms to defend the temple were to be found in the Stoa?[4]

It is not simply a matter for theology and philosophy. We must also concern ourselves with theology and ethics. Christendom in its various guises often failed and fails to account for the power of the cross: God wins people to faith by laying down his life rather than by taking others' lives. Perhaps such refusal to take seriously the historic claims of Christianity and the church led to the abuses on the part of the church during the medieval and Reformation ages. Along these lines, I would point out that it is ironic, curious, and troubling that a movement that was persecuted for its faith became the persecutor for the faith during the medieval and Reformation eras. We need to stick to our script: proclaiming and worshiping the crucified and risen Jesus and being the persecuted rather than the persecutor.[5] With this in mind, it is certainly important that as Christian apologists we take seriously our christological and trinitarian convictions, but it is equally and exceptionally important that we live them out.

Buckley points out that for the noted atheist Naigeon, "of all religious convictions the deism preached by Voltaire and swallowed whole by the Revolution disclosed itself to be the most savage and the most intolerant."[6] In his reflection on Buckley's point, Colin Gunton adds, "An immense stress on the single God of deism—ironically, a theology derived by means of a criticism of trinitarian Christian theology—came to be associated with the most repressive behavior of all."[7] Later, when discussing immanence, Gunton notes that the theological legacies of Immanuel Kant, Georg Hegel, and Friedrich Schleiermacher bequeathed to us a theology of immanence that is more subversive to the well-being of the many than any form of transcendence. Gunton argues that it is not transcendence that is the enemy (which much of modern theology and philosophy has maintained) "but forms of the one that fail to give space to the many."[8]

Monism (all is one) in whatever form collapses everything into the ultimate, including (and perhaps especially) its atheistic or materialistic version. There can be no sufficient safeguarding the creaturely sphere if there is no ultimate space or mediation between the One and the many, as is the case with deism and pantheism. The lack of sufficient safeguards extends to atheism. For example, while fascism is certainly gross evil, the atheistic socialist Joseph Stalin (and possibly Mao Tse-Tung and Pol Pot) committed even greater monstrosities than the religious Hitler. By no means do I wish to make light of Hitler's horrific oppression of people. He was truly a horror of a human being. However, the religiously destructive person at least maintains a pretension of righteousness, even while treating everyone and everything as an extension of his or her own being as the One. Hitler supposedly had daily quiet times; he spoke in very religious terms of his empire, appealing to the God of the Aryan people, and he also made a compact with the German church (albeit a counterfeit of the true and confessing church). These pious forms, while used for grave and unspeakable injustices, perhaps safeguarded in certain ways further horrific abuses being committed due to Hitler's pretense of affirming deity and historic German Christianity. My basic point is that being nonreligious and collapsing transcendence into immanence, even removing deity, will not solve the problem; in fact, removing deity altogether removes as well any safeguards from multiplying abuse exponentially.

Modern atheism is not the only form of atheism concerned about fascism and other forms of totalitarianism. The early Christians were called atheists, for they did not worship the pantheon of the Roman gods. In fact, Christianity at its best is a denial of the gods—those deities who lord it over humanity. Christianity is religionless in the sense that we deal here with the God-forsaken God on the cross, as Bonhoeffer (the Christian martyr under the fascist Hitler) maintained. As such the Christian faith at its best is the problematizing of religion, just as it poses the ultimate problem for evil. God does not lord it over us. He sent his Son to die and rise from the grave for us in order to destroy sin and death, and he sent his Spirit to live in us, opening us up, making us spacious people in the face of evil's hostile absorption of all things into itself. When the Spirit reigns within us, instead of taking space from others, we are marginalized for them, laying down our lives for them, just as the Lord did and does. Here is what Barth has to say of God revealed in Jesus' incarnate existence:

> God shows Himself to be the great and true God in the fact that He can and will let His grace bear this cost, that He is capable and willing and ready for this condescension, this act of extravagance, this far journey. What marks out God above all false gods is that they are not capable and ready for this. In their otherworldliness and supernaturalness and otherness, etc., the gods are a reflection of the human pride which will not unbend, which will not stoop to that which is beneath it. God is not proud. In His high majesty He is humble. It is in this high humility that He speaks and acts as the God who reconciles the world to Himself.[9]

Elsewhere Barth writes, "It is only the heathen gods who envy man. The true God, who is unconditionally the Lord, allows him to be the thing for which He created him."[10]

Jesus lays down his life for all people, even his enemies. While monistic religion and irreligion in its various forms is the problem of evil, trinitarian theism poses problems for evil, for this form of theism consumes hostility and hatred in sacrificial love. Instead of repaying evil, Jesus allows evil to push him into the void outside the city's gates at Golgotha and into the tomb. Together with the Spirit, who fills the void in our hearts as he enters them as the agent of God's love, Jesus saves us not only from dictators and fascist forces but also from the libertarian freedom of limitless choice that leads to self-consumption and oppression. Through the Spirit, Jesus lays down his freedom for us in love so that we might be set free in his embrace.

The acclaimed novelist Jonathan Franzen speaks of the problems with limitless choice and freedom in his book *Freedom*. One of his main characters, Patty, ponders her freedom and discovers that she "had all day every day to figure out some decent and satisfying way to live, and yet all she ever seemed to get for all her choices and all her freedom was more miserable."[11] In an interview with *Time* magazine, Franzen reasons that the freest person in the world is the individual with no moral values. "One of the ways of surrendering freedom is to actually have convictions." He adds, "And a way of further surrendering freedom is to spend quite a bit of time acting on those convictions." While freedom for Franzen is important, there is more to life than freedom. The interviewer remarks, "There is something beyond freedom that people need: work, love, belief in something, commitment to something. *Freedom* is not enough. It's necessary but not sufficient. It's what you do with freedom—what you give it up for—that matters."[12]

Freedom in Oppression

An American ethicist friend of mine who ponders the theme of freedom and the good life for a living as a seminary professor recently told me of a trip to Africa, where he, his daughter, and a missionary friend were robbed by a band of armed thugs while on their way to a slum to care for people in need. When they arrived at the slum, which was virtually a septic tank of raw sewage, and told the pastor there about their misfortune, he apologized profusely for what had happened to them. As the pastor grieved, he also shared of how he and his people are often robbed by similar bands of thugs, and that they pray that God will speak to their oppressors of his love for them and their need for Jesus as they spend his own and his people's money and use what they have taken from them. My friend said that he realized how different his value system was from this African pastor. When the thugs steal these African Christians' money, food, and belongings, these Christians offer up their prayers on empty stomachs and with bare backs. He, on the other hand, can simply go to the closest ATM machine and get replenished. These African Christians in this slum have very little freedom, especially when robbed at gunpoint; however, they are freer than we could ever imagine.

Whether it is being robbed by armed thugs in an African slum or hanging from a cross at Golgotha or being stoned to death outside the city's gates as Saul watched over the killers' belongings (Acts 7:58) or being chained in prison for the faith that sets people free through God's love, this is the kind of freedom to which true followers of Jesus aspire. Jesus cried out to his Father to forgive his enemies (Luke 23:34) and Stephen cried out the same to Jesus (Acts 7:60).

What about those who make others die for their causes and ambitions? I wonder if Hitler and Napoleon were not loved as children. I wonder if we "fascist" Christians who react and attack our political and cultural and atheistic enemies for harming us have come to terms with God's love that heals us of our wounds. Small people—small and wounded on the inside—cannot and will not make space for others, but can only take back America from their enemies. This has pertinence for any individual or movement inside or outside the church. Discerning followers of Jesus do not seek to take back America from their enemies by lobbying for one's own kind of people over against the common good; they lay their lives down for others, including their enemies, for the uncommon God who seeks after the common good of all.[13] We fight not as the world fights, and our battle is not with flesh and blood, but with the spiritual forces of evil in the heavenly realms (Ephesians 6:12). We wrestle through the Word and in prayer, not compelling people by force but loving them and appealing to them in view of God's mercies to be reconciled to God. Discerning Christians evangelize, not by pushing but by leading people to Christ, as one of my Buddhist friends so wisely stated.

True Christian faith centered in the Jesus revealed in the Bible is not the problem of evil. Rather it poses problems for evil because the love of the crucified and risen Jesus consumes evil and its self-absorbed ways of hatred in view of the Father's embrace of Jesus and Jesus' embrace of us in the Spirit. Jesus' followers wage war with compelling love that appeals to people through prayer as we take up our crosses to die to ourselves and live for God in true freedom, creating space so that others might live.

In discussions of Beethoven's *Eroica* the story is often told that Beethoven originally dedicated the piece to Napoleon for his creation of the French Republic, only to retract the dedication later after Napoleon declared himself emperor. Beethoven remarked that Napoleon was no more than a man after all. Not only was Napoleon small on the outside; he was small on the inside as well. In light of Jesus it is right to say that it is only a great person and a great God who will serve others. Common people as well as common gods will promote their own agendas and self-serving interests when given the chance.[14] One who has space within oneself is free to give space to others. One who has no such space must seek to find it by taking it from others. Only the true God, who has triune relational space within himself, grants space.

I don't mind if our cultural enemies call us Christians naive, but may they not call us nice, for nice won't lead us to die for our enemies. Only Jesus' selfless love will lead us to do that. And may they not call us fascist, for the sacrifice of oneself for one's enemies is the death of fascism, not its advance. I hope and pray that they will call us common followers of an uncommon God who lays down his life for his enemies and grants space to them in the freedom of his love.

PART IV

Responses from Diverse Traditions

CHAPTER 19

RESPONSE TO "THE JEWISH QUESTION"

Adam Gregerman

The dramatic contemporary changes in many Christians' views of Jews and Judaism have minimally affected evangelical Christians. While many Catholics and mainline Protestants have reevaluated millennia of anti-Jewish Christian teachings, evangelicals have often remained on the sidelines. Among the various reasons for this is the nature of the reevaluation. Other Christians' rejection of anti-Judaism prompts painful and even radical questions about, for example, exclusivist views on salvation, missions to the Jews, and the covenant between God and Israel. Evangelical beliefs about salvation through Christ alone and proselytism are potentially undermined by affirmations of the legitimacy of Judaism after the coming of Jesus. It is tempting for many evangelicals to dodge the hard questions raised by Judaism and especially by Jewish rejection of Christian claims.

I therefore welcome Paul Louis Metzger's essay and the chance to respond to it. While there remain profound and even unbridgeable disagreements between us, our honest and sometimes tough discussions are an achievement to celebrate. He plumbs some of the core theological issues that relate to Jews and Judaism, opening up a dialogue that should be encouraged. Though I have limited space to reply, this context is important, for my criticisms below should not detract from my endorsement of the project. My comments are intended to cultivate a more sympathetic awareness of what matters deeply to the other, especially as the Jewish-evangelical relationship takes its next steps.

I want to focus on a few tensions in the essay, beginning with Metzger's assessment of Judaism. He insists on the inherent and enduring value of Judaism, in which "God is at work." Briefly, he mentions the Jews' "profound sense of mystery, observance of Torah, and celebration of life" despite suffering. However, the bulk of his essay is an exploration of the claim that Jewish existence *as such* is essential for Christian faith. Jewish religious life, by contrast, is seldom mentioned. The closest he gets to an extended discussion of this inherent value of Judaism is his discussion of Jewish suffering (though it is largely connected with questions about Christ's passion). While it is not illegitimate to consider Judaism as he does—he is, after all, a Christian theologian—his praise for the value of Jewish survival sits awkwardly alongside the little attention actually given to Judaism itself. In light of his affirmations, then, I miss a fuller exploration of the ways that his faith life is enriched by contact with Jews and Judaism. He need not affirm Judaism's ultimate truth. However, I yearned for more reflection on Judaism as a "living tradition" and a vibrant covenantal reality beyond its relevance to claims about Jesus.

A related tension is present in Metzger's claim that Jews and Christians are "inseparably bound together." On the one hand, this has admirable practical implications. Christians are obligated to care about Jewish safety and security. I would add that this humanitarian obligation holds for Jews as well, in a duty to pursue social justice jointly with and in concern for Christians who face religious and social discrimination, most especially in places where they live as vulnerable minorities.

On the other hand, while I welcome Metzger's honest desire not only to end Jews' suffering but if necessary "to suffer with them," I am discomfited by his motivation. His emphasis on the threat to Christian belief posed by the suffering of the Jews reflects an overly abstract and theological rather than humanitarian or secular motivation for preventing this. He says Jewish

persecution and even extermination would be a victory for religious nihilism and would abrogate the "ontic basis for [Christians'] existence." I do
not want to offer a false dichotomy and deny any humanitarian motivation
for Metzger. However, the prominence given to theological justifications, in
which Jewish existence serves to safeguard Christian claims, is unsettling,
especially in light of our anguished history. Abrupt shifts in Christian theology, as Metzger rightly notes, have often entailed dangerous practical
consequences for Jews. My concern reflects my wariness of Christian theological scenarios in which Jews are assigned roles they did not ask for, even
ones favorable to Jews. I'd therefore prefer to see Christians emphasize an
ethical basis that honors and protects Jewish life.

Finally, on the freighted topic of the status of the Jewish covenant with
God, Metzger's views are puzzling. In a break with centuries of Christian
teaching, he accepts the Jewish no to Jesus without rancor and resentment.
Even more, he boldly insists, citing Paul, that God will "never" reject the
Jews despite their "unbelief." However, without further explanation, he
fails to explore the implications of this supposedly unconditional divine
acceptance. Are Jews ultimately saved even if they refuse to believe in Jesus?
In light of his insistence on Jesus as their "destiny," it seems unlikely that
unbelieving Jews can escape condemnation. If he expects that a "day will
come" when Christ will return and will be recognized by all, God's acceptance of the Jews seems not to be eternally unconditional, but only temporary.
That is, Jews will be expected to recognize Jesus and convert. If they do not,
how could rejection not follow? Metzger, like Paul before him, seems unable
to reconcile two (perhaps irreconcilable) claims. His defense of the Jewish
covenant is noteworthy but only partial, for his insistence that salvation is in
Christ alone—even at the end of days—must inevitably include the demand
that Jews cease to be unbelievers or face divine rejection. My enthusiasm for
his defense of the Jewish covenant is diminished by the idea that Jews must
eventually change their no to a yes.

I appreciate the generous invitation to respond to Metzger's essay. I
hope that my critical comments can be constructive. This young relationship between Jews and evangelicals is important to both communities and
will rest on a firmer foundation when we engage in frank and serious discussions. Rather than seek out simplistic areas of commonality, it is precisely

this type of inquiry—delving into complex and even painful issues—that holds the most promise for growth and learning.

Dr. Adam Gregerman is Jewish Scholar in Residence at the Institute for Christian and Jewish Studies and affiliate professor of theology at Loyola University Maryland in Baltimore.

CHAPTER 20

Response to "Whack Jobs"

Richard Reno

As I watch the campaigns during this political season from the comfort of my living room, during commercial breaks, I can't help but be disgusted by spin doctors on both sides attempting to convey to voters through a fifteen-second sound bite a solution to complex problems or an attack on their opponents' records and/or characters. The aim of these ads is either to activate the party base or convince a few independents to swing their way, with little or no concern for convincing their opponents.

Similar tactics have been employed in today's religious dialogues. Offensive terms such as "Crusaders" or "Islamists" are frequently used to describe one another as both sides attempt to preach to the choir and convince the uneducated among their respective parties to view the other as an extreme whole. How could one ever expect to sit down and have an honest and productive theological dialogue after creating such a hostile environment? Should the debate be over our own human weaknesses or the identity of the perfect God?

Dr. Metzger has done an excellent job of refocusing the dialogue to where it needs to be: on religion and away from politics. There is often a dual motivation of one's religion and politics as the influence of politics creeps into one's religious beliefs and principles. This melding of beliefs seems to harm both: diluting the concepts of kindness and compassion taught in all faiths and strengthening the division and conflict that are often seen in politics. Dr. Metzger rightly points out that this only increases hostility and enflames the "clash of cultures."

Drawing attention to the extreme elements of any religious or political perspective introduces a level of dishonesty to the dialogue because such attention is merely an attempt to misrepresent the faith of others with the views of a small minority. This dishonesty creates an atmosphere of distrust, which then makes religious dialogue all the more difficult. In order for fruitful dialogue to occur, it is important that we show respect and compassion for one another and create honest and genuine friendships. Dr. Metzger shares a nice story of a person who is doing just that, and as a result he is able to have a productive dialogue with someone who would have been hostile had he not shown those qualities or invoked his political views. There is certainly a need to engage face-to-face over tea so that we can see each other as human rather than stereotyping one another from a distance, which leads to animosity and warfare. It is only then that we can understand one another and self-reflect to see our own shortcomings, whether on a personal or national level.

Only when this honest and civil dialogue occurs can we begin to understand the real teachings of one another's faith. Then discussion on the real disagreements between Islam and Christianity can begin. This is when Christians can begin to understand why Muslims do not accept the death of Jesus on the cross, but rather accept him because God testified to his truth by saving him from his persecutors. A true prophet being killed (such as on the cross) is not acceptable to us as Muslims. It would be a sign of defeat. Thus we cannot accept the cross as central to our way of life and faith. Moreover, Christians can also begin to understand why Muslims believe that salvation does not depend on shedding the blood of the innocent, but on God's forgiveness through his principal attributes of grace and mercy. This is where the real discussion needs to begin, and let's keep the whack jobs out of it.

Richard Reno is the president of the Ahmadiyya Muslim Community of Portland, Oregon.

CHAPTER 21

RESPONSE TO "THE JESUS BOX"

Prema Raghunath

Dr. Metzger's article seeks to address issues that are germane to both Christianity and Hinduism.

First, I would like to clarify a few facts:

1. Hinduism is not an exclusivist religion, though, obviously, it has its share of fundamentalists as every religion does.
2. It is impossible to convert to Hinduism except through some reformist groups.
3. The cornerstone of Hinduism is tolerance for all religions.
4. Hinduism requires all its practitioners to attain individual spirituality before looking to "save" others.

Names are important in the Hindu tradition, and the idea of a god with form is as relevant as one without form. However, in the final stages of realization, name and form dissolve into Brahman, which is present in all living beings.

Two very important components of the religious experience are *bhakti* ("love of God") and *shraddha* ("faith"). Armed with these two beliefs, the ultimate aim of a human being, Sri Ramakrishna said, should be realizing God as a vital, living Presence in one's life.

Dr. Metzger displays great concern for those of other paths, who are really wayfarers with the same destination. Yes, it is true that it is a fundamental belief in Hinduism that the *atman* must dissolve in the *paramatman* because they are one and the same. The goal of human life is to realize this. However, Dr. Metzger's desire for his friend Bharat to "enter the fullness of life through Jesus" is contradictory to his assertion that he is willing to accept Bharat as he is. To a Hindu, this would smack of religious arrogance, and religion is certainly not about one-upmanship. To say that my God or my set of beliefs has greater power than yours to lead human beings forward in life's journey is certainly not within the beliefs of Hinduism.

Whether one thinks that, ultimately, there is face-to-face communion with God or dissolving (not disappearing!) into the ocean of eternity is a deeply personal choice and must be made with honesty and sincerity.

This article displays sympathy for Hinduism but not empathy or knowledge, which I define as processed information that leads, finally, to wisdom. Religious wisdom must have for its goal a total acceptance of every path.

Prema Raghunath is head of the English Department at M. CT. M Chidambaram Chettyar International School in Tamilnadu, India.

CHAPTER 22

RESPONSE TO "THE DEWDROP WORLD"

Kyogen Carlson

I appreciate my good friend Dr. Metzger's invitation to respond to this essay. As he says here, I do see evangelicals demonstrating great personal interest in their connection with others. I have also told him that many who find their way to Zen are refugees from the consequences when that interest is saturated with too much zeal. In turn, Paul praised the tolerance we Buddhists are known for, yet it is true that we can err on the side of coolness when detachment is excessive. So I agree with Paul that we can learn from each other, and in fact we have gained a great deal from our friendship within our differences.

The personal and the eternal are two themes Paul stresses in his essay. I see him approaching the eternal through the personal. I wouldn't say that our way is the opposite of that, exactly, but it is very different. When I let go of my personal, limited preferences and attachments, I open to something greater. My body relaxes, my heart warms, and I can turn toward the world in an open way. It responds and returns that warmth. Is this personal or not? Each moment is a new expression of this experience, so we call it *impermanent*. Yet it is also known as "eternal now." This effort, moment by moment, is how we find the Bodhisattva quality with which we engage the world. Personally, I think Issa understood that very well. There is warmth and kindness as he shows us his wounds. I humbly suggest it is a mistake to read too much into his wistfulness. Passages from St. Teresa of Avila's or Mother Teresa's diary can be used in powerful arguments against the efficacy of Christianity. Would they agree with them?

I once spoke about Zen meditation to a comparative religion class at a local Christian university. Afterward the professor asked me why we focus so much on the here and now. "What about eternity?" he asked. My answer was that if eternity is *all* of time, every bit of it, how can here and now be anything other than eternity? The only way to fully appreciate heaven or any "here and now" is to be fully present in it. Cultivating that attention is what our meditation is about.

Thinking of eternity as somewhere other than here and now is similar to seeing God as "other," and seeking salvation through someone or something else. I've found that some people open up to the sacred more readily when it is located in a sacred "other" and have trouble understanding it as immanent and always present. Some, like we Buddhists, are just the opposite. For us, going through an "other" is an awkward extra step. Perhaps the cataphatic and apophatic traditions arise in Christianity because people are just wired differently. I was raised as a Christian and struggled with the message. When I found Buddhism it made sense immediately. I felt as if I had found my own tribe and discovered my native language. Through it I have learned to appreciate Christianity much better. In closing, I say to my Christian friends, "go in peace" and find your way. May it go well. Please allow us to do the same.

Kyogen Carlson is co-abbot of Dharma Rain Zen Center in Portland, Oregon; a transmitted Soto Zen priest; and author of Zen in the American Grain *(Station Hill Press).*

CHAPTER 23

RESPONSE TO "WILL THE REAL JESUS PLEASE STAND UP—AND SIT DOWN?"

Marilyn Sewell

I appreciate Dr. Metzger's carefully reasoned essay in response to the talk I gave at the Multnomah Biblical Seminary, and I further appreciate his generosity in asking me to comment on his essay. In all our encounters, I have found him unfailingly profound of thought and generous of spirit.

In reading Dr. Metzger's essay, I found that we agree on much. A major theme of his essay is that according to the Bible, Jesus cares about the despised and rejected of this world. What was surprising to me is that Metzger feels obliged to convince Christians—Christians of any stripe—of this most obvious of conclusions. Have some evangelical Christians really come so far afield, so detached from Jesus and from the gospel?

Metzger also agrees with me that we must guard against moralism and piety. He believes, however, that I show a strong antinomian streak in my declaration, "Love trumps every law, every rule." What I was trying to say, perhaps awkwardly, is that the law of love is primary. It is the container and the arbiter, as it were, for all other law. When the law is called into question—e.g., should the disciples heal on the Sabbath?—then the primary law, the law of love, should prevail. Likewise, when the Mosaic law conflicts with the law of love—e.g., the law on stoning for adultery and various other sexual sins (Deuteronomy 22:20–24)—the law of love takes precedence.

The problem with treating law as the ultimate refuge is that people, fallen as we are, so easily interpret laws to our own benefit, and we use them as a club to condemn and punish others, rather than to assess our own shaky spiritual state. As Metzger so rightly points out, we shape Jesus according to our own upbringing and political orientation.

The only real difference between Dr. Metzger and me—and it is a significant one—is that we disagree about the nature of Jesus. Metzger quotes from Matthew 7:21–27 and says that Jesus is endowed with the very saving power and authority of God himself—i.e., Jesus *is* God. But this is Matthew speaking, scholars believe, not Jesus.

Jesus never said that he was God. Jesus never quizzed anyone about their theology. Though John the Baptist and Paul had an apocalyptic view of history, Jesus did not. In Jesus' sayings and parables the kingdom of God is always here and now. But we human beings—ever fearful of death and nonbeing, with guilt built into the human psyche—create the Jesus we need, a god who will save us.

What Jesus did ask us to do is to love God and to love our neighbor as ourselves (our neighbor meaning anyone in need of mercy). Given human fears and projections, this is the most difficult of commandments. And yet if we can keep this commandment as the star that we move toward, we needn't be so concerned about personal salvation and reaching heaven. We're headed there already.

Rev. Dr. Marilyn Sewell is the minister emerita at First Unitarian Church in Portland, Oregon, where she served as senior minister for seventeen years. Marilyn is known as a speaker and writer and social justice advocate. She is the subject of the documentary film Raw Faith, *which has garnered critical acclaim and has its television release in April 2012. She currently writes for* Huffington Post *and is touring with her film.*

CHAPTER 24

RESPONSE TO "THE BURNING BOSOM"

Robert L. Millet

According to sociologist Rodney Stark, Mormon founder Joseph Smith possessed a "creative imagination" that manifested itself in "ideas connected with what is deepest and most central in human experience, with special reference to the particular needs of their day and generation."[1] From a Latter-day Saint perspective, Joseph Smith, under divine direction, sought to reclaim the God of the ancients, the true God of the Old and New Testaments, first by renouncing the god of the philosophers, the distant deity and unknowable god of the neo-platonists. Fuller Seminary's Richard J. Mouw points out that Joseph's pronouncements and scriptural records seemed to represent a kind of "reduce-the-distance theology" that emerged "in an environment shaped significantly by the high Calvinism of New England Puritanism. I think it can be plausibly argued that New England theology, while rightly (from an orthodox Christian perspective) stressing the legitimate metaphysical distance between God and his human creatures, nonetheless at the same time fostered an unhealthy spiritual distance between the Calvinist deity and his human subjects. Thus it should not surprise us that movements arose to shrink the spiritual distance."[2]

Joseph Smith revealed a God who is approachable, knowable, and even comprehendible; a God with body, parts, and passions; a God who is the Father of the spirits of all men and women (Numbers 16:22; 27:16; Hebrews 12:9). Joseph unveiled a God who is fully divine and truly omnipotent, omniscient, and, by the power of His Spirit, omnipresent. A Being who possesses every divine attribute in perfection. Nevertheless, the God he revealed is material, has form and shape, and is in fact an exalted Man of Holiness. He is more than the ground of being, more than a holy essence, more than a great first cause, far more than a collection of laws. He was and is the Holy One who delights to reveal Himself—His mind and will and divine purposes—to His children. He is an actual Father in heaven, not a power in the great beyond who could only be conjured through philosophical speculation and the formulation of theological creeds.

For Latter-day Saints, true religion, revealed religion, is all about relationships: with God who is our Father in heaven in actuality, not myth or metaphor; with Jesus Christ through accepting and applying his atoning blood and thereby becoming members of the family of the Almighty by adoption and regeneration; with the Holy Spirit, the sanctifying and revelatory means by which we gain the mind of Christ (1 Corinthians 2:16); with all of humanity as our brothers and sisters in the most literal sense. Indeed, Mormons believe in the true Fatherhood of God and the actual brother- and sisterhood of man. Joseph Smith and his followers have sought to reclaim humanity's divine birthright and to reacquaint and re-link the human family, for, as Joseph Smith boldly declared in 1844, "If men do not comprehend the character of God, they do not comprehend themselves."[3]

Robert L. Millet is Abraham O. Smoot University Professor and professor of religious education at Brigham Young University.

CHAPTER 25

RESPONSES TO "ALL IN"

Thomas W. Clark

I appreciate the opportunity to comment on Paul Louis Metzger's challenge in "All In" to act in accordance with our worldviews. He makes many good points, but atheists (more broadly, naturalists) need not follow Nietzsche in abandoning conventional morality to live consistently with the claim that God is dead. Absent God, morality survives in us.

He is right that pragmatic grounds for belief are insufficient. We want to know what's true independent of what it might benefit us to believe, otherwise we might well deceive ourselves. This means putting epistemology first: What constitutes reliable grounds for belief? Theism and naturalism differ in their epistemic commitments, and from there diverge in their claims about the world.

Naturalists believe, on the basis of empiricism, that there is likely nothing supernatural, so no extra-natural foundations for morality exist. Instead, we find our moral instincts to be just that: hardwired dispositions for fairness, reciprocity, caring for the young and helpless, not inflicting unnecessary harm, and other naturally selected other-regarding propensities that make social life possible. Nietzsche's big mistake was to disown the moral side of human nature, to condemn it as a hindrance to total self-actualization. There's no reason naturalists must follow him in this, and I know of no contemporary secular philosophers who endorse the unchecked will to power as a force for good. If there are such, I will join Metzger in repudiating them.

That we are by nature moral creatures (and yes, selfish too) is why naturalists believe we don't need supernatural backup to justify the rightness of self-sacrifice. Generosity feels good, and is judged virtuous, because evolution has made concern for others one of our primary, basic values by which we evaluate action. This is why Republicans and the Right ignore economic inequality at their peril: their apparent lack of concern for the unlucky in life puts them in a morally untenable position as we instinctively judge it.

For Metzger good works only have meaning and value if God exists. The reduction in suffering here on earth isn't an intrinsic good, despite the manifest importance people place on reducing their suffering right now. This, perhaps, is why Metzger is humbled by atheists' altruism: they apparently don't need cosmic justification for good works, so their concern is in a sense more authentic, more direct. Altruistic naturalists are just doing what comes naturally, as they see it. And they are being epistemically consistent: since life on earth is all we reliably know we have, we can and should be fully engaged with terrestrial suffering.

The essential safeguard against nihilism, something Metzger thinks can only come from God, exists in the robust moral inclinations of each normally endowed human being. But because we are also naturally selfish, it's of course nearly impossible to go completely "all in" for the other. The tension between self-actualization and meeting the basic needs of others presents an inescapable moral dilemma that not even a god could resolve. Naturalists don't have it easy, but we are pretty sure it is real.

Thomas W. Clark is founder and director of the Center for Naturalism and author of Encountering Naturalism: A Worldview and Its Uses. *He hosts Naturalism.org, a comprehensive resource on worldview naturalism and its basis, implications, and applications.*

Austin Dacey

One of the worst things about being an atheist is not knowing whom to thank. Paul Louis Metzger thanks God for the apostle Paul and for Nietzsche. If I could sincerely thank God for Dr. Metzger, I would, for I appreciated reading his rich and engaging chapter on Nietzschean atheism. Instead, I should thank Dr. Metzger. And perhaps his parents. No doubt there are countless others who made their contributions to his life—some, like Paul Isihara, remarkable and indispensable, and others imperceptible even to their beneficiary. Hence the atheist's problem.

Some atheists also have a problem with humility. The chapters of Nietzsche's *Ecce Homo* were "Why I Am So Wise," "Why I Am So Clever," "Why I Write Such Excellent Books," and "Why I Am a Fatality." Dr. Metzger does not have a problem with humility. He is humble enough to say that he is failing to do what he believes he is called to do as a Christian. He is even humble enough to say that he is humbled by those atheists whose sacrificial care for others exceeds his own. The problem with these atheists, he says, is that they are inconsistent. They are not going "all in."

I want to believe that I am one of those atheists who aspires to live for others, to do what he can so that others might live more abundantly. Though I continually fall short of this aspiration, am I inconsistent for having it? I can think of worse things. Human beings are not axiomatic systems on which disaster descends at the first violation of the Law of Non-Contradiction. Couldn't an atheist's life of service to others be more valuable, admirable, and humbling for others to behold than a theist's life of selfishness, even if the atheist's life were "inconsistent"?

Philanthropic Nietzschean atheists may be inconsistent, but not all atheists are Nietzscheans, nor need they be. I am not a Nietzschean, at least not on Dr. Metzger's reading of Nietzsche, because I do not believe that in affirming life we must scorn the weak, the sick, the timid, and the slow. So, I am not acting contrary to my moral commitments. What would Dr. Metzger have to say about such atheists?

He could say that we have no reason to love our neighbors. This would make sense of his claim that self-sacrificing atheists are "not cutting off all ties to a Christian worldview." Now, unless one simply stipulates that any ethic of universal benevolence is a *Christian* ethic—which would, of course, beg the question against atheists, not to mention Jews or Jains—then one must hold that only Christianity gives one reasons to love one's neighbor. I found no argument for such a conclusion on these pages. Instead, I found the wise suggestion that the best life is "based not on quantitative rewards or punishments but on the reward of loving my neighbor." After all, Jesus wasn't a Christian. Yet he found in the downtrodden, the weak, and the despised something worthy of love. Let's give credit where credit is due.

Austin Dacey, PhD, is the author of The Secular Conscience: Why Belief Belongs in Public Life *and* The Future of Blasphemy: Speaking of the Sacred in an Age of Human Rights. *He is a representative to the United Nations for the International Humanist and Ethical Union. His website is www. austindacey.com.*

CHAPTER 26

RESPONSE TO "AVATAR"

Gus diZerega

Paul Louis Metzger's critique of me as a representative neo-pagan panentheist is a sincere and good-hearted effort to address my arguments from a Christian perspective. It is a pleasure to read. Critics such as Metzger deepen our understanding whether we are convinced or not. I hope I demonstrate equal fairness and open-heartedness.

As I read him, Metzger's criticisms fall into three basic areas: the weaknesses of panentheism; problems addressing evil, individuality, and freedom from a monistic perspective; and the supremacy of Scripture over experience. Any of these topics could generate a book, and I hope my brief replies will at least orient my readers toward a deeper understanding of how pagans might address these issues.

PANENTHEISM

Metzger quotes Kallistos Ware approvingly elsewhere in his essay, and so I shall as well: "While present everywhere in the world, God is not to be identified with the world. As Christians we affirm not pantheism but 'panentheism.'"[1] Ware also writes, "The whole universe is a cosmic Burning Bush, filled with the divine Fire yet not consumed."[2] Metzger's problem with panentheism is a problem between himself and Christians on whom he relies as authorities as well as a problem with pagans such as me.

MONISM

Panentheism is a kind of monism, and in important respects I think the doctrine of the Trinity is subject to objections remarkably similar to those he makes of pagan monists. In the Trinity we have a monotheism that claims the One is also Three *distinct* and therefore *individual* entities: Father, Son, and Holy Spirit. Since Metzger is neither Jewish nor Muslim, his deriving three individuals from One seems to me to settle this argument in my favor. But I will elaborate a little.

Even mundane phenomena such as photons manifest genuine individuality with a genuine lack thereof depending on the question you ask. Subjected to some tests, a photon manifests as an individual particle; other tests indicate it is a wave. From a human perspective a photon unites two incompatible concepts. Photons do not care.

From one perspective God (to use the Christian term) manifests as the One, and in some mystical experiences even as the NonDual. But from another perspective God manifests as love, which requires the beloved, and hence duality. To maximize the possible expressions of love, a universe of unimaginable variety and individuality *must* exist. Confusions arise when answers to one kind of question are applied to instances where different questions elicit different answers.

EVIL AND INDIVIDUALITY

I will apply these insights to a few issues Metzger raises. To be an individual there must be that which you are not, and so individuals are necessarily limited. Limited beings have limited knowledge, and so can err. Because of this what we call evil can arise from non-evil origins.

I imagine all of us have been upset with a person's words or actions, only to discover we were ill-informed or misunderstood. Upon learning so, our annoyance with that person evaporated. But what if we did not learn we were wrong? We might have become cold and distrustful. The other, innocent of wrongdoing, would then react negatively toward us, confirming our suspicions in our own minds. If this process escalated, as it sometimes does, what we call evil acts would result, all based on misperceptions on both sides.

The individuality required to experience and give love guarantees error, misunderstanding, and often nasty acts. Wisdom can prevent this, but limited beings become wise over time by learning from theirs and others' mistakes. A world where love can manifest in as many ways as possible, and as richly, is paradoxically a world where error and malice can and probably will arise. Error and malice are redeemed, the resulting love deepened, through compassion and genuine forgiveness, which I think is Christianity's most valuable contribution to the world's spiritual tapestry. "'Father, forgive them, for they do not know what they are doing'" (Luke 23:34).

Babies, children, even baby animals, are often loving, playful, and innocent. As experience trumps innocence they become far less open and far more calculating. Speaking for humans, this loss of innocence opens up the possibility for a qualitatively deeper love, deepened by wisdom and compassion. The loss of innocence can, and I think will, lead to a ripening and deepening of love.

As an alternative, Metzger argues self-love is the cause of evil, but I do not know what he means. The Old Testament says, "Love your neighbor as yourself" (Leviticus 19:18). Jesus repeats this teaching (Mark 12:30–31). Some kinds of self-love are praised. Until I know what Metzger means we cannot carry this discussion further, but I would argue the term *self* needs unpacking.

FREEDOM

This perspective also answers Metzger's concern with freedom. Beyond its use in political theory, freedom has proven difficult to describe. My own take is that freedom arises when the spirit of love, which is at the core of our individuality, encounters uncertainty and limitation. We begin as children with nearly complete ignorance. As the field of choices, correct and mistaken, expands and intertwines with others' similar choices, an environment of unimaginable complexity arises. This is the field of *free* acts. Freedom is not a fundamental category, but it is an important and inescapable part of our existence.

SCRIPTURE AND TEXTS

I place experience ahead of written texts. Metzger puts it the other way around. I will not go into why I have never found a written text suitable to consider an infallible guide because that is a matter everyone needs ultimately to puzzle out for themselves.

For over fifteen hundred years Christians have argued, fought, and often killed one another and others over competing interpretations of their Scriptures. So far as I can tell, combatants on all sides have been sincere. Here is a case where limited individuals seeking to act sincerely commit hideous acts. There never has been—and I think never will be—a universally agreed-upon interpretation of biblical texts.

Yet many individuals can deepen their spiritual understanding through thoughtful study of a text. But these individuals come to different conclusions. The same text speaks differently to different people. This is true in every religion. If reading scripture helps you grow in love, generosity, and compassion, you have found a good text for you. If it does not, you have not.

Nature is many a pagan's text. The cycles of the seasons; the eternal rhythm of birth, life, death, and new life; the beauty of a sunset; and the union of love, be it physical, emotional, or spiritual, are our texts. For many of us—and certainly for me—our meditation on them has made us more loving, generous, and compassionate.

As we respect and honor Christians who grow from their encounters with their sacred literature and their God, so we request a similar respect in our relations with our text and our Gods.

Gus diZerega is a Third Degree Wiccan Gardnerian Elder and political scientist/theorist. He is the author of Pagans & Christians: The Personal Spiritual Experience *and coauthor of* Beyond the Burning Times: A Pagan and Christian in Dialogue. *He lives in Sebastopol, California.*

AFTERWORD

AN APOLOGY FOR PRAYER

P rayer is where right brain and left brain meet, where intuition and logic wed. It is also where first-person and second-person and third-person discourse merge. It is not simply a matter of talking about God but of talking to God heart to heart on behalf of others. For example, "Dear God, I pray for John and Mary that they might come to know you personally and intimately." What Karl Barth says of theological work is also true of apologetics: all theological work must be done in the second person "in the form of a liturgical act, as invocation of God, and as prayer."[1] Prayer is more than a set of propositions that we utter before eating dinner or before beginning a service or officiating a ceremony. Prayerful living is a sphere where the heavens open up, the spirit soars, and lives are undone and transformed. Prayerful witness is where apologetics moves beyond head games to the heartfelt connection.

Prayer and apologetic witness are integrally related. Prayer that is more than perfunctory, like apologetics that is more than canned argumentation, is mysterious and drenched with the divine. Like vibrant prayer, vital apologetic witness is not something we could ever do alone. Our witness is communal, just like prayer. In fact, without the nurturing dynamic of prayerful communion within the life of the triune God and the fellowship of his Spirit-filled people, apologetic witness is stillborn.

Prayer is miraculous and so requires God's intervention, quickening, guidance, and empowerment. Ultimately Christian prayer is a trinitarian and ecclesial encounter; and given the significance of prayer for apologetic witness, apologetics is too. We pray in the Spirit, who himself intercedes for us. As the Scriptures say, "In the same way, the Spirit helps us in our weakness. We do not know what we ought to pray for, but the Spirit himself intercedes for us with groans that words cannot express" (Romans 8:26). The Father who knows the mind of the Spirit searches our hearts, and the Spirit intercedes for us in accordance with God's will: "And he who searches our hearts knows the mind of the Spirit, because the Spirit intercedes for the saints in accordance with God's will" (Romans 8:27). Jesus also prays for us as our great high priest: "Who is he that condemns? Christ Jesus, who died—more than that, who was raised to life—is at the right hand of God and is also interceding for us" (Romans 8:34). Jesus prays for his followers that they would be effective witnesses in the world. He wants them to experience holy communion with one another in and through him and his Father in the glory of their love: "I in them and you in me. May they be brought to complete unity to let the world know that you sent me and have loved them even as you have loved me" (John 17:23). As believers who participate in the life of the triune God—including through prayer—we are to pray for one another in our apologetic witness:

> Devote yourselves to prayer, being watchful and thankful. And pray
> for us, too, that God may open a door for our message, so that we may
> proclaim the mystery of Christ, for which I am in chains. Pray that I
> may proclaim it clearly, as I should. Be wise in the way you act toward
> outsiders; make the most of every opportunity. Let your conversation
> be always full of grace, seasoned with salt, so that you may know how
> to answer everyone" (Colossians 4:2–6).

Like prayer, apologetics is a spiritual and relational encounter with God (for whom and through whom we bear witness), with his people (with whom we bear witness), and with those who do not currently believe (to whom we bear witness). The Spirit through whom we pray illumines our minds and hearts to discern God's wisdom, for we have been given the mind of Christ. The Spirit who searches the deep things of God and who knows the mind of Christ reveals God to us. As we depend on the Spirit, God will use us to make Christ known to others (1 Corinthians 2).

We speak of spiritual truths in Christian apologetics, but so often I have been guilty of articulating those truths in unspiritual ways. Paul's approach was to preach with a demonstration of the Spirit's power, not with wise and persuasive words, so that people's faith would rest on God's power, not human wisdom (1 Corinthians 2:4–5). Paul is not speaking of discarding logical arguments or rigorous rhetorical strategies (in fact, he employs logic and rhetoric throughout his epistle to the Corinthians), but he is speaking of the need to seek approval from God and not from others. He is speaking of the need to boast not in our eloquence or human power or human wisdom that knows nothing of the foolish brilliance and frail omnipotence of the cross but, instead, in God's loving-kindness, justice, and righteousness revealed in the crucified and risen Jesus (as noted previously, 1 Corinthians 1:31 is an exhortation to boast in the Lord and is taken from Jeremiah 9:23–24, which speaks of boasting in God rather than human power, wisdom, and riches), and to put oneself under God's judgment, knowing that the One who makes divine judgments is not subject to human judgment.

How do we preach with a demonstration of the Spirit's power if we proclaim God's Word apart from prayer? I am not simply referring to propositional prayer. While praying to God is crucial, prayer in the Spirit goes beyond just speaking statements to God. It involves unceasing crying out to God from the depths of one's inner being.

A Ugandan student and friend of mine, Michael Badriaki, once said in class that Christians in the West are weak in prayer.[2] I believe I know what he meant: we may be strong in terms of our technology and tools and textbook knowledge, but we are weak in invocation and intercession. I am no exception. We are strong in church growth strategies, but are they ultimately strategies in converting the lost, or are they transferring people from one church to another? Most of the evangelistic growth in the global church is not in the developed North and West but in the developing South and East. Might there be a connection between our weakness in prayer and our weakness in evangelism and apologetics in the developed world?

Much is made of the New Atheism in the West and of how people are increasingly irreligious. However, I sense that this form of atheism is a latent spiritualism bound up with the worship of matter and mechanism and cynicism. Coupled with the growth of alternative spiritualities in ancient and new forms, it is vital that our spirituality deepens, including apologetics that is bathed in prayer.

What does this look like? Joan Chittister writes that "prayerfulness is the capacity to live intensely involved in the world and intensely immersed with the God who made it at the same time. It is a way of life that is aware of all of it in all its forms—both spiritual and material—at once."[3] My same African student would call this state of being one of living in the present. Such living in the present involves pursuing a lifestyle of prayer. Moreover a lifestyle of evangelism and a lifestyle of prayer are one, whereby we constantly submit our will to God's will, imploring God to align our hearts with his heart as we seek to live among people, laying down our lives for the world for Christ in word and deed. This allows us to see things and people here on earth as God does, no longer viewing anyone from a merely human point of view, living intensely and in the moment, not passing over people in their various complexities on account of our false ambitions and agendas, fallen propensities and drives that lead us to dismiss them hastily with oversimplifications and rigid categorizations.

I have been tempted so many times to dismiss people who react to my message in one way or another, but I am learning to reach out to them through prayer when my words appear to hit their chests and bounce off without penetrating their hearts. I am also learning now that as I enter into a dependent state of prayer in apologetic witness, their strong reactions are often clues to God's Spirit convicting them of their need for Jesus' love that will eradicate their hardness and heal them of their relational wounds. Such was the case at Portland State University, where a young woman reacted strongly to me. I was in the spirit of prayer throughout my guest lecture on the Christian faith because she was so distracting, talking incessantly to her classmates. When I finished my talk, she was the first to respond: "Do you think you're better than me?" As we dialogued about her question, she made clear what she was after (a point I had not addressed): she said that Christians believe that Jesus is the way, that they are insiders with Jesus, and that everyone else is outside. If it had not been for my being in the spirit of prayer that evening, I doubt I would have perceived what she was really thinking: *Does God love me? Christians in my past, by their words and acts of exclusion, have denied that he does.* As a result of being in the spirit of prayer, I was able to address her real question and invite her to know Jesus, informing her that Jesus breaks down insider-outsider divisions and wants to have a personal relationship with her—beginning that very night.

At other times I have not been in the spirit of prayer during my lectures, so I have not perceived well what was going on around me. Once while I was speaking at a secular university about Christ, an individual in the audience stood up and began shouting and calling me every name in the book (and I don't mean the Bible) before stomping out of the auditorium. It devastated me internally, especially since I was speaking from the heart. I did my best to regroup, as I was only halfway through my talk. A friend later shared with me that it was obviously an instance of spiritual warfare, and that I should not be taken by surprise by such reactions. However, my guard was down, and I failed to perceive what had just transpired. My own insecurities surfaced, and the evil one has a way of devastating us with his attacks on our confidence. The spiritual state of prayer is that safe place where we find our confidence in Jesus rather than ourselves. The spiritual state of prayer is where we look for God's affirmation rather than the praise of others.

The life of prayer involves drawing from the power of God's throne to contend against the fallen principalities and powers of the air. Every year in my world religions class, I invite the same guest speaker from another religion who is also an astrologer to share with my students. He often seeks to probe their spirits as he engages them one-on-one in dialectical discourse; students who had messed with the occult earlier in life have shared with me how traumatized they were by the encounter. (I am present to safeguard against such encounters getting out of hand and counsel these students afterward so that they may grow in their union and communion with Christ and his people.) I encourage my students to enter into the spirit of prayer and to wear the armor of God (being clothed in the righteousness and truth of Jesus in dependence on the Spirit), which Paul discusses in Ephesians 6:10–17. Paul exhorts the Ephesians to take to heart that our battle is not with flesh and blood but with the spiritual forces of evil in the heavenly realms. Paul then speaks of the life of prayer when he writes, "And pray in the Spirit on all occasions with all kinds of prayers and requests. With this in mind, be alert and always keep on praying for all the saints. Pray also for me, that whenever I open my mouth, words may be given me so that I will fearlessly make known the mystery of the gospel, for which I am an ambassador in chains. Pray that I may declare it fearlessly, as I should" (Ephesians 6:18–20).

The only way we Christians in the West will be prepared to engage spiritual forces beyond sheer intellect and technological controls is if we have a form of godliness that does not deny God's power. The state of prayer is where we experience God's power as we depend on him, not on our might or power or capacities. The spiritual battle can only be won if we do battle as Jehoshaphat did when faced with an overpowering army of overwhelming odds—through intercession and worship (2 Chronicles 20).[4]

I have already lost before beginning in apologetic debate—even if I win!—when I seek to demonstrate intellectual prowess or cleverness or charm rather than depend on God through prayer. I have already won before entering into apologetic debate—even if I lose!—when I depend on God for the victory through prayer. God's overwhelming goodness and faithfulness and truthful love quicken faithfulness in prayer and love for the people we seek to reach with God's life-giving message of love. That love is contagious, and prayer is God's resource for fanning the flame of passion for God's love in human souls.

◆ ◆ ◆

We now come to the end of the book. I hope you have realized that relational-incarnational apologetics does not mean you have all the bells and whistles or best gimmicks and best answers at every turn. I sure don't. At times you will fall on your face. I sure do. You will have people challenge you, saying you are arrogant and condescending. Sometimes these challenges and charges have been aimed at me. We need the discernment and humility to take on board people's challenges and repent and apologize if and when they are accurate. And when they are inaccurate? Even then we need to be willing to go the extra mile and suffer their claims, absorb their charges, and love these people with the love of Christ, not trying to prove ourselves and not viewing our dialogue partners from a merely human point of view (2 Corinthians 5:16). Instead we must approach them with Jesus' profound love for them as those created in God's image and wired for intimacy with him. We must also be willing to do anything to bear witness to Jesus and his love for them. In the spirit of prayer we understand that we—not simply they—are desperate for Christ; we understand that we stand only by the mercy and grace of God poured out in our lives. In the spirit of prayer we realize that we cannot muster the necessary spiritual bravado, courage, creativity, humility, and love to witness effectively to others. We come to comprehend that Jesus will make up for our lack and the Spirit will make the connections to Christ as we bear holistic witness to Jesus in word and deed in a spirit of prayer.

NOTES

Introduction: Wired for Relationships

1. Here are some significant examples of predominantly worldview-oriented apologetic texts: G. K. Chesterton, *Orthodoxy* (John Lane Company, 1908; San Francisco: Ignatius Press, 1995 rep. ed.); William Lane Craig, *Reasonable Faith: Christian Truth and Apologetics*, 3rd ed. (Wheaton, IL: Crossway Books, 2008); Tim Keller, *The Reason for God: Belief in an Age of Skepticism* (New York: Dutton, 2008); Peter Kreeft and Ronald K. Tacelli, *Handbook of Christian Apologetics* (Downers Grove, IL: IVP Academic, 1994); C. S. Lewis, *Mere Christianity*, rev. and enlarged ed. (San Francisco: HarperSanFrancisco, 2001); J. P. Moreland and William Lane Craig, *Philosophical Foundations for a Christian Worldview* (Downers Grove, IL: IVP Academic, 2003).

Generally speaking, market-driven apologetics are found in popular Christian circles as various churches and parachurch ministries seek to engage people's felt needs to attract them to the Christian faith and to church. The groups I have in mind are generally conservative theologically. While I would not consider their approaches market-driven or claim that they appealed to people's base instincts, nineteenth-century theologian Friedrich Schleiermacher and twentieth-century New Testament scholar Rudolf Bultmann were apologists who appealed to people's experience. Schleiermacher appealed to the cultured critics of Christianity in his day to find in religion the height of human culture. Writing in an age that esteemed feeling, Schleiermacher found in religion the highest form of feeling. He spoke of the essence of Christian faith as the feeling of absolute dependence. See his apologetic work *On Religion: Speeches to Its Cultured Despisers*, ed. Richard Crouter, Cambridge Texts in the History of Philosophy (Cambridge: Cambridge University Press,

1996). Bultmann also appealed to his audience's experiential instincts and sought to argue for the Christian faith's relevance in a modern age. He spoke of the need to demythologize the Bible in an age that could no longer accept the miraculous. See his work *Jesus Christ and Mythology* (Upper Saddle River, NJ: Prentice Hall, 1981). Schleiermacher and Bultmann were brilliant scholars and apologists who are often hailed as leading representatives of liberal Christian theology. Both scholars argue that faith is experiential at its core and must not be reduced to doctrine and rationality. While I argue that we must not reduce the faith to doctrine and must value experience, I contend for orthodox spirituality that weds piety and experience with orthodox doctrine. Jonathan Edwards, Blaise Pascal, Hans Urs von Balthasar, and Vladimir Lossky are notable figures who contend for the synthesis of vibrant relational experience and sound doctrine. See the following works: Jonathan Edwards, *The Works of Jonathan Edwards*, vol. 2, *Religious Affections*, The Works of Jonathan Edwards Series (New Haven, CT: Yale University Press, 2009); Blaise Pascal, *Pensées* [Thoughts], trans. A. J. Krailsheimer, rev. ed. (1966; London: Penguin Books, 1995); Hans Urs von Balthasar, *Love Alone Is Credible*, trans. D. C. Schindler (San Francisco: Ignatius Press, 2004); and Vladimir Lossky, *The Mystical Theology of the Eastern Church* (Crestwood: St. Vladimir's Seminary Press, 1976).

Lossky asserts that the totality of the early church's formulations on Jesus Christ were intended to safeguard "the possibility of attaining to the fullness of the mystical union" with God in Jesus Christ. For if he is not fully God and fully human, mystical union with God is unattainable. Lossky goes so far as to claim that the entirety of Eastern Orthodox theology has as its goal reflection on and attainment of union with God through Jesus Christ (Lossky, *Mystical Theology*, 9–10). Here we find the wedding of rationality and spiritual experience. I will list works that have a bearing on relational-incarnational and trinitarian apologetics in the endnotes to chapter 1.

2. Here is what my hip assistant and promising hipster scholar Beyth Hogue Greenetz says about hipsters: Hipsters reject a "polished" look (think "yuppies"— hipsters are not interested in fleece or REI or J. Crew), but they expend a significant amount of energy getting their "look" to look right. Hipsters reject corporate branding, like Old Navy or Gap, but they love to shop at corporations like American Apparel, which do not "feel" so corporate (and expenditures from AA can be justified because all their products are manufactured in the United States). Supporting "indie" organizations, be it apparel, filmmaking, or music, is a hallmark of being a hipster. Being "ironic" is very important to hipsters (though the actual definition of irony is a bit lost on the subculture), so they drink PBR even though they know how to appreciate a good microbrew and could afford one.

An article in *Time* refers to hipsters in the following way: "Hipsters are the friends who sneer when you cop to liking Coldplay. They're the people who wear T-shirts silk-screened with quotes from movies you've never heard of and the only ones in America who still think Pabst Blue Ribbon is a good beer. They sport cowboy hats and berets and think Kanye West stole their sunglasses. Everything about them is exactingly constructed to give off the vibe that they just don't care" (http://www .time.com/time/arts/article/0,8599,1913220,00.html; accessed on 10/26/11).

Here is an article that discusses the fact that core to being a hipster is *rejection of doing things just because they are cool*. They have to work to convince their subconscious that the things they do, buy, listen to, eat, etc., do not really represent who they are. "I wear trucker hats because I actually like them, not because it's cool" (http:// www.psychologytoday.com/blog/extreme-fear/201009/the-sad-science-hipsterism; accessed on 10/26/11). Here is a humorous illustration of this point (http://www .buzzfeed.com/peggy/the-accidental-hipster?awesm=5BDE7&utm_content=tweet-button-horizontal&utm_medium=awe.sm-twitter&utm_source=psychologytoday .com; accessed on 10/26/11).

Chapter 1: What Is Relational-Incarnational Apologetics?

1. *As Good As It Gets*, directed by James L. Brooks (1997; Culver City, CA: Columbia TriStar Home Entertainment, 1998), DVD.

2. Harper Lee, *To Kill a Mockingbird*, 50th Anniversary ed. (New York: Harper Luxe, 2010), 48.

3. Floyd McClung quoted in Joseph C. Aldrich, *Lifestyle Evangelism* (Sisters, OR: Multnomah Books, 1993), 35.

4. William Shakespeare, *Hamlet*, ed. David Bevington, in *Complete Works of Shakespeare*, 5th ed. (New York: Pearson/Longman, 2004), 1109.

5. Blaise Pascal, "The Memorial," in *Pensées* [Thoughts], trans. A. J. Krailsheimer, rev. ed. (1966; London: Penguin Books, 1995), 285.

6. C. S. Lewis, *Miracles: A Preliminary Study* (New York: Macmillan, 1948), 113–14.

7. Colin E. Gunton, *The Promise of Trinitarian Theology*, 2nd ed. (London: T. & T. Clark, 1997), 7.

8. Paul Louis Metzger, *The Gospel of John: When Love Comes to Town* (Downers Grove: InterVarsity Press, 2010), 59–63, 81–87, 287n12.

9. *As Good As It Gets*.

10. I am defining "post-Christendom" as a context in which Christianity no longer dominates the thought forms, moral consciousness, and rites of passage in a given culture. While there are still regions where Christianity appears to reign, such as the Bible Belt, the dissolution of Christendom as a dominant culture in the United States began with the onslaught and aftermath of the Civil War, where it was evident that the Christian North and South came to very different conclusions on the race question while using the same Bible. This is not to say that only one side was at fault. The United States as a nation has struggled with racism since its inception. North

and South together were deeply entrenched in racism. See the article by David von Drehle, "150 Years After Fort Sumter: Why We're Still Fighting the Civil War," *Time*, April 7, 2011, http://www.time.com/time/magazine /article/0,9171,2063869,00.html (accessed August 18, 2011).

It would be difficult to support the claim that the United States is post-Christian. It all depends on what one means by the term "post-Christian." Protestantism is still the majority religious group in the United States; the percentage of self-professed members of Protestant denominations is presently around 51 percent and Christianity as a whole is around 78 percent. See Pew Forum on Religion and Public Life, *U.S. Religious Landscape Survey: Diverse and Dynamic* (Washington: Pew Research Center, 2008), 5, http://religions.pewforum.org/pdf/report-religious -landscape-study-full.pdf (accessed August 18, 2011).

11. I am defining "postmodern" as that movement that serves paradoxically as both a hyperextension of modernity and as its antithesis. Postmodernity often includes antitraditional stances, including antagonism to organized religion. In this sense, it is similar to modernism. While some currents within postmodernity counter the claims of the revealed religions and their metanarratives, in other quarters there is a greater sensitivity to mystery and a rejection of antisupernaturalist trajectories.

12. There are numerous works that bear on our subject of developing a relational-incarnational model of apologetics in view of the triune God's engagement of his church and world. Here are but a few:

Rodney Stark speaks of relational and social dynamics in Christianity's rise in *The Rise of Christianity: How the Obscure, Marginal Jesus Movement Became the Dominant Religious Force in the Western World in a Few Centuries* (San Francisco: HarperSanFrancisco, 1997).

Paul Hiebert analyzes the transformation of people's worldviews from an anthropological perspective in *Transforming Worldviews: An Anthropological Understanding of How People Change* (Grand Rapids: Baker Academic, 2008). Toward the end of the work, he claims that a biblical view of transformation "is both a point and a process. . . . It is not simply mental assent to a set of metaphysical beliefs, nor is it solely a positive feeling toward God. Rather it involves entering a life of discipleship and obedience in every area of our being and throughout the whole story of our lives" (310).

See also Terry Muck and Frances S. Adeney, *Christianity Encountering World Religions: The Practice of Mission in the Twenty-First Century* (Grand Rapids: Baker Academic, 2009). There they focus on gift-giving as essential to building God's kingdom as his witnesses. See pages 7–10 for an initial discussion of this perspective and its implications for missional engagement.

Darrell L. Guder frames the church's witness in the world through the lens of Jesus' incarnation in *Be My Witnesses: The Church's Mission, Message, and Messengers* (Grand Rapids: Eerdmans, 1985).

Ravi Zacharias and his colleagues argue for the need for Christians to live out the faith we profess while also presenting arguments for the Christian faith in *Beyond Opinion: Living the Faith We Defend* (Nashville: Thomas Nelson, 2007).

David K. Clark calls for synthesizing traditional apologetics with evangelism that is person-centered in *Dialogical Apologetics: A Person-Centered Approach to Christian Defense* (Grand Rapids: Baker Books, 1999).

For a trinitarian approach to engaging our pluralistic culture, see Kevin J. Vanhoozer, ed., *The Trinity in a Pluralistic Age: Theological Essays on Culture and Religion* (Grand Rapids: Eerdmans, 1997).

Colin E. Gunton has provided a trinitarian apologetic for the faith in *The One, the Three and the Many: God, Creation and the Culture of Modernity, the 1992 Bampton Lectures* (Cambridge: Cambridge University Press, 1993).

Ninian Smart has argued that we should account for various dimensions in analyzing religion. For Smart, religion involves the distinct though inseparably related categories of doctrine, experience, ethics, and ritual, narrative/mythological, social, and material factors. See his work *Worldviews: Crosscultural Explorations of Human Beliefs*, 2nd ed. (Englewood Cliffs, NJ: Prentice-Hall, 1995). Of course, as Smart maintains, "The world religions owe some of their living power to their success in presenting a total picture of reality, through a coherent system of doctrines" (*The Religious Experience*, 5th ed. [Englewood Cliffs, NJ: Prentice-Hall, 1996], 5).

My argument in this book includes the claim that while worldview matters significantly, argumentation based solely on worldview is not sufficient for apologetic witness. As Smart maintains, there are numerous other dimensions for which we must account in analyzing religion and, I would add, for engaging other religions missionally.

I should make clear here that there is in my view only one incarnation: the eternal Word became human flesh (John 1:14). The church is not an incarnation of God. However, through the Spirit, the church participates in the life of the incarnate Christ—Jesus of Nazareth. As the church participates in the life of Christ, it bears witness to him with true words and sacrificial living. As such, the church is "incarnational." This is how the term "incarnational" is generally used in this book to refer to "relational-incarnational apologetics."

Chapter 2: What Are We Making an Apology for Anyway?

1. Ray Ortlund Jr., sermon (Westminster Presbyterian Church, Elgin, IL, 1992).

2. *The Works of Jonathan Edwards*, ed. Thomas A. Schafer, vol. 13, *The "Miscellanies," Entry Nos. a–z, aa–zz, 1–500* (New Haven, CT: Yale University Press, 1994), 741.

3. John Calvin, *Commentaries on the Epistles of Paul to the Galatians and Ephesians*, trans. William Pringle (Edinburgh: Calvin Translation Society, 1854), 324–25 (emphasis added).

4. Andrei Rublev, *Holy Trinity* (tempera on wood, State Tretyakov Gallery, Moscow, Russia, 1425–1427), http://members.valley.net/~transnat/trinlg.html (accessed August 18, 2011). In his depiction, Rublev uses angels to represent the persons of the Trinity because he wants to guard against making graven images of God.

5. Boris Bobrinskoy, *The Mystery of the Trinity: Trinitarian Experience and Vision in the Biblical and Patristic Tradition*, trans. Anthony P. Gythiel (Crestwood: St. Vladimir's Seminary Press, 1999), 12.

6. Ibid., 141.

Chapter 3: Who's the Stumbling Block—You and Me or Jesus?

1. "Heidelberg Disputation," in *Martin Luther's Basic Theological Writings*, ed. Timothy F. Lull (Minneapolis: Augsburg Fortress, 1989), 48.

2. Ibid., 48.

3. Ibid., 43–44.

4. Ibid., 44.

5. Blaise Pascal, "Excellence of This Means of Proving God," in *Pensées* [Thoughts], trans. A. J. Krailsheimer, rev. ed. (1966; London: Penguin Books, 1995), 86.

6. Friedrich Nietzsche, "The Antichrist," in *The Portable Nietzsche*, ed. Walter Kaufmann (New York: Viking Press, 1968), 633–44.

7. Like Pascal, I believe that reason has its rightful place, but not the only place. "If we submit everything to reason our reason will be left with nothing mysterious or supernatural. If we offend the principles of reason our religion will be absurd and ridiculous. . . . Two excesses: to exclude reason, to admit nothing but reason." See Peter Kreeft, *Christianity for Modern Pagans: Pascal's* Pensées *Edited, Outlined and Explained* (San Francisco: Ignatius Press, 1993), 236n173, 237n183. Note also Kreeft's discussion of Pascal on the heart, faith, and reason (228–42).

Like Pascal, I do not affirm blind faith, but I maintain that the guarded heart and true faith are foundational to right and rigorous thinking. James R. Peters draws from St. Augustine and Pascal and maintains that the appropriate use of reason, which the human heart guides, situates humans in the world and assists them in living according to wisdom. Peters seeks to restore the passionate use of reason to the Christian faith. James R. Peters, *The Logic of the Heart: Augustine, Pascal and the Rationality of Faith* (Grand Rapids: Baker Academic, 2009). I would add here that for Pascal, the wisdom and knowledge of God is displayed in the foolishness of the cross, as it was for Paul before him.

8. Pascal, "Excellence of This Means," 85–86.

9. See also the book of Galatians, where this problem is discussed at length, including Paul's rebuke of Peter for associating with the Jews and distancing himself from the Gentile believers based on Jewish peer pressure.

10. Pascal reminds us of God's approach to dealing with ignorant people who don't know God's ways: "The way of God, who disposes all things with gentleness, is to instill religion in our minds with reasoned arguments and into our hearts with grace, but attempting to instill it into hearts and minds with force and threats is to instill not religion but terror. Terror rather than religion" (Pascal, "Excellence of This Means," 83).

Jesus showed us the way of winning people's hearts—dying on the cross for their sins rather than condemning them and hanging them and their sins there. In contrast to Jesus and his servant Paul, the false teachers and Judaizers did just the opposite, imposing on people a reign of self-righteous terror.

Chapter 4: Why Should We Apologize?

1. Vine Deloria Jr., *God Is Red: A Native View of Religion* (Golden, CO: Fulcrum Publishing, 1994), 261–62. An example of such Christian involvement in genocide against Native Americans can be found in the words and actions of Methodist minister and US colonel John Chivington. Chivington was responsible for the 1864 Sand Creek Massacre. Chivington asserted, "I believe it is right and honorable to use any means under God's heaven to kill Indians." John Chivington quoted in Russell Means with Marvin J. Wolf, *Where White Men Fear to Tread: The Autobiography of Russell Means* (New York: St. Martin's Press, 1995), 518.

2. Deloria, *God Is Red*, 261.

3. Ibid., 262.

4. John M. Perkins, *Let Justice Roll Down* (Ventura, CA: Regal Books, 1976).

5. Here I am thinking primarily of the white, Anglo-Saxon, Protestant, middle- and upper-middle-class male persona, which I embody and benefit from in many respects.

6. Another form of rationalization against which we Christians must guard is quoting the common expression, "I'm not perfect, just forgiven." Such a statement can come across as trite and trivial and dismissive, suggesting an unwillingness to address one's personal failures, or when extended to the corporate sphere, the church's failings. Although we are forgiven, being forgiven by God leads us to seek after reconciliation with others, as in the case of Zacchaeus in Luke 19.

7. Robert W. Jenson, *America's Theologian: A Recommendation of Jonathan Edwards* (Oxford: Oxford University Press, 1988), 150.

8. Paul Louis Metzger, *Consuming Jesus: Beyond Race and Class Divisions in a Consumer Church* (Grand Rapids: Eerdmans, 2007), 148.

9. Gustav Niebuhr, "After the Attacks: Finding Fault; U.S. 'Secular' Groups Set Tone for Terror Attacks, Falwell Says," *New York Times*, September 14, 2001, 18.

10. Robert Franek, with Tom Meltzer, et al., *The Best 361 Colleges: The Smart Student's Guide to Colleges*, 2006 ed. (New York: Princeton Review, 2005). The

Princeton Review asks college students (more than 110,000 of them) what their schools are really like, and reports the most revealing answers in this book. For many years, Reed has maintained top rankings for academics and ignoring God. In the 2006 edition, Reed received the highest score among universities for "ignoring God on a regular basis."

11. Donald Miller, *Blue Like Jazz: Nonreligious Thoughts on Christian Spirituality* (Nashville: Thomas Nelson, 2003), 116.

12. Tony Kriz, personal conversation with the author.

13. Karl Barth, *Church Dogmatics*, eds. G. W. Bromiley and T. F. Torrance, vol. 3.1, *The Doctrine of Creation* (Edinburgh: T. & T. Clark, 1958), 200.

14. Ibid., 191–206.

15. For a radical treatment of the doctrine of sin, see Philip Melanchthon, *Loci Communes Theologici*, in *Melanchthon and Bucer*, eds. Wilhelm Pauck, trans. Lowell J. Satre (Philadelphia: The Westminster Press, 1969), 22–49.

16. This is the approach of Miroslav Volf in comparing Islam and Christianity: "Concentrate on what is common," and "keep an eye out for what is decisively different" (Miroslav Volf, *Allah: A Christian Response* [New York: HarperOne, 2011], 91). While I do not agree with Volf on some central points in his book, I do agree with his approach to addressing similarities and dissimilarities between the two religious traditions.

17. Apart from the Spirit's intervention and direction, given our fallen condition, we corrupt and distort the sense of the divine rather than follow it through to its end in Jesus. See Romans 1:21; John Calvin, *Book First: Of the Knowledge of God the Creator*, in *Institutes of the Christian Religion*, trans. Henry Beveridge (Edinburg: T. & T. Clark, 1863), 62–63.

18. Lesslie Newbigin, *The Open Secret: An Introduction to the Theology of Mission*, rev. ed. (Grand Rapids: Eerdmans, 1995), 175.

19. Look to my treatment of Karl Barth's Christocentric approach to accounting for similarities between the Christian faith and other faiths, as witnesses to Christ arise outside the realm of the church: *The Word of Christ and the World of Culture: Sacred and Secular through the Theology of Karl Barth* (Grand Rapids: Eerdmans, 2003), 121–57.

20. Rowan Williams, *Resurrection: Interpreting the Easter Gospel*, rev. ed. (Cleveland: Pilgrim Press, 2002), 73.

21. Christo Lombard, personal conversation with author, spring 2004.

Chapter 5: How Is Christ's Church God's Apologetic?

1. Josh McDowell, *Evidence That Demands a Verdict*, vol. 1, *Historical Evidences for the Christian Faith*, rev. ed. (Nashville: Thomas Nelson, 1992); Josh McDowell, *The New Evidence That Demands a Verdict: Evidence I and II, Fully Updated to*

Answer the Questions Challenging Christians in the 21st Century (Nashville: Thomas Nelson, 1999).

2. See the discussion of this theme in Paul Louis Metzger, "Beyond the Culture Wars: Contours of Authentic Dialogue," in *A World for All? Global Civil Society in Political Theory and Trinitarian Theology,* eds. William F. Storrar, Peter J. Casarella, and Paul Louis Metzger (Grand Rapids: William B. Eerdmans, 2011), 282–95.

3. G. K. Chesterton, *What's Wrong with the World,* repr. (San Francisco: Ignatius Press, 1994).

4. Metzger, "That Sense of Touch," in *Gospel of John,* 28–37.

5. "The Vacation," in *The Selected Poems of Wendell Berry* (Washington: HarperCollins, 1999), 157.

6. Ken Myers, "Dehumanizing Tendencies Should Be Put on Hold," *Dallas Morning News,* April 1, 2000.

7. *Crash,* directed by Paul Haggis (2004; Santa Monica, CA: Lions Gate Entertainment, 2005), DVD.

8. Eugene H. Peterson, *The Message: The Bible in Contemporary Language, New Testament with Psalms and Proverbs* (Colorado Springs: NavPress, 2007), 209.

9. Timothy Ware, *The Orthodox Church,* new ed. (London: Penguin Books, 1997), 208. Ware borrows the idea of the triune God as our social program from the Russian theologian Feodorov.

10. Stanley Hauerwas speaks of the church as being a social ethic rather than simply having a social ethic. For Hauerwas, the church as a social ethic involves witness through pacifistic practices. Stanley Hauerwas, *The Peaceable Kingdom: A Primer in Christian Ethics* (Notre Dame, IN: University of Notre Dame Press, 1991).

11. In Acts 1:1 Luke reminds his reader that his gospel recounted "all that Jesus began to do and to teach" (Acts 1:1). The implication is that Jesus continues to act in history, albeit most directly through his church in the power of the Spirit. The church is the concrete manifestation of God's presence in the world today as it participates in Christ's life through the Spirit.

12. Henri J. M. Nouwen, *The Wounded Healer: Ministry in Contemporary Society* (New York: Image, 1979), 92–93.

13. For Perkins's treatment of the three Rs of community development—relocation, reconciliation, and redistribution—see John M. Perkins, *With Justice for All: A Strategy for Community Development,* rev. ed. (1982; Ventura: Regal Books, 2007), 60–202.

14. King preached,

> To our most bitter opponents we say: "We shall match your capacity to inflict suffering by our capacity to endure suffering. We shall meet your physical force with soul force. Do to us what you will, and we shall continue to love you. We

cannot in all good conscience obey your unjust laws because noncooperation with evil is as much a moral obligation as is cooperation with good. Throw us in jail and we shall still love you. Bomb our homes and threaten our children, and we shall still love you. Send your hooded perpetrators of violence into our community at the midnight hour and beat us and leave us half dead, and we shall still love you. But be ye assured that we will wear you down by our capacity to suffer. One day we shall win freedom but not only for ourselves. We shall so appeal to your heart and conscience that we shall win you in the process and our victory will be a double victory.

Martin Luther King Jr., "Loving Your Enemies" (sermon, Dexter Avenue Baptist Church, Montgomery, Alabama, December 25, 1957), http://www.salsa.net/peace /conv/8weekconv4-2.html (accessed August 20, 2011).

15. Luther, "Heidelberg Disputation," 44.

16. However, chapter 6 will explain how Luther was grievously and horrifically inconsistent in his engagement of the Jewish community. This is why the church must continue to apologize, as discussed in chapter 4, even as we seek to be the apologetic.

17. Gary B. Ferngren, quoted in Rob Moll, "The Health Care Debate, Early Church Style," *Christianity Today*, September 19, 2009, http://www .christianitytoday.com/ct/2009/augustweb-only/134-31.0.html (accessed August 20, 2011); Gary B. Ferngren, *Medicine and Health Care in Early Christianity* (Baltimore: John Hopkins University Press, 2009).

18. See for example *Christianity Today*'s "This Is Our City" project, which highlights the Christian community's missional engagement in various cities around the country: http://www.christianitytoday.com/thisisourcity/. See also *Christianity Today*'s November 2011 issue.

Chapter 6: The Jewish Question (Judaism)

1. "The Church and the Jewish Question," in *Collected Works of Dietrich Bonhoeffer*, vol. 1, *No Rusty Swords: Letters, Lectures and Notes 1928–1936* (New York: Harper and Row, 1965), 217–25.

2. Ibid., 217.

3. Ibid., 218.

4. Ibid., 223.

5. "The Jewish Religion: Its Beliefs and Practices," in Louis Finkelstein, ed., *The Jews: Their History, Culture and Religion*, 3rd ed. (New York: Harper & Brothers, 1960), 2:1743.

6. In the 1960 edition of Finkelstein's *The Jews*, he lists the questions raised most frequently by numerous scholars and educators in response to his query, "What

questions should be answered in the book on Judaism and the Jews?" Three of the questions noted (and addressed in the two volumes) are, "What is the attitude of Judaism to Jesus?" "What is the Jewish concept of a Messiah?" and "How did World War II and the preceding events affect the Jews?" (Louis Finkelstein, ed., appendix to *The Jews: Their History, Culture and Religion*, 3rd ed. [New York: Harper & Brothers, 1960], 2:1804, 2:1805, 2:1810).

While "religion" should not be conceived exclusively in terms of beliefs, it should account for them, especially when approaching matters from a Christian perspective. Now, regarding an all-encompassing approach to religion, it is worth noting what Nicholas de Lange writes in *Judaism* (Oxford: Oxford University Press, 1986), 3:

> The use of the word "religion" to mean primarily a system of beliefs can be fairly said to be derived from a Christian way of looking at Christianity. The comparative study of religions is an academic discipline which has been developed within Christian theology faculties, and it has a tendency to force widely differing phenomena into a kind of strait-jacket cut to a Christian pattern. The problem is not only that other "religions" may have little or nothing to say about questions which are of burning importance for Christianity, but that they may not even see themselves as religions in precisely the way in which Christianity sees itself as a religion. At the heart of Christianity, of Christian self-definition, is a creed, a set of statements to which the Christian is required to assent. To be fair, this is not the only way of looking at Christianity, and there is certainly room for, let us say, a historical or sociological approach. But within the history of Christianity itself a crucial emphasis has been placed on belief as a criterion of Christian identity. . . . In fact it is fair to say that theology occupies a central role in Christianity which makes it unique among the "religions" of the world.

A theological approach to engaging other religions—in this instance Judaism—is not exhaustive (both in terms of Judaism and in terms of Christianity). I have focused consideration in part II of this volume on various religions from a theological point of view, albeit framed relationally and incarnationally. If I were to write an additional and complementary volume wherein I engage other religions, it would be important to speak primarily of the historical, cultural, and experiential forces, including discussions of the symbols, stories, and rituals of the diverse traditions, approaching these religions primarily from a sociological and historical vantage point. In light of de Lange's statement I maintain that it is important to differentiate between questions Christians raise from a particular theological perspective in addressing other traditions and the questions these other traditions pose in view of their own traditions (some of which are theological, but many which are not). It is important not to impose on the Jewish religious tradition (or any tradition, for that matter) Christian questions and categories while still approaching Judaism from the standpoint of one's Christian perspective. The Christian must seek to be true to issues of internal coherence pertaining to a particular tradition such as Judaism while also accounting for matters of external correspondence, namely, bearing witness to ultimate reality through the truth claims of one's tradition and assessing various traditions in view of these claims.

7. Martin Luther, "On the Jews and Their Lies," in *Luther's Works*, ed. Franklin Sherman, vol. 47, *The Christian Society IV* (Philadelphia: Fortress Press, 1971), 167.

8. Ibid., 268–70, 272.

9. Rabbi Joseph Telushkin, "Martin Luther and the Protestant Reformation," in *Jewish Literacy: The Most Important Things to Know About the Jewish Religion, Its People, and Its History*, rev. ed. (New York: William Morrow and Company, Inc., 2008), 210–11. He refers to Luther as "the most extreme example in history of a Jew-lover who turned into a Jew-hater when the Jews refused to convert to his ideology." It is worth noting that he also maintains that the Reformation, in spite of Luther's horrible attack on the Jews, brought about good for the Jews: after Protestantism's rise a plurality of religious traditions in Europe were eventually recognized; toleration was advanced; and the stage was eventually set for democracy's rise.

10. Marc H. Ellis, *Hitler and the Holocaust, Christian Anti-Semitism* (Waco, TX: Baylor University Center for Jewish Studies, Spring 2004), 35 mm slides, frame 14.

In his defense at the Nuremberg Trial, Streicher remarked: "Anti-Semitic publications have existed in Germany for centuries. A book I had, written by Dr. Martin Luther, was, for instance, confiscated. Dr. Martin Luther would very probably sit in my place in the defendants' dock today, if this book had been taken into consideration by the Prosecution. In the book *The Jews and Their Lies*, Dr. Martin Luther writes that the Jews are a serpent's brood and one should burn down their synagogues and destroy them" (International Military Tribunal for Germany, "Nuremberg Trial Proceedings," April 29, 1946 [New Haven: Yale University Avalon Project], 12:317, http://avalon.law.yale.edu/imt/04-29-46.asp [accessed August 20, 2011]).

11. See Hans J. Hillerbrand's caution about blaming Luther for the rise of anti-Semitism in Germany in "Martin Luther: Significance," in Hillerbrand, *Encyclopaedia Britannica*, 2007 ed., s.v. "Martin Luther: Significance."

12. Denis MacShane, "The New Anti-Semitism," *Washington Post*, September 4, 2007, http://www.washingtonpost.com/wp-dyn/content/article/2007/09/03/AR2007090300719.html (accessed August 20, 2011).

13. This statement should not be taken to mean that the church exists only for the Jewish people. The church is called to love and care for all people and their rights, including Jews, Palestinians, and others. I am not advocating blanket support for

the modern state of Israel's political actions, as some evangelical Christian Zionists tend to do. (See *Cultural Encounters: A Journal for the Theology of Culture* 7, no. 1 [2011], http://new-wineskins.org/journal/volumes/7/#number-1 [accessed August 20, 2011] for a wide-ranging engagement of the conflict involving a diverse group of contributors.) The Bible makes clear that the church comes from Israel and exists in relation to Israel in a unique manner in terms of God's covenantal designs for both Israel and the church. The church must be vitally concerned for the well-being and preservation of Israel.

14. See the *Jewish Study Bible*, ed. Adele Berlin et al. (New York: Oxford University, 2004), 1305. Commentary on Psalm 22 states, "Jewish tradition interprets this psalm as a lament by David over the future exile (*Rashi*), more specifically the threat against the Jews by Haman in the book of Esther (various *Rabbis*). For that reason there is a custom to read it on Purim." The Jews had an ongoing concern over the question of God's presence throughout their history as a people. Even Exodus 17 raises the question: "Is God among us or not?" The interpretation of Psalm 22 as a lament by David over the future exile intensifies the question and takes it to a new level.

15. Matthew emphasizes that Jesus is "God with us" or "Immanuel" (harking back to Isaiah 7:14), who will be with us throughout the ages (Matthew 1:23; 28:18–20).

16. My view on Jesus as ultimate truth in relation to other truths resonates with Karl Barth's discussion of Jesus as the light of the world in relation to other lights in *Church Dogmatics*, eds. G. W. Bromiley and T. F. Torrance, vol. 4.3, *The Doctrine of Reconciliation* (Edinburgh: T. & T. Clark, 1961); Paul Louis Metzger, *Word of Christ*, 121–57. See also Pope John Paul II, "Dominus Iesus" (encyclical letter, Rome, June 16, 2000).

17. "Elie Wiesel (b. 1928)," in Telushkin, *Jewish Literacy*, 430–31. Wiesel's works include *Night*, trans. Marion Wiesel, rev. ed (New York: Hill and Wang, 2006); *The Jews of Silence: A Personal Report on Soviet Jewry*, rev. ed. (New York: Schocken Books, 2011); and *Legends of Our Time* (New York: Schocken Books, 2004).

18. Wiesel, *Night*, 64–65.

19. See Ellen Norman Stern's account of how Wiesel's ordeal (including the execution of the "sad angel") affected his faith, in her biography, *Elie Wiesel: Witness for Life* (New York: Ktav, 1982), 79–84. There she writes that Wiesel had formerly "believed that his fervent prayers were the direct key to God. It had been up to him—through the intensity with which he appealed to God—to influence Him, to ask Him for blessings for his family and for himself. Elie's belief had undergone the most drastic of changes. Not only had he been disappointed by God; after the cruel events which had befallen them during the past year, Elie had every reason to doubt the very existence of God. His whole former life had been a love affair with the idea of a beneficent God. His every day had been devoted to the service of religion.

But now . . ." As Stern makes clear, Wiesel does not deny God, but did experience extreme disappointment and anger with God, feelings with which any honest human being would empathize given Wiesel's harrowing experiences.

20. Wiesel, *Night*, 67.

21. Ibid., 68. Rabbi Telushkin claims, "No event in the last two thousand years of Jewish history has shaken the faith of so many Jews as the Holocaust" (Telushkin, "The 614th Commandment: Not to Grant Hitler Posthumous Victory," *Jewish Literacy*, 432–33).

Emil L. Fackenheim, who is often referred to as the philosopher of the Holocaust, has reflected at great length on the significance and impact of the Holocaust on world history and the Jewish and Christian faiths. Fackenheim claims that the 614th commandment (beyond the 613 commandments of the law of Moses) is that there must not be any weakening of faith among Jews. To do so would grant Hitler a victory after the grave (Emil L. Fackenheim, "The 614 Commandment," in *The Jewish Thought of Emil Fackenheim: A Reader*, Michael L. Morgan, ed. [Detroit: Wayne State University, 1987], 157–60; Emil L. Fackenheim, "Holocaust," in *The Ways of Religion: An Introduction to the Major Traditions*, ed. Roger Eastman [New York: Oxford University Press, 1999], 327–35).

22. See for example Wiesel's sobering and deep reflection on the Midrashic and mystical teaching of God accompanying his people into exile in "God's Suffering: A Commentary," *All Rivers Run to the Sea: Memoirs* (New York: Shocken Books, 1995), 101–5.

For all our differences regarding views on the Messiah and the interpretation of various biblical texts such as Isaiah 53, we Christians should see Judaism as a living faith. In addition to learning from the Jewish people on such topics as theodicy and providence, we must also see that the encounter with the Jewish community is essential to understanding who we are as the church. Judaism's differences as a community from the church reveal to us our distinctiveness, and their distinctiveness as the Jewish community reminds us of where we come from and where we are going and who we are—ever in relation to them. We come to know ourselves better the more we come to know them. This is true of any vital encounter with another tradition; true knowledge is always relational and participatory, dialogical and dialectical. All too often in the Western context, there has been a disparaging of the non-Western other (rather than a meaningful dialogical and mutually beneficial encounter), epitomized in the West's treatment of the Jewish community. One of the greatest wrongs committed by the Western church has been to turn an Oriental faith into an Occidental one, suppressing the former, failing to sense the fundamental Jewish quality of the Christian faith. This is grievously evident in the Christendom era as the West attacked the Jewish people, viewing the Jews as an intrinsic contamination that needed to be removed. A similar move was made against the Arabs, seeing both as enemies of the West. See Gil Anidjar, *The Jew, the Arab: A History of the Enemy* (Stanford: Stanford University Press, 2003); J. Kameron Carter, "Epilogue," in *A World for All? Global Civil Society in Political Theory and Trinitarian Theology*, ed. William F. Storrar, Peter J. Casarella, and Paul Louis Metzger (Grand Rapids: Eerdmans, 2011). The agenda of Christendom is extremely problematic and dangerous. Among other things, Judaism in its distinctive and profound particularity rightly and profoundly reminds us of who we once were as the church (and still should be), and rightly serves as a witness that rebukes us, simply through its presence in our midst, for not maintaining our distinctive particularity in relation to our Jewish sources and destiny through the Jewish Jesus.

23. Elie Wiesel, quoted in Stern, *Elie Wiesel*, 172. For a discussion of theodicy in the Jewish tradition, see Rabbi Joseph Telushkin, "Theodicy," in *Jewish Literacy*, 622–25.

24. Dietrich Bonhoeffer, *Letters and Papers from Prison*, ed. Eberhard Bethge, rev. ed. (New York: Macmillan, 1967), 188.

25. Ibid., xxiii.

26. For Bonhoeffer, the "God" who would sweep into town and save the day by taking care of all our problems "forsakes" us. This was his experience: God did not deliver Germany from the Nazis during his lifetime. It is important to note that Bonhoeffer did not believe that the God of Jesus Christ abandons us. For Bonhoeffer, we have not taken seriously enough God's presence on the cross.

I believe that if Bonhoeffer were to have survived imprisonment and witnessed Hitler's demise, he would have modified his position to suggest that God also delivers us dramatically through other acts of power; such acts of power would include the liberation of Germany by the Allies. The *Letters and Papers from Prison* are important existential reflections written "in the moment."

27. Elie Wiesel, *After the Darkness: Reflections on the Holocaust* (New York: Schocken Books, 2002), 10.

28. Bonhoeffer models for Christians today a profoundly redemptive engagement of the Jewish community (in contrast to the German Christians of his day and the founder of his Christian tradition in Germany, Luther).

29. In 1970 (about twelve years after writing *Night*), Wiesel gave a lecture at a conference focusing on the history of the church struggle and the Holocaust at Wayne State University. The proceedings were eventually published in the volume *The German Church Struggle and the Holocaust*, ed. Franklin H. Littell and Hubert G. Locke (Detroit: Wayne State University Press, 1974). In his essay titled "Talking and Writing and Keeping Silent," Wiesel comments on his own spiritual state of being. After sharing that he never engages in "God-is-dead" language, he goes on to say, "I never speak of God now. I rather speak of men who believed in God or men who denied God. How strange that the philosophy denying God came not from the

survivors. Those who came out with the so-called God is dead theology, not one of them had been in Auschwitz. Those who had never said it. I have my problems with God, believe me. I have my anger and I have my quarrels and I have my nightmares. But my dispute, my bewilderment, my astonishment, is with men" (271–72). Later in the same essay Wiesel reacts to a point made by an earlier conference presenter who claimed that it is more difficult today to live in a world without God; in response Wiesel exclaims, "NO! If you want difficulties, choose to live with God. Can you compare today the tragedy of the believer to that of the nonbeliever?! The real tragedy, the real drama, is the drama of the believer" (274). Wiesel closes his address explaining that to be a Jew is to have all the reasons in the world to hate the Germans and the church and not to hate them, and "to be a Jew is to have all the reasons in the world not to have faith in language, in singing, in prayers, and in God, but to go on telling the tale, to go on carrying on the dialogue, and to have my own silent prayers and quarrels with God" (276–77).

30. The biographer Ellen Norman Stern has commented on the centrality of hope and also of joy in Wiesel's mature life as reflected in his communion with his wife and children and his passion for young people for whom he writes. See Stern, *Elie Wiesel*, 167, 173, 175–76.

31. In the New Testament, it is only a select group of Jewish leaders (and not the people as a whole) who actually deliver Jesus to the Gentile Pilate, who as the Roman governor sentences Jesus to death by crucifixion at the hands of his Roman forces.

32. The major Jewish rabbis of the medieval era such as Rashi (Rabbi Shelomo ben Isaac, 1040–1105) commented on Isaiah 53 against the backdrop of the persecution of the Jews at the hands of Christians during the Crusades. The theme of the presence of God sparked Rashi's comments on Isaiah 53: Has God abandoned the Jewish people? One solution was to interpret Isaiah 53 to refer to the nation; it wasn't about God abandoning his people but about God having a distinctive role for his people in suffering on behalf of the Gentiles. It is in modern times in the debate with Christians that Jews have often virtually abandoned the idea of Isaiah 53 as messianic. However, between AD 100 and the mid-nineteenth century, documents from many rabbis emphasize that the text of Isaiah 53 was messianic. They also deal with Psalm 22 in this way. In other words, not all substantial figures accepted the "national-collective interpretation" developed by Rashi.

The messianic dimensions of the text are important to many Jews throughout history. Regarding the messianic interpretation from the second through the nineteenth centuries, see Samuel R. Driver and Adolf Neubauer, eds., *The Fifty-Third Chapter of Isaiah According to the Jewish Interpreters*, 2 vols. (New York: Ktav, 1969). In particular, see the following references (all in volume 2), which allude to or discuss Isaiah 52 and 53 in messianic terms: II:9 (Yalkut Sh'moni, ascribed to Rabbi Simeon Kara, twelfth century); II:10–11 (Siphre, second to third century); II:14–15

(Rabbi Simeon ben Yochai, second century); II:34–35 (Rabbi Moses, Ha-Darshan, eleventh century); II:99–100, 114 (Rabbi Moshe Kohen Ibn Crispin, fifteenth century); II:374–75 (Rabbi Moses ben Maimon [Maimonides], 1135–1204); II:399 (Prayer for the Day of Atonement, c. ninth century AD); II:400–1 (Herz Homberg, 1749–1841); II:568 (Levi ben Gershon, 1288–1344). See also pages 890–91 of the *Jewish Study Bible* for the discussion of Isaiah 53. While providing a good overview, it does not do justice to the multifaceted level of interpretation within Rabbinic interpretation (it can be both/and, not either/or in terms of the nation and individual). If anything, the widespread distancing from the individual Messiah is a modern phenomenon, not ancient or medieval. In view of the influence of Rashi (his commentary on the whole Bible is basically incorporated into the Rabbinic Bible), especially in the last three hundred years, many Jews today do not know that the messianic-individual interpretation was a dominant view through much of the common era (post-Christ). Whether or not the predominant number of Jewish people today read Isaiah 53 messianically, I believe they should do so (while not ceasing to account for a national dimension). As Rabbi Telushkin claims, "among traditional Jews, the belief in a personal Messiah seems to have grown more central in recent years" ("Messianism" in *Jewish Literacy*, 614–16).

Joel Rembaum points to an instance of Rashi interpreting Isaiah 53 in messianic terms: "The Development of a Jewish Exegetical Tradition Regarding Isaiah 53," *Harvard Theological Review* (1982): 294n19. Rembaum argues that "the Servant as messiah is the dominant theme in the rabbinic sources. In the Middle Ages, Jewish exegetes tended to view the Servant as the Jewish people suffering in exile" (291–92). Rembaum offers several reasons for the shift: first, "Christian anti-Jewish propaganda . . . pointed to the Jewish exile as proof of God's punishment and abandonment of the Jewish people." In contending against such propaganda the Jewish respondents claimed that the Jewish people were God's Suffering Servant functioning as a light to the nations while in exile, thus affirming their special significance as God's covenantal people. In the face of Christian attempts to prove the christological reading of the Suffering Servant prophecy in Isaiah 53, they reacted "by avoiding the messianic interpretation altogether, so as not to give their adversaries even the slightest pretext for arguing their point." In its place, they put forth the collective-national view of the Suffering Servant.

There is at least one more reason why the collective-national interpretation became so prominent among the Jewish people in medieval Europe. Having experienced horrible persecution during the first Crusade, the Jewish community wrestled with questions of the status of God's covenant with his people Israel and matters of theodicy. They came to see themselves as God's faithful people suffering in exile, bearing witness to the indelible bond between God, Torah, and Israel as the highest form of religious truth, for which they would be greatly rewarded in the future as God's Suffering Servant (Rembaum, "Development of Jewish Exegetical Tradition," 292–94). While not wishing to dismiss a collective dimension to Isaiah 53, I am deeply burdened and troubled by the realization that the church was largely responsible for the widespread rejection of Isaiah 53 as a messianic prophecy.

33. This is not to say that all Jewish people have rejected Jesus. Many have not even been introduced to him or encountered him personally, no doubt in part because of the church's failure in most circles throughout the centuries to engage God's chosen people meaningfully. In the use of words such as "rejection," I am speaking of Israel's rejection in the Pauline sense, that as a corporate entity Israel has rejected Jesus. In discussions of Paul, it is always important to maintain that in spite of this rejection, God in Jesus has not and will not reject the Jewish people (Romans 9–11).

34. Elie Wiesel (interview by Academy of Achievement, Sun Valley, Idaho, June 29, 1996), http://www.achievement.org/autodoc/printmember/wie0int-1 (accessed August 20, 2011).

35. According to Wiesel, in Midrashic and mystical Jewish thought, God accompanies his people into exile (Wiesel, "God's Suffering," 103).

36. I do not make these claims lightly. It has been asserted that Bonhoeffer said that as a result of the Holocaust, the Germans could never evangelize the Jews again. One person who makes this assertion, Theodore A. Gill, extends it to cover all Gentiles. See his essay "What Can America Learn from the German Church Struggle?" in *The German Church Struggle and the Holocaust*, ed. Franklin H. Littell and Hubert G. Locke (Detroit: Wayne State University Press, 1974), 288. Emil Fackenheim quotes from Gill's essay in his own article previously cited, titled "Holocaust." A footnote in Fackenheim's piece claims that Bonhoeffer is quoted in *The German Church Struggle and the Holocaust* as saying that Christians as a whole "can no longer speak evangelically to the Jews." Here is the context for the statement in Fackenheim: "Is the Holocaust a rupture for Christianity? German Christians, and possibly Christians as a whole, 'can no longer speak evangelically to Jews'" (Fackenheim, "Holocaust," in *The Ways of Religion*, 331). According to Gill's essay, it is not Bonhoeffer who declares that Christians as a whole cannot present the gospel to the Jewish people but Gill himself (Fackenheim does nuance the point with the use of the word *possibly*). The actual statement from Bonhoeffer is likely a paraphrase, given that there are no quote marks around the statement in Gill's essay (Gill, "What Can America Learn from the German Church Struggle?," 288). Nonetheless it is important that Gentile Christians reflect on Fackenheim's contextual remarks: "Is the Holocaust a rupture for Christianity?" Drawing from other writers, mostly German theologians, Fackenheim declares, "The Jewish stance toward Christian missionizing attempts directed at them, in any case, cannot be what it once was. Prior to the Holocaust, Jews could respect such attempts, although of course considering them misguided. After the Holocaust, they can only view them as

trying in one way what Hitler undertook in another" (Fackenheim, "Holocaust," 332). Lastly, see Fackenheim's "Letters on Bonhoeffer," and "Concerning Post-Holocaust Christianity," in *The Jewish Thought of Emil Fackenheim* (241–43; 244–54). We Gentile Christians must be very sensitive to the past and be very diligent that the Holocaust does not occur again. We must also assert that Hitler and his so-called German Christians' distortion of Christianity was the teaching of "the antichrist." In keeping with Karl Barth, we must exclaim that the Hitler enterprise was that "of an evil spirit" and that it must be unreservedly and rigorously opposed. See Karl Barth, "A Letter to Great Britain from Switzerland," in *This Christian Cause* (New York: Macmillan, 1941), 11.

For Bonhoeffer and later for Barth, the Jewish question was vital. Eberhard Bethge speaks of the Jewish problem being the first and fundamental question for Bonhoeffer in 1933 in *Dietrich Bonhoeffer: A Biography* (Minneapolis: Augsburg Fortress Publishers, 2000). Bonhoeffer wrote the important and controversial essay discussed earlier, "The Church and the Jewish Question," in 1933. See the discussion of Bonhoeffer and this 1933 essay at the United States Holocaust Memorial Museum website: http://www.ushmm.org/museum/exhibit/online/bonhoeffer/?content=3 (accessed August 20, 2011).

Going beyond Bonhoeffer, from the standpoint of the New Testament (which was written almost exclusively by Jewish men), Jesus is the culmination of the Jewish faith. According to the New Testament, the gospel or good news of Jesus Christ (a righteousness by faith from first to last) is from the Jews and for the Jews—by faith—and then for the Gentiles as equal sharers in this good news by faith (Romans 1:16–17; 9–11). With great sensitivity and love, we must share our faith with the Jews and share in their suffering from this New Testament vantage point.

37. Tevye says to God, "I know, I know. We are Your chosen people. But, once in a while, can't You choose someone else?" *Fiddler on the Roof,* directed by Norman Jewison (1971; Century City, CA: United Artists, 2007), DVD.

Chapter 7: Whack Jobs (Islam)

1. Richard Reno, "Islam" (lecture, Rizwan Mosque, Portland, Oregon, October 2009). While some may question the legitimacy of engaging Mr. Reno, who is a Western convert to a form of Islam considered suspect to many Muslims, I beg to differ. Islam is a living and global religion. As with any religious tradition that is living and global, there are diverse perspectives and people advocating those perspectives. We must learn to move beyond stereotypical and generalized views, and deal with concrete manifestations and embodiments. This point is especially pertinent when dealing with folk religion (not to be confused here with Mr. Reno's branch of Islam), which does not represent the received orthodoxies of the various religions.

2. Daniel W. Brown, "Clash of Cultures or Clash of Theologies? A Critique

of Some Contemporary Evangelical Responses to Islam," in *Cultural Encounters: A Journal for the Theology of Culture* 1, no. 1 (2006): 69–84. Brown is also the author of *Rethinking Tradition in Modern Islamic Thought*, Cambridge Middle East Studies (Cambridge: Cambridge University Press, 1999); and *A New Introduction to Islam* (Oxford: Blackwell Publishing, 2004).

3. Two classic texts on Islam are Frederick Mathewson Denny, *An Introduction to Islam*, 4th ed. (1985; Upper Saddle River, NJ: Prentice Hall, 2010); and Fazlur Rahman, *Islam*, 2nd ed. (Chicago: University of Chicago Press, 1979). Edward W. Said, in *Covering Islam: How the Media and the Experts Determine How We See the Rest of the World* (New York: Pantheon Books, 1981), reflects upon the bias of the Western world toward Islam and internal movements that seek to homogenize Islam.

4. Many Christians maintain that the Quran speaks of Jesus as the only truly "sinless" prophet. It is the meaning of the word translated "sinless" that is debated. The sinlessness of all prophets in Islam may only mean that God preserved their words from error, not that they never made errors in life.

5. For a discussion of various non-Christian and Christian sources concerning the life and death of Jesus Christ, see *Catholic Encyclopedia Online*, s.vv. "Early Historical Documents on Jesus Christ," http://www.newadvent.org/cathen/08375a .htm (accessed August 22, 2011).

6. In this portion of his lecture, Mr. Reno claimed that there are six core tenets of Islam: living and loyal faith in God's absolute unity, belief in angels as important messengers of God, belief in revealed books culminating in the Quran, belief in prophetic messengers culminating in Muhammad, belief in the final judgment, and belief in the divine decree and with it predestination. On the subject of the various classes of Islamic doctrine, see Denny, *An Introduction to Islam*, 92–98.

7. Ibid., 105–23.

8. "The Official Website of the Ahmadiyya Muslim Community," Al Islam, http://www.alislam.org/ (accessed August 22, 2011). See also *Encyclopedia of Islam and the Muslim World*, ed. Richard C. Martin (New York: Macmillan Reference, 2004), s.v. "Ahmadiyya."

9. While jihad is often translated as "holy war" in the West, there are other meanings to it. Denny speaks of a greater and a lesser jihad: "The greater is the individual's personal struggle with his or her base instincts and lack of faith and devotion." This is spiritual in nature. Denny also speaks of the lesser jihad, which "involves, if necessary, armed struggle against the enemies of Islam, although it should be only in self-defense. . . . The Quran commands that 'there shall be no compulsion in religion.' Jihad as exertion is definitely aimed at the spread of Islam, but by peaceful means like preaching, travel, establishing educational institutions, and setting a good example. Jihad as warfare is generally aimed at righting a wrong and has even been proclaimed by one Muslim group with reference to another. Even

today, sometimes such a call to jihad is heard in troubled parts of the Islamic world." Denny mentions that jihad is sometimes referred to as the "sixth pillar" (Denny, *An Introduction to Islam*, 123). Rahman notes that "among the later Muslim legal schools, however, it is only the fanatic Khārijites who have declared jihad to be one of the 'pillars of the Faith'" (Rahman, *Islam*, 37).

10. One source on Islam claims, "Despite the fact that jihad is not supposed to include aggressive warfare, this has occurred as exemplified by early extremists like the Khārijites and contemporary extremists such as Osama Bin Laden and his jihad against America as well as jihad organizations in Lebanon, the Persian Gulf, and Indonesia" (John L. Esposito, Darrell J. Fasching, and Todd Lewis, *World Religions Today* [New York: Oxford University Press, 2002], 213).

11. See these sources on Islam's rise, expansion, and conquest of different lands, as well as their approach to other religions: Denny, *An Introduction to Islam*, 88–89, 125–49; Fred McGraw Donner, *The Early Islamic Conquests* (Princeton: Princeton University Press, 1981); *Encyclopedia of Islam and the Muslim World*, s.v. "Conflict and Violence."

See these sources for diverse perspectives on Islam's rise: Karen Armstrong, *Muhammad: A Biography of the Prophet* (San Francisco: HarperOne, 1993); Efraim Karsh, *Islamic Imperialism: A History* (New Haven: Yale University Press, 2006).

12. Brown, "Clash of Cultures or Clash of Theologies?" 83–84.

13. Ibid., 84n71. See also Esposito et al., *World Religions Today*, 189, for their discussion of Muhammad as "the living Quran."

14. See Kenneth Cragg, *Muhammad and the Christian: A Question of Response* (Maryknoll: Orbis Books, 1984), 45. While Jesus is highly honored in Islam, he does not enjoy the prominence Muhammad does. Although God delivers him from his enemies by rapturing him to heaven, he makes "no triumphal entry into a capitulating Mecca" as Muhammad did. "Muhammad's more 'effective' destiny is further seen as indicating his 'finality' as 'the seal of the prophets.'" If Cragg is correct in his comparison (and I believe he is), Christians in the West must not seek to have success at combating Islam but be willing to suffer for Muslims out of Christ's sacrificial love for them and all other people.

Brown draws attention to Kenneth Cragg's delineation of the cardinal difference between Christianity and Islam as being one of suffering versus success (Brown, "Clash of Cultures or Clash of Theologies?" 84).

15. Brown, "Clash of Cultures or Clash of Theologies?" 84.

16. Ibid., 69–72.

17. Deloria, *God Is Red*, 261.

18. Esposito, et al., *World Religions Today*, 184–85.

19. I have changed the names of the individuals in this account to Rick and Ahmed for the sake of confidentiality.

20. Stephen Neill, *Christian Faith and Other Faiths: The Christian Dialogue with Other Religions* (London: Oxford University Press, 1960), 69.

21. In keeping with a point made later in this chapter, one danger in telling this story is that it perpetuates a stereotype that Rick is obviously a well-intentioned and peace-loving Christian whereas Ahmed is an angry, militant Muslim with an AK-47. This is just one of Rick's stories of life among Muslims, many about peace-loving and gracious Muslims like the ones I encounter at Rizwan Mosque. Moreover, as the story indicates, once Ahmed and Rick connected on a personal level, Ahmed became a very hospitable host.

For an inviting account of life among Muslims in Pakistan, refer to Greg Mortenson and David Oliver Relin's book, *Three Cups of Tea: One Man's Mission to Promote Peace One School at a Time* (London: Penguin Books, 2006). While Mortenson has come under intense scrutiny, the story of what occurred there is profound. Also see the article on the Navy Seal who was protected by a village in Afghanistan from the Taliban: Laura Blumenfeld, "The Sole Survivor," *Washington Post*, June 11, 2007, http://www .washingtonpost.com/wp-dyn/content/article/2007/06/10 /AR2007061001492.html?hpid=artslot (accessed August 22, 2011).

22. Brown, "Clash of Cultures or Clash of Theologies?" 84. Volf's point on the distinctiveness of love in Christianity by way of enemy love resonates with Brown's claim in that the cross signifies enemy love; Miroslav Volf, *Allah: A Christian Response* (New York: HarperOne, 2011), 183.

23. Of course, on account of the fall, there is a real sense in which all of us are God's enemies (Romans 5:6–11). The good news is that God does not treat us as enemies; rather he laid down his life for us so that we can become his friends.

24. Miroslav Volf claims that although it is not accurate to assert that normative Christianity is a religion of love and official Islam is a religion of war, and while Muslims "insist" that we should be kind to all people—even those who mistreat us—"most reject the idea that [for Islam] the love of neighbor includes the love of enemy" (Volf, *Allah*, 183).

25. "Is America Islamophobic? What the anti-mosque uproar tells us about how the U.S. regards Muslims," *Time*, August 30, 2010, cover.

26. John Howard Yoder, "Armaments and Eschatology"; quoted in Stanley Hauerwas, *With the Grain of the Universe: The Church's Witness and Natural Theology* (Grand Rapids: Brazos Press, 2001), 6.

27. Cragg, *Muhammad and the Christian*, 45.

While Cragg does not speak of the cross but of God delivering Jesus by rapturing him to heaven (according to a Muslim account), Jesus did not conquer his enemies by way of their capitulation to him, but by suffering for them.

28. There are rich resources in the Christian and Muslim traditions bound up with neighborliness and hospitality that make possible peaceful and sacrificial coexistence,

as illustrated in the Muslim named Mohammed's sacrifice of his life for his Christian friend, Christian de Chergé, and Christian's solidarity with the Muslim community unto the death in Algeria as recounted in John W. Kiser's historical account, *The Monks of Tibhirine: Faith, Love, and Terror in Algeria* (New York: St. Martin's Griffin, 2002). While the lead monk, Christian, saw closer connections than I do between the teachings of Christianity and Islam (in part because he was less inclined to doctrinal discussions and focused primarily on religious ethics—how religion helps people live together well; p. 68), his humility, sense of solidarity with his Muslim neighbors, and commitment to Jesus' ethic stand out as exemplary and worthy of imitation.

Chapter 8: The Jesus Box (Hinduism)

1. "Ten Questions People Ask About Hinduism," *Hinduism Today Educational Insight* (Kapaa, HI: Himalayan Academy, 2006), 3.

2. Bharat Naik, "Hinduism" (lecture, Multnomah Biblical Seminary, Portland, OR, November 4, 2009).

It is worth noting what Heinrich Zimmer says of the anthropomorphic personifications of ultimate reality in Hinduism: In contrast to the Greeks who in later times became quite critical of anthropomorphic representations of the divine, India "retained its anthropomorphic personifications of the cosmic forces as vivid masks, magnificent celestial personae, which could serve, in an optional way, to assist the mind in its attempt to comprehend what was regarded as manifested through them. . . . What is expressed through the personal masks was understood to transcend them, and yet the garb of the divine personae was never actually removed. By this tolerant, cherishing attitude a solution of the theological problem was attained that preserved the personal character of the divine powers for all the purposes of worship and daily life while permitting an abstract, supreme and transcendent concept to dominate for the more lofty, supraritualistic stages of insight and speculation" (Heinrich Zimmer, *Philosophies of India*, ed. Joseph Campbell, Bollingen Series [Princeton: Princeton University Press, 1969], 342–43). This orientation stands in contrast to trinitarian thought, which sees the persons as constitutive of divine being. In trinitarian thought, God is interpersonal and communal in the divine life and interpersonal and communal in relation to the world. There is no division between God's eternal being and God's engagement of us. The goal of worship and reflection in trinitarian monotheism is interpersonal union and communion with God. For further reading on Hinduism in general, see Thomas J. Hopkins, *The Hindu Religious Tradition*, The Religious Life of Man (Belmont, CA: Wadsworth, 1971).

3. "God in Hindu Dharma and Temples," Hindu Universe, http://www.hindunet.org/god/ (accessed August 22, 2011).

4. "The Same Water, Different Names: A Parable by Ramakrishna," Ramakrishna Mission Pamphlet (Calcutta, 1976); quoted in Esposito et al, *World Religions Today*, 316.

5. Edward Gibbon, *History of the Decline and Fall of the Roman Empire* (London: Jones and Co., 1826), 1:18.

6. R. Kendall Soulen, "Go Tell Pharaoh, Or, Why Empires Prefer a Nameless God," *Cultural Encounters: A Journal for the Theology of Culture* 1, no. 2 (Summer 2005): 49–59.

7. According to the authors of *Patterns of Religion*, the spiritual progeny of Hindu poets Ravidas and Kabir maintained that God "cannot be encompassed in form or, especially, in the social and religious organizations that temples and the priestly hierarchy involve." This orientation stands in marked contrast to other Hindu traditions, which assert that God is associated with various forms, such as a deity in a temple image or the image in a sacred object of nature. The authors go on to say that "this form of devotion provides a religious basis for the criticism of caste privilege" (Roger Schmidt et al., *Patterns of Religion* [Belmont, CA: Wadsworth, 1999], 212–13).

While I can certainly appreciate their point about stratification being tied to particular forms of deity, I still do not believe that namelessness moves us beyond social stratification and oppression because one can commodify a nameless deity and its people, and a people whose deity is ultimately nameless is itself ultimately a nameless people. In contrast to the formed deities found in temples associated with priestly hierarchy and in contrast to the formless deity noted here, the named God revealed in Jesus Christ breaks down divisions between Jews and Gentiles, males and females, and slaves and free—all as a result of this named God's atoning work on their behalf (Galatians 3:28). This same named deity lifts up the widow and orphan in their distress and causes them to ascend by faith rather than by social status or human decision to reign with the resurrected and ascended Jesus.

8. Niels C. Nielsen Jr. et al., *Religions of the World* (New York: St. Martin's Press, 1983), 144.

Chapter 9: The Dewdrop World (Buddhism)

1. Paul Louis Metzger, "Mutuality and Particularity: Contours of Authentic Dialogue," in *Cultural Encounters: A Journal for the Theology of Culture* 3, no. 1 (Winter 2006): 51–59; Sallie Jiko Tisdale, "Beloved Community," in *Tricycle: The Buddhist Review* 16, no. 1 (Fall 2006): 54–59, 114–15.

2. Thich Nhat Hanh, *Living Buddha, Living Christ*, 10th anniversary ed. (New York: Riverhead Books, 2007). The author talks about how Buddhism and Christianity intersect at compassion and holiness.

3. Kyogen Carlson, "Zen Buddhism" (lecture, Zen Center, Portland, OR, October 28, 2009).

Abbot Carlson recommends the following sources for further study: for general Buddhism, see Steve Hagen, *Buddhism Plain and Simple* (New York: Broadway Books, 1997). For Soto Zen Buddhism, see John Daido Loori, *The Heart of Being: Moral and Ethical Teachings of Zen Buddhism*, Tuttle Library of Enlightenment (Rutland, Vermont: Charles E. Tuttle Company, Inc., 1996); Shunryu Suzuki, *Zen Mind, Beginner's Mind*, ed. Trudy Dixon (Boston: Shambhala Publications, Inc., 2006); Dainen Katagiri, *Returning to Silence: Zen Practice in Daily Life* (Boston: Shambala Publications, Inc., 1988).

For further study, see Daisetz Teitaro Suzuki, *An Introduction to Zen Buddhism* (New York: Grove Press, Inc., 1964); D. T. Suzuki, *Essays in Zen Buddhism* (1949; New York: Grove Press, 1994). In their work, *Buddhism: A Christian Exploration and Appraisal* (Downers Grove: IVP Academic, 2009), Keith Yandell and Harold Netland speak of D. T. Suzuki's role in popularizing Zen in the West, and claim that his "characterization of satori and Zen is not accepted by all Buddhists" (62). See also chapter 3 of their work, where they discuss Suzuki's influence in Zen's transmission to the West in more recent times. The authors recommend the following for the historical development of Zen: Heinrich Dumoulin, *Zen Buddhism: A History*, vol. 1 (India and China), trans. James W. Heisig and Paul Knitter (New York: Macmillan, 1988); Heinrich Dumoulin, *Zen Buddhism: A History*, vol. 2 (Japan), trans. James W. Heisig and Paul Knitter (New York: Macmillan, 1990).

4. The Noble Eightfold Path involves "Right View, Right Aspiration, Right Speech, Right Conduct, Right Means of Livelihood, Right Endeavor, Right Mindfulness, and Right Contemplation" (Heinrich Zimmer, "Buddhahood," in Roger Eastman, ed., *The Ways of Religion: An Introduction to the Major Traditions*, 3rd ed. [New York: Oxford University Press, 1999], 84).

5. Heinrich Zimmer sets forth the following as the "Four Noble Truths" of Buddhism: first, "All li[f]e is sorrowful"; second, "The cause of suffering is ignorant craving"; third, "The suppression of suffering can be achieved"; and fourth, "The way is the Noble Eightfold Path." Heinrich Zimmer, "Buddhahood," 84.

6. According to Walpola Rahula, Buddhism is atheistic: there is no place for an almighty creator. He also asserts the doctrine of "no-self" (*anatman*); there is no enduring self. What perpetuates rebirth is the mistaken view that we are enduring selves with enduring egos. There is nothing substantial that passes on from this life to the next. Karmic effects are what pass on, not the soul. See his work, *What the Buddha Taught*, rev. ed. (New York: Grove Press, 1974). On "God," see for example pages 52 and 56; for examples on the "ego," "self," and "soul," see pages 21, 23, 33, 39, 51–52, 55–57. On karma, see pages 31–32.

7. Harold Netland maintains that if you take Buddhist metaphysics seriously, there is no ultimate difference between good and evil. For Netland, this trivializes

our experience of suffering and our sense of doing right and not wrong. See Harold A. Netland, *Encountering Religious Pluralism: The Challenge to Christian Faith & Mission* (Downers Grove: InterVarsity Press, 2001), 306–7 for his discussion of Masao Abe. For Netland, if there is no ultimate distinction between good and evil, why be compassionate? What is so good about being compassionate? If one says that through compassion we put ourselves in a better position to attain enlightenment, one can respond by saying that this is a utilitarian reason, and not one grounded in reality.

8. Paul Tillich asked some Buddhist dialogue partners how essential it was for Buddhism that Gautama Buddha existed. The response was that it wouldn't matter at all. This runs contrary to Jesus and the gospel. See Robert E. Wood, "Tillich Encounters Japan," *Japanese Religions* 2 (May 1962): 48–50.

9. See Yandell's and Netland's helpful discussion of key similarities and fundamental differences between traditional Buddhism and Christianity pertaining to the dharma and the gospel: *Buddhism*, 177–81.

10. See Paul Williams's discussion of the Buddhist doctrine of rebirth and how rebirth is conceived in the West in *The Unexpected Way: On Converting from Buddhism to Catholicism* (Edinburg: T&T Clark, 2002), 198–203. There he writes, "Rebirth, in Buddhism and other early Indian systems of liberation, was seen as horrific. To point out that 'my' rebirth involves among other things the destruction of everything that counts as me would have been seen simply as emphasizing how horrible rebirth is, and the need to escape from it through spiritual liberation, nirvāna." See also Williams's critical reflections on the Buddhist view of persons and other entities as ultimately "conventional constructs" in his other work, *Altruism and Reality: Studies in the Philosophy of the Bodhicaryāvatāra* (Richmond: Curzon, 1998), 104–74.

11. Os Guinness, *The Dust of Death: A Critique of the Establishment and the Counter Culture and the Proposal for a Third Way* (Downers Grove: InterVarsity Press, 1973), 222–23.

12. See also my discussion of these and similar themes in Paul Louis Metzger, "The Migration of Monism and the Matrix of Trinitarian Mediation," *Scottish Journal of Theology* 58/3, no. 2, 302–18. On page 317, I set forth the following fundamental difference between orthodox Christianity and Buddhism: "How radically different is the Christian vision from that of Buddhism? Whereas Gautama Buddha sought to rid himself and others of the world of pain by withdrawing from it, Christ sought to rid the world of pain by entering into it. Whereas Gautama departed so as to deny being, Christ came so as to deny the denial of being. Whereas Gautama sought to become what we are not so that we might become nothing, too, Christ became what we are so that we might become what he is, and enter into the sacred dance of communion in the trinitarian life of God."

Chapter 10: Will the Real Jesus Please Stand Up—and Sit Down? (Unitarian Universalism)

1. Marilyn Sewell, "Will the Real Jesus Please Stand Up?" *Cultural Encounters: A Journal for the Theology of Culture* 3, no. 1 (Winter 2006): 36. A movie has been made of her, called *Raw Faith*, www.rawfaith.com. Reverend Sewell is the author and editor of several works. She edited *Cries of the Spirit: A Celebration of Women's Spirituality* (Boston: Beacon Press, 1991), which is an anthology of women's poetry on spiritual themes. She also edited the companion volume, *Claiming the Spirit Within: A Sourcebook of Women's Poetry* (Boston: Beacon Press, 2001). Her latest Beacon book is the edited volume *Breaking Free: Women of Spirit at Midlife and Beyond* (Boston: Beacon Press, 2004). Her most recent publications are *A Little Book on Prayer* (Boston: Fuller Press, 2009) and *A Little Book on Forgiveness* (Boston: Fuller Press, 2009).

2. Sewell, "Will the Real Jesus Please Stand Up?" 36.

Rev. Dr. Sewell recommends the following works for a deeper understanding of Unitarian Universalism: John A. Buehrens and Forrest Church, *A Chosen Faith: An Introduction to Unitarian Universalism*, rev. ed. (Boston: Beacon Press, 1998); David E. Bumbaugh, *Unitarian Universalism: A Narrative History* (Chicago: Meadville Lombard Press, 2001).

3. *Talladega Nights*, directed by Adam McKay (2006; Culver City, CA: Sony Pictures Home Entertainment, 2006), DVD.

4. See Stephen J. Nichols, *Jesus Made in America: A Cultural History from the Puritans to the Passion of the Christ* (Downers Grove: IVP Academic, 2008).

5. Gordon Fee and Douglas Stuart, *How to Read the Bible for All Its Worth*, 2nd ed. (Grand Rapids: Zondervan, 1993), 125.

6. Sewell, "Will the Real Jesus Please Stand Up?" 37.

7. Ibid.

8. Ibid.

9. John R. W. Stott, "The Message of the Sermon on the Mount (Matthew 5–7): Christian Counter-Culture," *The Bible Speaks Today* (Downers Grove, IL: Inter-Varsity Press, 1978), 104.

10. Ibid., 108.

11. Ibid., 113. Stott views Martin Luther King Jr. as the greatest modern representative of this ethic disclosed in this text.

12. I do not have in mind here Martin Luther's biblically framed antinomian position of grace over works, but rather that antinomian (anti-law) orientation that would dismiss a biblically governed ethic of love, grace, and affection.

13. See Sewell, "Will the Real Jesus Please Stand Up?" 37.

14. Stott, "The Message of the Sermon on the Mount," 39.

15. Moll, "Health Care Debate."

16. Robert H. Gundry, *A Survey of the New Testament*, 3rd ed. (Grand Rapids:

Zondervan, 1994), 103. For a contemporary and unique introduction to the historical Jesus debate involving a representative of liberalism and a representative of orthodoxy, see Marcus J. Borg and N. T. Wright, *The Meaning of Jesus: Two Visions* (New York: HarperOne, 2000). For works focusing on the historical reliability of the gospel accounts and the historical Jesus, see F. F. Bruce, *The New Testament Documents: Are They Reliable?* 6th ed. (1943; Grand Rapids: Eerdmans/Downers Grove: InterVarsity Press, 1981); I. Howard Marshall, *I Believe in the Historical Jesus* (Grand Rapids: Eerdmans, 1977); Craig S. Keener, *The Historical Jesus of the Gospels* (Grand Rapids: Eerdmans, 2009).

17. Stott, "Sermon on the Mount," 222.

18. C. S. Lewis, *Miracles* (New York: HarperCollins, 2001), 174.

Chapter 11: The Burning Bosom (Mormonism)

1. Rather than speaking of Mormonism as a cult, it is best to speak of Mormonism as a culture. I am indebted to John Morehead and the Western Institute for Intercultural Studies, who focus on engaging Mormonism and the like from the standpoint of dynamic religious subcultures that need to hear the gospel in their own context. John has been an important dialogue partner in the formation of this chapter. See his essay, "From 'Cults' to Cultures: Bridges as a Case Study in a New Evangelical Paradigm on New Religions" (paper, CESNUR Conference, Salt Lake City, UT, June 11, 2009), http://www.cesnur.org/2009/slc_morehead.htm (accessed August 22, 2011).

2. For an example of a relational approach to engaging Mormons, see David L. Rowe, *I Love Mormons: A New Way to Share Christ with Latter-day Saints* (Grand Rapids: Baker Books, 2005). The relational dynamic is critical to missional engagement. Rodney Stark speaks of how important social networks are for Mormons in making religious tenets believable. This relational dynamic is typical of growing religious movements. See Rodney Stark, *The Rise of Mormonism*, ed. Reid L. Neilson (New York: Columbia University Press, 2005).

3. For a groundbreaking encounter between evangelicals and Mormons, see Carrie A. Moore's article chronicling an "Evening of Friendship" in Salt Lake Tabernacle, "Evangelical Preaches at Salt Lake Tabernacle," *Deseret News*, November 15, 2004, http://www.deseretnews.com/article/595105580/Evangelical-preaches -at-Salt-Lake-Tabernacle.html?pg=1 (accessed August 22, 2011). The "Evening of Friendship" took place on November 14, 2004. In addition to Ravi Zacharias, who spoke of theological differences and shared concerns of evangelicals and Mormons in a culture of relativism, Richard Mouw addressed the capacity crowd: "Taking the pulpit to speak of the event's historic nature, Fuller Theological Seminary President Richard Mouw addressed a capacity crowd of several thousand, offering a stunningly candid apology to members of The Church of Jesus Christ of Latter-day Saints and

noting that 'friendship has not come easily between our communities.' He dubbed the evening 'historic' and apologized that evangelicals 'have often misrepresented the faith and beliefs of the Latter-day Saints.' 'Let me state it clearly. We evangelicals have sinned against you,' he said, adding both camps have tended to marginalize and simplify the others' beliefs." Without taking aim at others, I confess that I resonate with Mouw's confession personally, having been guilty of the very problems he notes. I also appreciated how Zacharias emphasized biblical truth and spoke to differences between evangelicals and Mormons while also seeking common ground. *The Salt Lake Tribune* reports that Zacharias "acknowledged there are doctrinal differences—including some that are deep—between traditional Christianity and the LDS faith. His hour-long sermon emphasized aspects of Christian doctrine for which Mormons have a different understanding, such as sin, salvation through the Cross, and the Trinity. But his overarching message—that Jesus Christ is the answer to the longing in all human hearts—was one that resonated with both evangelical Christians and Mormons." This quotation is taken from "Weblog: Ravi Zacharias, Rich Mouw Speak in Mormon Tabernacle," compiled by Ted Olsen and posted on November 16, 2004 (http://www.standingtogether.org/itn_111604.html; accessed on October 8, 2010). The event called to mind Moody's historic visits to speak there in 1871 and 1899.

4. *The Doctrine and Covenants of the Church of Jesus Christ of Latter-Day Saints: Containing the Revelations Given to Joseph Smith, Jun., the Prophet, for the Building Up of the Kingdom of God in the Last Days*, section 9:8 (Westport, CT: Greenwood Press, 1971), 96, http://scriptures.lds.org/en/dc/9 (accessed August 22, 2011).

5. *Encyclopedia of Mormonism*, ed. Daniel H. Ludlow, vol. 3 (New York: Macmillan Publishing Company, 1992), s.v. "revelation." This article lists "burning in the bosom as an indication of the will of God" under "types of revelation." The explanation under "types of revelation" reads as follows: "A DISPENSATION of the GOSPEL OF JESUS CHRIST is a series of personal revelations from God. These revelations may be direct manifestations from God." The burning in the bosom is classified as one of these direct manifestations.

6. *God's Army*, directed by Richard Dutcher (2001; Thousand Oaks, CA: Ventura Distribution, 2004), DVD.

7. LeRoi C. Snow, "Devotion to a Divine Inspiration," *Improvement Era* 22, no. 8 (June 1919): 656. The same basic theme or concept as it pertains to God's progression or exaltation is found in Robert L. Millet and Joseph Fielding McConkie's claim: "Our Father's development and progression over an infinitely long period of time has brought him to a point at which he now presides as God Almighty." For the full statement, see their work, *The Life Beyond* (Salt Lake City: Bookcraft, 1986), 148–49.

8. For the debate over the primacy of this phrase, see Ronald V. Huggins, "Lorenzo Snow's Couplet: 'As Man Now Is, God Once Was; As God Now Is, Man

May Be': 'No Functioning Place in Present-Day Mormon Doctrine?' A Response to Richard Mouw," *Journal of the Evangelical Theological Society* 49, no. 3 (September 2006): 549–68. Huggins is responding to Richard Mouw's claim that the couplet by Snow has no place of prominence today in Mormon teaching. Among other items he uses in support, Huggins quotes from Stephen E. Robinson in his book with Craig L. Blomberg, *How Wide the Divide? A Mormon and an Evangelical in Conversation* (Downers Grove: InterVarsity Press, 1997), 85. See Huggins, "Lorenzo Snow's Couplet," 560–61. Referring to Snow's couplet along with the King Follett Discourse, Robinson states, "Neither statement is scriptural or canonized in the technical sense, and neither has been explained or elucidated to the church in any official manner, but they are so widely accepted by Latter-Day Saints that this technical point has become moot" (*How Wide the Divide?* 85). Snow's couplet is reproduced in *The Life and Teachings of Jesus & His Apostles* (Religion 211 and 212), 2nd ed. (Salt Lake City: The LDS Church, 1978), 60.

It is important to note in the debate on the centrality of the Snow couplet that Mormonism, like any other living religious tradition, is not a monolithic movement. In *Mormon Neo-Orthodoxy: A Crisis Theology*, O. Kendall White points to differences between some contemporary Mormons and traditionalists in terms of emphases. "By emphasizing the differences rather than the similarities between God and humanity, Mormon neo-orthodoxy aligns itself more closely with Protestant neo-orthodoxy than with traditional Mormon thought. For instance, traditional Mormon theology teaches that humans were created in the physical and spiritual image of God and may themselves become gods. In contrast, Hyrum Andrus, an early neo-orthodox theologian and professor of religion at Mormon-owned Brigham Young University, lamented in a 1960 address at the school the Mormon preoccupation with anthropomorphic descriptions of God. Arguing that Mormons pay too little attention to the greatness of God, Andrus urged listeners to acknowledge divine uniqueness, or God's otherness. In fact, an emphasis on the 'glory of God' generally characterized much of Andrus's writings" (O. Kendall White Jr., *Mormon Neo-Orthodoxy: A Crisis Theology* [Salt Lake City: Signature Books, 1987], http://www.signaturebookslibrary.org/theology/chapter4.htm#Mormon [accessed on October 26, 2010]).

9. *Encyclopedia of Mormonism*, ed. Daniel H. Ludlow, vol. 4 (New York: Macmillan Publishing Company, 1992), s.v., "War in Heaven."

10. Evangelicals and Mormons share a common religious vocabulary, though the terms have different meanings. Take, for example, *salvation*. According to Mormonism, salvation is understood in a variety of ways ("Salvation," in *Preach My Gospel: A Guide to Missionary Service* [Salt Lake City: Church of Jesus Christ of Latter-day Saints, 2004], 59), but it is commonly understood by many Mormons as a general resurrection. This view is different from the evangelical conception of salvation.

The goal for Mormonism is exaltation. Mormons do not hope that others will receive "salvation" after death because everyone will experience salvation in terms of the general resurrection. Instead, Mormons hope that non-Mormons will embrace the gospel as taught by Mormonism in the afterlife, which would entail freedom from bondage in spirit prison and the movement toward one of the glorious states postmortem. Mormons also speak of exaltation or progression beyond the individual in terms of having an eternal family. It is this theme to which Snow's couplet refers and which clarifies the meaning of becoming like God for Mormonism.

An orthodox Protestant Christian approach to exaltation involves the claim that believers become like God in his communicable attributes or perfections as we share in his life. We experience such exaltation as the fruit of our salvation. Here I have in mind Peter's declaration in 2 Peter 1:3–4: "His divine power has given us everything we need for life and godliness through our knowledge of him who called us by his own glory and goodness. Through these he has given us his very great and precious promises, so that through them you may participate in the divine nature and escape the corruption in the world caused by evil desires."

This view of exaltation is bound up with an orthodox view of Christ and our union with him. St. Athanasius speaks of Christ's incarnation and our exaltation through union with him in this way: "He [the Word of God] indeed, assumed humanity that we might become God" (St. Athanasius, *On the Incarnation: De Incarnatione Verbi Dei*, rev. ed., with an introduction by C. S. Lewis, Popular Patristics Series [New York: St. Vladimir's Seminary Press, 1996], 93). The Eastern Orthodox distinguishes between Jesus as God and saints as gods. Jesus is God by nature, whereas we become gods by grace. For the Eastern Orthodox, deification (our becoming "God" or "gods") is an exalted state of sanctification.

11. *Preach My Gospel*, 53.

12. Ibid.

13. Ibid.

14. *Encyclopedia of Mormonism*, ed. Daniel H. Ludlow, vol. 2 (New York: Macmillan Publishing Company, 1992), s.v. "hell."

15. N. T. Wright also frames consideration of the Christian notion of God by beginning with Jesus' incarnation. See Wright's chapter, "The Divinity of Jesus," in Marcus J. Borg and N. T. Wright, *The Meaning of Jesus: Two Visions* (San Francisco: HarperSanFrancisco, 1999), 157–68. In *Man of Holiness: The Mormon Search for a Personal God* (Salt Lake City: Sacred Tribes Press, 2010), John L. Bracht provides an alternative perspective and suggests approaching Mormons with a reminder of the intimacy and reality of God as incorporeal as understood by Israel through any number of Old Testament texts. Lastly, see the discussion involving Mormon dialogue on the subject of divine embodiment in *Sacred Tribes Journal* 6, no. 2 (Fall 2011). The discussion will include focused consideration of Stephen Webb's work,

Jesus Christ, Eternal God: Heavenly Flesh and the Metaphysics of Matter (Oxford: Oxford University Press, 2011).

16. St. John Damascene, *On Holy Images*, trans. Mary H. Allies (London, Thomas Baker, 1898), 15–16.

17. Edwards, *Miscellanies*, 741.

18. In their interaction with Mormon missionaries, evangelicals have often understood that Mormons have an expanded view of Scripture. These evangelicals have stated that biblical claims such as those made here may not convince Mormons of their position. Reflecting upon their encounters, these evangelicals maintain that for the Mormons they have engaged, the Bible is the Word of God as long as it is correctly translated, and that wherever the Bible contradicts Mormon teaching, it has been corrupted. These evangelicals have suggested that it is probably wise to engage Mormons using the King James Version of the Bible since Mormons have a high regard for this translation. Their other Scriptures are the Book of Mormon, Doctrine and Covenants, and the Pearl of Great Price. Mormons also give weight to the Living Prophet.

19. Calvin, *Commentaries on Galatians and Ephesians*, 324–25 (italics added).

20. See Heiko A. Oberman, *The Dawn of the Reformation: Essays in Late Medieval and Early Reformation Thought* (Grand Rapids: Eerdmans, 1992), 124.

21. "The Freedom of a Christian," in *Martin Luther's Basic Theological Writings*, ed. Timothy F. Lull (Minneapolis: Fortress Press, 1989), 619.

22. The medievals spoke of three forms of love: uncreated love, created love, and acts of love. Uncreated love is the Holy Spirit, who is the mutual love of the Father and Son. Created love is sacramental grace. Acts of love are meritorious acts. For a discussion of these themes, see Steven Ozment, *The Age of Reform, 1250–1550: An Intellectual and Religious History of Late Medieval and Reformation Europe* (New Haven: Yale University Press, 1980), 242.

23. See David A. Weir's treatment of Federal Theology in the introduction to *The Origins of the Federal Theology in Sixteenth-Century Reformation Thought* (Oxford: Clarendon Press, 1990), 1–50.

24. Luther, "Freedom of a Christian," 604.

25. Heiko A. Oberman, *Luther: Man Between God and the Devil* (New York: Image Books, 1992), 185.

26. Administration, "The Unexpected Reformation," *CrossAlone Lutheran District* (blog), December 7, 2010, http://crossalone.us/?page_id=215.

27. Luther, "Freedom of a Christian," 623.

28. Joseph Smith, *Teachings of the Prophet Joseph Smith*, comp. Joseph Fielding Smith (Salt Lake City: Deseret Book Company, 1938), 348.

29. Spencer W. Kimball, *Teachings of Spencer W. Kimball* (West Valley City, UT: Bookcraft, 1995), 153.

30. Spencer W. Kimball, *The Miracle of Forgiveness* (West Valley City, UT: Bookcraft, 1969), 207.

31. *The Journal of the Rev. John Wesley*, vol. 1, ed. Nehemiah Curnock (Whitefish, MT: Kessinger Publishing, 2006), 475–76.

32. Paul Louis Metzger, "Mystical Union with Christ: An Alternative to Blood Transfusions and Legal Fictions," *Westminster Theological Journal* 65, no. 2 (Fall 2003): 212n60.

33. Here I am drawing from missiologist Paul Hiebert's work in discussing bounded and centered sets. He contrasted the bounded set—who is in and who is out—with the centered set. The centered set is not so much concerned with building the defense as it is with focusing on the center. See Paul G. Hiebert, *Anthropological Reflections on Missiological Issues* (Grand Rapids: Baker Academic, 1994). Our center is the Word of God enfleshed, and we are to point people to him as John the Baptist did, encouraging Protestants like me, Mormons, Catholics, and Orthodox to look only unto him. Traditional Christians have often persecuted Mormons, and so understandably Mormons feel persecuted. When we question them on their doctrine, that sense of persecution often surfaces. I grieve over having challenged them doctrinally in bounded terms rather than centering discussion on Jesus. It is far better to speak with them in centered rather than bounded terms. And given that Mormonism is not to be defined primarily by doctrinal systems but by sacred story, testimony, and ethics, I must engage them in this way, using my story with Jesus and his impact on my life and community. In this essay, I use Luther's, Wesley's, and my own personal stories and testimonies on salvation and assurance. I also make use of Paul's testimony (Philippians 3) and the reigning story or central narrative of Scripture—Jesus in his union with the church (Ephesians 5).

34. Richard Mouw quoted in *Bridges: Helping Mormons Discover God's Grace*, produced by WIIS (2001; Salt Lake City: Salt Lake Theological Seminary, 2001), DVD. Mouw demonstrates concern for Mormons regarding faith and salvation in keeping with *Bridges'* approach to engaging Mormons relationally and with cultural sensitivity.

35. Certainly there are many evangelicals who have views of the Trinity and of Jesus that do not always line up with Nicea and Chalcedon, which in my estimation reflect well upon the Bible's view of God and Jesus. Having said that, I do not intend to argue that one is saved only if one can articulate well these doctrines. Our confidence is not in our faith or beliefs, but in the God in whom we believe and have faith. Paul speaks of the critical importance of right doctrine and right living for the Christian leader (1 Timothy 4:16). But I do not want to put on the average Christian an intellectual weight that so many cannot bear. For Luther, faith was an empty hand. Faith is not something we bring to the table. God creates faith. It is not a work;

in fact, faith itself is our assurance, signifying to us by the Spirit of truth that we who believe in Jesus for eternal life are God's children and are saved.

36. http://wesley.nnu.edu/john-wesley/john-wesley-the-methodist/chapter-vi-to-america-and-back.

Chapter 12: All In (Nietzschean Atheism)

1. While I am focusing on Nietzsche's orientation in this essay, I believe the following points bear significance for atheists at large:

Many atheists are moral, but why are they moral? The problem for atheism in regard to morality is primarily not one of moral failure (as in hypocrisy) but one of philosophical inconsistency; to be specific, their commitment to metaphysical naturalism offers insufficient grounds for their moral practices. Some atheists have sought to ground their sense of normative morality in evolutionary ethics, appealing to the narrative of biological and correspondingly cultural evolution as a basis for morality. But this, too, seems inadequate. For instance, on the basis of evolutionary ethics, why should we care for the elderly? I suspect that many atheists do in fact see it as a moral duty to care for the elderly when they are unable to care for themselves, but is this consistent with an evolutionary approach to ethics? One can easily make the case that the elderly at a certain point can be and are burdens to society and offer nothing in terms of enhancing the survival of our biological species. It seems reasonable and consistent with an evolutionary ethic that our duties are no longer to the elderly, and possibly even worse. While certainly affirming morality and championing concern for those in need, atheist Michael Ruse offers the following reflection on evolutionary ethics: "What I believe is that claims of normative ethics are like the rules of a game. In baseball, it is true that after three strikes the batter is out; but this claim does not have any reference or correspondence in absolute reality. . . . What right have I to say, as an evolutionist, that normative ethics has no foundation? . . . I have argued that normative ethics is a biological adaptation, and I would argue that as such it can be seen to have no being or reality beyond this. We believe normative ethics for our own (biological) good, and that is that" (Michael Ruse, "Evolution and Ethics: The Sociobiological Approach," in Louis Pojman ed., *Ethical Theory: Classic and Contemporary Readings*, 2nd ed. [Belmont: Wadsworth Pub., 1995], 103–4).

Fellow atheist Sam Harris takes issue with Ruse and E. O. Wilson for maintaining that our moral beliefs are biological adaptations set forth to advance the human species' "biological ends" in Sam Harris, *The Moral Landscape: How Science Can Determine Human Values* (New York: Free Press, 2010). Harris contends that we must look to neuroscience and psychology for answers to questions concerning moral values, not to religion or "evolutionary pressure and cultural invention" (2). Among other things, Harris seeks to persuade his readers that scientific knowledge and human values can no longer be kept apart, and that science can address values and morals from the vantage point of the brain's operations. While I certainly agree with Harris that the good life is to be preferred to the bad life as he defines them (15–16), I am left asking about foundations or grounds for what I take to be his and my moral intuitions. Can the brain alone be determinate in accounting for moral values? I think not, but this is the question I will need to explore further as I reflect upon Harris's highly controversial study.

As in the essay on physicalism, I would argue here that while science can investigate morality from the vantage point of I-It, it cannot evaluate morality from the vantage point of the I-Thou interpersonal encounter. I share Harris's disdain for Stephen J. Gould's thesis about "nonoverlapping magisteria" concerning science and religion (6), but would claim that science can only account for the objective I-It aspects of moral actions and not what I take to be the subjective interpersonal encounter involving the will bound over to the affections, which shape moral actions. While Harris prizes the mind and appears to view reason as foundational to human identity, I maintain that the will grounded in the affections is the ultimate foundation. Thus I resonate with Nietzsche when he claims that the will to power shapes society.

2. Paul Tillich, *The Shaking of the Foundations* (New York: Penguin, 1962), 60–70.

3. Friedrich Nietzsche, "The Gay Science," in *The Portable Nietzsche*, ed. Walter Kaufmann (New York: The Viking Press, 1968), 95–96.

4. Friedrich Nietzsche, "The Antichrist," in *The Portable Nietzsche*, 612.

5. Friedrich Nietzsche, "Thus Spoke Zarathustra," in *The Portable Nietzsche*, 307.

6. Fyodor Dostoevsky, *The Brothers Karamazov*, vol. 2, trans. Constance Garnett (London: J. M. Dent & Sons, 1927; repr., London: J. M. Dent & Sons, 1961), 288.

I am not claiming through the reference to Dostoevsky that we must believe in God for the pragmatic purpose of safeguarding morality, but to indicate that adherence to Nietzsche's atheism requires more than pragmatic and blind assent.

7. *Groundhog Day*, directed by Harold Ramis (1993; Culver City, CA: Sony Pictures Home Entertainment, 2004), DVD.

8. Edward Craig, *The Mind of God and the Works of Man* (Oxford: Clarendon Press, 1987), 281.

9. Nietzsche, "The Antichrist," 633–44.

10. See Karl Barth's account of Nietzsche in *Church Dogmatics*, 3.2: 231–42.

11. Friedrich Nietzsche, *Ecce Homo*, in *Basic Writings of Nietzsche*, edited by Walter Kaufmann (New York: The Modern Library, 1992), 762, 783, 784.

12. Walter Kaufmann, "Editor's Introduction to *Ecce Homo*," in *Basic Writings of Nietzsche* (New York: The Modern Library, 1992), 665.

13. Walter Kaufmann has argued that there is no bifurcation in Nietzsche's thought, contrary to what is often claimed. See *Encyclopedia of Philosophy* (New York:

Macmillan, 1967), s.v. "Friedrich Nietzsche." I disagree with Kaufmann. I do believe that a bifurcation in humanity does exist for Nietzsche, resulting from something being *gained* (*aufgegeben*) rather than something being *given* (*gegeben*). (See Kaufmann's discussion of these terms.) Over against the Judeo-Christian claim that we find our identity and worth in relation to our Creator in whose image we are made as equals, and from whom we receive life as a gift, Nietzsche maintains that our identity is something to be attained. One's own creative activity shapes and determines our identity and value. Now, since for Nietzsche there is no God, the individual is alone responsible for determining its identity and destiny, acting alone and attributing values to its actions. However, given that Nietzsche calls on people to be creators rather than mere creatures and imitators, is not the individual led to look at others as objects, which the individual must seek to bring under its control? For is not the world about the individual simply the playing field for its own creative exploits? And does not the individual find its value solely in the sheer act of creating? If the individual's identity is somehow dependent on the imposition of its will on its surroundings, as Craig argues (Craig, *Mind of God*, 277), is it not the case that to retain its identity and self-worth the individual must impose its creative will on others whose own identity and worth are nothing more than the products of the individual's own creative judgment? At least, there is nothing to safeguard against this move. In the end, does not this supposedly innocuous bifurcation, if employed by less-than-virtuous souls, become the most sinister division of all? This footnote is taken largely from my work *Word of Christ*, 102n77.

14. On this model, one could never resort to coasting, propelled forward by the force of energy. The ongoing, ceaseless, creative striving is essential to the continuance of meaning and significance. From the Christian vantage point, rest has its place, not in terms of slothfulness, idleness, and waste, but in terms of security. If I am secure in knowing I have inherent value as one created in God's image and loved as his handiwork and as one for whom Christ died and rose again, I will work all the harder, not to prove my worth, but to reflect his creativity and glory in gratitude for his love poured out on me through the Spirit, and caring for the downtrodden just as he has cared for me. This is what I mean by rest.

Chapter 13: Avatar (Neo-Paganism)

1. *Avatar*, directed by James Cameron (2009; Century City, CA: 20th Century Fox, 2010), DVD.

I am not suggesting in the essay that *Avatar* offers us a definitive understanding of neo-paganism, but that it provides inroads for analysis of this movement given the movie's resonance with neo-paganism at key points.

2. See Freda Matchett, *Krishna, Lord or Avatara? The Relationship Between Krishna and Vishnu* (Richmond, Surrey: Curzon Press, 2001).

3. Science here is to be distinguished from scientism (where science, technological progress, material well-being, and efficiency, all void of humanitarian and creaturely aims, rule).

4. Gus diZerega in Philip Johnson and Gus diZerega, *Beyond the Burning Times: A Pagan and Christian in Dialogue*, ed. John W. Morehead (Oxford: Lion, 2008), 78. The reader is also encouraged to read the selections from *Beyond the Burning Times* coauthor Philip Johnson, who offers a Christian perspective in dialogue with diZerega. Their joint effort is a highly valuable contribution to developing understanding between neo-pagans and Christians.

DiZerega does not claim to speak for all pagans or neo-pagans (21). He is a Third Degree Wiccan Gardnerian Elder. I have considered diZerega as a representative who embraces what I take to be key themes (such as his panentheistic perspective) reflective of neo-paganism in general. My points of critique are directed toward those tenets that he embraces, and are of pertinence for all neo-pagans who share those perspectives.

Sometimes diZerega refers to the movement he represents as pagan, and at other times, as neo-pagan. But there is a difference according to diZerega: "The term 'NeoPaganism' differentiates us from Pagan traditions with unbroken roots to traditional and often pre-Christian cultures." So while there may be links to the past depending on the branch of neo-paganism, there is not unbroken continuity (11). For further study on neo-paganism and Christianity from diZerega's perspective, see his work *Pagans and Christians: The Personal Spiritual Experience* (St. Paul: Llewellyn, 2001).

5. DiZerega, *Beyond the Burning Times*, 77–78.

6. Joseph Epes Brown signifies a non-objectified view of Nature from a Native American standpoint. While I certainly would not go so far as to say with Brown that "I am the universe," I would maintain that humanity is vitally and integrally connected to the universe, and so should not objectify it as an artifact to use in a detached and exploitive manner. See the following work: Joseph Epes Brown, "Becoming Part of It," reprinted from *I Become Part of It: Sacred Dimensions in Native American Life*, eds. D. M. Dooling and Paul Jordan-Smith (New York: Parabola Books, 1989); quoted in Roger Eastman, *The Ways of Religion: An Introduction to the Major Traditions*, 3rd ed. (New York: Oxford University Press, 1999), 526.

7. DiZerega, *Beyond the Burning Times*, 68.

8. Ibid.

9. Ibid., 44.

10. Ibid., 47.

11. Ibid., 24.

12. Ibid., 43.

13. Ibid., 29.

14. Ibid., 54.

15. See Lynn White Jr., "The Historical Roots of Our Ecological Crisis," *Science* 155 (1967): 1203–7. In this famous essay identifying the Christian religion as a chief historical contributor to the growing ecological crisis, Lynn White claims that Christianity is the most anthropocentric religion in the world, and that creation exists simply for human use from this vantage point. But it is not so easy to contend that Christian thought and the church are to blame for the environmental crisis, though certainly environmental considerations are absent from a great number of theological treatises. The church's view of the environment throughout Christian history is a complex one. In keeping with Irenaeus's view of Christ as the mediator of all creation, it is possible to develop a theology of creation that guards against an exclusively anthropocentric orientation. Christ did not come to earth simply to redeem fallen humanity; he was incarnated to redeem the whole of creation, whose pinnacle is humanity (though never in isolation and abstraction from the nonhuman sphere).

H. Paul Santmire has argued that the environment has throughout Christian history been susceptible to theological threat and also showered with theological promise. See his work *The Travail of Nature: The Ambiguous Ecological Promise of Christian Theology*, Theology and the Sciences (Philadelphia: Fortress Press, 1985), 8–12. See also Sarah Koetje, "Green Christianity: A Response to 'The Historical Roots of Our Ecological Crisis,'" in *Cultural Encounters: A Journal for the Theology of Culture* 2, no. 1 (Winter 2005): 53–64.

16. Barth, *Church Dogmatics*, 3.1: 187–88.

17. DiZerega, *Beyond the Burning Times*, 29; Martin Buber, *I and Thou*, 2nd ed. (New York: Charles Scribner's Sons, 1958). DiZerega argues that we cannot truly know subjects by impersonal means; if we treat them as objects, we will never be able to account for their subjectivity. While impersonal standards of knowing have their place in technological and scientific analysis, they do not constitute the whole of knowing (69–70). Although I would not want to personalize or humanize the creation, we will see later in this essay how people have often humanized creation and possessions in a psychological sense. Although personalizing creation goes too far (in an ontic sense), it is important to emphasize the intimate relation of humanity to the rest of the creation.

18. Maltbie D. Babcock, "This Is My Father's World" (Lockport, NY, 1901), http://www.hymnsite.com/lyrics/umh144.sht (accessed August 23, 2010).

19. St. Francis of Assisi, "The Canticle of the Sun," trans. Bill Barrett, http://www.webster.edu/~barrettb/canticle.htm (accessed August 23, 2011).

20. Irenaeus, *Against Heresies*, vol. 4, no. 20 (repr.; Whitefish, MT: Kessinger, 2004). See Robert M. Grant, *Irenaeus of Lyons*, The Early Church Fathers (London: Routledge, 1997), 150.

21. Irenaeus, *Against Heresies*, vol. 3, no. 16 (repr.; Whitefish, MT: Kessinger, 2004), 56.

22. The great exponent of orthodox Christology, Athanasius, models well the trinitarian theistic framework that guards against the extremes and polar opposites of pantheism and deism when he writes of Christ Jesus that he is distinct from the creation, not being contained by it, and yet containing it even as he exists wholly in his Father. See Athanasius, *De Incarnatione Verbi Dei*, trans. T. Herbert Bindley (London: Religious Tract Society, 1903), 72.

23. While I appreciate Sallie McFague's concern for fostering a more ecologically sensitive theology in *Models of God: Theology for an Ecological, Nuclear Age* (Philadelphia: Fortress Press, 1987), especially as she seeks to base her model on consideration of the doctrine of God, her panentheistic account (the world is God's body, though God is greater than the world) is problematic. A panentheistic account, like its pantheistic counterpart, fails to account adequately for sin and evil and the need for Jesus as Savior to deliver us from them for life with the one true God who is good and in whom there is no evil; moreover, a panentheistic (as well as pantheistic) account does not allow the creation to be truly free as creaturely; instead the creation is viewed in some manner as divine in its ontic relation to God—it is part of God. Often in liberal and Gnostic Christian circles, Christ ultimately serves as a midwife, helping humanity bring forth what has always been there within it, albeit implicitly, namely, its own participation in the divine nature. Søren Kierkegaard refers to this heretical notion as "the Socratic view." "Every human being is himself the midpoint, and the whole world focuses only on him because his self-knowledge is God-knowledge" (Søren Kierkegaard, *Philosophical Fragments*, ed. and trans. Howard V. Hong and Edna H. Hong [Princeton: Princeton University Press, 1985], 11). For the historical Socrates, the knowledge of the eternal lies dormant in the human person, and needs only to be recalled through a process of dialectical reasoning, which Socrates initiates. Tied to Socrates's belief that the truth lies within the human soul is Plato's doctrine of the soul's eternality. A soul only needs to recall the eternal forms, from whose presence it eternally proceeds. In rightful opposition to this framework, Kierkegaard exhorts his reader to look beyond oneself, for within oneself one only "discovers his untruth." "For the learner is indeed untruth" (Kierkegaard, *Philosophical Fragments*, 14). Over against a midwife who simply serves as the occasion for the discovery of truth (Socrates referred to himself as a midwife, who helps us get in touch with ourselves through the process of dialectical reasoning; on this view the divine spark lies within us), or really untruth, Kierkegaard sets forth Jesus as the teacher who is much more than a teacher; he is "the god himself" (15). This "teacher" and "god" provides the truth and the condition for understanding, even transforming the learner. The teacher of whom Kierkegaard speaks is "savior," "deliverer," "reconciler," "judge" (17–18).

He is the wisdom of God, but foolishness to the Greeks and their descendants. Over against those who would question that the incarnation is essential to the Christian faith, I maintain that the gospel perishes without it. (The question of the incarnation's indispensability is raised by Maurice Wiles in "Christianity Without Incarnation?" in *The Myth of God Incarnate*, ed. John Hick [Philadelphia: Westminster Press, 1977], 1–10.) Apart from the incarnation, there is no salvation if we are separated from God due to sin, or else there is no need for salvation if God and the world are one. And without the incarnation, Jesus Christ's uniqueness is lost and he is dispensable. Marcus Borg of the Jesus Seminar questions Jesus Christ's uniqueness. See Marcus J. Borg, *Meeting Jesus Again for the First Time: The Historical Jesus & the Heart of Contemporary Faith* (San Francisco: HarperSanFrancisco, 1994), 37. Jesus' significance is bound up with his being "one of many mediators of the sacred" (37). According to Borg, Jesus does not save us from sin, but invites us to experience the transformative life found in Spirit (119). Elsewhere Borg argues that Jesus is a lens for viewing one's relationship with God; however, "what matters is not believing in the lens but seeing through the lens" (Marcus J. Borg, "A Vision of the Christian Life," in Marcus J. Borg and N. T. Wright, *The Meaning of Jesus: Two Visions* [San Francisco: HarperSanFrancisco, 1999], 240). Borg certainly views Jesus as significant for Christians, and yet he is ultimately dispensable. Jesus experiences life in the Spirit in a way that is quantitatively greater than what we experience, but Jesus is not qualitatively or ontically different from us. How can Jesus be different if he is not literally the incarnation of God, as in Borg's model? For Borg, Christians simply *experience* Jesus as the Son of God from the perspective of post-Easter faith. After Easter, "increasingly he was spoken of as having all of the qualities of God" (Borg, *Meeting Jesus Again*, 16). On Borg's account each of us ultimately has the potential to mediate the sacred to other humans. In contrast the gospel includes the following fundamental conviction: Jesus Christ is not simply a particular of history or an illustration of the eternal ideal. He is the universal, even as the historical particular that he is. This particular universal who is Jesus Christ is scandalous to humankind, robbing it of its supposed claim to divinity, yet affirming and honoring humanity as Jesus gives himself to us as our loving redeemer and saving Lord. See Lesslie Newbigin's discussion of the universal and particular in *The Gospel in a Pluralist Society*, 2.

24. DiZerega, *Beyond the Burning Times*, 55.

25. While objectivism is problematic, concern for objectivity is vital: it guards against merely subjective bases for ethical decisions that are relativistic and unsustainable in preserving justice.

26. Kallistos Ware, *The Orthodox Way*, rev. ed. (Crestwood: St. Vladimir's Seminary Press, 1998), 53. Ware speaks of panentheism at a few places. However, his use of the term as an Orthodox theologian signifies a close connection between

God and his creation, not identification. For instances of the term's appearance in his volume, see *Orthodox Way*, 46, 118.

27. DiZerega, *Beyond the Burning Times*, 27.

28. I cannot accept diZerega's appeal to Karen Armstrong's assessment that the three hypostases of Father, Son, and Spirit were not taken by St. Gregory of Nyssa to be "objective facts but simply 'terms that we use' to express the way in which the 'unnameable and unspeakable' divine nature (ousia) adapts itself to the limits of our human minds" (Karen Armstrong, *The Battle for God* [New York: Ballantine Books, 2000], 69; quoted in diZerega, *Beyond the Burning Times*, 122]. While there was certainly a strong element of the apophatic, the kataphatic was equally pronounced for one such as Gregory. God is supra-personal *par excellence*; his personal being in its perfection and ultimacy transcends the limitations and distortions of our personal identities as humans; we speak analogically, not equivocally. In my reading of Gregory and the Cappadocians, the terms are not vacuous of content, but refer adequately and accurately though not exhaustively to the divine subject. Among other problems in the quotation from Armstrong is that it makes Gregory out to appear modalistic: the three "persons" are simply modes through which the divine nature adapts itself to accommodate itself to us. Modalism is not only foreign to Gregory but also problematic in that we don't really know God if the persons are modes (the same is true of any view that contends that God is beyond personhood). Gregory and others in his tradition were not modalistic, and would not have given so much attention to terms such as hypostasis in argumentation if these terms were not to be treated as objective facts, albeit analogically conceived.

29. Buber, *I and Thou*, 7.

30. Paul Tournier, *The Gift of Feeling* (Atlanta: John Knox Press, 1981), 8–9.

31. C. S. Lewis, *Surprised by Joy: The Shape of My Early Life* (London: Geoffrey Bles, 1955), 222.

32. I am not alone in this Christocentric framing of creation. Byzantine theologian Maximus the Confessor speaks not simply of the transfiguration of humanity but of the entire cosmos through Christ. His is a Christocentric cosmological framework. See St. Maximus the Confessor, *On the Cosmic Mystery of Jesus Christ: Selected Writings from St. Maximus the Confessor*, transs. Paul M. Blowers and Robert Louis Wilken, Popular Patristics Series (Crestwood, New York: St. Vladimir's Seminary Press, 2003), 38, 100nn2, 4.

33. For the Orthodox, man is the "microcosm" of the world, and as such the "mediator," reconciling and harmonizing "the noetic and the material realms" (Ware, *The Orthodox Way*, 50). As the one made in God's image, he is "priest and king of the creation," who is not simply a logical creature but ultimately a "Eucharistic" creature who sees the world as a divine gift and sacrament and offers "the world back

to God in thanksgiving" (Ware, *The Orthodox Way*, 50, 53, 54). Ultimately, given the Christocentric framing of creation and humanity in Orthodox thought, it appears appropriate to claim that Christ as the archetypal human is this priestly king and mediator who serves God and creation as the ultimate Eucharistic creature.

34. Some of the biblical texts that I have in mind when articulating these claims at the close of this essay are John 1:18; 3:16; 14–16; 17:3; and Colossians 1:15–20. Far from engaging neo-paganism in merely doctrinal terms in this chapter, I have sought to show doctrine's connection to practice and experience (values that neo-paganism also esteems). I espouse experiential theology and rigorous practice rooted in Christ's incarnation and interpersonal communion in the life of the triune God. Rational analysis is birthed and nurtured and consummated in spiritual encounter as we share in God's life through Christ in the Spirit. With this in mind, I would return to the words "I see you" in *Avatar*: I affirm the intimate relation of people, things, and God. Intimate connections should make us humble and care for the world. However, if the phrase "I see you" as used in this movie signifies the ultimate divinity of each individual and that we are ultimately the same, it proves problematic for preserving the dignity of the creation. The denial of distinctiveness along with the emphasis within the neo-pagan framework that God is beyond personhood and beyond incarnation respectively undermine the particularity of otherness and fail to provide assurance that God affirms the world. Apart from the incarnation of the interpersonal God in the flesh, how would we know that the world is not ultimately a dark abyss and nothingness, given all the chaos in the world? What would guard us against the pessimism of a Schopenhauer or a Marcion?

Chapter 14: All Roads Lead to Wall Street

1. Religious pluralism is more than an acknowledgment of religious diversity in culture, and more than legal and social tolerance of diverse religious perspectives. Here I am speaking of pluralism as the notion that all paths are basically equally valid and true and appropriate ways of engaging God (however "God" may be defined). Here is how Harold Netland defines the technical use of the expression *religious pluralism*. "As a technical term in religious studies and theology . . . 'religious pluralism' refers to a view that goes well beyond just the social acceptance of religious others. *Religious pluralism* in this sense is the view that all of the major religions are (roughly) equally true and provide equally legitimate ways in which to respond to the divine reality. No single religion—including Christianity—can legitimately claim to be uniquely true and normative for all people in all cultures at all times." See Harold A. Netland, "One Lord and Savior for All? Jesus Christ and Religious Diversity" (published by the "Christ on Campus Initiative" and available through the Carl F. H. Henry Center at Trinity Evangelical Divinity School, Deerfield, IL.), 6; http://henrycenter.org/pdf/netland-pluralism.pdf (accessed on November 25, 2010).

2. J. A. DiNoia, O. P., "Pluralist Theology of Religions: Pluralistic or Non-Pluralistic," in *Christian Uniqueness Reconsidered: The Myth of a Pluralistic Theology of Religions*, ed. Gavin D'Costa, Faith Meets Faith Series in Interreligious Dialogue (Maryknoll, NY: Orbis, 1990), 129. For a key text expounding the religious pluralist perspective, see John Hick and Paul F. Knitter, eds., *The Myth of Christian Uniqueness: Toward a Pluralistic Theology of Religions* (Maryknoll, NY: Orbis, 1987).

3. John Hick, "A Personal Note," *Disputed Questions in Theology and the Philosophy of Religion* (New Haven: Yale University Press, 1993), 133.

4. Ibid.

5. Ayn Rand's objectivist approach to ethics promotes rational selfishness. Over against the selfish barbarism of those who are driven by human sacrifice and the desire to conquer and loot, this rational and objective form of selfism rejects the need for sacrifice on the part of anyone. Rejecting altruism, Rand maintains that humans do not clash when they pursue interests that are rational. Humans who desire only that which is earned experience no conflict of interest and "do not make sacrifices nor accept them." They "deal with one another as traders, giving value for value" (Ayn Rand, *The Virtue of Selfishness* [New York: Signet, 1964], 31).

6. Sallie McFague frames theology in terms of particular models' import for the flourishing of life in a nuclear age. Models are accepted and rejected based on how they foster an ecologically minded theology. A monarchial view of God gives way to God as Mother, Lover, and Friend; for McFague, espousing motherly qualities for God and a view of the world as God's body are more promising for nurturing creation care. See McFague's *Models of God: Theology for an Ecological, Nuclear Age* (Philadelphia: Fortress Press, 1987). See especially what McFague says of theology as *"mostly* fiction" (xi–xii): "Admitting theology is mainly fiction, mainly elaboration, we claim that some fictions are better than others, both for human habitation and as expressions of the gospel of Christian faith at a particular time . . . metaphorical theology is a postmodern, highly skeptical, heuristic enterprise, which claims that in order to be faithful to the God of its tradition—the God on the side of life and its fulfillment—we must try out new pictures that will bring the reality of God's love into the imaginations of the women and men of today" (xii). Here the basis for judgment is pragmatic: the respective models' usefulness for promoting such matters as environmental stewardship in a nuclear age is what determines their appropriation. As noted here, the models function as heuristic devices; they are seen as useful projections that help us view the world in environmentally conscious ways.

7. Gordon Bigelow, "Let There Be Markets: The Evangelical Roots of Economics," *Harper's* 310, no. 1860 (May 2005): 33.

8. Lesslie Newbigin, "Religion for the Marketplace," *Christian Uniqueness Reconsidered: The Myth of a Pluralistic Theology of Religions*, ed. Gavin D'Costa,

Faith Meets Faith Series in Interreligious Dialogue (Maryknoll, NY: Orbis Books, 1990), 152.

9. The religious pluralist may very well hold to one particular path and tradition for his or her own faith and practice, never seeking to mix and match. The individual adherent may view the particular path as crucial to maturation in spirituality, thinking one should finish what one started, while affirming different paths chosen by other spiritual seekers as equally valid and salvific.

10. "Let your vision be world embracing . . . ," Baha'i International Community, http://www.bahai.org/ (accessed August 23, 2011). Here is what the official website for Baha'i claims about itself: "Throughout history, God has revealed Himself to humanity through a series of divine Messengers, whose teachings guide and educate us and provide the basis for the advancement of human society. These Messengers have included Abraham, Krishna, Zoroaster, Moses, Buddha, Jesus, and Muhammad. Their religions come from the same Source and are in essence successive chapters of one religion from God. Bahá'u'lláh, the latest of these Messengers, brought new spiritual and social teachings for our time. His essential message is of unity. He taught the oneness of God, the oneness of the human family, and the oneness of religion." Founded on his teachings, adherents of Baha'i "believe the crucial need facing humanity is to find a unifying vision of the nature and purpose of life and of the future of society. Such a vision unfolds in the writings of Bahá'u'lláh."

I am using "Baha'i" here in a loose sense. The person in question was simply very pluralistic. Beyond the immediate context of this essay, it is important to note that orthodox Muslims reject Baha'i as a heresy. Shia Muslims in Iran have heavily persecuted Baha'is. While I do not ultimately know the religious affiliation of the man I nicknamed "Billy Baha'i," his presence there that day was unusual given his apparent convictions.

11. Often the pluralist approaches religious texts nonliterally or metaphorically while claiming that the traditional religions' approaches to the ultimate derive from their cultural contexts. These considerations enable them, in their estimation, to speak of the unity of religions in the midst of their apparent differences and disagreements. See Harold Netland's discussion of key tenets and approaches involving religious pluralism's explanation of religious diversity in "Religious Pluralism as an Explanation for Religious Diversity," *Philosophy and the Christian Worldview: Analysis, Assessment and Development*, ed., David Werther and Mark D. Linville, Continuum Studies in Philosophy of Religion (New York: Continuum, 2012). See also John Hick's summative remarks of the mythological and cultural facets of his pluralistic hypothesis in *An Interpretation of Religion: Human Responses to the Transcendent* (New Haven: Yale University Press, 1989), 240–49, 358–59, 375–76; John Hick, "Religious Pluralism," *The Routledge Companion to Philosophy of*

Religion, eds. Chad Meister and Paul Copan (London: Routledge, 2007), 221. It is also important for this discussion to take into account Hick's particular adaptation of Kant's epistemology regarding the real in itself and how it is experienced through our concepts in *An Interpretation of Religion,* 240–49.

12. W. A. Visser 't Hooft, *No Other Name: The Choice Between Syncretism and Christian Universalism* (Philadelphia: Westminster, 1963), 86.

13. Hick, "A Personal Note," 534–35.

14. Keith Yandell, "How to Sink in Cognitive Quicksand: Nuancing Religious Pluralism," in *Contemporary Debates in Philosophy of Religion,* eds. Michael L. Peterson and Raymond J. Vanarragon (Oxford: Blackwell, 2003), 193; John Hick, *The Metaphor of God Incarnate* (Louisville, KY: Westminster/John Knox, 1993).

15. For an evangelical presentation of the particular truth claims of the Christian faith in the context of engaging other religions, see Ravi Zacharias, *Jesus Among Other Gods: The Absolute Claims of the Christian Message* (Nashville: Thomas Nelson, 2000).

16. Paul Molnar has argued similarly in his critique of the mythological or projectionist theologies espoused by Gordon Kaufman and Sallie McFague. According to Molnar, instead of serving to liberate humanity, projectionist theologies lead to deeper alienation from God, self-justification, and self-imposed oppression, which removes the hope of salvation. Molnar affirms their efforts in pointing out the authoritarian excesses of past orthodox theologians, and yet goes on to maintain that they are guilty of the same. Molnar maintains that Kaufman displays an authoritarian approach by removing from consideration the traditional conception of God's independence and Jesus' significance as God's Son. While Molnar maintains that Kaufman rightly critiques instances of Christian imperialism, Molnar contends, nonetheless, that Kaufman fails to recognize that these instances arise not from asserting Jesus' singular uniqueness but rather arise when Christians do not take to heart his distinctiveness as the one and only Lord of life. If imperialism is to cease, we must not promote that form of agnosticism that gives rise to projectionism, but an activism that results from taking seriously the God revealed in Jesus Christ. See Paul D. Molnar, "Myth and Reality: Analysis and Critique of Gordon Kaufman and Sallie McFague on God, Christ, and Salvation," in *Cultural Encounters: A Journal for the Theology of Culture* 1, no. 2 (Summer 2005): 23–48. See also Metzger's discussion of Molnar's essay in the "Editor's Introduction" of the same issue.

17. Tolerance and its opposite do not function as properties of beliefs but of behaviors. If tolerance were to be framed as a matter of acceptance of another person or tradition's belief system, then anyone who rejects my belief system as true would be intolerant. My Zen Buddhist friends reject my Christian worldview but do not reject me personally. Rather they are very tolerant of me. I believe the same is true of my approach to them.

Harold Netland also makes the distinction between behavior and belief concerning tolerance. Netland claims, "It is not accepting or rejecting a particular belief that marks one as tolerant or intolerant. For if this were the case, then any time one disagreed with someone's beliefs one would be intolerant; the only way to be tolerant would be to accept all beliefs or withhold judgment about competing beliefs. If religious exclusivism is necessarily intolerant for the Christian exclusivist, then it follows that anyone—Buddhist, Wiccan, atheist, or religious pluralist—who maintains that her beliefs about religious matters are true and other incompatible beliefs false is also similarly morally blameworthy. But surely this is intellectual suicide, not tolerance." See Harold A. Netland, "Religious Exclusivism," in *Philosophy of Religion: Classic and Contemporary Issues*, eds. Paul Copan and Chad Meister (Oxford: Blackwell, 2008), 71. It is worth noting here that just as an evangelical Christian can be tolerant, so, too, he or she can be affirming of various aspects of other religions. While I believe that no truth found elsewhere adds to or negates the truth found in Jesus as revealed in the Bible, and that salvation is only found through personal faith in Jesus (and that no one who ultimately rejects Jesus will be saved), such claims do not prohibit me from finding the teachings of other religions of value and their practitioners' lives profound. All people are created in God's image and by God's grace in creation often bear witness to God revealed in Jesus. As the Alpha and Omega, the triune God is the one in whom we live and move and have our being (Acts 17:28).

18. I believe that American Christians often see their individual political activism as public engagement, but do not view their ecclesial engagement as public. See the discussion of the church as a public engaging other publics in Brad Harper and Paul Louis Metzger, *Exploring Ecclesiology: An Evangelical and Ecumenical Introduction* (Grand Rapids: Eerdmans, 2009), 123–46, 217, 321nn35–36. See also chapter 7, which includes a discussion of the church viewed as a voluntary association along these lines.

19. For example, John Hick believes the ultimate is beyond good and evil. See John Hick, "Ineffability," *Religious Studies* 36 (March 2000): 44. Now, if this is so, why favor divine reality-centeredness over self-centeredness, which involves moral transformation? On this view, how could one adequately contend against a view of salvation that involves the commodification of human identity where all human relations are matters of contractual arrangements and business exchanges where value is conceived in terms of supply and demand? The reader is encouraged to look to Don Slater's helpful discussion of how consumerism gives rise to the commodification of human life and reality in *Consumer Culture and Modernity* (Cambridge: Polity, 1997), 8, 10, 27.

20. Colin Gunton maintains that modernity has been guilty of greater forms of oppressiveness than the medieval era. While rightly contending against monistic

forms of the divine where a wrongly conceived personally transcendent deity
suppresses the many, the immanentist alternatives of impersonal forces have proven
to be even more oppressive (Colin E. Gunton, *The One, the Three and the Many:
God, Creation and the Culture of Modernity, the 1992 Bampton Lectures* [Cambridge:
Cambridge University Press, 1993], 38–39; Richard John Neuhaus, *The Naked
Public Square* [Grand Rapids: Eerdmans, 1984]).

21. The political tradition of democratic liberalism demands that the church be
tolerant of "competing" institutions; yet democratic liberalism refuses to tolerate
or make space for the church and its particular truth claims in the public sphere,
cordoning it and other religious institutions off to the private domain. Stanley
Hauerwas critically analyzes this problematic state of affairs in *After Christendom*
(Nashville: Abingdon Press, 1999). In *Democracy and Tradition*, Jeffrey Stout
reasons that religion is not inherently a political "conversation-stopper," contrary to
what Richard Rorty maintains (Jeffrey Stout, *Democracy and Tradition* [Princeton
University Press, 2004], 10). While Stout critiques Hauerwas's particular brand
of theological traditionalism, Stout affirms Hauerwas's concerns about the secular
liberal democratic enterprise and how its proponents like Rorty claim religious
beliefs are best privatized. See Stout, *Democracy and Tradition* (Princeton University
Press, 2004), 10–11.

22. William T. Cavanaugh calls for the demystifying of the state in "Killing for
the Telephone Company: Why the Nation-State Is Not the Keeper of the Common
Good," in *Modern Theology* 20, no. 2 (April 2004): 243–74.

23. See Gavin D'Costa's article, "The Impossibility of a Pluralist View of
Religions," in *Religious Studies* 32 (1996): 223–32. There he claims that "pluralism
must always logically be a form of exclusivism and that nothing called pluralism
really exists" (225). Two representative pluralist exponents whom he engages are
John Hick and Paul Knitter. D'Costa draws from the following samples of their
work in the exposition of his argument: John Hick, *An Interpretation of Religion:
Human Responses to the Transcendent* (London: Macmillan, 1989); Paul F. Knitter,
"Dialogue and Liberation: Foundations for a Pluralist Theology of Religions," in *The
Drew Gateway*, vol. 58/1 (1988): 1–53; and Knitter's co-authored part in Leonard
Swidler et al., *Death or Dialogue? From the Age of Monologue to the Age of Dialogue*
(New York: Continuum, 1990). John Hick responds to D'Costa, claiming that
there are very significant differences between the religious exclusivists, inclusivists,
and pluralists, which must not be forgotten. See John Hick, "The Possibility of
Religious Pluralism: A Reply to Gavin D'Costa" in *Religious Studies* 33 (1997):
161–66. Harold Netland maintains that the basic taxonomy of the three terms of
religious exclusivism, inclusivism, and pluralism have some limited merit, but that
these terms lack clarity and cannot be used in precise ways: "the three positions
should not be understood as clearly defined, mutually exclusive categories so much as

distinct points on a continuum of perspectives, with particular thinkers falling into one or another category depending upon the particular issue under consideration" (Netland, "Religious Exclusivism," 70). See also his footnote discussion of these three terms in the essay "Religious Pluralism as an Explanation for Religious Diversity" in the forthcoming volume *Philosophy and the Christian Worldview*. There he writes, "Although use of the three categories is today widespread, the taxonomy is misleading and simplistic. The broad range of questions concerning religious others and the many, often highly nuanced and sophisticated, perspectives on these issues cannot be forced into just three neat categories." See also his article "Inclusivism and Exclusivism," in *The Routledge Companion to Philosophy of Religion*, eds. Chad Meister and Paul Copan (London: Routledge, 2007), 226–32.

24. No doubt, in keeping with what is argued here, there is a need for Christians to present a worldview that makes the best rational and moral sense of life. Along these lines, see Ninian Smart, "The Philosophy of Worldviews, or the Philosophy of Religion Transformed," in *Religious Pluralism and Truth: Essays in Cross-Cultural Philosophy of Religion*, ed. Thomas Dean (Albany, NY: SUNY Press, 1995), 17–31. See also Netland, "Religious Exclusivism," 20. While a relational-incarnational approach to apologetics goes beyond worldview formulation and argumentation, it does involve it.

25. John Hick, *God Has Many Names* (Philadelphia: Westminster, 1982).

Chapter 15: Dead Metaphors and Living Hell

1. "Sinners in the Hands of an Angry God," in *Jonathan Edwards: Basic Writings*, ed. Ola Elizabeth Winslow (New York: New American Library, 1966), 159.

2. Amy Plantinga Pauw speaks of a significant tension in Edwards's thought between his doctrine of union and communion and his view of divine judgment in *The Supreme Harmony of All: The Trinitarian Theology of Jonathan Edwards* (Grand Rapids: Eerdmans, 2002), 132–33.

3. Refer to the helpful contextualization of the sermon in Edwards's ministry and theology at http://edwards.yale.edu/research/major-works/sinners-in-the-hands-of-an-angry-god (accessed on July 3, 2010). I make use of this "Consumers in the Lap of a Feel-Good God" imagery in Paul Louis Metzger, *Consuming Jesus: Beyond Race and Class Divisions in a Consumer Church* (Grand Rapids: Eerdmans, 2007), 106.

4. C. S. Lewis, *The Problem of Pain* (New York: Macmillan Publishing Company, 1962), 120. While language used to describe hell is often figurative, the referent to which such language points is literal.

5. In discussing hell, Lewis suggests that "even mercy can hardly wish" to an evil and horribly deceived person "his eternal, contended continuance in . . . ghastly illusion" (Lewis, *Problem of Pain*, 122).

6. Bertrand Russell, *Why I Am Not a Christian: And Other Essays on Religion*

and Related Subjects, ed. Paul Edwards (New York: Simon and Schuster Publishing, 1952), 42.

7. Ibid., 107.

8. John Steinbeck, *Travels with Charley in Search of America* (New York: Penguin Books, 1962), 60–61.

9. "Evening Prayer from *The Book of Common Prayer*," Church of England, http://www.churchofengland.org/prayer-worship/worship/texts/principal-services /word/mornevebcp/eveningbcp.aspx (accessed on August 25, 2011).

10. Alan Lewis speaks of the need to recognize Holy Saturday not simply as a preamble to Christ's victory but also as a sequel to his defeat on the cross in its hellish agony and despair (Alan E. Lewis, *Between Cross and Resurrection: A Theology of Holy Saturday* [Grand Rapids: Eerdmans, 2001], 39–41). If we see Holy Saturday simply as a preamble to victory and not also as a sequel to Christ's defeat as he experiences God's judgment and God-forsakenness in hell, we will not be able to appreciate all that Jesus has done for us. Expanding this point, I believe the church's common failure (addressed by Alan Lewis) of downplaying or dismissing the belief that Christ's "humiliation is intensified and made most hellishly complete" (39) through his descent into hell in favor of the view that his humiliation ceases with the descent as he triumphs over his enemies in hell makes it more difficult for people to appreciate the magnitude of what Jesus has done in their place. It also intensifies the inaccurate critique that damnation is the cold and merciless act of a distant divine judge.

11. Lewis, *Problem of Pain*, 127.

12. Ibid., 122.

13. Ibid.

14. Ibid., 127; C. S. Lewis, *The Great Divorce* (New York: Macmillan, 1946), 69–70, 72–73.

15. I resonate with the atheist Sartre's depiction of hell as self-absorption, but I would contend that the door to the room where the three solitary figures in his play eternally reside can be opened from the inside but will never be tried. While wishing to flee the agony of the hellish presence of "the other"—divine and human—the individuals in question in my view would never want to depart from the freedom of their own solitary confinement that they forever relish in hell. Instead of self-abandonment leading to true liberation, they prefer the distorted and oppressive freedom of self-enslavement (Jean Paul Sartre, *No Exit*, in *No Exit and Three Other Plays* [New York: Vintage International, 1989], 45). Compare this perspective with Lewis's discussion of the damned in *Problem of Pain*, 127–28.

16. Lewis approaches the matter somewhat differently, though agreeably, I believe. If God sensed that there was hope in giving people innumerable chances, he would give them. As omniscient, he knows what would be the outcome and so has determined that one life is indicative of one's eternal course (Lewis, *Problem of Pain*, 124).

17. Lesslie Newbigin, *The Gospel in a Pluralist Society* (Grand Rapids: Eerdmans, 1989), especially page 177; Lesslie Newbigin, *The Open Secret: An Introduction to the Theology of Mission*, rev. ed. (Grand Rapids: Eerdmans, 1995), especially page 173.

18. Jesus addressed many of his warnings to the religious leaders who thought they were "in" and who looked with scorn on the outsiders, like tax collectors and prostitutes and other pagans, many of whom were responding to Jesus and finding life. One should also take note that Jonathan Edwards addressed his warning in *Sinners in the Hands of an Angry God* to people in his church. See also Newbigin, *Open Secret*, 79.

19. C. S. Lewis, *The Screwtape Letters*, rev. ed. (New York: Macmillan, 1982), 37–38. See also Lewis's discussion of heaven as a state that fulfills our humanity whereas hell is the abode of human "remains" (Lewis, *The Problem of Pain*, 125).

20. As dangerous as dead metaphors can be, there is nothing more dangerous than deadly metaphors, such as the devil Mephistopheles in Goethe's *Faust*. Lewis speaks of Mephistopheles as "humourous, civilized, sensible, adaptable." Lewis goes on to write that this literary figure "has helped to strengthen the illusion that evil [is] liberating." For Lewis, this devil is the most pernicious literary symbol for the demonic (Lewis, *Screwtape Letters*, ix).

21. Lewis, *Screwtape Letters*, xii.

Chapter 16: The Missing Link

1. David Bentley Hart critiques many such "tensions" as misreadings of history in *Atheist Delusions: The Christian Revolution and Its Fashionable Enemies* (New Haven: Yale University Press, 2009).

2. Stephen Hawking and Leonard Mlodinow, *Design* (New York: Random House, 2010).

3. See Lonnie D. Kliever's discussion of this evolution in *The Shattered Spectrum: A Survey of Contemporary Theology* (Atlanta: John Knox Press, 1981), 3–7. Building on the arguments of Graf Reventlow in *The Authority of the Bible and the Rise of the Modern World*, Lesslie Newbigin maintains that the origins for the attack on the Christian worldview in the West are found in the humanist tradition, emerging from Greece and Rome, and not modern science. See Newbigin, *Gospel in a Pluralist Society*, 1–2.

4. Harold Nebelsick, *The Renaissance, the Reformation and the Rise of Science* (Edinburgh: T & T Clark, 1992), 154–56. Nebelsick writes that the Reformation teaching on the Word highlighted the distinction between God and the cosmos: "God is God and the world as the world is secular" (154–55). Nebelsick then quotes T. F. Torrance: "It is the sheer differentiation between God and nature which definitively overcomes both the sacramentalism of Augustinianism and the *aeternitas mundi* (the eternality of the universe) of Aristotelian philosophy. Thus the concept

of *deus sive natura* is finally dispensed with" (155, quoting Thomas F. Torrance, *Theological Science* [London: Oxford University Press, 1969], 65–66).

5. William T. Jones, *A History of Western Philosophy*, vol. 1 (New York: Harcourt, Brace and Co., 1952), 524.

6. For example, Jones is wrong to claim that Thomas maintains that everything is sacramental. Only the incarnation and the ecclesial rites such as the Mass are sacramental. For Thomas, the cosmos is filled with signs, but not with sacraments. Thomas makes a distinction between sacrament and sign. A sacrament is a particular kind of sign, which pertains to the incarnate Lord. Thus there is no sacrament outside the ecclesial sphere. Jones is also mistaken in claiming that for Thomas the world is only a sign. Rather the cosmos is a sign that is fully real. While Jones's criticism does not apply to Thomas, it does have pertinence for those later medievals who claim that the world is full of sacraments. For a treatment of the later medievals' sacramental mind-set, see J. Huizinga, *The Waning of the Middle Ages: A Study of the Forms of Life, Thought and Art in France and the Netherlands in the XIVTH and XVTH Centuries* (London: Edward Arnold & Co., 1937).

7. Nebelsick argues, "Like Plato who viewed nature as unreal, a shadow of the ideal, Aristotle considered matter to be of secondary importance. It was an 'accident' of the *substance* of reality. Added to that, Aristotle's 'metaphysics' so circumscribed his 'physics' with the contradictory characteristics of rigidity and capriciousness that investigation of nature was discouraged. The rigidity resulted from its claim that first and final causes both determined reality and interpenetrated it in such a way that all solutions could be gained from present principles by the simple application of deductive logic. At the same time and equally important, Aristotle's understanding of reality in organismic terms subjected nature to the unpredictable and capricious intervention of living and divine principles" (Nebelsick, *The Renaissance, the Reformation and the Rise of Science*, x–xi). Nebelsick draws attention to Stanley Jaki's claim that the evolution of physics was influenced by Greek theology (xii). Jaki argues, "To a large extent, it was religious motivation that helped decide the course of physics for almost two thousand years when Aristotle, following Socrates' and Plato's lead, made physics serve the 'living and divine principles' that were believed to rule the cosmos" (Stanley L. Jaki, *The Relevance of Physics* [Chicago: University of Chicago Press, 1966], 412).

8. Sir Francis Bacon, "First Book of Aphorisms," in *The Age of Reason: The 17th Century Philosophers*, ed. Stuart Hampshire, The Mentor Philosophers (New York: Meridian Classic, 1956), 27–29. For Bacon, empirical observation and efficient recording were the essential traits of scientific study. However, he failed to appreciate the roles of hypothesis and theory formulation for scientific analysis.

9. Michael Foster, "The Christian Doctrine of Creation and the Rise of Modern Natural Science," in *Science and Religious Belief: A Selection of Recent Historical*

Studies, ed. C. A. Russell (1964; London: Open University, 1973), 311. For other treatments of how natural modern science owes much to its Western Christian context, see R. Hooykaas, *Religion and the Rise of Modern Science* (Edinburgh: Scottish Academic Press, 1972); Stanley Jaki, *Cosmos and Creator* (Edinburgh: Scottish Academic Press, 1980).

10. Michael Polanyi and others, such as Thomas Kuhn and Karl Popper, have emphasized that science isn't really purely "objective." I do not wish to overplay the distinction between "objective science" and "relational trinitarian theology." A theology framed by way of trinitarian relationality can raise questions of science, challenging what it takes to be a less-than-*objective* scientific procedure. Conor Cunningham gives a particular theological interpretation of recent evolutionary theory in *Darwin's Pious Idea: Why the Ultra-Darwinists and Creationists Both Get It Wrong* (Grand Rapids: Eerdmans, 2010). There he seeks to demonstrate that Richard Dawkins and others do not present the objective evidence of evolution but actually reconstruct it through an interpretive grid, which results in changing the evidence. For a definitive work by Polanyi pertaining to the theme of objectivity, see *Personal Knowledge: Towards a Post-Critical Philosophy* (Chicago: University of Chicago Press, 1974).

11. Jonathan Edwards, "Treatise on Grace," *Treatise on Grace and Other Posthumously Published Writings*, ed. Paul Helm (Cambridge: James Clarke, 1971), 48–49.

12. Paul Tournier, *The Gift of Feeling* (Atlanta: John Knox Press, 1981), 12.

Tournier comments on how he had made very silly mistakes in diagnosing family members because of being blinded by feelings for them, and speaks of how important it is to defer to one's fellow medical practitioners to treat his or her loved ones.

13. Gilbert Ryle, *The Concept of Mind* (Chicago: University of Chicago Press, 1949), 22.

14. Tournier, *The Gift of Feeling*, 11.

15. See Martin Buber, *I and Thou*, 2nd ed., with a postscript by the author added, trans. Ronald Gregor Smith (New York: Charles Scribner's Sons, 1958).

16. See Immanuel Kant, *Selections*, ed. Lewis White Beck, in *The Great Philosophers*, ed. Paul Edwards (New York: Macmillan, 1988). Kant spoke of denying knowledge in the realm of metaphysics in order to make room for faith (103), and of standing in awe of the starry sky above (which reveals to him how trivial people are against the backdrop of the universe), and in awe of the moral law within people (which reveals to us our supreme value as lawgivers of moral ends) (303, 325–26).

17. Kant spoke of how we readily think about matters beyond the realm of fact, though we cannot have knowledge of them. While not rejecting this move, it must be done reasonably and with the awareness that such moves will never lead to knowledge of facts, as he defines facts in his first *Critique*. We can never know things

in themselves, for "theoretical knowledge of reason is limited to objects of experience." However, we can think about them, albeit rationally. I do not limit this move simply to analysis of items in the spatial-temporal sphere but also take it to pertain to God as well for Kant. See Kant, *Selections*, 102, for his discussion of knowledge of things in the empirical sphere.

18. Clark H. Pinnock makes a similar claim in *Reason Enough: A Case for the Christian Faith* (Eugene, OR: Wipf & Stock, 1997).

19. Hans Urs von Balthasar, *Love Alone Is Credible*, trans. D. C. Schindler (San Francisco: Ignatius Press, 2004), 141–42.

20. Ibid., 142.

21. Stephen Jay Gould, *Rocks of Ages: Science and Religion in the Fullness of Life* (New York: Ballantine Books, 2002).

22. Richard Dawkins, "When Religion Steps on Science's Turf," in *Free Inquiry* 18, no. 2 (1998), http://www.secularhumanism.org/library/fi/dawkins_18_2.html (accessed August 25, 2011).

23. Gunton, *The One, the Three and the Many*, 43. The quotation from Polyani is taken from *Personal Knowledge: Towards a Post-Critical Philosophy*, 2nd ed. (London: Routledge, 1962), 139–41.

24. Jonathan Edwards also conceived of the world in relational terms in view of the trinitarian doctrine of God and his view of dynamic creation. God continues to create the universe out of nothing at every moment. Edwards would come to conceive the creation's beginning and ongoing existence as the result of God's continual conscious awareness of it, seeking to guard against materialist philosophy. Rather than viewing the creation as a copy of abstract and static ideals in the supra-sensible world, as in Platonism, the creation exists so that God can communicate his interpersonal, triune being of love and happiness and beauty to his creatures in a universe consisting of personal beings and also relationships. See George M. Marsden's discussion of Edwards's doctrine of creation in view of the Trinity and his engagement of materialist philosophy in *Jonathan Edwards: A Life* (New Haven: Yale University Press, 2003), 73–77.

25. Edwin A. Abbott, *Flatland: A Romance of Many Dimensions*, 6th ed. (New York: Dover, 1952), 102.

26. I am indebted to Wink Chin for his insights and interaction with me as I wrote this chapter.

Chapter 17: Homosexuality, Holy Matrimony, and Hospitality

1. Oscar Wilde to More Adey, MS Princeton, November 29, 1897, in *The Complete Letters of Oscar Wilde*, eds. Merlin Holland and Rupert Hart-Davis (New York: Henry Holt, 2000), 996.

2. One must also account for the christological and ecclesial framing of the image in Colossians 1:15 and following. Christ is the ultimate image of God, which he shares

with his church as his body. The imaging of God in the church includes men and women as Christ's ecclesial body, not just Christian husbands and wives in their particular marital unions.

3. John F. Harris, "God Gave Us 'What We Deserve,' Falwell Says," *Washington Post*, September 14, 2001, http://www.washingtonpost.com/ac2/wp-dyn/A28620 -2001Sep14 (accessed August 25, 2011).

4. James Montgomery Boice, "Our All-Too-Easy Conscience," *Modern Reformation* 7, no. 5 (September/October 1998): 44.

5. See Joe Dallas's discussion, *The Gay Gospel? How Pro-Gay Advocates Misread the Bible* (Eugene, OR: Harvest House Publishers, 2007).

6. See also Jesus' teaching recorded in Mark 10:1–12, where he is building on Genesis 1:27 and 2:24.

7. Jeffrey Satinover, *Homosexuality and the Politics of Truth* (Grand Rapids: Baker Books, 1996), 146–47, 153.

8. Derrick Sherwin Bailey, *Homosexuality and the Western Christian Tradition* (New York: Longmans, Green & Co., 1955), 3–4.

9. Martti Nissinen, *Homoeroticism in the Biblical World* (Minneapolis: Fortress, 1998), 48–49. See Robert A. J. Gagnon's response in *The Bible and Homosexual Practice* (Nashville: Abingdon, 2001), 78n101.

10. This has not kept people from making a connection. Note the origin of the word *sodomy* in the English language, perhaps implying the close association many have made between Sodom and homosexuality.

11. Paul Jewett with Marguerite Shuster, *Who We Are: Our Dignity as Human: A Neo-Evangelical Theology* (Grand Rapids: Eerdmans, 1996), 318. The authors also point to the following references to Sodom on 318: Deuteronomy 29:23; 32:32; Isaiah 3:9; 13:19; Jeremiah 23:14; 49:18; 50:40; Lamentations 4:6; Ezekiel 16:46–48; Amos 4:11; Zephaniah 2:9; Matthew 10:15; Luke 17:29; Romans 9:29; 2 Peter 2:6; Jude 7. See also John Boswell, *Christianity, Social Tolerance and Homosexuality: Gay People in Western Europe from the Beginning of the Christian Era to the Fourteenth Century* (Chicago: University of Chicago Press, 1980), 94. Boswell remarks: "There are, moreover, numerous other references in the Old Testament to Sodom and its fate, and scholars have failed to accord this facet of the controversy the importance it deserves. Sodom is used as a symbol of evil in dozens of places, but not in a single instance is the sin of the Sodomites specified as homosexuality." Contrast Boswell with Gagnon's discussion on these biblical passages on pages 79–91 of *The Bible and Homosexual Practice*.

12. Gagnon, *Bible and Homosexual Practice*, 75.

13. Jewett, *Who We Are*, 319–20.

14. The terms *arsenokoitai* and *malakoi* appear in the vice list of 1 Corinthians 6:9; the former term also appears in 1 Timothy 1:10's vice list. Gagnon claims that

"in 1 Corinthians 6:9, the term *malakoi* has most in view males who actively seek to transform their maleness into femaleness in order to make themselves more attractive as receptive or passive sexual partners of men; *arsenokoitai* has most in view men who serve as the active sex partners of the *malakoi*. Neither term can be widened in meaning to include heterosexuals or narrowed in meaning to exclude certain non-exploitative forms of homosexual intercourse" (Gagnon, *Bible and Homosexual Practice*, 338). See his full discussion of the terms on pages 306–39. See Boswell's alternative take on these terms in *Christianity, Social Tolerance, and Homosexuality*, 338–53.

15. See Gagnon's discussion of implicit references to same-sex intercourse in accounts of Jesus' teaching in Gagnon, *Bible and Homosexual Practice*, 191–93.

16. See Gagnon's discussion of Jesus' supposed leniency in *The Bible and Homosexual Practice*, 196–209.

17. Boswell, *Christianity, Social Tolerance, and Homosexuality*, 109.

18. In keeping with Gagnon's remarks on the biblical and contemporary warnings, to warn people of the severity of God's judgment concerning homosexual behavior (if uttered with concern and not in spite and cruelty) is an act of love; in contrast, to refuse to warn those engaging in such acts can be deemed an abuse of power (Gagnon, *Bible and Homosexual Practice*, 331–32).

19. Nissinen claims that Paul's principal concern (regardless of the kind of sexuality in view in such texts as 1 Corinthians 6:9) is the exploitation of others in *Homoeroticism*, 118. In contrast, Gagnon claims that the combination of the terms *malakoi* and *arsenokoitai* in 1 Corinthians 6:9 "are correctly understood in our contemporary context when they are applied to every conceivable type of same-sex intercourse" (Gagnon, *Bible and Homosexual Practice*, 325–32. See also 347–50).

20. See Gordon Fee and Douglas Stuart's discussion of the cultural and universal in *How to Read the Bible for All Its Worth: A Guide to Understanding the Bible*, 2nd ed. (Grand Rapids: Zondervan, 1993), 70–76.

21. This is not to take away from Paul's repudiation and visceral reaction to homosexuality. For Paul, his declaration concerning homosexuality in Romans 1 sets the stage for everything that follows. As Gagnon remarks, "Same-sex eroticism functions as a particularly poignant example of human enslavement to passions and of God's just judgment precisely because it parallels in the horizontal-ethical dimension a denial of God's reality like that of idolatry in the vertical-divine dimension. In other words, idolatry is a deliberative suppression of the truth available to pagans in the world around them, but so too is same-sex intercourse" (Gagnon, *Bible and Homosexual Practice*, 254). Homosexual behavior is a clear denial of our creaturely design, and more visible and concrete than our sinful passions, bearing clear witness to human rebellion against God. See Gagnon, *The Bible and Homosexual Practice*, 264.

22. Barth, *Church Dogmatics*, 3.1:183–206; 3.2: 286.

Colin Gunton claims that Barth's discussion of the image as exclusively male and female is too narrow. It does not give rise to a full theology of communion, although he acknowledges that there are elements of a communal anthropology (Colin E. Gunton, "Trinity, Ontology and Anthropology: Towards a Renewal of the Doctrine of the Imago Dei," in *Persons, Divine and Human*, ed. Christoph Schwöbel and Colin E. Gunton [Edinburgh: T & T Clark, 1991], 57–58).

23. Donald Miller, "Building the Bridge Back," in *Cultural Encounters: A Journal for the Theology of Culture* 3, no. 1 (Winter 2006): 79.

24. Jann S. Wenner, "Bono: The Rolling Stone Interview," *Rolling Stone*, November 3, 2005.

25. Brad Harper, "Lesbians: A Biblical and Personal Reflection," in Scott Dawson, ed., *The Complete Evangelism Guidebook: Expert Advice on Reaching Others for Christ* (Grand Rapids: Baker, 2006), 358.

26. Ibid., 359.

27. Ibid.

28. Ibid., 358.

29. Ibid., 359.

30. Ibid.

31. We are not living in a theocracy, which was the backdrop to the presentation of the Mosaic Law. While the Law certainly has universal and ever-binding features (such as the Great Commandments and the Ten Commandments), it is also important to note that in our democratic society, we champion the basic human rights of all people apart from such matters as sexual orientation.

32. One of the best presentations I have heard concerning the church's role in assisting people in the gay community live celibate lives was delivered by Tim Otto (lecture, San Francisco Faith Leaders' Collective, San Francisco, CA, May 12, 2011). Associate pastor at Church of the Sojourners in San Francisco, Otto spoke of how we need to move beyond fixation with the nuclear family in the local church context and view the church as an extended family. He spoke of the role the church plays in loving people of a homosexual persuasion into celibacy and holiness where they find their relational needs for intimacy met by caring brothers and sisters in Christ. The church is the ultimate family, and it is to live as such.

Chapter 18: Beyond Ned Flanders and the Fascists

1. Michael Spencer, "The Coming Evangelical Collapse," in *Christian Science Monitor*, March 10, 2009, http://www.csmonitor.com/Commentary /Opinion/2009/0310/p09s01-coop.html (accessed on August 25, 2011).

2. Christopher Hitchens, *God Is Not Great: How Religion Poisons Everything* (New York: Twelve, Hachette Book Group, 2007), 25, 230, 235–37, 240–42, 244–47.

3. Karl Barth, *Church Dogmatics*, 2.1: 468–69, 472.

4. Michael J. Buckley, S. J., *At the Origins of Modern Atheism* (New Haven and London: Yale University Press, 1987), 33. See also 55, 64–67, 350–69.

Lesslie Newbigin offers a similar reflection: "It has been said that the question of the Trinity is the one theological question that has been really settled. It would, I think, be nearer to the truth to say that the Nicene formula has been so devoutly hallowed that it is effectively put out of circulation. It has been treated like the talent that was buried for safekeeping rather than risked in the commerce of discussion. The church continues to repeat the trinitarian formula but—unless I am greatly mistaken—the ordinary Christian in the Western world who hears or reads the word 'God' does not immediately and inevitably think of the Triune Being—Father, Son, and Spirit. He thinks of a supreme monad. Not many preachers, I suspect, look forward eagerly to Trinity Sunday. The working concept of God for most ordinary Christians is—if one may venture a bold guess—shaped more by the combination of Greek philosophy and Islamic theology that was powerfully injected in the thought of Christendom at the beginning of the High Middle Ages than by the thought of the fathers of the first four centuries" (Newbigin, *Open Secret*, 27–28).

5. It is not that Christians in the medieval and Reformation eras failed to believe in the triune God—they did believe. They failed to practice what they believed. The bloodshed within the church and outside the church at the church's hands signifies a triumphalism that the apostolic community in the New Testament period would have rejected wholesale given their participation in the life of the crucified and risen Jesus as his victorious people through their own suffering and death. It is worth noting a claim made by Miroslav Volf: "*Commitment to the properly understood love of God and neighbor makes deeply religious persons*, because they are deeply religious, *into dedicated social pluralists*" (Volf, *Allah*, 32 [italics in original]).

6. Buckley, *At the Origins*, 323.

7. Gunton, *The One, the Three and the Many*, 25.

8. Ibid., 36–37.

It is worth discussing the trajectory along immanentist lines arising from one of these leading modern(ist) representatives, Hegel. Hegel has been hailed as a/the father of modernism. J. N. Findlay has gone so far as to call Hegel "the father of 'modernism'" (J. N. Findlay, *Hegel: A Re-examination* [London: George Allen and Unwin, Ltd., 1958], 139). As support for his claim, Findlay argues that Hegel's belief that the "realization" in Christ that God must attain "self-consciousness" in humanity was more significant for Hegel than Christ being the "vehicle" for making this truth explicit (139). Hegel's immediate descendants have been classified according to two groups: right-wing and left-wing Hegelians. Left-wing Hegelians, in contrast to those on the right, who attempted to defend Hegel's orthodoxy, interpreted Hegel's theology along pantheistic lines (see Frederick Copleston, S. J.,

A History of Philosophy, bk. 3, vol. 7, *Fichte to Nietzsche* [New York: Image Books, 1985], 245–47); on the subject of Hegel's orthodoxy, Charles Taylor writes that Hegel's rational "interpretation" of Christian faith, where it is argued that the ideal must become historical, "restores the decisive events of Christian faith to their central historical importance" (Charles Taylor, *Hegel* [Cambridge: Cambridge University Press, 1975], 493); for Hegel, the real is the rational, and the rational is the real. But for the rational to be fully true or real, it cannot remain in the realm of the ideal but must become incarnate in history (see G. W. F. Hegel, *Phenomenology of Spirit*, trans. A. V. Miller [Oxford: Clarendon Press, 1977], 586). There is evidence in Hegel's philosophy to support the pantheistic trajectory. In Hegel, God or Spirit requires human consciousness to attain self-consciousness. That is to say, God becomes conscious of himself through human consciousness through the course of history. And since thought coupled with historical process, or development, are keystones in Hegel's thought, no higher praise could be awarded humanity. For Hegel, human consciousness is in effect an incarnation of God, for human consciousness is the historical vehicle through which God becomes self-conscious (see Hegel's discussion of "world-historical persons" who served the "World-Spirit" in this way in Georg Wilhelm Friedrich Hegel, *Introduction to the Philosophy of History*, in *The European Philosophers from Descartes to Nietzsche*, ed. Monroe C. Beardsley [New York: The Modern Library, 1960], 564). Edward Craig writes of Hegel's doctrine that, "In so far as it is consciousness that is in question, there is nothing to God's thought but what is in our minds—our conscious thought *is* the consciousness of the deity. The Image of God doctrine, the thesis of the divinity of man, reaches its climax" (Edward Craig, *The Mind of God and the Works of Man* [Oxford: Clarendon Press, 1987], 180). It was not long, however, before this pantheistic viewpoint gave way to naturalism and atheism (Copleston, *A History of Philosophy*, 247). Ludwig Feuerbach, who did not so much interpret or develop Hegel's thought as transform it (Copleston, *A History of Philosophy*, 293), turned Hegel's philosophy upside down or, rather, set it on its feet (see Copleston, *A History of Philosophy*, 295). For Feuerbach, humanity's God is divinized humanity, whereas for Hegel, God's humanity is ultimately humanized deity. (For Feuerbach's view, see Ludwig Feuerbach, *Lectures on the Essence of Religion*, trans. Ralph Manheim [New York, Evanston, and London: Harper & Row, Publishers, 1967], 17). In place of "Idea," Feuerbach substituted "Nature" (Copleston, *A History of Philosophy*, 295). Instead of Spirit or God or Idea coming to self-consciousness through human consciousness in human history, humanity comes to self-consciousness through the objectification of itself through conceiving God. It requires very little to make the transition from claiming that God comes to self-consciousness through human consciousness to argue that God is but the projection of human consciousness or reason. For Feuerbach the sense of ultimate dependence that humanity experiences is grounded not in God but in nature, which is the fundamental ground of reality, including human consciousness (Copleston, *A History of Philosophy*, 295–96). For all their differences from one another, Hegel and Feuerbach were very much alike. For the former the incarnation is the realization in history of the truth that God and humanity are ultimately one. Here one finds the deification of humanity. For Feuerbach, on the other hand, God is but the projection of one's own humanity, infinitely extended. In Feuerbach one finds the total secularization of theology and life. Theology becomes anthropology (Feuerbach, *Lectures on the Essence of Religion*, 17). Friedrich Engels and Karl Marx, who propagated dialectical materialism, further developed this transformation of Hegel's thought along materialistic lines. Unlike Hegel and Feuerbach, however, the chief thing was not thought but activity (Karl Marx, "Theses on Feuerbach," in *The Age of Ideology: The Nineteenth Century Philosophers*, ed. Henry D. Aiken [New York: The New American Library, Inc., 1956], 195). With Nietzsche and Freud, Feuerbach, Marx, and Engels raised suspicion of the existence of God to a new level, calling for the abandonment of the concept in favor of human progress. Nietzsche's prophet, Zarathustra, speaks for all of them when he claims, "Dead are all the Gods: now do we desire the Superman to live" (Friedrich Nietzsche, *Thus Spake Zarathustra*, trans. Thomas Common [New York: The Heritage Press, 1967], 72). We have already chronicled how Nietzsche's particular philosophy does not permit space for the other.

9. Barth, *Church Dogmatics*, 4.1:159.

10. Ibid., 3.3:87.

11. Jonathan Franzen, *Freedom* (New York: Farrar, Straus and Giroux, 2010), 181.

12. Lev Grossman, "Jonathan Franzen: The Wide Shot," *Time*, August 23, 2010, 46.

13. *Christianity Today*'s new multimedia project, "This Is Our City," highlights a movement of Christians who believe God has called them to love their cities and to labor for their cities' shalom: http://thisisourcityoverview.com/Welcome.html (accessed October 17, 2011). *Christianity Today* will feature Christian engagement in several cities nationwide, beginning with Portland, Oregon. My essay, "The Gospel for Portland," highlights wonderful labors of love on the part of the church and calls for continuing and deepening efforts to foster shalom for the common good in view of our uncommon God. Many ministries have been reaching out to the community. Here are a few examples: www.secondstories.org, www.compassionconnect.com, www.imagodeicommunity.com/article/love-portland/, and www.seasonofservice .com. A wonderful ministry in the Portland, Oregon, area, called 11:45, is challenging the community to serve in what they call the "There-Share-Care-Prayer" method. The challenge is to serve in strategic areas for a commitment of one year, once a week, for forty-five minutes (hence, 11:45), in an effort to stop gang violence and its aftermath.

14. Paul Louis Metzger, "The Migration of Monism and the Matrix of Trinitarian Mediation," *Scottish Journal of Theology* 58, no. 3 (2005): 302–18.

Chapter 24: Response to "The Burning Bosom" by Robert L. Millet

1. Rodney Stark, *The Rise of Mormonism*, ed. Reid L. Neilson (New York: Columbia University Press, 2005), 32.

2. Richard J. Mouw, "The Possibility of Joseph Smith: Some Evangelical Probings," *Joseph Smith, Jr.: Reappraisals After Two Centuries*, eds. Reid L. Neilson and Terryl L. Givens (New York: Oxford University Press, 2009), 195.

3. *Teachings of the Prophet Joseph Smith, selected by Joseph Fielding Smith* (Salt Lake City: Deseret Books, 1976), 343.

Chapter 26: Response to "Avatar" by Gus diZerega

1. Bishop Kallistos Ware, *The Orthodox Way* (Crestwood, NY: St. Vladimir's Seminary Press, 1979), 46.

2. Ibid., 118.

Afterword: An Apology for Prayer

1. Karl Barth, *Evangelical Theology: An Introduction* (Grand Rapids: Eerdmans, 1963), 164.

2. Michael Badriaki, comment in IS 642 Theology of Cultural Engagement, Multnomah University, spring semester, 2010.

3. Joan Chittister, *The Breath of the Soul: Reflections on Prayer* (New London, CT: Twenty-Third, 2009), 47.

4. Edward M. Bounds, *Power Through Prayer* (New York: Cosimo, 1997).

ABOUT THE AUTHOR

Paul Louis Metzger, PhD is professor of Christian theology and theology of culture at Multnomah Biblical Seminary, Multnomah University. He is also the founder and director of the seminary's Institute for the Theology of Culture: New Wine, New Wineskins. Integrating theology and spirituality with cultural sensitivity stands at the center of Dr. Metzger's ministry vision. Dr. Metzger received his PhD from King's College London and is a member of the Center of Theological Inquiry, Princeton, New Jersey. He is the author of numerous works, including the award-winning *Consuming Jesus: Beyond Race and Class Divisions in a Consumer Church*.

Dr. Metzger is married with two children. He has a keen interest in the art of Katsushika Hokusai and Georges Rouault and the writings of John Steinbeck.